The Splendid Drunken Twenties

The Splendid Drunken Twe

SELECTIONS FROM

THE DAYBOOKS,

1922–1930

Carl Van Vechten

Edited by Bruce Kellner

University of Illinois Press
Urbana and Chicago

© 2003 by the Carl Van Vechten Trust

All rights reserved

Manufactured in the United States of America

C 5 4 3 2 1

♾ This book is printed on acid-free paper.

Library of Congress Cataloging-in-Publication Data

Van Vechten, Carl, 1880–1964.

The splendid drunken twenties : selections from the daybooks,

1922–1930 / Carl Van Vechten ; edited by Bruce Kellner.

p.   cm.

ISBN 0-252-02848-1 (cloth : alk. paper)

1. Van Vechten, Carl, 1880–1964—Diaries.

2. Novelists, American—20th century—Diaries.

3. Music critics—United States—Diaries.

4. Photographers—United States—Diaries.

5. Nineteen-twenties.

I. Kellner, Bruce.

II. Title.

PS3543.A653Z474   2003

813'.52—dc21   2002154448

The world of the nineteen-twenties
was a narrow one easily encompassed
without the aid of a bicycle, glamorous
with literary "teas" . . . and bathtubs so
full of synthetic gin that ablutions had
to be performed extramural.

    —CARL VAN VECHTEN

Ce n'est pas dans la nouveaute, c'est
dans l'habitude que nous trouvons les
plus grands plaisirs.

    —RAYMOND RADIGUET

1926   Saturday 4,   Sept.

up at 8.15; clear & cool. Wonderful
letter from Arthur Spingarn anent
nigger Heaven. — Finished Reading
the Romantic Comedians. Before
lunch I went to the post office.
Lunch in with marinoff. In the
afternoon I wrote first draft of
review of Ellen's book, lay down
for a while & then read in Smoke.
Victor Wittgenstein comes to
take marinoff out to dinner.
Edna Kenton comes to dine
with me. We talk about
nigger Heaven all the evening.
She leaves at midnight. I
go to bed about one & dream
I am a nigger, being chased in
race riots.

CONTENTS

Illustrations follow pages 104, 188, and 272

ACKNOWLEDGMENTS

The title for this book comes from Carl Van Vechten's "Joseph Hergesheimer as I Knew Him," an essay first published in the *Yale University Library Gazette* 22:3 (January 1948) and reprinted in his *Fragments from an Unwritten Autobiography* (1955). The first epigraph is drawn from the same source; Van Vechten used Raymond Radiguet's epigraph for his final novel, *Parties.*

The cooperation of the staff in the Beinecke Rare Book and Manuscript Library at Yale University and the staff of the Manuscripts and Archives Division of the New York Public Library, Tilden, Lenox, and Astor Foundations, eased my chores considerably.

For many favors, large or small, my thanks to the late Desmond Arthur, Emily Bernard, Lisa Browar, A'Lelia Bundles, Patricia Everett Ellenhorn, the late Donald Gallup, the late Eric Garber, George Hutchinson, Stephen Jones, Carla Kaplan, Ann Marie Menta, Francis M. Naumann, Priscilla Oppenheimer, Jack Sharrar, the late Joseph Solomon, Dieter Ullrich, Patricia Willis, and Donald Windham.

My best thanks to my wife, Margaret Wilcox Kellner, for her scrupulous proofreading, and my friend J. Joel Farber, for programming the text and illustrations. They did so with remarkable patience and good cheer.

Carl Van Vechten was seventy-one and I was twenty-one when we met. I am fortunate to have called him my friend for the last thirteen years of his productive life. His candor and the meticulous records of his collections have informed this selection from his daybooks and my annotations to them.

His wife, Fania Marinoff, and five of his close friends—Ann Andrews, Donald Angus, Nora Holt, Aileen Pringle, and Prentiss Taylor—were extraordinary sources on whom to draw in retrospect for this book and for earlier books at the time of their writing. I am fortunate to have called them my friends as well.

The Carl Van Vechten Papers in the Collection of American Literature in the Beinecke Rare Book and Manuscript Library at Yale University, the Carl Van Vechten Collection in the Manuscripts and Archives Division of the New York Public Library, the Carl Van Vechten Memorial Collection of Afro-American Arts and Letters at Millersville University, and the Estates of Donald

Angus, Fania Marinoff, and Aileen Pringle have supplied photographs, caricatures, and illustrations. Miguel Covarrubias's caricatures of Van Vechten are reproduced through the courtesy of Maria Rico Covarrubias. The photograph of A'Lelia Walker is reproduced through the courtesy of A'Lelia Bundles; the photograph of John Floyd is reproduced through the courtesy of Jack Sharrar. Selections from the daybooks are published by permission of the New York Public Library as owner of the physical property and through the Estate of Carl Van Vechten, for which I am successor trustee.

· · ·

The facsimile facing the table of contents appears courtesy of the Carl Van Vechten Papers, Manuscripts and Archives Division, New York Public Library, Astor, Lenox and Tilden Foundations. Illustrations on the various section pages appear courtesy of the Van Vechten Trust unless otherwise indicated:

1922: Drawing by Ted Scheel.
1923: Drawing by Ruth Hammond.
1924: Drawing by Tonio Salazar.
1925: Drawing by Eve Merriman.
1926: "A Prediction," drawing by Miguel Covarrubias, courtesy of Maria Rico Covarrubias.
1927: Drawing by Ralph Barton, courtesy of Diana Barton Franz.
1928: "In Hollywood," drawing by Miguel Covarrubias, courtesy of Maria Rico Covarrubias.
1929: Drawing by Luis Saravi.
1930: "Carl Van Vechten with and without a Hat," drawing by E. McKnight Kauffer, courtesy of the Yale Collection of American Literature, Beinecke Rare Book and Manuscript Library, Yale University.

INTRODUCTION

Between 1922 and 1930—the years during which Carl Van Vechten published his seven novels—he kept a daily account of his activities but without any explanation of why he started and why he stopped. Then he sealed up this record of what he later called "The Splendid Drunken Twenties" in one of several locked metal file boxes and deposited it with his papers in the Manuscripts and Archives Division of the New York Public Library, along with his letters to and from his wife, the Russian actress Fania Marinoff, some other family papers, and mementos. The boxes were designated to be opened on 17 June 1980, the one-hundredth anniversary of his birth.

During the subsequent twenty-odd years, the small daybooks have proven of inestimable value to a number of writers on various subjects, although the entries are almost entirely free of literary or social observation and commentary. Instead, they record the daily comings and goings—as well as the drinking habits, feuds, and love affairs—of a wide number of significant figures of the period. Taken as a collective accretion over their nine years, they make clear that the twenties passed—for many people, including Van Vechten himself— in an alcoholic haze, cheerfully at first and then desperately, as the decade's denizens stumbled from one cocktail party to another on an almost daily and nightly basis, until the long bender wound down to the sobering silence that gradually followed the stock market crash in October 1929. At the end of 1930, when Van Vechten stopped keeping his daybooks, the party was over.

Even a partial list of Van Vechten's acquaintances suggests the value of the daybooks to future biographers and historians in supplying dates for the associations and alliances of many friends and enemies in a long list of luminaries of the early twentieth century.[1]

Furthermore, these hasty summaries account for the rise and fall—in popular terms anyway—of what has come to be called the Harlem Renaissance; of Hollywood at the end of its silent heyday; of the artists' colonies in Santa Fe and Taos, New Mexico; of the Lost Generations in Paris and the decadent Weimar Republic in Berlin during Van Vechten's holidays there. On his home turf in New York, the daybooks account for bootlegging, literary teas, shifting cliques of artists and writers, cabaret slumming, sexual and social peccadilloes, and a seemingly endless catalog of parties—and their hangovers—in Greenwich Village studios, Harlem buffet flats and brothels, and private residences and salons, including the apartments Van Vechten shared with Fania Marinoff. Also, they offer a fascinating eavesdrop on an amazing marriage. It was as volatile as it was loving. They were married for fifty years, and—as the daybooks all too clearly reveal—Marinoff and Van Vechten were emotionally dependent on each other in what was surely a sometimes difficult alliance for them both. Finally, the daybooks chronicle one writer's processes and progress through the series of novels that made Carl Van Vechten a popular writer in the twenties.

• • •

He wrote his daybooks hurriedly, often illegibly, with a cheerful and sometimes apparently drunken disregard for conventional punctuation and capitalization, and clear abbreviations. The earliest of the daybooks often are made up of separate lines for separate subjects; in later ones, everything is run into single paragraphs. Also, entries for the earlier years are brief and less detailed than those from the later ones. As Van Vechten's reputation as a popular novelist grew and as his celebrity spread, introducing him to a wide number of social circles, the daybooks increase in interest as well as content. Inevitably, then, the number of entries from the later years included in the following selection is much higher.

Because the daybooks are hardly stylistic masterpieces in form or thought and are valuable largely for their factual information and the atmosphere that they offer of their period, my editing is designed to assist the reader in search of dates, names, and places, rather than in the vagaries of Van Vechten's hasty holograph. This selection deletes material that is repetitious, is without interest, or merely catalogs guest lists at an interminable number of parties. Van Vechten's lifelong habit of name-dropping indicates that he was a lion hunter, from his early days until his death, always ready to document in letters as well as in these daybooks whom he had met or seen, even if only fleetingly. Dozens of people—famous or forgotten—turn up, some of them repeatedly, some only once. Eventually the lists of guests at parties begin to grow suffocating, for often the same people who attended an afternoon cocktail party then attended an evening party on the same day. For periods of several weeks or months, these lists seem to have constituted a series of cliques. Limiting names to avoid repetition sometimes overlooks people, but the daybooks themselves are always available on microfilm, in Van Vechten's holograph as well as in a complete transcription, which I typed without annotations some years ago for the Manuscripts and Archives Division of the New York Public Library. Anybody who wants to check out the *ur*-version, in preference to these selections, may surely do so.

I have indicated every deletion with conventional ellipses. I have deleted many of the routine weather reports and the times of day at which Van Vechten arose and went to bed. I have identified names in the notes but generally only on their first appearance in the daybooks and only if Van Vechten's text did not identify them. Moreover, I have identified restaurants, speakeasies, hotels, plays, and films only when some clarification was necessary. I have added missing last names in brackets when only first names appear in the text until their repetition has clearly identified them. On the other hand, I have added missing first names after initial footnote identifications only when necessary to avoid confusion. I have guessed at no identities without some substantiating evidence, and—with several exceptions to preserve the sense of an entry—I have deleted the names of people whom I could not identify.

Van Vechten was a compulsive reader—sometimes reading four or five books simultaneously, over a period of time—although in the daybooks he rarely commented on what he was reading beyond the title. Similarly, he regularly attended plays and saw many films without assessing them. Usually, I have included only those on which he passed opinions.

I have freely repunctuated, often ignoring Van Vechten's all-purpose dash, which seems to substitute for commas, periods, semicolons, and colons, as well as frequent pauses to think; I have added possessive apostrophes and moved others from singular to plural or vice versa; I have capitalized or lowercased words and names as appropriate. Sometimes Van Vechten underlined titles, but just as often he put them in quotation marks or did not mark them at all, and often he used partial titles. I have put all titles of full-length works (published and unpublished alike, complete or incomplete) in italics; I have put titles of stories and songs in quotation marks; I have excised words that Van Vechten wrote in error and then crossed out; I have truncated his repetition, "etc etc" at the ends of guest lists and after his routine accounting for morning chores.

I have transcribed each day as a single paragraph, in accordance with Van Vechten's practice in the later daybooks. I have not spelled out words such as "Street" and "Company" or names such as "Geo." when he abbreviated them, but I have silently corrected punctuation, misspellings, and variant spellings, especially of names, without riddling the pages with [*sic*]. I have followed Van Vechten when he used either the maiden names (usually used for professional reasons) or the married names of women. I have retained Van Vechten's English spellings, popular during the twenties with Alfred A. Knopf and some other writers in his stable. Also, I have corrected Van Vechten's grammatical slips in agreement or number and his factual slips, the latter either silently when unimportant or in brackets or footnotes when substantive. In every case my annotations have been designed for the lay reader rather than for the scholar, identifying many people whom my generation will immediately recognize without any assistance but with whom later readers may not be familiar. However, I have not troubled to identify those whose names—Charlie Chaplin, Booker T. Washington, or the author of *Twelfth Night,* for instance—are sufficiently recognizable without my assistance.

In writing for publication, Van Vechten was meticulous, so it seems to me of negligible value to reproduce errors he would have corrected himself had he intended to publish these daybooks. It is hardly crucial for the reader to know that Van Vechten first encountered a young black poet named "Kingston Hughes" instead of Langston Hughes, although in this case and a few others I have retained his first guesses just as historical curiosities.

Usually Van Vechten wrote in black or purple ink. His sometimes pale turquoise ink (mercifully little used) often proved impossible to read. Occasionally, Van Vechten's handwriting proved equally impossible to decipher, regardless of the ink. Words or names of which I was uncertain I have bracketed with a question mark, thus [*Smith?*]; illegible words and names I have indicated as [*name*] or [*names*] and [*word*] or, for example, [*three words*]. I have added words and letters of my own in brackets only when sense demanded them, but I have not added missing parts of speech in Van Vechten's frequent sentence fragments or altered his sometimes bewildering locutions unless, again, sense demanded them. Part of the flavor of the daybooks lies in the haste in which he wrote them.

• • •

As a musical, dramatic, and literary critic—and he achieved some stature in these roles early in his career—Carl Van Vechten is largely forgotten. But during his stints on the *New York Times* as assistant music critic (1906–13) and the *New York Press* as drama critic (1913–14), and in seven books of essays and periodical articles (1914–20), he called early attention—and arguably the earliest serious attention in the United States—to Igor Stravinsky, Erik Satie, Richard Strauss's early operas, Isaac Albéniz and the music of Spain, Isadora Duncan and modern dance, Anna Pavlova, Waslav Nijinsky and the Russian Ballet, George Gershwin and the evolution of ragtime and jazz, Negro spirituals and blues, Countee Cullen, Ronald Firbank, Henry Blake Fuller, Langston Hughes, Nella Larsen, Herman Melville, Bessie Smith, Gertrude Stein, Wallace Stevens, and Ethel Waters. He advocated musical scores composed expressly for films at a time when pit pianists or orchestras in movie theaters vamped 'til ready with familiar selections instead of playing from prepared scores; he sought to classify stage decoration and set design as a fine art; he urged the establishment of an African American theater, beginning in 1914 and through the twenties, during which time serious black playwrights had no forum in commercial theater on or off-Broadway. Van Vechten was largely responsible for sparking popular if not always intellectual interest in what has come to be called the Harlem Renaissance, through a series of articles about African American arts and letters in *Vanity Fair* and other influential magazines and with *Nigger Heaven*, his novel detailing a cross-section of contemporary Harlem life.

In addition to *Nigger Heaven*, three other novels chronicle the high jinks of his era in New York, with sometimes discomfiting fidelity: *The Blind Bow-Boy*, *Firecrackers*, and *Parties*. *Spider Boy* is a spoof on Hollywood just before the silent screen began to talk. Taken as extensions of his daybooks, all these offer palpable evidence that flappers and bootleggers and apparently nearly everybody else really did roar through the twenties. *Peter Whiffle: His Life and Works* is a faux biography of a writer who never wrote anything and, instead, raised appreciation itself to an art, and the novel offers first-hand accounts of Paris before World War I and of the Greenwich Village salon maintained by Mabel Dodge (later Luhan). *The Tattooed Countess* is a story of 1890s life in Iowa—Van Vechten was born and reared there—when a middle-aged demimondaine spirits away to Paris a conniving boy of seventeen who can't wait to get out of town. There is little likelihood that any of these novels will spark a Van Vechten revival, although a new Van Vechten biography is under way, *Parties* has been produced as a play, *Nigger Heaven* is being turned into a musical, and *The Tattooed Countess* (already transformed into a silent movie, an opera, and a musical comedy) is being readied for television.

Also, *The Tiger in the House*, written just before he turned to fiction, is as influential on other books about cats as it is timeless.

After he concluded his career as a novelist—and at the same time stopped keeping these daybooks—Carl Van Vechten took up photography as a hobby in 1932. That resulted in at least five images so recognizable that they have become national icons: F. Scott Fitzgerald, Zora Neale Hurston, Eugene O'Neill, Bessie Smith, and Gertrude Stein. Several others lag not far behind. Four volumes of his photographs have been posthumously published, his photographs of George Gershwin and Zora Neale Hurston have been reproduced on U.S. postage stamps, and requests to include his photographs in books and television documentaries are steady. Van Vechten was an amateur in the best sense of the word: he loved making photographs and he loved giving them away to friends; he never sold his photographs, he never took commissions, and he never photographed anybody he didn't want to.

Over a period of thirty-two years, until his death in 1964, he amassed an impressive catalog of celebrated subjects, including nearly every African American of note or promise. He established the James Weldon Johnson Memorial Collection of Negro Arts and Letters at Yale University, collected materials for it for the rest of his life, and willed all posthumous income from his work to its endowment fund. His photographs preserve for posterity an otherwise lost generation of African American images in addition to memorable portraits of many other of the century's artists, writers, actors, composers, musicians, dancers, and singers, plus a few prizefighters and politicians, full documentations of the 1939 World's Fair and the 1942–45 Stage Door Canteen, and many friends and acquaintances simply because they were promising subjects.

Some of his nude photographs found their way into the series of scrapbooks he kept over a period of thirty-five years that documented a history of homosexuality—largely limited to New York and the manner in which the law operated to subvert or persecute it—through newspaper and periodical clippings. But the scrapbooks also contain a remarkable collection of erotic photographs by others, such as the Baron Wilhelm Von Gloeden and George Platt Lynes; scabrous drawings by Richard Banks and Elwyn Chamberlin; and miscellaneous Uranian memorabilia, including a series of juxtapositions of pictures and headlines as hilarious as they are vulgar.

Also, Carl Van Vechten kept nearly every letter he ever received. He corresponded extensively with many of the people who turn up in his daybooks and with some who followed in later years, such as writers Baroness Karen Blixen, Chester Himes, James Purdy, Donald Windham, and Richard Wright; artists George George and Karl Priebe; and ballet dancers Hugh Laing and Alicia Markova. Many of his own letters to a wide variety of correspondents have been deposited by their recipients in the Beinecke Library or in other university libraries.

Carl Van Vechten's musical and literary criticism often is perceptive and even visionary, his novels are certainly diverting, many of his photographs are masterful, and the immediacy of his correspondence and the material in his daybooks offer a palpable recreation of his time. Taken en toto, this is an extraordinary legacy to American arts and letters.

Note

1. For example, Gertrude Atherton, Tallulah Bankhead, Ralph Barton, Cecil Beaton, Gladys Bentley, Neith Boyce, Ernest Boyd, Witter Bynner, James Branch Cabell, Frank and Bertha Case of the Algonquin Hotel, Charlie Chaplin, Emily Clark and Hunter Stagg of *The Reviewer,* Miguel Covarrubias and Rose Rolanda, Noel Coward, Frank Crowninshield of *Vanity Fair,* Countee Cullen, Charles Demuth, Muriel Draper, Theodore Dreiser, W. E. B. Du Bois, Arthur Davison Ficke, Ronald Firbank, F. Scott and Zelda Fitzgerald, George Gershwin, Ellen Glasgow, Isa Glenn, Hutchins Hapgood, Joseph Hergesheimer, Avery Hopwood, Langston Hughes, Fannie Hurst, Zora Neale Hurston, James Weldon Johnson, Edna Kenton, Alfred and Blanche Knopf, Nella Larsen, Sinclair Lewis, Horace Liveright, Robert Morss Lovett, Mabel Dodge Luhan, Arthur Machen, W. Somerset Maugham, Claude McKay, H. L. Mencken, George Moore, Georgia O'Keeffe, Eugene O'Neill, Channing and Anna Marble Pollock, Aileen Pringle, Paul and Essie Robeson, Bill "Bojangles" Robinson, Bessie Smith, Clara Smith, Gertrude Stein and Alice B. Toklas, Carrie, Ettie, and Florine Stettheimer, Wallace Stevens, Virgil Thomson, Wallace Thurman, Louis Untermeyer, Carl and Irita Van Doren, A'Lelia Walker, Hugh Walpole, Ethel Waters, Rebecca West, Walter White, Thomas Wolfe, and Elinor Wylie.

1922

"Everything in the world to drink"

In 1922, after several years of obscurity and periodic penury—Carl Van Vechten's annual volumes of literary and musical criticism had produced little income—he published his first novel, *Peter Whiffle: His Life and Works,* which proved to be an unexpected best-seller. As a result, Van Vechten became a minor celebrity, with healthy royalties, and the social circle he shared with his wife, Russian actress Fania Marinoff, began to expand. At the Algonquin Hotel, where various writers regularly congregated; in Richmond, Virginia, where the literary fortnightly *Reviewer* was published; and in a growing number of speakeasies that had begun to flourish almost immediately after the Nineteenth Amendment outlawed the sale and consumption of liquor, Van Vechten was a familiar figure. That same year, he began his second novel, *The Blind Bow-Boy,* and completed it with little effort.

Sunday, 8 January 1922

Calvé, Carnegie Hall at 3.[1] Theatre Guild at 8.30: *He Who Gets Slapped*[2] Pepe Schildkraut[3] at 4 to meet Ernst Lubitsch.[4]

1. Emma Calvé, celebrated Metropolitan Opera French soprano who by 1922 had migrated to the recital stage.

2. A circus allegory by Russian dramatist Leonid Andreiev. This performance probably would have been a preview or dress rehearsal; as intimate friends of executive director of the Theatre Guild, Lawrence Langner, Carl Van Vechten—hereafter referred to in annotations as CVV—and Fania Marinoff were regularly invited.

3. German stage and film actor Joseph Schildkraut.

4. German film director who had come to the United States to direct popular movie star Mary Pickford.

Saturday, 4 February 1922

Señor Ismael Smith[1] party after nine & dinner, but did not go. Miss Emily Clark, editor of *The Reviewer* of Richmond, Va.[2] Lunch, English tea-room, Sat. at 12.30. Party at the Stettheimers'.[3]

1. Spanish book dealer who had supplied CVV with material for *The Music of Spain* (Knopf, 1918).

2. A literary journal, to which it had become fashionable for celebrated and cult writers alike to contribute free of charge, was edited by Emily Clark and Hunter Stagg and shepherded by James Branch Cabell. Ronald Firbank, Ellen Glasgow, Joseph Hergesheimer, H. L. Mencken, Gertrude Stein, CVV, Hugh Walpole, Elinor Wylie, and many other then popular or respected and now forgotten writers appeared in its pages during its four-year run.

3. Three American eccentric spinster sisters who maintained a salon in New York's high bohemia, holding elaborate dinner parties in their over-decorated apartment. Ettie wrote novels now long out of print; Florine painted fancifully sophisticated canvases, largely ignored during her lifetime and now in many museums; Carrie furnished an elaborate dollhouse with an art gallery of original miniatures by Marcel Duchamp, Constantin Brancusi, Gaston Lachaise, and others, now on permanent display in the Museum of the City of New York.

Thursday, 16 February 1922

Evening with Edna[1] & *Frank Fay's Fables.*[2] Midnight material. Dinner with Ralph & Fannie,[3] Pierre's, 290 Park Ave.

1. American feminist Edna Kenton, an intimate friend since CVV's days in Chicago from the turn of the twentieth century until 1934, when he cut her from his circle of friends without explanation. A member of the Heterodoxy, a group of independent women in Greenwich Village before the First War, Kenton wrote fiction and histories.

2. A musical revue, titled for its star, comedian Frank Fay, and featuring Fania Marinoff. It may have failed in part because she was without musical talent.

3. CVV's older brother (by eighteen years), a prosperous Chicago banker, and his wife.

Friday, 10 March 1922

Vernissage of the Salon des Indépendants.[1] Florine Stettheimer has sent me tickets. Lunch with Thomas Beer[2] at the Yale Club, 12.45. Burton Rascoe[3] was there. Mabel Reber[4] entertains in the evening for Dustan Hellström[5] who sails for Sweden tomorrow. Louise Hellström, Edwin Björkman,[6] Jane Heap,[7] Philip Moeller,[8] Edna Kenton, . . . and Helen Westley.[9] Fania[10] signs contract with Klauber.[11]

1. An American equivalent of the Salon des Indépendants in Paris, where avantgarde artists could show their work. Stettheimer had entered a piece in the exhibition, *Zinnias,* that CVV subsequently purchased for $150.00. It was her first sale.

2. American novelist and short story writer, also author of a Stephen Crane biography and an influential study of the 1890s titled *The Mauve Decades.*

3. Prolific American literary critic, journalist, and apparent sycophant, although he did much to popularize a number of writers, notably James Branch Cabell.

4. Edna Kenton's sister, married to Neil Reber, with whom she raised and boarded cats in their Greenwich Village apartment.

5. Brother of Louise Hellström, a interior decorator and popular figure in the twenties, mistress of artist Robert Chanler, and the model for CVV's "Simone Fly," who "resembled a gay death," in his 1930 novel *Parties.*

6. Swedish-American writer and critic responsible for introducing American audiences to the plays of August Strindberg and Arthur Schnitzler.

7. American writer and editor who with Margaret Anderson edited *The Little Review,* responsible for first publishing James Joyce's *Ulysses,* in installments, until the police stepped in.

8. American playwright, translator, and later director with the Theatre Guild.

9. American actress and executive of the Theatre Guild, notable as Ftatateetah in George Bernard Shaw's *Caesar and Cleopatra* and later in films, a friend of CVV's from circa 1906.

10. Fania Marinoff, CVV's second wife. He met her two months after his first wife, Anna Snyder, divorced him in 1912 for adultery. He and Marinoff were lovers for two years before their marriage in 1914. Their alliance was fully sexual from 1912 until circa 1919 and occasionally so afterward until circa 1931, interrupted sporadically by his homosexual liaisons. Born a Russian Jew in 1887, Marinoff made her acting debut at age eight in Denver. She steadily appeared on stage in New York from 1903 until 1923, including roles in plays by Shakespeare (as Ariel in *The Tempest*), Shaw (in *Arms and the Man* and *You Never Can Tell*), and Wedekind (in *Spring's Awakening,* a production closed for obscenity after a single performance) and in many silent films. She continued to act periodically for another twenty years.

During most the time covered by CVV's daybooks, however, she was more steadily a party-goer and social hostess.

11. Ernst Klauber, theatrical producer of *The Charlatan,* by Leonard Paskins and Ernst Pascal, starring Marinoff in 1922.

Sunday, 12 March 1922

Back to Methuselah, Part III.[1] Dinner with Marie Doro[2] at Americans, and supper after the theatre with her. . . . Marinoff writes Yiddish poems for Jewish war sufferers.

1. The Theatre Guild was mounting George Bernard Shaw's ten-hour play in sections.

2. English-born Marie Kathryn Stewart changed her name to Marie Doro when she began her stage career in 1900. She was celebrated for her startling beauty long after she retired in 1921.

Sunday, 26 March 1922

After dinner Marinoff and I went to call on Edna Aug,[1] in bed, as usual, at the Brevoort.[2] Then to see Ernest A. and Madeleine Boyd.[3] She has just returned from the hospital after an operation for appendicitis. Home-brew beer.[4]

1. Minor American actress in early vaudeville, usually languishing because of her languishing career when her broad comedic style went out of fashion in the twenties.

2. Greenwich Village hotel near Washington Square, well known as a haven for artists and writers. Its popular restaurant was frequented by a broad cross-section of New Yorkers.

3. Irish literary critic who lived in New York, and his wife, who served as copyeditor and proofreader for writer friends.

4. At the beginning of Prohibition it was not unusual for people to make their own beer and spirits: gin in bathtubs and beer in kitchen crockery. Professional bootlegging did not become a major industry for about another year, although speakeasies already dotted the city.

Monday, 27 March 1922

Saw Rendisoff (artist of the *Chauve-Souris*)[1] exhibition at Wildenstein Galleries. His caricatures are amazing: Pop-eyed Frank Crowninshield,[2] fatuously amazed at something that occurred ten years ago, the lustful, mean, leering face of Morris Gest,[3] a demonical caricature, & the dried-up academic piddling countenance of Christian Brinton.[4]

1. A popular Russian musical entertainment, notable for its intermission curtain by Ralph Barton, featuring caricatures of about one hundred literary and theatrical celebrities.

2. Editor of the popular and influential magazine *Vanity Fair*.

3. Theatrical producer who imported *Chauve Souris* for its New York run.

4. Widely published American academic art historian.

Monday, 10 April 1922

Georgette Leblanc.[1] 10 o'clock, 123 Washington Place. George Antheil,[2] the youthful composer, plays his "Valse Profane" & "Sonata." Very much under the influence of Stravinsky.[3] Believes in "mechanistic" music as opposed to "rhapsodic." De Segurola,[4] Señor Ismael Smith, Margaret Anderson,[5] Dr. Berman, the youthful author of a new book on glands.[6] I took Ernest Boyd with me. And he and I had dinner together at the Brevoort. *The Charlatan*[7] opens for a week in Washington.

1. French singer, the wife of Belgian playwright Maurice Maeterlinck.

2. American avant-garde composer.

3. Russian composer, whose work CVV was first in America to champion.

4. Spanish singer Andres de Segurola.

5. American avant garde editor who with Jane Heap published *The Little Review*, responsible for first publishing James Joyce's *Ulysses*, in installments.

6. Louis Berman, M.D., *The Glands Regulating Personality* (Macmillan, 1922).

7. An out-of-town run for the play in which Marinoff was appearing.

Saturday, 15 April 1922

Tea, Florine Stettheimer's studio at 4.30: Baron and Baroness de Meyer,[1] Henry McBride,[2] . . . Marcel Duchamp,[3] & 3 Stettheimers. After dinner to Mabel [Reber]'s & later to a Provincetown party, celebrating last performance of *The Hairy Ape* at the Provincetown Theatre, before it moves to the Plymouth. I met Eugene O'Neill.[4]

1. German fashion and celebrity photographer Adolphe and his wife, Olga.

2. American art critic for *New York Sun, Dial,* and other publications, an early champion of artist Charles Demuth and writer Gertrude Stein, both of whom CVV tried to popularize.

3. French Dadaist innovator and artist whose fractured abstract painting *Nude Descending a Staircase* had caused a popular furor at the 69th Regimental Armory Exhibition in 1913.

4. Destined to become America's premiere playwright, O'Neill had written an expressionist play that had proven successful enough to move from the Provincetown Playhouse in Greenwich Village to Broadway.

Saturday, 22 April 1922

Letter from Arthur Machen[1] in regard to *Peter Whiffle*.[2] Geraldine Farrar sings her farewell at the Metropolitan Opera House in *Zaza*,[3] a full account of this in my scrap book.[4] Fania arrives from Stamford & appears at Jack's Big Stick Concert at the Manhattan Opera House.[5] Yorska arrival.[6]

1. Obscure English writer and mystic for whom CVV was creating an American audience with assistance of his publisher, Alfred A. Knopf.

2. *Peter Whiffle: His Life and Works* (Knopf, 1922), CVV's first novel.

3. Popular American soprano, singing Pietro Mascagni's now rarely produced opera. She inspired the "Gerryflappers," arguably the first organized fan club in America.

4. CVV was an inveterate scrapbook keeper: a series devoted to his own writings, beginning circa 1903 with his newspaper articles and, later, reviews of his books; a series about musical and theatrical matters such as the Farrar opera performance; and later a series devoted to homosexual subjects.

5. Jacob Marinoff, Fania's older brother, was a poet and editor of *Der Groyser Kundas* (*The Grand Prankster*), a satirical Yiddish journal, for which a fund-raising concert was given.

6. "Madame Yorska," French comedienne making her first American appearance.

Monday, 15 May 1922

Saw Stieglitz[1] & he is lyric in his praise of *Peter Whiffle*. Cocktails & dinner with Avery Hopwood & John Floyd.[2] Evening at Mabel Reber's. Edna Kenton, Ida Rauh,[3] Andrew Dasburg.[4] . . .

1. Alfred Stieglitz, American photographer whose 291 and American Place galleries offered exhibitions of the work of many young American painters, notably Charles Demuth, Arthur Dove, Marsden Hartley, John Marin, and most prominently his wife and photographic muse, Georgia O'Keeffe.

2. Phenomenally successful American playwright of light comedies. Floyd, an occasional actor and playwright, was Hopwood's longtime lover in a mutually abusive relationship. CVV and Hopwood had been intimate friends since 1906. Hopwood considered Marinoff his closest woman friend.

3. American modern dancer, former wife of Greenwich Village poet and novelist Max Eastman.

4. American abstractionist painter, current husband of Ida Rauh, with whom he migrated to the artists' colony in Taos, New Mexico.

Friday, 19 May 1922

Lunch with Tom Beer at Yale Club, 12.30–1.00. Meade Minnegrode, who is writing a bibliography of Melville, present. Says that *The Refugee* is printed from Putnam plates (not pirated) & that there is a versified version of *Redburn*—under title *Redburn* in N.Y. Pub Lib.—formerly attributed to Melville, 1844–45.[1] Dinner with Hutchins Hapgood, Neith Boyce,[2] & E. Kenton. At Edna's after dinner. The Boyds came in. We dined at Fior O'Italia on MacDougal Street.

1. CVV was among the earliest writers to spearhead the Herman Melville revival, having reviewed Raymond Weaver's *Of Herman Melville: Mariner and Mystic* in 1921. Two months earlier, in the September 11 issue of *Die Zeit*, available only in a Yiddish translation, he had written enthusiastically about Melville. Arguably then, he was first to begin the Melville revival.

2. American socialist writer and his novelist wife. CVV and Boyce were compatriots in escaping from Italy when war broke out in 1914.

Wednesday, 31 May 1922

Mabel Reber's at 8 o'clock. Donald Angus,[1] . . . Edna Kenton, Helen Westley. Party at Hamilton Revell's.[2] . . . About a hundred others were there.

1. Interior decorator, minor actor, department store window dresser. Half CVV's age, Angus became the first of his *jeunes gens assortis*, a phrase invented by Mabel Dodge Luhan that CVV appropriated to assign to his coterie of young men during the decade. He and Angus were lovers, 1919–20, and intermittently until circa 1930; afterward, Angus was an intimate friend of both CVV and Marinoff until their deaths in 1964 and 1971, respectively. Marinoff was aware of CVV's homosexual affairs. She was not herself homosexual, nor did she ever engage in any known extramarital affairs.

2. American actor who appeared with Marinoff in *Captain Applejack* and in Avery Hopwood's *Fair and Warmer*.

Wednesday, 14 June 1922

Saw part of Nazimova's film *Salome*[1] in evening, invitation of Alfred Kuttner & Board of Censors. Film stopped because of defective instrument. Saw *Music Box Revue* with Fania in afternoon. I left after first act. Lunch with Ettie Stettheimer to talk about mss. of her new book [*Love Days*], English tearoom.

1. Russian actress Alla Nazimova had made a film version of Oscar Wilde's play, with sets and costumes based on Aubrey Beardsley's illustrations.

Monday, 10 July 1922

Fania comes back from the country. Lunch with Alfred Knopf, he tells me he has made up his mind to do Ettie Stettheimer's *Love Days*.

Friday, 14 July 1922

Dinner at Beaux-Arts—with Ettie Stettheimer . . . & Marinoff. Marcel Duchamp came in later. Ettie took her book away from Knopf today because he won't publish it for a year.[1]

    1. Knopf published *Love Days* in 1923. Ettie was the most impatient of the Stettheimer sisters.

Sunday, 23 July 1922

Dinner with Marinoff at Town House, 67 & Central Park West. Later Regina[1] came in. Willard Wright[2] came to table & introduced us to Ralph Barton & his daughter, Natalie. We went to his apartment. Barton is living with this child by his first wife. His second wife & her child by him have left him & he is at present intrigued by Carlotta Monterey.[3]

    1. Regina Wallace, American actress and Marinoff's oldest and closest friend. She appeared in many plays and films but is best remembered as Mrs. Freddie Eynsford-Hill in *My Fair Lady,* the musical version of George Bernard Shaw's *Pygmalion.*

    2. As "S.S. Van Dyne," Willard Huntington Wright was the creator of the popular Philo Vance murder mysteries.

    3. Ralph Barton was the most popular and successful caricaturist of the twenties. Carlotta Monterey was an actress admired for her surpassing beauty rather than for her talent. She gave up her tenuous career for an all-consuming affair and later marriage to Barton until she discovered him in flagrante delicto. Subsequently, she married Eugene O'Neill, and Barton married French composer Germaine Tailleferre. Monterey and Marinoff had been friends since 1917.

Wednesday, 26 July 1922

Lunch with Norman Bel Geddes at the Crillon & after lunch he takes me up to his studio & shows me his remarkable drawings & masks for his Dante pageant, & his model for a theatre. This boy is a genius.

Sunday, 30 July 1922

Ettie Stettheimer celebrates her birthday, which occurred at midnight between 30 & 31 so that she celebrates either day at case. They have taken her aunt (Mrs. [Frances] Sternberger)'s house for the summer at Sea Bright, N.J. & Fania & I go down for the day.

Friday, 4 August 1922

Claire Schermerhorn,[1] Marinoff & myself dine with Ralph [Van Vechten] at Leone's where I take him. He wants a card to the place, which is difficult to enter on account of drink, signs his name D. Ankersheim, [and] says, when I tell Jean that he is my brother, that he is my half-brother, and otherwise makes a provincial ass of himself.[2]

    1. Actress Claire Burke Schermerhorn, who left her husband to form a long alliance and brief marriage with American verse writer Samuel Hoffenstein. Poet Donald Evans, publisher of Gertrude Stein's *Tender Buttons,* named his Claire-Marie Press after her.

    2. Despite his fortune—more than $6,000,000 when he died five years later—CVV's older brother never outgrew his homespun Iowa roots.

Saturday, 5 August 1922

Fania goes to visit Jack Marinoff in New Jersey. I see a negro show, *The Whirl of Joy,* at the Lafayette Theatre.[1]

    1. The Lafayette Theatre in Harlem regularly staged variety shows, vaudeville, and musical revues. CVV was largely indifferent to its resident stock company, which often produced all-black performances of plays that had been successful downtown on Broadway.

Monday, 14 August 1922

Lunch at the Algonquin[1] with Marinoff. Sinclair Lewis & Harcourt[2] came to sit at our table.

    1. The Algonquin Hotel was a popular place for many writers and performers to have meals. It is best remembered for its "Round Table," which included poet Dorothy Parker, humorist Robert Benchley, theater critic Alexander Woollcott, journalist Franklin P. Adams, playwright Marc Connelly, novelist Edna Ferber, and others, but never CVV.

    2. American novelist, best remembered for *Main Street* and *Babbitt* and his Nobel prize, and his publisher, Alfred Harcourt. Lewis and CVV had known each other since 1906.

Friday, 25 August 1922

Went to Hergesheimer's,[1] West Chester. Dower House being remodelled & they are living in a Victorian house in town.[2] Emily Clark there.

    1. Joseph Hergesheimer, prolific American writer whose upholstered novels are now out of fashion, was one of the most popular as well as critically admired writers in America from 1917. With the Depression he lapsed into obscurity.

2. Hergesheimer and his wife, Dorothy, often had literary guests for weekends at their home in West Chester, Pennsylvania, first in an eighteenth-century Dower House and later in a nineteenth-century townhouse they were refurbishing.

Sunday, 10 September 1922

Meade Minnegrode came in afternoon to see my Melvilles for his bibliography.[1] Tom Beer came with him. Joe Hergesheimer turns up & has dinner with me at Leone's (raided 2 nights ago, but we still have cocktails). Afterwards he came down to the house. Fania, who has been at Jack [Marinoff]'s in the country all day, returns & Tom Beer and Ernest Boyd come in. They stay till one o'clock. I work all day on 4th chapter.[2]

    1. An inveterate collector, CVV had amassed a complete collection of Melville first editions, including the rarest items. He gave this archive to Yale University, where it is currently part of the Collection of American Literature in the Beinecke Rare Book and Manuscript Library.

    2. CVV was writing his second novel, *The Blind Bow-Boy.*

Tuesday, 19 September 1922

Henry Sell turns down *The Blind Bow-Boy* for *Harper's Bazar.*[1] Lunch at Algonquin with Muriel Starr,[2] Irene McIver,[3] & Marinoff. Wrote 3rd draft of 5 chapters of *Bow-Boy.* Dinner at Leone's with Marinoff. Went to see *Banco*— with Regina Wallace. . . .

    1. Sell had considered serializing the novel in his magazine, the name of which in 1922 was spelled *Bazar* rather than *Bazaar.*

    2. Muriel MacIver, Canadian actress who appeared professionally as Muriel Starr.

    3. Marinoff's niece.

Monday, 25 September 1922

Lunch with Joseph Hergesheimer at the Algonquin. Worked on Rimsky proofs.[1] Joe had dinner with us at Leone's—& after dinner I gave a party for him. Rita Romilly,[2] Alfred Kuttner, Ernest & Madeleine Boyd, Tallulah Bankhead (who stood on her head, disrobed, gave imitations & was amusing generally),[3] Phil Moeller, Helen Westley.

    1. CVV had edited the autobiography of Nikolay Rimsky-Korsakov as *My Musical Life* for Knopf.

    2. American dancer, actress, and teacher, later prominently engaged in Harlem Renaissance circles.

    3. Flamboyant American actress, generally better remembered for her off-stage

antics. "Regina Giddens" in *The Little Foxes* and "Lily Sabina Fairweather" in *The Skin of Our Teeth* are exceptions.

Wednesday, 4 October 1922

Wrote Chapter X of *Bow-Boy*. Lunch at Algonquin with Virginia Hammond. Tallulah Bankhead & Blythe Daly came to the table.[1] Saw *On the Stairs* [by William Hurlbut] in evening & went back to see Arnold Daly,[2] a wreck, with drink or drugs. . . .

    1. Hammond and Daly were minor American actresses of the period.
    2. American theatrical producer and actor, married to Blythe Daly.

Friday, 6 October 1922

Wrote Chapter XI of *Bow-Boy*. Horace Liveright[1] gives a dinner, . . . pushes me off a piano stool, & breaks my arm. T. R. Smith,[2] Ernest Boyd, George Jean Nathan,[3] Scott Fitzgerald (whom I meet for the first time),[4] Charles Brackett (first time). . . .[5]

    1. Eccentric American publisher. In partnership with his brother Otto, Liveright was responsible for establishing several notable careers and founding the Modern Library, later purchased by Bennett Cerf for Random House.
    2. Thomas R. Smith, Horace Liveright's second in command and largely responsible for the publisher's success. He was an inveterate party-giver and -goer and occasional escort for Marinoff.
    3. Influential American theater critic, co-editor with H. L. Mencken of *The Smart Set* and *The American Mercury*.
    4. American novelist and short story writer, at the time in the first flush of his popularity.
    5. American novelist and playwright, later better known as a screenwriter in Hollywood.

Friday, 20 October 1922

Lunch at the Algonquin. Saw Joe [Hergesheimer] and Boyds. Boyd is coming frequently now. Bandage off today. Arm in sling. Ralph [Van Vechten] gives a dinner in his room at Algonquin. . . . Mencken[1] just back from Europe & Nathan, both drunk, turn up. Mencken soon dead to the world, snores. Joe has a crying jag. Very amusing party. Met Basil Thompson of *The Double Dealer*[2] in Goldsmith's shop in afternoon.

    1. Henry Louis Mencken, arguably the most influential social, political, and literary critic of the period and through Knopf a friend and correspondent of CVV.
    2. A journal published in New Orleans that had featured articles by CVV on obscure literary figures Henry Blake Fuller and Ronald Firbank.

Sunday, 22 October 1922

Lunch at Algonquin solo. Afternoon at Mrs. Atherton's.[1] She tells me that she visited Philadelphia at time of Walt Whitman's funeral, "Everybody was drunk but Agnes Repplier."[2] Fania goes to Leo Lane's for dinner & I dine at Avery [Hopwood]'s. John Floyd there. We visit The Jungle, 11 Cornelia Street in the [Greenwich] Village, a tough gangster resort. Avery loses his overcoat. On way to police station to report loss we run into a murder.

    1. Gertrude Atherton who wrote popular romance novels, primarily with California settings and subjects.

    2. Knowledgeable and witty old-school essayist and biographer of Catholic subjects.

Sunday, 29 October 1922

Went to Edna Kenton's in afternoon. Dinner at Arrowhead Inn (old-fashioned whiskey cocktails) with Avery Hopwood, Marinoff, John Floyd & Ralph Glover.[1] Party at Avery's, 850 Park Ave. The above and Marie Dressler[2] (met for first time), Boyds, Gertrude Atherton, Edward Knoblauch,[3] Gladys Unger,[4] Edna Aug, Grace George,[5] Edgar Selwyn,[6] Mickey Harrison,[7] Mr. & Mrs. Gilbert Miller,[8] Anita Loos & John Emerson,[9] T. R. Smith, Philip Moeller.

    1. Minor actor who had appeared in Hopwood's *The Demi-Virgin* in 1921.

    2. Popular film actress, from *Tillie's Punctured Romance* (1914) through *Dinner at Eight* (1933) and other notable movies.

    3. German American Edward Knoblauch (which he altered to Knoblock in 1917), novelist and playwright best known for *Kismet*, with Otis Skinner, and an adaptation of Vicki Baum's *Grand Hotel*, both later made into successful films and musical plays.

    4. Playwright who adapted *The Love Habit* by Louis Verneuil, in which Marinoff appeared.

    5. American actress, the star of Hopwood's first success, *Clothes*, 1907.

    6. Theatrical producer, responsible for many of Hopwood's successful plays.

    7. Probably Bertram Harrison, Hopwood's stage manager.

    8. Theatrical producer and his wife. Miller produced *The Captive*, an adaptation of a serious and subtle French play about lesbians, but the district attorney ordered the police to close it down. A jury acquitted it of immorality charges, but only seven to five, and Miller did not reopen it.

    9. American humorist and, later, playwright, best known for one of the most enduring books of the twenties, *Gentlemen Prefer Blondes;* and her husband, with whom she later wrote screenplays.

Thursday, 2 November 1922

Ruth Shepley[1] has lunch with us at the Algonquin, a particularly brilliant day. Among those in the room: Robert Benchley, Connelly[2] & Kauffman[3] (author of *Dulcy*), Douglas Fairbanks, Mary Pickford, Flora Zabelle,[4] Roberta Arnold, Carol McComas,[5] Horace Liveright, Tallulah Bankhead, Anita Loos, Heywood Broun,[6] Alec Woollcott, Joseph Hergesheimer, Louis Untermeyer,[7] . . . and others. Frank Case puts "Onion Soup with Cheese, Rascoe"[8] on the bill. I take Joe Hergesheimer to see Marie Doro in the afternoon.

    1. American actress.

    2. Marc Connelly, American playwright best remembered for *The Green Pastures* in 1930, with an all-black cast, based on Garland Roark's *Ole Adam and His Chillun*.

    3. George S. Kauffman, prolific and successful American playwright (*Dulcy* was the current hit of the season), often in collaboration with other playwrights.

    4. Older actress and partner of Raymond Hitchcock, on stage and off.

    5. Arnold and McComas were both established but minor American actresses.

    6. American journalist and critic, with liberal sympathies toward social injustices.

    7. American poet and poetry anthologist.

    8. Named for newspaper critic Burton Rascoe because he was such a faithful customer at the Algonquin.

Sunday, 5 November 1922

Father & Addie's anniversary.[1] Dinner at William Hurlbut's,[2] 63 West 48 Street at 8 o'clock. Marie Doro, Fania, Joseph & Dorothy Hergesheimer. Lunch at 1.15 at Stettheimers' family. Cocktail party at Sylvia Joslyn's—all the kept women & brokers in New York. I divide my time between the butler's pantry—where Maitland d'Arcy the Irish butler mixes cocktails & the piano where George Gershwin[3] plays his "Swanee" & "I'll Build a Stairway to Paradise."

    1. Charles Duane Van Vechten and his second wife, Addie Lawton.

    2. Prolific playwright in the Twenties.

    3. Young composer on the cusp of becoming—with his brother Ira—the most popular and enduring songwriter in America. CVV was his earliest public champion, in *Vanity Fair*.

Monday, 6 November 1922

Tea at 5 at Waldorf with Hugh Walpole.[1] (No tea. We sit in his room and talk.) I give a lunch at the Russian Inn for Boyd & Ettie Stettheimer. Andrew Dasburg & Antonio de Sanchez[2] join us. I give *The Blind Bow-Boy* to Alfred

[Knopf].³ Tom Beer at the Yale Club at 7, gives me a bottle of absinthe. Cocktail with Joe Hergesheimer at Algonquin. Dinner at Algonquin with Fania. . . .

1. Popular English novelist who became an intimate but solely literary friend. Walpole was homosexual, but according to CVV they never discussed the subject.

2. J. A. M. De Sanchez, a Hispanic statistician with J. P. Morgan & Company. He and his wife, Dorothy, were inveterate theater-goers.

3. CVV's only publisher (seventeen books) after 1915. He refers here to the finished manuscript of his second novel.

Friday, 10 November 1922

Dinner at Muriel Draper's,¹ 21 E. 89 Street, at 8 o'clock. Lunch with A. B. MacCaughy, Ralph [Van Vechten]'s Chicago friend at Algonquin. Walked home with Ernest Boyd. Bobby Locher comes in in the morning to discuss frontispiece for *Blind Bow-Boy*. . . . We went on to . . . birthday party for the Lochers. . . .²

1. Prominent social patron of the arts, in London before the war and then in New York. She was later identified as "The White Negress" because of her physical appearance and her patronage in Harlem Renaissance circles.

2. Interior and stage decorator Robert Locher and his wife, Beatrice.

Saturday, 11 November 1922

MacCaughy was to give a party tonight for Walpole, Hergesheimer, Knoblock, etc. but I am tired of parties and called it off. Marie Doro calls up & wants to give a party.

Thursday, 16 November 1922

Lunch at Algonquin with Marinoff, T. R. Smith, Tallulah Bankhead, Horace Liveright. Helen Westley brings her brother in. Tom Beer asked me some time ago to see John Barrymore's opening in *Hamlet* tonight but he is unable to get seats & calls it off today. Very Tom Beerish! I am re-reading *The Buffoon* by Louis Wilkinson.¹

1. This novel, published by Knopf circa 1916, was considered obscene and originally suppressed.

Monday, 20 November 1922

I have a bad cold. Lunch at the Algonquin. Bertha & Frank Case¹ & Mrs. Atherton came to the table. Wallace Stevens came in in the afternoon with the mss of his book *Harmonium* which I have gotten for Knopf.² He talked about

Pitts'[3] jealousies—Pitts it seems thinks I have kept him out of Knopf's—and after drinking half a quart of my best bourbon Wallace told me he didn't like me. Dinner at home. Reading [Charles] Brockden Brown's *Ormond.*

    1. The Cases owned and operated the Algonquin Hotel, often mixing as friends with their guests.

    2. The first collection of Stevens's poems was published by Alfred A. Knopf at the behest of CVV, who had first published Stevens himself in *Trend,* an arts and letters journal he edited for three months at the end of 1914.

    3. American music critic John Pitts Sanborn, a friend of CVV since circa 1910.

Friday, 24 November 1922

Read Mary Heaton Vorse's *Growing Up.* Lunched with Arthur D[avison] Ficke,[1] just divorced, at Hotel Brevoort. Still have bad cold. Dinner with Ralph V. V. at Giarbini de Caserta. Regina Wallace[2] & Roger Hyatt of Cleveland. They came down to the house after dinner. . . .

    1. American poet and Asian art connoisseur. With American poet Witter Bynner, Ficke is responsible for having perpetrated the *Spectra* hoax, passing off a collection of deliberately obscurantist work as the inspired verse of "Anne Knish" and "Emanuel Morgan." Literary critics took *Spectra* seriously for a time.

    2. Regina Wallace never married, but she had an extensive roster of beaux.

Monday, 27 November 1922

Still have bad cold. Sent "On Visiting Fashionable Places Out of Season" to Emily Clark for *The Reviewer.* Lunch at Algonquin with Marinoff & Claire Schermerhorn. Rita Romilly & Helen Westley came in after lunch. Dinner with Marinoff at Ceylonese Restaurant. We went to the premiere of Gertrude Saunders[1] in *Liza* at 63 St. Theatre, a negro review. Wonderful![2]

    1. Popular black comedienne and singer who opened in *Shuffle Along* in 1921, the first African American entertainment on Broadway, sometimes cited as having sparked the Harlem Renaissance.

    2. Although CVV saw all-black shows early in the century, this is his first recorded response to the new interest in African-American matters. *Liza* was pronounced "unbelievably crude and rough-hewn" by the *New York Times,* but it was notable for introducing the Charleston to white audiences for the first time.

Tuesday, 5 December 1922

Silver Society Cat Show, Biltmore, Dec 5, 1922. Took Phil Moeller. . . . Dinner at Yale Club, spent evening with him [and] David Kirkpatrick Esty Bruce,[1] nephew of Thomas Nelson Page, cousin of James Branch Cabell, [and] collector of Ouida[2] & Carl Van Vechten. Lunch at Algonquin with Marinoff. Phil

[Moeller] & Helen [Westley] came in. Reading [Theodore] Dreiser's *A Book About Myself.*

> 1. The son of Senator Cabell Bruce, he wrote criticism for *The Reviewer*, collected books, and aspired to be a serious writer. Emily Clark described him as "extremely attractive, not a bit like his father, and the best looking man in the twenties, I think, that I have seen." CVV had met him in Richmond and immediately adopted him as one of his *jeunes gens assortis.*
>
> 2. Marie Louise de la Ramée, a nineteenth-century novelist of whom CVV was fond.

Wednesday, 6 December 1922

David Bruce came to lunch with me at Algonquin. Phil Moeller & Helen Westley, Tallulah Bankhead & Blythe Daly sit with us. Afterwards I take Tallulah, Blythe, & Bruce over to see Florine's picture of me.[1] . . . Avery [Hopwood] & John Floyd go to dinner with us at Ceylonese Restaurant.

> 1. Florine Stettheimer had painted one of her fanciful portraits, in which a glamorized CVV, svelte and effete in black with purple stockings, is surrounded by his familiar enthusiasms: cats, a piano, a mask of Fania Marinoff on the wall, Broadway nightlife outside the window, a typewriter, and haute cuisine.

Friday, 8 December 1922

Finished Dreiser's *awful* book & read Forrest Reid's *Pender Among the Residents.* Lunch at Algonquin. Dinner home.

Sunday, 10 December 1922

Here all day. Reading proofs on *Bow-Boy.* In the afternoon Sinclair Lewis telephoned to ask if he & his wife might come in in the evening . . . first time he has ever set foot in any of my apartments![1]

> 1. Lewis's wife in 1922 was Grace Hegger, a former *Vogue* editor.

Monday, 25 December 1922

Actors' Equity Play, Jessye Lynch Williams's *Why Not?* Algonquin for dinner. Tallulah Bankhead & Freddo Sides[1] dine with us. T. R. Smith party—Boyds, Edna Kenton, John D. Williams,[2] Tallulah & Freddo. We go on to John Murray Anderson's[3] where we find Bert Savoy,[4] Philip Bartholomae[5] & twenty others. We go to Mendes, the architect's, where we find Yvonne George,[6] Bob Chanler, Louise Hellström, Marcel Duchamp, and many others. Home at 7 A.M. . . .

> 1. Alfred Sides, minor actor.

2. Theatrical producer, responsible for Eugene O'Neill's *Beyond the Horizon*.

3. Musical theater revue producer.

4. Popular transvestite entertainer who appeared with Jay Brennan in vaudeville.

5. Donald Angus's first partner in New York. Insanity cut short Bartholomae's career as a playwright of farces, 1911–22, and occasional director.

6. Minor actress in musical revues of the period.

Saturday, 30 December 1922

Stettheimers', after 9 o'clock. Hugh Walpole lunches with me at Algonquin. We pick up Joe Hergesheimer & I take them to Florine's studio to see my portrait. Then Walpole comes home with me to spend afternoon. Dinner with Joe at Algonquin. I take him to Stettheimer party: . . . Marcel Duchamp, Marie Sterner,[1] Pitts Sanborn, Hugo Seligman,[2] . . . Joe & I meet Walpole at the Algonquin & go up to the Cases'.

1. Curator at the Knoedler art gallery, wife of artist Albert Sterner.

2. A Stettheimer relative and a member of another wealthy family dynasty, Seligman and his wife, Frances, were frequent dinner guests.

1923

"All greeted me cordially.
This must mean fame!"

In 1923, Van Vechten wrote his third novel, *The Tattooed Countess,* requiring some research into the past, at the New York Public Library, for he was recreating the 1897 milieu of his home town in Iowa. In the twenties, 1897 seemed to have occurred a century rather than only a quarter of a century before. Simultaneously, he continued his unearthing of undiscovered, underrated, or forgotten literary figures such as Ronald Firbank, Henry Blake Fuller, Edgar Saltus, M. P. Shiel, and Gertrude Stein. Van Vechten took a second trip to Richmond, Virginia, and Fania Marinoff made her last appearance on the New York stage for a decade. Meanwhile, Van Vechten had begun to explore more widely the range of speakeasies that had opened in New York in the wake Prohibition, including several in Harlem.

Friday, 5 January 1923

F.P.A.[1] dinner at 7.00. Ill with abdominal influenza—unable to go. Went to see Dr. Livingstone & found that there was an epidemic. Letter from H. B. Fuller saying he is returning the first six of his books, autographed.[2] *The International Book Review* for February is out with *Peter Whiffle* in Hugh Walpole's list of the six best books of 1922. Lunch, alone, on way to doctor's, at The Kloster Cloche on 4 Ave. Dinner home.

    1. Franklin P. Adams, popular American journalist and humorist whose columns, always signed "F.P.A.," chronicled New York's literary and theatrical life through the twenties.

    2. CVV had written favorably about the forgotten Chicago novelist Henry Blake Fuller and had accumulated all of his books, including the rare (because Fuller destroyed most copies of the only edition when it failed) *Bertram Cope's Year*, a novel resurrected by Turtle Point Press in 1999 that is now required reading in some college literature courses in gay and gender studies. CVV's Fuller collection is in the Beinecke Rare Book and Manuscript Library at Yale University.

Saturday, 13 January 1923

Stettheimers' party: Boyds, D'Alvarez,[1] Phil Moeller, Zorachs,[2] Louis Bouché & wife,[3] Marcel Duchamp, Hergesheimer, Charles Brackett, Pitts Sanborn, . . . Henry McBride, . . . Walkowitz,[4] Andrew Dasburg, Marie Doro, . . . etc. Dasburg took a lot of us down to Louise Hellström's where we found the painter [Joseph] Stella, Jane Heap, Margaret Anderson, Eva Gauthier[5] & a pianist friend of Jane's—a woman. Lunch at Algonquin with Marinoff, Ernest & Madeleine Boyd. Reading Aleicester Crowley's *Diary of a Drug Fiend*.

    1. Marguerite D'Alvarez, Peruvian contralto whose monumental proportions and flamboyant manner limited her appearances in staged operas (although she concertized for many years) but not as herself in public.

    2. American sculptor William Zorach and his painter wife, Marguerite.

    3. French painter and his wife, Marion.

    4. German American artist Abraham Walkowitz, notable for his hundreds of ink-wash sketches of dancer Isadora Duncan.

    5. Canadian soprano first to introduce jazz—by way of a group of songs by George Gershwin in 1924—into a recital program, at the instigation of CVV.

Wednesday, 17 January 1923

Lunch with Horace Liveright at Algonquin. Talked with Mencken and Edna Ferber.[1] To the office with Horace & got a copy of Mrs. [Gertrude] Atherton's *Black Oxen*, which I started to read when I got home. Dinner with Madeleine & Ernest Boyd at Brevoort—Fania dining out. . . . Madeleine went to *The God of Vengeance*[2] & Boyd took me to Theodore Dreiser's[3] where I met Sherwood Anderson[4] & Dr. [A. A.] Brill (psychoanalyst) for first time. Mencken, Llewelyn Powys,[5] Scott Fitzgerald were also there.

    1. Prolific American writer and member of the Algonquin Round Table, later notable for her novel *Showboat.*

    2. This play, based on a novel by Sholem Asch, was closed by the police after a few weeks because it mixed religion and prostitution.

    3. American novelist who published CVV's first article (about Richard Strauss's *Salome*) in New York in 1906 in *Broadway Magazine*, of which he was then editor.

    4. American writer and, with CVV, a supporter of experimental expatriate writer Gertrude Stein.

    5. Member of a trio of prolific Welsh writing brothers, with John Cowper Powys and Theodore Powys.

Thursday, 18 January 1923

Horace Liveright's luncheon for Theodore Dreiser at the Beaux Arts: private room. Henry Mencken, George Jean Nathan, T. R. Smith, Dreiser, Gilbert Cannon,[1] Hendrick Van Loon,[2] Flaherty,[3] etc. . . . After Cannon had gone I gave my imitation of him at Horace's lunch party. Home in a taxi & to bed at 4.30.

    1. English writer better known for his translation of Romain Rolland's *Jean Christophe* than for his own novels.

    2. Dutch American journalist and prolific popular historian.

    3. Robert Flaherty, pioneering documentary filmmaker.

Tuesday, 23 January 1923

Lunch at the Algonquin with Madeleine Boyd, Otto Liveright, . . . Tennessee Anderson (Mrs. Sherwood Anderson) whom I met. Frank Case & Charlie Brackett. Saw Ralph [Van Vechten] for a cocktail. Then Fania & I dined at Leone's & to see [Luigi] Pirandello's *Six Characters in Search of an Author,* left after first act. Reading Marcel Proust's *Swann's Way.*[1]

    1. Proust's novel *A la recherche de temps perdu* had commenced publication in English in semiannual volumes.

Wednesday, 24 January 1923

Lunched at Algonquin with Ralph Van Vechten & Charles Brackett. . . . Dinner at 7 with Gertrude Atherton at Madison Square Hotel. She told me the marvelous history of her father & mother, & of her husband George Atherton, who died on a man-o-war &, as a guest, was not buried at sea but was brought home in a keg of rum.

Friday, 26 January 1923

Lunch at the Algonquin with Otto Liveright & Fania. Reading page proofs on *Blind Bow-Boy.* To Edna Kenton's in evening. Party at Louise Hellström's—after 10 o'clock—for Yvonne George. Margaret Anderson, Jane Heap, Kitty Kelly.[1] . . . Stella (painter), Phil Moeller, Helen Westley, Georgette Leblanc.

    1. American comedienne, primarily in films.

Saturday, 3 February 1923

. . . Dinner with Horace Liveright called off because Horace's children are ill. In the morning saw Georgia O'Keeffe's exhibit[1] & talked with Stieglitz & Jules Pascin.[2] . . . Read Ronald Firbank's *Flower Beneath the Foot.* We had dinner home. Gertrude Atherton called me up to take me to dinner . . . but I could not go.

    1. Although O'Keeffe's work had been shown earlier at Stieglitz's gallery, this was her first solo exhibition in New York.
    2. French Post-Impressionist painter.

Saturday, 10 February 1923

Lunch with Rosamund & Leah Ach[1] & Marinoff at the Algonquin. To Marie Doro's after lunch for an hour, with some Chinese & Spanish gipsy records, & magazines with papers by me. . . . Lawrence [and Estelle] Langner's,[2] after 9.30 party for Edna St. Vincent Millay,[3] Jane Cowl,[4] Rollo Peters,[5] John Emerson, Anita Loos, Phil Moeller, Mrs. Waldo Frank (met),[6] Heywood Broun.[7] . . . Talked for first time in years with Henrietta McCry Metcalf (Pam).[8] Jay Kaufman,[9] Freddo Sides, Helen Westley, Helen Sheridan,[10] Louis & Jean Untermeyer,[11] etc. Nigger[12] orchestra: dancing.

    1. Marinoff relatives.
    2. Lawrence Langner was founder of the Theatre Guild. He and his second wife, the actress Armina Marshall, were close friends of CVV and Marinoff.
    3. American poet popular with both readers and critics in the twenties.
    4. Popular American actress noted in her lucrative run in *Smilin' Thru,* a sentimental romance she wrote with Jane Murfin. Her "tears and treacle" approach to acting, according to CVV, was less successful when she appeared in Shakespeare's plays.
    5. American actor, a sometime co-star of Fania Marinoff.
    6. Like CVV, Waldo Frank was an Iowan who had escaped the Midwest to become a writer, but unlike CVV, he was a left-wing, radical poet, polemicist, and novelist, notable for his association with early black writer Jean Toomer, with whom his wife later eloped.

7. American journalist and Algonquin Round Table member, married to feminist writer Ruth Hale.

8. CVV met the daughter of American painter Willard Metcalf in Paris in 1908 when he was beset with a fit of giggles because of her bad singing during a vocal recital. They became fast friends and remained so for many years.

9. Probably S. Jay Kaufman, American theatrical producer.

10. American actress who appeared in *He Who Gets Slapped, Don Juan,* and *Fata Morgana.*

11. Husband and wife poets and anthologists.

12. CVV's use of this epithet at the time is not unusual. Many white Americans used the word in ignorance more often than in malice. There was no public outcry against the word in the black press until circa 1926, although African Americans had always fiercely resented its use by the white race. Like others after him, CVV had to be taught.

Thursday, 15 February 1923

Lunch at Algonquin with Marinoff. Talked with Frank Case and Helen Westley. [Theatre] Guild may do [George Bernard] Shaw's *[Caesar and] Cleopatra* with Marinoff.[1] Lunch—Marie Doro, 12.30, called off. Marie sick. Dinner at home & early to bed.

1. Marinoff refused the role of the teenaged Cleopatra; in 1923 she was thirty-six years old. Long afterward, Armina Marshall Langner claimed that Marinoff had effectively killed her own career by refusing the role.

Sunday, 18 February 1923

Lunch at home. Charles Brackett came at 3 o'clock and we went to Arthur Davison Ficke's for cocktails. Found Edna St. Vincent Millay there. Also discovered Arthur was a painter. Brackett, Ficke, & I go to baptize kittens for Arthur Ficke at a [*word*] on West 47 Street. . . .

Friday, 9 March 1923

Fania rehearsing.[1] Lunch with Marinoff, Ernest Boyd, & Charles Brackett at Algonquin. Dinner at Claire Burke Schermerhorn's. Regina Wallace & Marinoff. To M. M. Baths.[2] Home alone. Marinoff at the Algonquin so that she can sleep late in the morning.

1. In *The Love Habit,* Marinoff's penultimate stage appearance in New York for nearly a decade.

2. The Mount Morris Bathhouse in Harlem catered to rough trade. This is the only reference in CVV's papers to his patronizing the African American emporium for homosexuals.

Sunday, 18 March 1923

In all day, lunch at home. Fania stays in bed & does not go to dinner at Marie Doro's. Phil Moeller, Helen Westley, Fannie Cottenet,[1] Marie et moi. Theatre Guild rehearsal. Elmer Rice's *The Adding Machine*. Edna Kenton, Sue Glaspell,[2] Marie Doro & Phil in box with me.

> 1. Director of the Three Arts Club for forty years, which strongly supported young women in the theater. Cottenet was also a privately generous philanthropist.
>
> 2. American playwright who founded—with her husband, dramaturg George Cram Cook—The Provincetown Players on Cape Cod in 1914 and subsequently in Greenwich Village.

Monday, 26 March 1923

Wrote title page of *Tattooed Countess*.[1] Working on preface for Ouida's *In a Winter City* which I reread. Sent to Horace Liveright. London reviews of *Peter Whiffle*—all good—continue to come in. Lunch alone at Algonquin. . . . Reading Bjorkman's *Gates of Life*.[2] Marinoff & I dine at Leone's. Sarah Bernhardt dies.[3]

> 1. CVV's third novel, about his hometown, Cedar Rapids, Iowa, just before the turn of the twentieth century.
>
> 2. Edwin August Björkman, Swedish novelist whom CVV had recently met through the Stettheimer sisters.
>
> 3. The most celebrated actress in the Western world, still performing at seventy-eight, always in French, and latterly minus one leg. CVV had met her at the turn of the twentieth century in Chicago and reported on her anorexic figure, her golden voice, and her breakfast—including two bottles of beer—in his gossip column for the *Chicago American*.

Friday, 30 March 1923

Marinoff signed contract with Cromwell for *Tarnish*.[1] Lunch at Algonquin. Guest of Antonio de Sanchez. . . . My plate proofs of *The Blind Bow-Boy* came and I worked on them. Dinner at the Elysée, guest of John Floyd (who is sailing on the *Majestic* tomorrow to rejoin Avery in Venice). Marinoff who dined with us went to Everard Baths.

> 1. John Cromwell, theatrical producer of *Tarnish*, by Gilbert Emery.

Sunday, 1 April 1923

In all day, cataloguing letters. Read in *World* how Frank Case has barred the Jews from Algonquin. Dinner at Lee Simonson's,[1] 71 West 68 St. Louis & Jean

Untermeyer, Maurice & Alma Wertheim,[2] Clarence & Gladys Axman,[3] . . .
Philip Moeller, Helen Westley.

　　1. American set designer, later a Theatre Guild director, still later an editor for
Creative Art.
　　2. Wealthy American patrons of the arts.
　　3. Insurance editor and his wife, an occasional soprano.

Monday, 2 April 1923

Madeleine returned the proofs of *The Bow-Boy,* very enthusiastic. Lunch at
Algonquin, with Marinoff & Madeleine Boyd. Talked with Frank Case about
the Jew story. Broun, Woollcott,[1] & Liveright have all refused to lunch there.
Cataloguing letters. Dinner home alone, and then to Edna Kenton's. Teddie
Ballentyne[2] has left Stella Corman. Neil & Mabel Reber come in. I go [to] the
theatre to get Marinoff.

　　1. Alexander Woollcott, dyspeptic theater critic, charter member of the
Algonquin Round Table.
　　2. E. S. Ballentyne was an established actor early in the century.

Tuesday, 3 April 1923

Reading plate proofs of *Bow-Boy.* Went to office & saw Sam Knopf.[1] Lunch
alone at Algonquin. Saw Connelly & Woollcott: An attempt is being made
to treat the pogrom as a joke.

　　1. The "office" refers to CVV's publisher's office. Samuel Knopf was Alfred
Knopf's father and a senior advisor.

Monday, 9 April 1923

Mailed corrected *Peter* [*Whiffle*] to Richards.[1] Ettie [Stettheimer] to lunch
with us, 12.45, Algonquin, also C[harles] Brackett. . . . Luncheon party moved
on to see Stieglitz photo exhibition at Anderson Galleries. . . . To Edna
Kenton's before dinner. Dinner with Marinoff at Leone's.

　　1. Grant Richards, London publisher of CVV's first two novels, the second of
which contained passages that he censored slightly because of their homosexual
innuendo and some similes that offended him.

Monday, 23 April 1923

Reading M. P. Shiel's *Unto the Third Generation.*[1] Lunch at Algonquin with
Ernest Boyd & Marinoff. Talked with Gertrude Atherton, H. Liveright, &
T. R. Smith.[2] Joffe brought Rimsky-Korsakoff page proofs & stayed all the af-

ternoon. Dinner alone at Luchow's. In the evening Edmund Wilson, Jr., called to look at my Gertrude Steins.[3]

1. Matthew Phipps Shiel, the English novelist, is one of several obscure writers CVV resurrected in the twenties.
2. Judah A. Joffe, translator of *My Musical Life* by Nikolay Rimsky-Korsakov, which CVV was editing for Knopf.
3. Then a young critic, Wilson was already gathering material for his study of literary modernism, *Axel's Castle* (1931), arguably the first serious consideration of Stein's work. CVV her earliest public advocate and had already amassed an impressive collection of her publications to date.

Thursday, 3 May 1923

Wrote review for [*New York Herald*] *Tribune* of G. Stein's *Geography and Plays*.[1] Lunch alone at Algonquin. Talked with Stuart Rose,[2] Horace Liveright, Ernest & Madeleine Boyd. I've been suffering with poor indigestion for past few days.[3] Dinner with Tom Smith at the Brevoort. Marinoff, Ernest & Madeleine Boyd. We go to Boyds' after dinner for a little while.

1. Stein had financed her first major collection into print through the Four Seas Company in Boston.
2. American literary critic who first introduced CVV to the work of English fantasist Ronald Firbank, which CVV then began to publicize in America.
3. CVV apparently was unable or unwilling to connect his increasing bouts of physical discomfort with his overindulgence in food and liquor in the twenties.

Sunday, 6 May 1923

Still with indigestion. Finished my review of Stein's *Geography & Plays* & sent it off to Rascoe. Rereading *The Flower Beneath the Foot* for review. Lunch at the Brevoort with Tony de Sanchez. Claire [Burke Schermerhorn] came in. We dropped her & came over to the house. At 4.30 W. Sterling Suftin, a young Philadelphia boy who has been writing me, came in. I sent him away at 6.15 and joined Phil Moeller & Helen Westley at the Brevoort for dinner. Party at Mabel Reber's. Edna Kenton, Andrew Dasburg, Ida Rauh, Otto & Bernardine[1] Liveright, Phil & Helen. Harry Kemp[2] brought a new girl in. Andrew & Ida just returned from New Mexico & Mabel Dodge's wedding.[3] Marinoff in N.J. at Jack [Marinoff]'s.

1. Under her maiden name, Otto Liveright's wife, Bernardine Szold, wrote a regular column for the *New York News*.
2. Iconoclastic American poet and playwright who lived as a tramp, a familiar Greenwich Village figure, whose novel *More Miles* includes a thinly disguised CVV as "Jarl Loring."

3. American art patron Mabel Ganson Evans Dodge Sterne had just married a Taos Pueblo Indian, Antonio Lujan, thereafter identified as Tony Luhan. She and CVV had known each other intimately for a decade and maintained a lifelong friendship (interrupted by long periods of estrangement) until her death in 1961.

Thursday, 10 May 1923

Wrote part of Chapter IX of *The Tattooed Countess.* Went to office to see Alfred & Blanche [Knopf] at 12. Had lunch with Alfred. We talked over everything. I took up mss. by Charles Brackett[1] & Gertrude Stein.[2] Alfred says he will print *The Blind Bow-Boy* intact in America. It is to be expurgated in England. Dinner with Marinoff at Leone's . . . & home to bed.

1. *Weekend,* a novel later published at CVV's instigation by Brentano's.
2. *The Making of Americans.* Knopf actually issued a subscription flyer for this nearly one thousand-page novel, but the return was insufficient to persuade him to publish it. The book was first published two years later in Paris.

Tuesday, 29 May 1923

Lunch at Algonquin with T. R. Smith. Talked with Tony de Sanchez & Ernest Boyd. Worked in library.[1] Tony, Ernest, & Louis Sherwin[2] came in for cocktails & dine with me at Leone's. We go to Jack Catlin's[3] & at 10 o'clock I pick up Bert Savoy at the Palace where he is playing & bring him up. He amuses us for 3 hours & then takes Ernest away with him. Louis, Tony & I go down to Louis (Mabel Reber's apt.), wake up his sister & her husband there.[4] Dinner at Brevoort alone, & home to bed.

1. CVV was doing period research for *The Tattooed Countess,* set in 1897.
2. American journalist and theater critic, one of Marinoff's earliest champions, noted for a scatological sense of humor.
3. A speakeasy briefly popular.
4. Sherwin lived in the same apartment house as his actress-sister Jeannette and her husband, James Jolly.

Tuesday, 5 June 1923

I made my list for *Vanity Fair* of the ten authors who bore me most.[1] Finished <u>first</u> draught of *The Tattooed Countess.* Lunch at Algonquin, alone but saw Sam Hoffenstein, Burton Rascoe, Horace Liveright, Julian Messner,[2] Mrs. Jelliffe.[3] . . . Dinner alone at Leone's. Saw Chamberlain Brown.[4] Then to Jack & Lucile's,[5] where I passed the evening drinking gin & got very drunk.

1. A symposium, including H. L. Mencken, George Jean Nathan, Elinor Wylie, James Branch Cabell, Christopher Morley, Burton Rascoe, Ernest Boyd, and Edna Ferber. CVV's choices were Sigmund Freud, Gabriele d'Annunzio, Edith Wharton,

Walter Pater, Gerhart Hauptmann, James Joyce, Pierre Loti, D. H. Lawrence, Amy Lowell, and J. M. Barrie.

2. Originally an editor with Boni & Liveright, then an independent publisher in partnership with his brother Kendall.

3. Rowena Jelliffe and her husband, Russell, managed the Gilpin Players, a repertory company in Cleveland, Ohio that specialized in African American drama and performers.

4. Theatrical agent who at one time founded his own stock company to employ the actors he represented. In partnership with his brother, Lyman, he represented Fania Marinoff, among many others.

5. Lucile and Jack Harper owned and operated CVV's favorite speakeasy for some years. CVV usually called the place "Lucile's." Jack served as one of CVV's regular bootleggers.

Tuesday, 19 June 1923

At work rummaging over first chapter of *The Tattooed Countess*. Lunch with Hugh Walpole at 12.30. The Crillon. I met him with Stark (Young Boswell)[1] in the Harriman Bank. At the Crillon we met Avery Hopwood, John Floyd, & Mrs. Hopwood,[2] just back from Europe. . . . Hugh & I went to see the swimmers at Madison Square Garden & then came down to the house for a while. I gave him *Bertram Cope's Year*.[3] He had never heard of Fuller. After he left I went to Lucille's. Eddie Mayer[4] came in. I took him to dinner at Algonquin. Then home. Hunter Stagg[5] came & stayed till 1.30.

1. Stark Young, theater critic. CVV is making a private joke about Samuel Johnson's biographer, James Boswell, because Young wrote biographies. Later he became theater critic for the *New York Times* and the *New Republic*.

2. Avery Hopwood's mother and close companion, Julie, sometimes spelled Jule.

3. Henry Blake Fuller's novel had sunk into obscurity on publication in 1919, misunderstood by critics and causing embarrassment to his friends, and was not republished until 1999.

4. American playwright Edward Justus Mayer, best known for *The Firebrand* and *Children of Darkness*.

5. With Emily Clark, Stagg edited *The Reviewer* in Richmond, Virginia. He was an early admirer of CVV's novels; also, he was wealthy, high strung, handsome, and homosexual, one of CVV's group of *jeunes gens assortis*, five of whom he called "Famous Beauties of the XXth Century," having their photographs reproduced on a series of postcards. The others were Donald Angus, Max Ewing, Tom Mabry, Prentiss Taylor, Edward Wassermann, and himself.

Wednesday, 20 June 1923

Went to office & collected $600. Met Hunter Stagg who walks with me to 5th Avenue. Lunch alone at Algonquin. Avery Hopwood came in to sit with me.

Talked with Ernest Boyd & Tony de Sanchez (who were lunching together), Otto & Bernardine [Szold] Liveright, Burton Rascoe (with 6 women), & Horace Liveright. Excessively hot—95—I spend the afternoon at home & begin 2nd draught of *The Tattooed Countess*. Get my own dinner. After dinner Hunter Stagg comes in with Young Montgomery Evans[1] of Philadelphia, with whom he is going to Europe.

    1. A New Orleans friend of Hunter Stagg, a valuable diarist, and a devotee of diabolic cults.

Sunday, 24 June 1923

Fania and I visit the Stettheimers at Sea Bright. There for the day. Come back in the evening. No one else on this week-end. We motor to Asbury Park & observe the beaches, black & white.[1] Reading Shiel's *Cold Steel*.

    1. The Stettheimers often rented summer houses away from the city. Mixed races bathing together on public beaches was an anomaly in 1923.

Wednesday, 27 June 1923

Lunch at Algonquin with Marinoff. She leaves to go to first rehearsal of *Tarnish*. I talk with Burton Rascoe, . . . Otto Liveright, Henry Mencken, . . . Horace Liveright. . . . I go to Horace's office with him & sit through a meeting in which he borrows $150,000 in stock belonging to his wife's father. Then Horace asks me to leave Knopf & offers me $12,500 on my next book. I refuse but he prophesies I'll be with him in 18 mos. Working on 4 chapter of *The Countess*. Dinner with Marinoff at Leone's. We go to see *Sweet Nell* at Equity Theatre & back to see Lynn Fontanne[1] & Laurette Taylor.[2]

    1. English-born American actress later well known for her regular appearances with her husband, Alfred Lunt. "The Lunts," as they were routinely called, reigned on Broadway until their joint retirement in 1960.

    2. American actress whose alcoholism ended her early career. Some years later she made a successful comeback on Broadway as Amanda in the first production of Tennessee Williams's *The Glass Menagerie*.

Tuesday, 3 July 1923

Mailed *Bow-Boy* to [Grant] Richards. Saw Alfred [Knopf] at office who tells me there isn't enough paper for the first edition of *Bow-Boy*, so I select three other papers to fill in.[1] Lunch at Algonquin. Ben Ray Redman[2] joins me. Then I go to table with Carrie & Ettie Stettheimer, Muk de Jari[3] & Gilbert Adrian[4] (met latter). Marinoff joins us. Marinoff goes out to dinner with Orchidee[5]

& I go to Taormina's new place alone, then to Lucile's, where I stay until midnight & come home.

    1. The binding for *The Blind Bow-Boy* had decorative paper over its boards, with a linen spine. CVV is referring here to alternative designs. Eventually, there were more than four variations because of the success of the book.

    2. American poet and translator as well as influential critic in his *Herald Tribune* column, "Old Wine in New Bottles," and later a similar column in the *Saturday Review of Literature.*

    3. An acquaintance through the Stettheimer sisters, self-described as minor royalty and an artist, although no record of his work seems to have survived.

    4. An aspiring artist at the time, Gilbert Grahame had changed his name to Adrian. He went on to become one of the leading costume designers in Hollywood.

    5. The stage name of Lucille Hoff, a dancer with Loie Fuller, the choreographer who performed at the turn of the twentieth century, manipulating huge and billowing silk butterfly wings attached to hand-held rods.

Monday, 23 July 1923

Wrote Chapter XI of *The Countess.* Lunch at Algonquin with Ernest Boyd. Sat next to Bernardine [Szold] Liveright. Talk to Eddie Knopf & Mary Ellis,[1] just back from Berlin. Walk home with Boyd. Dinner alone at Algonquin. Go to Lucile's where I find Arnold Daly.[2] He goes to play in *Fashions of 1924,* comes back after a while, fired because he was drunk. Reading Shiel's *Shapes in the Fire.* Marinoff opens in *Tarnish* in Newport.

    1. Theatrical producer and his popular musical comedy actress wife.

    2. American actor and theatrical producer, responsible for introducing several of George Bernard Shaw's plays in America, one of them (*You Never Can Tell*) with Marinoff.

Wednesday, 25 July 1923

Finish Chapter 13. Alfred Knopf tells me that *The Bow-Boy* has already sold 4,500 copies! Also that on Jan 1 he is to start a magazine to be called (if possible) *The American Mercury.* Mencken, Nathan, editors. Lunch at Algonquin with Ernest Boyd, Ben Ray Redman. Cocktails at Claire [Burke] Schermerhorn's. We go to a Chinese restaurant for dinner. Then to Lucile's, joined there by Sam Hoffenstein.[1] Marinoff plays in New London, Conn.

    1. American writer of light verse, also a humorist, lyricist, and parodist. This may be the first time that he and Claire Burke Schermerhorn met; subsequently she left her husband and married Hoffenstein.

Friday, 10 August 1923

President Harding's funeral. Everything closed. Finished papering the hall.[1] Lunch at Algonquin. Marinoff, Otto Liveright, Bernardine Szold, Doris Rebera,[2] Ernest Boyd. Talked with Horace Liveright, Julian Messner, Mary Ellis, Blythe Daly. Claire Schermerhorn dines with us at Leone's. Saw Robert M. Lovett.[3] Claire & I go to Lucile Harper's for a drink & then down to Edna Kenton's, where we find Helen Westley just back from Europe. Bernardine & Otto Liveright & Marinoff arrive later.

    1. Almost invariably, when Marinoff was out of town for tryouts or performing, CVV became engaged in major renovations to their apartment on East Nineteenth Street just off Gramercy Park. This time he wallpapered the living room with gold Chinese tea-paper but without moving any of the furniture, simply outlining it as he proceeded.

    2. Probably Neil Reber's sister. Because she aspired to a career as an opera singer, CVV added an *a* to her name, which she then adopted. However, she never stopped preparing to perform and therefore never did. Whether she and Louis Sherwin were married is unclear.

    3. Robert Morss Lovett, a scholarly writer and novelist on the faculty of the University of Chicago when CVV was a student there. Later Lovett was an infrequent social companion.

Saturday, 25 August 1923

Went to office at noon and signed large paper copies of *The Bow-Boy* which had just arrived.[1] Lunch at Algonquin with Ernest Boyd and Burton & Hazel Rascoe. Signed a book for Rita Romilly, talked with Raymond Hitchcock,[2] Edwin Knopf[3] & Dagmar Godowsky.[4] Late in afternoon went to see Lucile Harper at the hospital. She is very sick. Then went to see Jack [Harper] at his house. Dinner at Leone's with Marinoff. We came home and to bed early.

    1. In the twenties, Knopf issued limited, signed editions in extravagant bindings for several of his authors, including CVV.

    2. Musical comedy actor who first appeared with his wife, Flora Zabelle, and then regularly thereafter, notably in Victor Herbert's *The Red Mill*, 1911.

    3. Actor and director in whose Baltimore stock company Marinoff later appeared.

    4. Silent film actress; daughter of pianist and composer Leopold Godowsky.

Wednesday, 29 August 1923

Went to office. *Bow-Boy* & *Peter* [*Whiffle*] both in Knopf's list of 10 best sellers last week. Lunch at Crillon with Hunter Stagg. We went up to Lucile

[Harper]'s. She is back from hospital. Dinner at Leone's with Louis Sherwin, . . . Marinoff. Marinoff goes to theatre with Henriette Metcalf & we go to Lucile's where we are joined later by . . . Jim Jolley & Jeanette Sherwin. Party at Robert Morss Lovett's, 229 E 48 St. Vanderbilt 0119, under name of Grimes, postponed.

Wednesday, 12 September 1923

Alfred Knopf's birthday. I begin 3rd draught of *The Tattooed Countess.* Go to the office. Lunch at Algonquin with Phil Moeller & Helen Westley. Boyd back from a visit with Tom Beer. Talked with Ben Ray Redman, Woollcott, Dagmar Godowski, Rita Romilly, Mrs. Sherwood Anderson, Bernardine Szold, etc. Ernest Boyd walked home with me, had drinks here. Sherrill Schell[1] & Miguel Covarrubias[2] come in, latter to caricature me. Dinner at Henriette Metcalf's: Marinoff & Nickolas Muray.[3] We went to see *Earl Carroll's Vanities.* Then to opening of Club Colbert where we were joined by Charlie MacArthur[4] (met), Arthur Hornblow, Jr.[5] . . . Talked with Dagmar Godowsky, . . . Margaret Case,[6] Crowninshield, Muriel Draper, Martha Lorber,[7] Johnnie McMullin,[8] Barney Gallant,[9] Percy Hammond,[10] . . . etc.

1. English artist, photographer, and travel writer with a strong interest in Mexico.

2. Mexican artist whose successful career in New York began with a series of caricatures of celebrities with whom CVV arranged sittings. Later, Covarrubias became a noted anthropologist and, with photographs by his wife, the dancer Rose Rolanda, produced a series of books on Balinese, Mexican, and native American cultures.

3. Arguably the most successful celebrity and fashion photographer of the twenties.

4. American playwright and director, later married to the actress Helen Hayes.

5. Translator of several French plays that appeared on Broadway, notably *Les Hannetons,* by Sasha Guitry, and *The Captive,* by Edouard Bourdet.

6. Writer and editor for Condé Nast and *Vanity Fair;* daughter of Bertha and Frank Case.

7. American dancer, a protégée of both Ruth St. Denis and Martha Graham.

8. Author of a syndicated column about fashion and, later, Paris editor of *Vogue.* McMullin was the adopted son of interior decorator Elsie de Wolfe.

9. Legendary proprietor of the Greenwich Village Inn at Sheridan Square. Gallant was the first person to be convicted for selling liquor after Prohibition took effect, but he was out of jail in three weeks to open the Washington Square Club. Other speakeasies followed in his long career.

10. American playwright of an older generation and later a drama critic; a friend of CVV's since the turn of the twentieth century.

Wednesday, 19 September 1923

Worked on Chapter III of *The Countess*. Reading Shiel's *The Evil That Men Do*. Marinoff & I lunch at the Algonquin with Claire Schermerhorn. Talked with Bernardine Szold, Laurence Stallings,[1] Frank & Bertha Case, Dagmar Godowsky, George Oppenheimer.[2] . . . Took Stuart Rose at Brentano's Brackett's *Weekend* mss. We talked about Brentano doing Firbank & I wrote to Firbank. Donald Angus comes down for drinks & he dines with me at Algonquin where we sit next to Edwin Knopf & Mary Kennedy[3] & Deems Taylor.[4] At nine I go to a party at Robert Morss Lovett's. . . . Marinoff spends night in country at her brother's.

    1. American playwright best remembered for *What Price Glory?*, which he co-wrote with Maxwell Anderson.
    2. An editor at Alfred A. Knopf, Inc., later press agent there and eventually a vice president.
    3. Actress appearing in Eva LeGallienne's *Not So Long Ago*.
    4. American composer of musical comedy, opera, and symphonic music. He was a widely published and influential music critic as well.

Saturday, 22 September 1923

Working on Chapter IV of *The Countess*. Reading *The Dragon*.[1] Lunch with Marinoff at Algonquin. Miguel Covarrubias comes in with his caricatures. I introduce him to Woollcott, Broun, Eddie Mayer & The Round Table generally. He goes to sit at Round Table. With me he does Elinor Wylie. Talked with Margaret Case, Pam Metcalf, Ernest Boyd. Boyd walks home with me. Marinoff & I dine at Louis Sherwin's. Jolleys are there. Waldo Frank telephones Marinoff.

    1. Yet another novel by the prolific M. P. Shiel, whose books CVV was reading systematically as part of his eventual effort to popularize him in the United States.

Sunday, 23 September 1923

Newspaper strike still on. Strange odds and ends of paper come out, dramatic supplement of one, library supplement of another. Lunch at home. Worked on Chapter IV of *The Countess*. . . . Started to read *The Chronicles of Clovis* by Saki. At 4, Bernardine Szold & Otto Liveright, Pam Metcalf & Nickolas Muray, James Jolly & Jeannette Sherwin & T. R. Smith come in for drinks. When they go we have dinner at Luchow's & home to bed. Stomachache!

Saturday, 29 September 1923

Lunch at Algonquin. Mary Ellis and Edwin Knopf. Joe Hergesheimer comes in unexpectedly & sits with us. Then Covarrubias comes in & draws Joe. . . . Home arranging papers. At 7, Pam Metcalf & Nickolas Muray come for me. We go to Algonquin for Marinoff. Nik takes us to a bad dinner at Bertolotti's. Then they bring me home & take Marinoff back to Algonquin.[1]

 1. Marinoff infrequently stayed at the Algonquin while she was in rehearsals because of erratic hours, her chronic insomnia, and CVV's own misbehavior.

Monday, 1 October 1923

Finished *The Yellow Wave*. Began Shiel's *This Knot of Life*. Wrote Chapter VIII of *The Countess*. Lunch at Algonquin with Marinoff. . . . Charlie Chaplin lunches here today. Opening of *Tarnish*, with Marinoff at Belmonte Theatre. . . . Guest reception on the stage after performance. Henriette Metcalf, Marinoff & I have supper at Algonquin in Cases' apt. where Fania spends the night.

Sunday, 7 October 1923

In all day working at papers. . . . We have lunch in. Late in the afternoon I wandered up to Lucile Harper's. Then to the Piccadilly to dinner, with Pam Metcalf, Phil Moeller, Marinoff. Fania plays a benefit performance for Japanese earthquake sufferers. Rest of us go to Theatre Guild rehearsal of *Windows* [by John Galsworthy]. . . . Pam takes us home in her car. We call for Marinoff.

Wednesday, 10 October 1923

Wrote Chapter XI of *The Countess*. Lunch at Benedusi's alone, but met Guy Holt[1] & a poet named Owen. Reading Mallock's *Romance of the 19 Century*. Cocktails at Claire Schermerhorn's. Sam Hoffenstein was there. Dinner with Marinoff at Pam Metcalf's. After dinner while Marinoff was at the theatre, I helped arrange Pam's books, & she told me how her brother had killed himself after trying to shoot her father. Marinoff came back after theatre & we went home. Wrote M. P. Shiel.

 1. James Branch Cabell's editor at McBride & Company.

Friday, 12 October 1923

Reading Saki's *The Toys of Peace.* Letter from Sinclair Lewis about *The Bow-Boy* arrived. Writing Chapter XIII of *The Countess.* Lunch at Algonquin with Ben Ray Redman, Ernest Boyd, T. R. Smith, Burton Rascoe, etc. . . . Cocktails at Ralph Barton's with his wife Carlotta Monterey.[1] I went to theatre for Marinoff & we had dinner at Leone's with Chamberlain & Lyman Brown. Then I went to Lucile's. Pokey Murray[2] (later with his big blonde girl), Louis Sherwin, Ruth Hammond,[3] Claire Schermerhorn, Stuart Rose came in with Lewis Baer,[4] and after I [*get?*] Marinoff, Baer drove us home at 1.15.

    1. Barton did not marry actress Carlotta Monterey until 1925, but they called themselves Mr. and Mrs. Ralph Barton at least two years before that.
    2. A bootlegger.
    3. Minor American actress and cartoonist.
    4. Editor at Albert & Charles Boni Publishers.

Sunday, 21 October 1923

Our 9th wedding anniversary. Sam Hoffenstein & Claire Schermerhorn came to lunch. After lunch Bernardine Szold & Otto Liveright, Lynn Fontanne, Florine Stettheimer, Miguel Covarrubias, Ralph Barton, Carlotta Monterey, Burton Rascoe, Tom Powers,[1] Ruth Hammond, Louis Sherwin, Pam Metcalf, Max Ewing,[2] Margaret Case,[3] Helen Simonson.[4] Some of us went on to the Liverights for supper.

    1. Actor with whom Marinoff was appearing in *Tarnish.*
    2. A student who had written about CVV in his University of Michigan newspaper and soon was one of the *jeunes gens assortis.* He was the composer for annual editions of the *Grand Street Follies,* had an art gallery in a closet in his apartment, served as Muriel Draper's frequent escort, wrote one Firbankian pastiche, *Going Somewhere* (Knopf, 1934), and committed suicide.
    3. Daughter of Frank and Bertha Case of the Algonquin, later a writer of memoirs.
    4. Mrs. Lee Simonson, wife of the stage designer with the Theatre Guild.

Wednesday, 24 October 1923

Started reworking *The Tattooed Countess.* Rain all day. Lunched with Marinoff at Benedusi's. Avery [Hopwood] came down in afternoon, and took me uptown at 6 o'clock. Dinner with Marinoff, Ralph & Fannie Van Vechten at Algonquin. Avery there with John Floyd, Clifton Webb.[1] I talked with Texas Guinan,[2] etc. Mabel Reber's party at 8. . . .

1. Effete American musical comedy actor whose greater success lay ahead of him in Hollywood.

2. Popular speakeasy queen who greeted her customers, "Hello, sucker!" CVV invited her to witness his contract with Knopf for his last novel, *Parties*, because so much of it took place in speakeasies.

Saturday, 27 October 1923

Working on mss of *The Countess*. Lunch at Benedusi's. Read Firbank's *A Drama in Sunlight* in mss.[1] Ralph & Fannie [Van Vechten] came to dinner & after dinner Percy & Florence Hammond, Henry B. Fuller, Theodore Dreiser, . . . Helen Westley, Pam Metcalfe, Nik Muray, Philip Moeller, Robert Morss Lovett, Regina Wallace, . . . Carrie & Ettie Stettheimer came in.

1. Ronald Firbank's novel was published in England as *Sorrow in Sunlight* and in the United States as *Prancing Nigger*, after a phrase in the book.

Tuesday, 30 October 1923

Working on papers, writing letters, etc. Marinoff reading *The Countess*. Brentano's decides definitely to publish Firbank's new book. I have suggested a change in title to *Prancing Nigger*. Lunch solo at Algonquin but talked with May Vokes,[1] Madeleine Boyd, Margaret Case. Dinner at Leo Lane's with Marinoff. Then to Ralph Barton's & Carlotta Monterey's. Marinoff came in after theatre.

1. American actress associated primarily with comic roles, earlier in vaudeville.

Friday, 2 November 1923

At the Ritz in Philadelphia. To Leary's Book Shop & then to Gimbel's to get [Stuart] Suftin. At 12.30 Joe Hergesheimer arrived with James Branch Cabell.[1] We went to the Franklin Inn for dinner with a group of men which included Leicester Holland[2] whom I haven't seen for 12 years. . . . Then to the Centaur Book Shop.[3] . . . Then to the West Philadelphia Station for Margaret Case & motored to Dower House where Dorothy Hergesheimer & Priscilla Cabell awaited us. . . .

1. American fantasist whose mannered and indirectly and elegantly obscene novel *Jurgen* had brought him a popular audience, including CVV, with whom he had been corresponding for some time.

2. An English friend whom CVV had known briefly in Paris circa 1910.

3. The Centaur Book Shop was then engaged in preparing bibliographies of popular writers. Scott Cunningham compiled CVV's bibliography in 1924.

Monday, 5 November 1923

Saw Joe's new office in West Chester, gaily papered with old American paper. Joe, Dorothy, Emma Gray Trigg,[1] & I lunch at Dower House. Reading Sinclair Lewis's *Our Mr. Wrenn*. . . . A gay meal with champagne. She & I talk while others play Mah Jong.

    1. Richmond, Virginia society matron whom CVV liked to call Emigré.

Tuesday, 6 November 1923

Got up & packed and at 11 Emma Gray (Mrs. William) Trigg, Joseph Hergesheimer, & I motored to Wilmington [Delaware] where we caught the express to Richmond—at 12.14. We had a drawing-room & many drinks on the way down. Emigré and I lunched together. Billy Trigg met us at the station & took his wife away. Then Joe and I motored to the Jefferson Hotel, where I am installed in 242. Met Richard Barboree & Alfred Lunt in the lobby. They were playing in *Robert E. Lee* [by John Drinkwater]. Hunter Stagg came to dinner & spent evening with me.

Wednesday, 7 November 1923

Joe and I walked about this very ugly town in the morning. He introduced me to some book-sellers, showed me the capitol, etc. Emily Clark came to lunch with me & took me to the [Edgar Allan] Poe Shrine where *The Reviewer* is installed. At 4 Josephine Pickney[1] came for us & drove us to the Cabells' house at Dumbarton where there was a party in my honour. . . . The strange Cabell child, Ballard.[2] Dinner with Joe at the Westmoreland Club. [Hunter] Stagg came in at 10. . . .

    1. Charleston, South Carolina poet, founder of the Poet Society there, and later a novelist.
    2. The Cabells' only child, Ballard, was mildly retarded, both physically and mentally.

Saturday, 10 November 1923

High Richmond dinner at 2.30 at Tompkins'. . . . Mint juleps. Priscilla Cabell came for us & drove us over. Called on Emily Clark at 4.30. Dinner talk with Dick . . . & Bertie Trigg. I met Trigg's Mammy.

Monday, 12 November 1923

I leave Hergesheimer & Richmond in the morning. Arrive in Baltimore at 3.56, met by David Bruce who brings me to Maryland Club. Then we go to . . . Hotel Rennert & dinner with Mencken. Oysters, canvasback, terrapin. Then we go to Baum's & drink until 11.00.

Thursday, 6 December 1923

Lunch at Algonquin at a quarter of one for Dorothy. Dorothy Hergesheimer, Noma Way,[1] Alfred & Blanche Knopf, Philip Moeller. Alfred tells me he is crazy about *The Tattooed Countess*. "What you did to Scott Fitzgerald with *The Blind Bow-Boy* you have done to *Main Street* [by Sinclair Lewis] with *The Tattooed Countess*" were his words. Walked down the street & celebrated by buying a copy of *Clarel* [by Herman Melville] at Dreschil for $65.00. Marinoff & I dine at Benedusi's. Boyds come in. I go to party at Sam & Lelia Hoffenstein's: . . . Claire Burke, Percy & Florence Hammond, T. R. Smith, . . . Louis Sherwin, Burton Rascoe, Helena Rubinstein.[2]

1. A leading socialite in West Chester, Pennsylvania and Dorothy Hergesheimer's close friend.
2. Fashion and makeup doyenne of the period.

Saturday, 8 December 1923

D'Alvarez for lunch, Benedusi's at 12.45. Louis Sherwin, Marinoff & Pam Metcalf. Arthur Ficke married Gladys Brown. 5, Arthur's, at 42 Commerce St. Floyd Dell, . . . Witter Bynner,[1] Louise Norton, Varèse,[2] . . . Edna Millay, Eugen Boissevain (met),[3] F.P.A., etc. Dined alone at Brevoort. After 9, Hallie Schlesinger's. Sam & Lelia Hoffenstein, . . . Claire [Burke] Schermerhorn, Louis Sherwin, Pam Metcalf, Charles MacArthur, Glenway Wescott,[4] Otto & Bernardine [Szold] Liveright, . . . & a young man called Marcus Aurelius Goodrich, Percy Hammond's assistant.

1. Although CVV confessed neither interest in nor comprehension of much contemporary poetry, he and Witter Bynner began a warm friendship in the twenties that persisted until death. Bynner was known as "Hal."
2. Poet (and later journalist for the *New York World*) Allen Norton's divorced wife, Louise, had married the composer Edgard Varèse. The Nortons had been responsible for the little magazine *Rogue*, in 1915, to which CVV contributed.
3. Edna St. Vincent Millay's husband.
4. Precocious American novelist who had recently had his first success with *The Grandmothers*.

Monday, 31 December 1923

Finished first reading of proofs of *The Countess*. Reading Mencken's *More Prejudices*. Dinner with Marinoff at Algonquin. Then to Lucile's for three hours, a rainy-chilly night. Party at Pam [Metcalf]'s. . . . An awful party.

1924

"No one knows the agony I
suffer over the birth of a book."

The success of three novels in row allowed the Van Vechtens to move from the three-room flat they had rented on East Nineteenth Street since 1915 to larger quarters at 150 West 55th Street and begin entertaining on a more lavish scale than in the past. Van Vechten completed a fourth novel, *Firecrackers,* and began editing *Red* and *Excavations,* two collections of his earlier essays and articles about musical and literary subjects and figures. George Gershwin fulfilled Van Vechten's early predictions about jazz with the premiere of *Rhapsody in Blue* this year. Van Vechten's growing interest in African American entertainments expanded to include intellectual Harlem through new acquaintances Walter White, James Weldon Johnson, and other black writers. Within weeks, his imagination had been fired sufficiently for him to begin what would become a personal crusade.

Saturday, 5 January 1924

. . . 100 copies of *The Tow-Headed Blind Boy*[1] arrived from Chicago. . . . Steichen,[2] Robert & B[eatrice] Locher, . . . Peggy Bacon (met),[3] . . . Louis Bouché, etc., Marinoff & 3 Stettheimers at party at Florine Stettheimer's studio. To show Louis Bouché's portrait. Dinner with Marinoff at Algonquin. . . . Phil Moeller party. Rebecca West (met),[4] Stark Young (met) Winafred Lanihan (met),[5] Lawrence and Estelle Langner, Lee Simonson, Theresa Helburn,[6] Burton & Hazel Rascoe, Helen Westley, . . . Ettie Stettheimer, Arnold Daly, . . . Robert Nathan,[7] etc., A. Woollcott, Maurice Wertheim.

> 1. Ralph Van Vechten had Samuel Hoffenstein's review of *The Blind Bow-Boy* in the *New York Tribune Book News*, 2 September 1923—written as a parody of the novel—printed up as a pamphlet in an edition of 250 copies to give to friends.
> 2. Edward Steichen, pioneering American experimental photographer who had commanded photographic forces during World War I.
> 3. Illustrator and satirical artist, married to the American painter Alexander Brook.
> 4. Born Cecily Isabel Fairfield, Rebecca West was a prolific English novelist and critic.
> 5. Winifred Ellerman, an English novelist whose name CVV had misunderstood. She wrote under the pen name "Bryher" and was married to Robert McAlmon, Contact Editions publisher.
> 6. Lawrence Langner's producer and partner in the Theater Guild.
> 7. American writer whose popular novels were marked by sentimentality, fantasy, or satire, sometimes simultaneously. His *Portrait of Jennie* and *The Bishop's Wife* were later filmed.

Monday, 7 January 1924

Marinoff goes to court in Willy Pogany versus David Belasco case.[1] Ernest Boyd lunches with me at Algonquin. I talk with Bertha, Frank & Margaret Case, B[unny, i.e., Edmund] Wilson, George Oppenheimer, etc. Two new bookcases came & I work on books all afternoon & evening. Dinner with Bernardine & Otto Liveright at Benedusi's.

> 1. Pogany, a Hungarian illustrator and stage designer (and Marinoff's French coach), was in litigation with Belasco, an *éminence grise* in theatrical circles.

Saturday, 12 January 1924

Worked all day on proofs of *The Countess*. Lunch with Marinoff at Benedusi's. . . . Finished *The Golden Asse* and read Whitley's essay on Apuleius. Dinner alone at Benedusi's. Party at Lawrence Langner's. Marinoff, Rebecca West (whom I call Toto), Doris Stevens,[1] [Marcus Aurelius] Goodrich, . . . Phil Moeller, Helen Westley, Phyllis Povah (met),[2] . . . Edna Kenton, . . . T. R. Smith, Louis Sherwin, . . . the Boyds, . . . Horace Liveright & Lucile Liveright, Bernardine & Otto Liveright. Party at Isa Glenn Schindel's.[3] Didn't go.

1. Mrs. Dudley Field Malone, a militant feminist writer and economist, jailed briefly for picketing the White House over women's suffrage.

2. American actress.

3. Mrs. Bayard Schindel was a young widow who had recently settled in New York with her son Bayard Jr. Two years later she became one of CVV's protégées and began her career as a successful novelist, writing under her maiden name, Isa Glenn. CVV appears as "Charles Glidden" in her novel *East of Eden*. (1932).

Monday, 14 January 1924

Took corrected galley proofs of *The Countess* to the office. Lunch, 12.45, Horace Liveright at Algonquin. Claire Schermerhorn & Sam Hoffenstein lunching with Marinoff. Home: cleaning out closets, etc. Dinner with Marinoff at Benedusi's. After dinner Ben Ray Redman came over for the evening.

Thursday, 17 January 1924

Working on papers, for binding, etc. Lunch at Benedusi's with Marinoff. Eva Gauthier sings at Mrs. Walter Rosen's, at 4, 35 W. 54 St. Sings most of her Boston program, including the jazz group with Geo. Gershwin at the piano. He plays part of his *Rhapsody in Blue* which he is to play at Paul Whiteman's concert. Olin Downes (met),[1] Arthur Bliss (met)[2] & 2 others there. Dinner with Marinoff at Algonquin. . . . I go to Lucile Harper's for some gin & then go home.

1. Music critic for the *New York Times,* also a pianist and musicologist.

2. Prolific English composer visiting the United States.

Wednesday, 23 January 1924

Wrote the preface for *Prancing Nigger*. Lunch with Ernest Boyd at Benedusi's, talked with Guy Holt. To Charlotte Ives[1] for cocktails. Mencken, Rebecca West, Doris Stevens, Dudley Field Malone,[2] . . . Marinoff. We stay to dinner. Took Ernest Boyd to D'Alvarez concert. Madeleine bought a seat & followed us. Talked with Donald Angus & his two friends. . . .

1. Early silent film actress.

2. American divorce lawyer best known for his speech about truth at the 1925 Scopes trial. Later Malone played small roles on stage and in films.

Thursday, 24 January 1924

Wrote second & last draught of preface to *Prancing Nigger*. Received semi-annual statement from Knopf, largest I've ever had. Lunch with Avery Hopwood at Voisin's. Dinner at Virginia Hammond's with Marinoff. Mencken, 9 P.M., came in to sign books, also Boyd . . . and . . . at 11 . . . we went to a nigger joint in Harlem with Eddie Knoblauch, . . . Rebecca West, Lucile Harper. Home at 6 A.M.

Friday, 25 January 1924

Felt terribly hungoverish all day. Marinoff spent last night at Virginia Hammond's. . . .

Wednesday, 30 January 1924

Received $2,000 advance from A. A. Knopf in morning mail & paid up my Cedar Rapids note.[1] Cold & feeling rotten. Working, not very hard, on *Red*.[2] Lunch at Algonquin with Marinoff & Virginia Hammond. . . . In afternoon Scott Fitzgerald telephoned. He was at Ernest Boyd's. I went over there & found him & Zelda[3] with Ernest, later Madeleine. Cocktails. . . .

1. In desperate straits, circa 1917–19, CVV had borrowed money against his principal at the Cedar Rapids (Iowa) Guaranty Bank and Trust, still under the control of the Van Vechten family.
2. A collection of CVV's musical criticism, revised, published in 1925.
3. F. Scott Fitzgerald's wife.

Saturday, 2 February 1924

. . . Lunch with Mrs. Cabell at Algonquin at one o'clock. . . . Dinner with Triggs and Delia Carrington.[1] We took them to Leone's. Claire Schermerhorn party: Sam Hoffenstein, . . . T. R. Smith, Edna Kenton, . . . Burton & Hazel Rascoe, Louis Sherwin, Jim & Jeannette Jolly, Ruth Hammond. . . . I insult Madeleine Boyd.[2]

1. Mrs. Richard Carrington, another visiting Richmond, Virginia matron, with Emma Gray and William Trigg, also from Richmond.
2. Mrs. Boyd was neither the first nor the last person to find herself under verbal attack when CVV had drunk too much. Invariably he sent flowers in apology the next day, but that did not always excuse him, and more than once his bad behavior permanently severed friendships.

Tuesday, 5 February 1924

Worked on *Red* in the morning. Lunch alone at Benedusi's. Paul Whiteman's rehearsal, 2.30, heard George Gershwin play his *Rhapsody in Blue* twice. Also heard Victor Herbert's *Serenade* written for this concert and Zez Confrey play the piano. Talked with Whiteman, Gershwin, Confrey, Gilbert Seldes[1] & Olin Downes. Pouring rain. I had dinner alone at home. Marinoff went to Algonquin to dine with Beverly Sitgreaves.[2] Ralph V.V. telephoned me, but I stayed home & worked on proofs of *Countess*, etc.

   1. American social, literary, and theater critic who championed the popular arts, best represented by his lively defense, *The Seven Lively Arts* (1924).
   2. Older stage actress still active in the twenties.

Saturday, 9 February 1924

Lunch with Elinor Wylie,[1] one o'clock at the Algonquin. William Rose Benét (met),[2] Robert Nathan & his girl, [and] Marinoff. After lunch we were joined by Mary Colleen & Lloyd Morris.[3] Then Mrs. Wylie, Benét & I went upstairs to see Joe Hergesheimer. The Knopfs were there & later Richard Barthelmess.[4] To library, then home & met Marinoff at Algonquin for dinner. Then home. Read until she came.

   1. American poet whose novel *Jennifer Lorn* CVV rescued from oblivion with a one-man publicity campaign that he liked to describe in later years as a "torch-light parade" through the streets of Manhattan. Subsequently, he lured her away from her publisher to become a Knopf author.
   2. American writer and publisher of the *Saturday Review of Literature;* Wylie's husband.
   3. American biographer, playwright, and social historian. CVV appears as "Paul Follet" in Morris's novel, *This Circle of Flesh* (1932). Morris was never married.
   4. Popular American silent film star.

Friday, 15 February 1924

Joe Hergesheimer's birthday. To Algonquin for lunch. Sat with Bertha & Frank Case. Collected Joe (Richard Barthelmess was there) & we left for West Chester at 2. Arrived at West Philadelphia at 4. Motored to Joe's. Then Dorothy, Joe & I motored to Phoebe Gilkyson's at Phoenixville for dinner & party. . . . The girls dressed as the characters in Joe's books.

Monday, 18 February 1924

Working all day on *Red*. Lunch alone at Benedusi's. Sent Knopfs flowers as they moved into their new quarters at 730 Fifth Ave. on Sat. . . . Started to read *The Beautiful & Damned* which Scott Fitzgerald just sent to me.

Tuesday, 19 February 1924

. . . Ralph Barton & Carlotta Monterey dine with us at Crillon & Ralph takes me to Jane Cowl in *Antony and Cleopatra*.[1]

    1. Barton and CVV went regularly to witness the performances of this actress, whose trademark weeping in every role they found hilarious, although their affection for her apparently was genuine.

Saturday, 1 March 1924

Working on *Red*. Lunch with Marinoff at Benedusi's. Plate proofs of *The Countess* arrived. . . . Met Ernest Boyd (first time since I insulted Madeleine) & we walked up to Horace Liveright's together. Party at Horace's: T. R. Smith, Conrad Bercovici,[1] Edna Ferber, Otto & Bernardine Liveright, Heywood Broun, Julian Messner, Madeleine Boyd, etc. Madeleine brought me a clipping from *Le Figaro* concerning *The Blind B.B.* Otherwise we did not speak. Dinner at Algonquin with Marinoff. . . .

    1. Romanian American social historian of immigrant life on the Lower East Side.

Sunday, 2 March 1924

. . . Reading *These Charming People* by Michael Arlen. . . . I took Donald Angus to see the *Andre Charlot Revue*, the very best entertainment of its kind I've ever seen. Beatrice Lillie & Gertrude Lawrence splendid.[1]

    1. These two popular British performers were making their American debuts.

Thursday, 13 March 1924

Tarnish Co. asked last night to take a cut. Marinoff tells me about it today. Probably closing.[1] Lunch with Marinoff at Benedusi's. Working on *Red*. Dinner with Marinoff at the Little Tavern. Then to the theatre where we discussed situation with Marion Lord, Ann Harding & Tom Powers.[2] Home in evening.

    1. Marinoff had had a personal success in an unsavory play. Although chosen as one of the best plays of the year, *Tarnish* closed after a modest run.
    2. The other actors in *Tarnish*. They were given two weeks' notice two days later.

Saturday, 29 March 1924

Packing to go to Richmond. Lunch with Marinoff at Benedusi's. Donald Angus came in in afternoon. Dinner at Leone's with Marinoff. Robert Morss Lovett there. . . . Down to Edna Kenton's & drove uptown with her. Jane Heap & Margaret Anderson. Then to Lucile Harper's for an hour. Then to theatre for a party. Last night of Tom Powers, Marion Lord, Mildred McLeod, & Marinoff in *Tarnish*. . . . Ann Harding who leaves next week drove us home.

Sunday, 30 March 1924

Rose early and took the 9.15 train to Richmond. Joe Hergesheimer joined me at Wilmington [Delaware]. We took a compartment & drank all the way into Richmond, where we arrived at 7. Hunter Stagg came to dinner.

Tuesday, 1 April 1924

Rain all day. Joe has lunch with me at the Jefferson, and we spend most of the afternoon together. I started reading Rebecca West's *The Judge*. Dinner at Miss Ellen Glasgow's (met),[1] her companion Miss [Ann Virginia] Bennett, dog Jeremy, etc., Dr. & Mrs. Beverly Tucker,[2] Emily Clark, & Hunter Stagg.

> 1. Novelist and formidable head of Richmond's social hierarchy, a "great Southern Lady," CVV wrote, who never allowed the city to forget that "she was an ignominious 'lady writer.'"
> 2. A Richmond neurologist interested in Southern folklore. He served as an advisor to *The Reviewer*.

Friday, 4 April 1924

Alfred & Blanche Knopf's wedding anniversary. I go to their room to speak with them. Hunter Stagg comes in before he goes to lunch with E. Wylie. Joe and I go to Mrs. Christopher Tompkins.[1] I brought her a bottle of brandy & she makes mint juleps, before a high Richmond dinner at 2.30. Joe Hergesheimer, Elinor Wylie, Alfred & Blanche Knopf motor over to the Poe shrine to a tea given by Mrs. Archer ([*Tikerus?*] Goucher) Jones.[2] She was drunk again. . . .

> 1. Mary Tompkins was another member of Richmond's social register; her unmarried daughters, Nellie (who had published some stories) and Delia, lived with her.
> 2. This Richmond dowager turned an old stone house into a shrine to Edgar Allen Poe and then entertained there to memorialize her late husband.

Friday, 11 April 1924

... Went to Dorothy Harvey's[1] for cocktails. A crowd but I spent 2 hours talking to her & Dreiser. Glenway Wescott was there & John Dos Passos,[2] who as usual I did not meet. Dinner at Zoë Akins'.[3] W. Rose Benét, Elinor Wylie, Willa Cather.[4] I spent about the entire evening talking to Miss Cather whom I took home. A number of other people arrived after the theatre. ...

    1. Dorothy Dudley and her sisters, Caroline and Katherine, were Chicago friends from CVV's college days. Dorothy (Mrs. Harry) Harvey wrote *Forgotten Frontiers;* Caroline (Mrs. Dan) Reagan mounted the first black musical show, *Revue Nègre,* in Paris; Katherine did not marry and lived permanently in Paris.

    2. One of the Lost Generation novelists of the twenties, strongly leftist in his views; later he grew conservative.

    3. American playwright, best remembered for her adaptation of Edith Wharton's *The Old Maid,* the Pulitzer Prize winner in 1935.

    4. Nebraska novelist, Alfred A. Knopf's most critically successful writer, with the arguable exception of H. L. Mencken. His most commercially successful writer was the Eastern mystic Kahlil Gibran.

Sunday, 13 April 1924

Worked all day on papers. Lunch in. Reading *Sodom & Gomorrah* (Proust). Went to Edna Kenton's at 4 o'clock. We had dinner with Philip Moeller & Helen Westley at the Brevoort. Theatre Guild rehearsal of Ernst Toller's rotten play, *Man and the Masses.* Spent most of my time in the lobby smoking. Besides dinner party, Ettie & Florine Stettheimer were in the box. ...

Monday, 14 April 1924

Worked on papers, wrote letters, etc. Lunch at Benedusi's with Arthur Ficke. Went to bookshops with him. He comes home with me to get two gallons of wine. Blanche Knopf telephones me that Elinor Wylie has signed a contract to come with us. Proofs of *Red* arrive & I begin to read them. Marinoff returns from Atlantic City.[1] Dinner at Lawrence Langner's & we go to *The Show-Off*[2] together. To Lucile Harper's for 2 quarts of gin. She is in bed again, very ill.

    1. At about this time, Marinoff began a series of periodic holidays—weekends in Atlantic City or with relatives or the Langners, sometimes cruises to Europe—that continued until a few years before her death.

    2. Music, lyrics, book, and leading role by George M. Cohan.

Monday, 21 April 1924

. . . Lunch at Algonquin with Pam Metcalf & Marinoff. Talked with Louis Bromfield[1] & Ben Ray Redman. Marie Doro, back from Europe, telephones. Party at 4 for Marjorie Seiffert.[2] Arthur Davison Ficke & Gladys Brown, William Rose Benét, Elinor Wylie, Samuel Hoffenstein, Claire Schermerhorn, T. R. Smith, Horace Liveright, Ralph Barton, Carlotta Monterey, Philip Moeller, Helen Westley. Marjorie & I went to Moskowitz for dinner & and to . . . Garden Burlesque, & to Jack Harper's. Lucile is better.

    1. Popular and prolific American novelist.
    2. Mrs. Otto Seiffert, a minor poet and writer of light verse. She and CVV shared a strong interest in cats.

Friday, 2 May 1924

Signed lease for 150 W. 55 St.[1] . . . Lunch at Benedusi's with Marinoff. . . . Then to Ralph Barton's. Ralph was putting finishing touches on his cover design for *The Tattooed Countess*. When it was dry I snatched it out of his hands & carried it up to Knopf. Gertrude Atherton, Margaret Freeman[2] & Hunter Stagg dine with us at Benedusi's.

    1. A spacious apartment with a large foyer, drawing room, dining room, Marinoff's bedroom, CVV's bedroom doubling as a library, and two bathrooms.
    2. Business manager for *The Reviewer*. Subsequently she became James Branch Cabell's second wife.

Tuesday, 6 May 1924

Marinoff & I carried the suit-cases full of stuff to apartment. Lunch at the Little Tavern. Dinner at 7, Edwin Knopf's. Mary Ellis,[1] Marinoff. After dinner Pam Metcalf comes in. Marinoff goes home with her to spend the night. I came home.[2]

    1. Knopf and Ellis lived two floors above CVV and Marinoff.
    2. This is not the first occasion on which Marinoff had gone to spend the night with a friend because CVV's drinking was out of hand and he had become abusive. To what degree this was verbal and to what degree physical it is impossible to determine, although Marinoff's best friend, Regina Wallace, believed CVV capable of both.

Sunday, 11 May 1924

Finished *Sandoval* [by Thomas Beer], a tawdry melodrama smothered in 1870 plush. There is no <u>important characterization, no philosophy, no overtone,</u>

but one cannot deny the brilliancy of the writing, or the pictorial beauty of the novel. Packing. Took two pictures to Mabel Reber. Saw the Seabrooks.[1]

    1. American writer William Seabrook and his wife, Katie.

Tuesday, 13 May 1924

Moved from 151 E. 19 Street where we have lived 9 years to 150 West 55 Street. Dinner at Lawrence Langner's. Helen Westley there.

Tuesday, 20 May 1924

Took Ralph Barton's picture for jacket of *The Countess* to him for him to put colors in it. Carlotta Monterey there. Went to see Alfred & Blanche Knopf on business connection with Starrett's piracy in *Et Cetera*.[1] Lunch with the Knopfs: May Sinclair,[2] Willa Cather (I sat between them), Mencken, Margaret Freeman, Mr. & Mrs. Carl Van Doren,[3] Tom Beer, Alfred & Blanche. Dinner at Stettheimers'—all of them. Wittgenstein,[4] Marinoff.

    1. Vincent Starrett had reprinted CVV's essay on Edgar Saltus from *The Merry-Go-Round* (Knopf, 1918) in *Et Cetera,* an anthology, but without permission.
    2. American-born English poet and novelist.
    3. American journalist and his wife, Irita, book editor for the *Herald Tribune*.
    4. Victor Wittgenstein, a teacher of piano and composition, who often served as an escort for Fania Marinoff on theater dates.

Saturday, 24 May 1924

Our apartment is settled enough to entertain callers & we telephone several people. Marinoff goes out to lunch & I have a vile lunch at the Hotel Cumberland. At 2 o'clock Ralph Barton & Carlotta Monterey, our first callers, appear. At 4, Edwin Knopf & Mary Ellis, a little later Edna Kenton & Mabel Reber. Still later Regina Wallace. Regina stays to dinner. She is, consequently, our first dinner guest.

Saturday, 31 May 1924

Catherine's day off.[1] Reading page proofs of *Red*. Read Ruth Suckow's *Country People*. It seems to me that Miss Suckow has a talent for observation & characterization, but none for novels. She should stick to short stories. Marinoff goes out to lunch & I lunch alone at the Plaza. Dinner home. Marinoff cooks it, & to bed early.

    1. Catherine James, a new cook described elsewhere in the daybooks as "dirty, slow, plausible, & good-natured." CVV fired her the next day.

Monday, 16 June 1924

Wrote Chapter VII of new book which I may call *Firecrackers*.[1] Lunch in with Marinoff. Reading [Sacheverell] Sitwell's *Southern Baroque Art*. At 5 John Floyd comes in & later he takes Marinoff to dinner & to the movies. Donald Angus dines with me at the Little Tavern. Then we spend the evening chez moi. Floyd & Marinoff return at 1.

    1. More than one columnist registered in print that CVV's next novel would be called *The Divine Monkey*, a title he never registered in his daybooks.

Thursday, 19 June 1924

Wrote Chapter VIII of *Firecrackers*. Read Frank Harris's *Undream'd of Shores* & *The Fire in the Flint* [by Walter White], a great negro novel that Knopf is to publish in Sept.[1] Ben Ray Redman comes to lunch & stays until 4. I go to N.Y. Edison Co. & then walk home. . . .

    1. This novel fired CVV's enthusiasm for African American arts and letters. White, whom he met through Knopf, was responsible for introducing CVV to black culture beyond its music and speakeasies.

Thursday, 3 July 1924

. . . At 3.25 Marinoff leaves for Sag Harbor to spend the Fourth with the Cases. I meet Margaret Freeman on 5 Avenue. Donald Angus comes to dinner. At 9 o'clock we go to Avery Hopwood's at the Ambassador. John Floyd comes in.

Friday, 4 July 1924

Worked on old receipts & cheques all day. . . . Lunch with Donald Angus at the Ritz. Join Avery Hopwood at the Ambassador at 7. John Floyd, Bob Hundley, Ralph Glover, Jack Morony.[1] Avery in a terrific temper. Leaves party flat before the door of Divan Parisienne at 8.30. John & Bob had gone in. I turn around & go home. Avery sails at one on the *Olympia*.

    1. Hundley, Glover, and Morony were minor actors in Hopwood plays.

Saturday, 5 July 1924

Still working on papers. Lunch alone at Reuben's. Donald Angus comes in at 6 & we go to the Divan Parisienne for dinner where we meet John Floyd & Jack Morony. Ralph Glover and Ty Boyz[1] turn up later & we all go to John's room in the Gotham. Donald goes home, & later so do the others & John Floyd comes home with me to talk about Avery till 12.30.

1. Another member in CVV's growing circle of homosexual acquaintances, although these gatherings were primarily homosocial.

Sunday, 6 July 1924

In all day working on papers, & alone. Saw nobody & nobody called up. Got my own lunch. Read Michael Arlen's *The Green Hat*. This young Armenian is a false alarm. . . . Dinner at the Algonquin solo. Home: furious. The evening hot & went to bed.

Wednesday, 8 July 1924

Worked all day on notes for *Firecrackers*. Toward evening the tangle of the book which has held me up for several days begins to be straightened out in my mind. I think I can finish it now. Marinoff gets lunch for me. John Floyd comes in at 5.30 & stays for dinner. Marinoff gets dinner.

Friday, 11 July 1924

Alfred [Knopf] tells me that *The Tattooed Countess* has already gone over 5,000, & publication day over a month away. Working all day revising my preface to my bibliography[1] & *Firecrackers*. The latter is coming along very badly & I feel sick & discouraged. I wonder if I can't write any more. Lunch alone at Benedusi's. Dinner in with Marinoff. Read the preface to [George Bernard] Shaw's *Saint Joan*, & Algernon Blackwood's *Episodes Before Thirty*, a wonderful book.

1. Compiled by Scott Cunnningham for David Jester's Centaur Book Shop and Centaur Press in Philadelphia, published in 1924.

Saturday, 12 July 1924

Awful heat continues. I feel rotten. *Firecrackers* continues to baffle me. Lunch in. Marinoff cooks. After lunch I go to post office & bank. Returning, I begin to drink Tom Collins. Margaret Freeman, Rita Romilly, Regina Wallace, & John Floyd come in. All except Margaret stay for a cold supper which Marinoff prepares. We go up to Edwin Knopf's & Mary Ellis's 2 floors above us, for Bacardi cocktails, etc.

Tuesday, 15 July 1924

. . . In the morning I write Chapter XI of *Firecrackers*. Lunch in. After lunch I visit the Aquarium & other downtown districts for notes for *Firecrackers*.

Reading Pio Baroja's *The Quest.* Dinner home & then Marinoff & I go to see Ramon Novarro in *The Arab.* Horrible. I think I'm through with pictures. Wrote half a dozen letters.

Saturday, 19 July 1924

Marinoff & I cleaned the house. Then I went to office & got 6 copies (the first) of *The Tattooed Countess,* & a new edition of *The Tiger in the House.*[1] Talked with [John] Mullen, the head-salesman who was most encouraging. Lunch in, with Marinoff. Sent first 4 copies of *Countess* to Edna Kenton, Elinor Wylie, Florine Stettheimer, & Stuart Rose. Finished *Mark Only.* Altho [T. F.] Powys writes of English peasant life he has a philosophy much like mine. At 4 Joseph Schildkraut came in & pulled a tragic scene about his loss of his bride, Elise Bartlett. John Floyd appears & both stay to dinner.

> 1. CVV's *The Tiger in the House* (Knopf, 1920), a vast compendium of material about domestic cats and their role in art, music, literature, and superstition. Originally published in an edition of 2,000 copies, it has sold steadily for more than eighty years and has never been long out of print.

Friday, 25 July 1924

Up at 8.30. Hot! Spend morning cleaning house & packing up more books to mail. Alfred telephones me that second edition [i.e., printing] of *The Countess* will be ordered next week. Go over my bibliography. Read *Psychic Messages from Oscar Wilde.* Go to dinner at Dorothy Harvey's at Sneeden Point on the Hudson. Katherine Dudley, . . . Theodore Dreiser, Miguel Covarrubias. Dreiser witnesses signing of *Tattooed Countess* contract.[1] Home at midnight.

> 1. It was CVV's habit to have his contracts witnessed by celebrated people.

Friday, 1 August 1924

Cooler. Nothing going on. Read . . . Herman Melville's "Billy Budd" in a type-written mss. Raymond Weaver sent me.[1] Went out for a few minutes in the morning. Lunch in with Marinoff. Ernestine[2] cooking. . . .

> 1. *Billy Budd* was first published in 1925.
> 2. Another in a growing list of unsatisfactory domestics.

Sunday, 3 August 1924

Wrote a note to Ernestine, discharging her. A cool day. Lunch in. In the afternoon I made corrections of Chapter I of *Firecrackers* & went over first draught of Chapter II. Marinoff & I go to John Floyd's apartment at 6.30. Avery Hopwood & a youth named Metcalfe. Avery takes us (sans Metcalfe) to dinner at Leone's. . . .

Monday, 4 August 1924

Note from Ellen Glasgow about *The Countess*. Wrote Chapter II of 2nd draught of *Firecrackers*. Lunch in. Avery Hopwood comes in battered after another row with John. . . . We go to see *Cobra*, & Judith Anderson,[1] leave after second act.

> 1. Australian actress, later an intimate friend of CVV and Marinoff. Subsequently, he photographed her in nearly all of her roles as well as nude.

Wednesday, 6 August 1924

Hot again, 92. The hottest day of the summer. I remain undressed all the day but manage to struggle through the rest of Chapter III of *Firecrackers*. . . . Avery telephones. He has been beaten up again, thoroughly this time. . . .

Tuesday, 26 August 1924

Wrote Chapter X & started on chapter XI of *Firecrackers*. Lunch in. In the afternoon Walter P. White,[1] the Negro author of *The Fire in the Flint*, came to see me (met) & stayed until seven. Dinner home. Then I went alone to the Hippodrome. Avery Hopwood & John Floyd appeared, drunk at 5 o'clock, but I sent them away. . . .

> 1. Powerful gadfly of the National Association for the Advancement of Colored People (NAACP), White began a productive interracial friendship with CVV. Until that time, CVV's acquaintance in African American life had been limited to the performing arts. White introduced him to its intellectual life as well, and by the end of the year CVV had begun his one-(white)-man campaign to spur what has come to be called the Harlem Renaissance.

Monday, 8 September 1924

Went to Knopf office this morning. Had business with everybody. . . . Lunch with Marinoff at Algonquin. Met Ruth Donnelly[1] & Judith Anderson. Talked with Margalo Gilmore,[2] Ben Ray Redman, Laurence Stallings, Guy Holt, Margaret Case, etc. Clifton Webb sat at our table. Marinoff & I go to Wanamaker's & buy a phonograph. Home, wrote a little on Chapter XV of *Firecrackers*. Dined in & then went to see moving picture, *Open All Night*. Terrible, dreadful and worthless.

1. American actress, appearing in George M. Cohan's *The Meanest Man in the World.*

2. American actress, first notable for her performance in Sidney Howard's *The Silver Cord* when she replaced one of the first cast members.

Wednesday, 10 September 1924

Fine day again. I write the <u>new</u> sixteenth & last chapter for the present version of *Firecrackers,* good or bad I don't know. But this book is a strange combination of farcical extravagance, melodrama, & mystic allegory. We have lunch in. I'm <u>very</u> depressed. . . . Our new phonograph arrives & first record played is *Caprice Viennois,* our nuptial record. Avery Hopwood & his mother come to dinner. . . .

Saturday, 4 October 1924

Charming, cool day. Letter from M. P. Shiel,[1] thanking me for the preface. Letter from lawyers regarding my income tax. Lunch in with Marinoff. At 3 Marie Doro comes in. She takes me out in the car. . . . A little later Avery Hopwood comes for me & takes me to meet Somerset Maugham[2] at Hotel Gotham. . . . Dinner home. Regina Wallace here. Marinoff goes to theatre, spends night with Reg. I go to a party at Lewis Baer's.[3] Richard Barnett, Harry Block,[4] Maynard Farley, Gordon Nielsen, "Buddie" Barber, Frank Pierce, etc.[5] Home at 5.30 A.M.

1. English novelist whose American career CVV fostered with reviews and a preface to *The Lord of the Sea.*

2. Prolific, popular English novelist and playwright William Somerset Maugham.

3. An editor at *Survey Graphic* magazine, also a regular all-male party-giver.

4. Senior editor at Alfred A. Knopf, Inc. and an early enthusiast for African American arts and letters. Also, Block served as a frequent escort for Fania Marinoff.

5. This is not the first all-male gathering documented in CVV's daybooks. Of those guests listed for the party, only Harry Block can be positively identified.

Thursday, 9 October 1924

Bright & cool, furnace heat. . . . Lunch at Chinese place. Look for Columbia records. Wonderful letter from Somerset Maugham [about *The Tattooed Countess*]. Working on Chapter XI until 6.30. Finished all but last page of this chapter. . . . We went to see Ina Claire in *Grounds for Divorce.* . . . Mary Ellis & Edwin Knopf came in & Murray Taylor played the piano until 1.30 when he was requested to stop by the superintendent. Mrs. Edgar Saltus calls up & wants to give me the bed Edgar was born in.[1]

1. The Chicago novelist Edgar Saltus was another writer of an earlier period whose work CVV had resuscitated with essays and reviews.

Friday, 10 October 1924

In a terrible temper all day, but I finished Chapter XI & wrote Chapter XII. . . . In the evening George Gershwin calls up & comes down & stays an hour. Later Edwin Knopf. Marinoff returns from seeing Gladys Axman in *Tosca*.[1] George plays all the evening. After he is gone I accompany Edwin upstairs & have supper with him & Mary Ellis.

1. Mrs. Clarence Axman was making one of her rare appearances, with the San Carlo Opera Company in Puccini's *Tosca*.

Monday, 13 October 1924

Bright cool day. This is a marvelous autumn. Up at 7.30. Wrote Chapter XIII of *Firecrackers*. Lunched at home. Then went down town. Saw Stuart Rose and Herold of Brentano's who want me to do a Saltus preface. Went up to see Alfred & Blanche, also talked to Sam Knopf, Harry Block & G[eorge] Oppenheimer. Engagement with Walter White changed until tomorrow. At 5 o'clock Covarrubias comes in with his marvelous Negro drawings, & my caricature at last. Mary Ellis & Edwin Knopf come down to see these. Marinoff & I dine alone & then I go to the Hippodrome. . . .

Tuesday, 14 October 1924

. . . Dinner at Marie Doro's. Then we join Walter White & Gladys [White] at *The Chocolate Dandies*. White introduces me to Sissle & Blake.[1] Whites & Marie come up after the show.

1. Noble Sissle and Eubie Blake had written *Shuffle Along* in 1921, which sparked a broad white interest in African American entertainment. Their subsequent shows were not so successful, although *The Chocolate Dandies* drew audiences because of three racehorses on a revolving platform. Otherwise, it merely perpetuated racial stereotypes.

Thursday, 16 October 1924

Cloudy. I woke up at half-past-six. Reading [Marmaduke] Pickthall's *Pot au feu* & George Moore's *Pure Poetry*. . . . Worked all day on *Firecrackers* & finished last draught. Charlie Brackett comes in in afternoon. George

Gershwin to dinner. Also Eva Gauthier. In the evening, Mercedes de Acosta,[1] Marie Doro, Walter & Gladys White, Mary Ellis, Edwin Knopf, Mr. & Mrs. Ernest Newman,[2] Dorothy Harvey. . . . Gershwin plays the entire *Rhapsody in Blue* for Newman. He plays all the evening from 9 to 3. A historical occasion!

    1. Failed playwright and Hollywood screenwriter, later intimate companion of celebrated women, including Greta Garbo and Marlene Dietrich.

    2. English musicologist and his wife. Newman was a prolific and catholic writer, but his speciality was opera by Richard Wagner.

Saturday, 18 October 1924

An idea came to me for the Gershwin opera.[1] Up at 8. Bright, charming day. Wrote letters & worked over papers. Lunch in with Marinoff. In the afternoon I went to bank & for phonograph records. Marinoff finished *Firecrackers*. Dinner with Reg Wallace at Lily's. Ben Ray Redman comes in & stays till 11. Party at Mary Ellis's. We go. Jascha Heifetz,[2] Knopf, Covarrubias, . . . Rita Romilly, Nickolas Muray, Dennis King,[3] George Oppenheimer, . . . Heifetz plays jazz on piano. Finished *Straws & Prayer books* [by James Branch Cabell].

    1. For *George White's Scandals of 1922*, Gershwin had written a serious one-act opera about Harlem with white singers in blackface makeup, called *Blue Monday*, which audiences and critics sufficiently despised to cause its cancellation after one performance. He continued to want to compose a serious musical play or opera with an African American theme and in 1924 proposed that he and CVV collaborate on such a work. "I've been thinking more about the opera & I have more ideas," CVV wrote to Fania Marinoff a few days later, on 23 October 1924, "but I'm sure Gershwin wants something different, and nothing will come of it. In that case I think I'll write a Negro novel."

    2. Russian violinist, a child prodigy at five and apparently a master at fifteen.

    3. Musical comedy and operetta tenor.

Sunday, 19 October 1924

Bright, sunny day. Up at 9. We got home last night at 3. Working on papers, etc. Lunch in. Tried to sleep but couldn't. Harry Block came in at 4, and stayed till 6.30. I had dinner with Marie Doro. . . . Home at 10.30. Covarrubias comes to take me to Harlem. Met Eric Walrond.[1] We go to Clara Smith's[2] & Small's.[3] Home at 4.30.

    1. Guyana-born writer identified with the Harlem Renaissance and CVV's first close friend in the younger generation of writers associated with that movement.

    2. African American blues singer, adept at wailing and moaning.

    3. Small's Paradise was a Harlem speakeasy serving Chinese food, bootleg liquor, and raunchy floorshows. CVV's introduction to black life did not begin or end in literary pursuits.

Thursday, 23 October 1924

Up early. Arrived at 9.45 in Chicago. Telephoned Ralph [Van Vechten]. Then took the *Colorado Special* (not the *Overland Limited*) at 10.30 for Cedar Rapids [Iowa]. This is the train the Countess took in 1897. Arrived home at 3.55. . . . Angevine & Van Vechten[1] & Father appear. Dinner & bed early. The whole town apparently is stirred by *The Countess.*

    1. Van Vechten Shaffer was the son of CVV's sister Emma. Angevine was his wife.

Friday, 24 October 1924

Breakfast at 8 with family. . . . At 10 . . . the *Gazette* & . . . the *Republican* came to interview me. Then I walked out through the cemetery with Gareth and the Countess by my side. . . .[1]

    1. In *The Tattooed Countess,* Gareth is a conniving teenager who allows himself to be seduced by Ella Nattatorrini, a glamorous demimondaine of fifty-three, so he can escape with her from the stifling atmosphere of 1897 Iowa by running off together to Paris.

Tuesday, 28 October 1924

A cloudy day. Arrived at 8.25. Met by Claude, Mahala Douglas's[1] chauffeur in the grey Simplex. He motored me out to Walden, the Douglas estate in Minnetaka [Minnesota] where I have breakfast with Mahala. . . . We lunch together at the Minneapolis Club. Then arrange pumpkins & lanterns at a tea room for a Coolidge Halloween celebration. . . . Mahala & I dine alone in the country. . . .

    1. Mahala Dutton Benedict Douglas, an heir to the Quaker Oats industry in Cedar Rapids, was thought by many to be the model for the tattooed countess because she had scandalized the town in the 1890s. CVV always denied this because Douglas was a sophisticated and intelligent woman, whereas the countess was, in his words, a "sex-beset moron."

Saturday, 1 November 1924

I left a call for six [at Chicago hotel], but they didn't wake me up. Ralph [Van Vechten] stopped for me at 6.45 & by dressing like lightning & putting some of my clothes on in the motor I managed to make a seven o'clock train . . . to Ade, Indiana, to George Ade's farm.[1] 150 luncheon guests and 1 or 3000 farmers on the lawn to hear General Dawes speak. . . . Got back to Chicago at 10 o'clock. . . .

    1. George Ade was a turn-of-the-century American humorist and playwright.

Wednesday, 5 November 1924

Arrived home at 9.40 and found a pile of mail waiting. Lunch in with Marinoff & spent the day putting things in order. . . . Dinner at Knopfs'. Marinoff, George Gershwin, Henry B. Sell[1] & wife, Covarrubias, Farrell (prof. golfer), Miss Madison (professional rider). Gershwin plays all the evening. Then without Gershwin or Sell we all go to Nigger joints in Harlem. . . . Home at 4.

> 1. Editor of *Harper's Bazar.*

Thursday, 6 November 1924

Up early. Working on papers, scrap-books, etc. . . . A lot of people called up & I wrote a lot of letters. Dummy of *Red*[1] arrived. Marinoff and I dine with Avery Hopwood at Leone's with a detective at another table to protect Avery who had just had another fight with John Floyd. Claire Schermerhorn & Sam Hoffenstein came in. Later we all go to Lucile Harper's. . . .

> 1. It was the habit of many publishers—Knopf included—to issue a proof copy of a book, to preview its binding, with only the first signature printed, followed by blank leaves.

Friday, 7 November 1924

Working all day on letters & papers & get pretty nearly straightened out. Lunch in with Marinoff. At 4 Arthur Ficke comes in with some extraordinary pornographic Japanese prints. Reading Eric Walrond's manuscripts.[1] Tea at Knopfs' for Wanda Landowska[2] at 5. Didn't go. Edna Kenton comes to dinner & spends the evening here.

> 1. These stories were published by Knopf, at CVV's urging, as *Tropic Death* (1926).
> 2. Russian harpsichordist and pianist who had made her American debut the year before.

Monday, 10 November 1924

Bright clear, coolish day. Up early, working on papers, etc. Reading *Hadrian VII* [by Baron Corvo]. Lunch at Biltmore with Mabel [Dodge] Luhan. Started revising *Firecrackers*. Went through 2 chapters. Dinner home with Marinoff. Party with Walter Whites, 9 o'clock. Marinoff & I & Covarrubias met at his house. Then to James W. Johnson's[1] where Miss Ovington[2] comes in. Then to party at Happy Rhone's.[3] W. E. B. Du Bois (met),[4] Countee Cullen (met),[5] Kingston Hughes (met),[6] Florence Mills (met),[7] Rosamond Johnson (met),[8]

Bill Robinson (met),[9] [Noble] Sissle, etc. Fletcher Henderson's Orchestra. Alberta Hunter sang.

1. James Weldon Johnson, poet and black activist, field secretary of the NAACP, soon to become CVV's closest friend.

2. Mary White Ovington, white activist for African American causes, writer, humanitarian, and one of the founders of the NAACP.

3. Stylish Harlem cabaret, sometimes rented out (as on this occasion) to the NAACP.

4. Powerful black activist and writer, editor of *Crisis*, publication of the NAACP.

5. African American poet whose early work CVV got into print in *Vanity Fair.*

6. African American poet Langston Hughes, whose name CVV misunderstood. He fostered Hughes's early career, and the two remained warm friends for forty years.

7. The leading African American musical comedy star of the Harlem Renaissance.

8. J. Rosamond Johnson, composer and musician, James Weldon Johnson's brother and sometime collaborator.

9. Better known as Bojangles, a greatly beloved dancer in Harlem and, later, in Hollywood.

Saturday, 15 November 1924

. . . Alfred & Blanche Knopf came to dinner & went with us to Whiteman concert. George Gershwin plays *Rhapsody* again. Blanche, Mrs. Ernest Newman, & I go back to see him. Equity Ball. Edwin Knopf's box party. . . . Mary Ellis sick & could not come.

Sunday, 16 November 1924

Still have a rotten cold. Worked on papers. Lunch in with Marinoff. Continued revisions of *Firecrackers*. At 4 Eric Walrond comes to see me. He left at 6. Mary Ellis, Edwin Knopf came down & we all had supper together. Mary & Edwin have an emotional scene.[1]

1. Mary Ellis had begun an affair with George Gershwin.

Wednesday, 19 November 1924

Woke at 7.30. Still have an awful cold. Finished revising *Firecrackers* at 4 P.M. . . . Dinner with Lewis Baer, Dick Barnett & Gordon Nielsen at the Tavern. Then party at Baer's. . . . Ronald McRae,[1] Dwight Fiske,[2] Harry Block, etc. We went to Gordon's for breakfast. Home about 5.

1. Minor illustrator who designed the dust jacket for CVV's *Spider Boy* (1928), a frequent guest at Uranian gatherings, where he supplied part of the entertainment.

2. Popular cabaret entertainer who wrote his own scabrous material.

Friday, 21 November 1924

Up at 8.30. Mary Ellis comes to lunch. After lunch I walk down town, meet Ronald McRae on the street. Eric Walrond & Countee Cullen to dine with me at the tea-room in Harlem. I come home early & sleep badly. Marinoff goes to dinner with Ralph Van Vechten.

Saturday, 22 November 1924

Up early. Rain. I am in a depressed mood. Jack Marinoff comes in, bearing gifts. Lunch in with Marinoff. It pours all day. At 5.30 we go to a cocktail party at Tom Smith's. Eddie Mayer, Ben Hecht,[1] Emerson Whithorn,[2] Jack Colton[3] (who tells me he wants to dramatize *The Tattooed Countess*). . . . We dine together. Come home & go to Mary Ellis's where I stay till two. Read *A Story Teller's Story* by Sherwood Anderson. According to Ben Hecht this is a tissue of romantic fiction.

    1. American journalist and novelist.
    2. Prolific but now largely forgotten composer and London music critic.
    3. John Colton, American playwright best known for *Rain* (1922) and *The Shanghai Gesture* (1928).

Friday, 28 November 1924

Up at 5. . . . Finished "[On Visiting] Fashionable Places [Out of Season]" for *Excavations,* and started "Edgar Saltus."[1] Harry Block came to lunch. Eric Walrond calls up. I go for a walk & meet Henry McBride, Gerald Kelly,[2] Kathleen Norris[3] & Elinor Wylie. . . . Marinoff brings D'Alvarez home with her. Donald Angus comes to dinner. Later D'Alvarez, Eric Walrond & Mary Ellis come in. Party until 2.30. Marinoff goes to a ball with Daniel Frohman[4] but returns.

    1. These two essays appeared in CVV's *Excavations* (Knopf, 1926).
    2. Braun Art Gallery manager, later a curator at the Metropolitan Museum of Art, not to be confused with Gerald Kelly, the English artist whom CVV met about a year later.
    3. Prolific and popular novelist of the twenties and wife of Charles Norris, author of many sociological novels.
    4. Theatrical producer who helped foster Marinoff's early stage career.

Saturday, 29 November 1924

Rainy morning. Up at 9.30. . . . Wrote five or six pages of a note on Philip Thicknesse[1] for *Excavations.* Dinner in with Marinoff. George Gershwin telephones that he may be at Mary Ellis's tonight. Edwin Knopf spends the evening with me. Gershwin telephones he cannot come. Bed shortly after 11.

    1. Eighteenth-century English rake, vagabond, traveler, soldier, and prolific autobiographer and travel writer whom CVV admired.

Sunday, 30 November 1924

Bright and cooler. Up a little after 8. Working on papers all morning. Lunch with Marinoff. Working on *Excavations* in afternoon. Went to Lewis Baer's. Richard Barrett, Gordon Nielsen—and two other boys.[1] To Mary Ellis's for dinner. Edwin Knopf & Marinoff. It becomes increasingly evident that Mary is wild about G. Gershwin.

    1. Another instance of CVV's growing involvement with a homosexual circle at a number of subterranean parties.

Wednesday, 3 December 1924

Working on Ouida[1] for *Excavations*. Marinoff fires Sophie Palmer,[2] & Ella Jackson, her old theatre maid, comes in for the day. Lunch at Henri's with Marinoff, and then we went to *Lady, Be Good*. Saw George Gershwin. Between acts he introduced me to Jimmy Lee & Eddie Cantor.[3] Mary Ellis sat with us until she had to go to the theatre. After dinner Florence Reed,[4] Marie Doro, Glenway Wescott, Donald [Angus], Nik Muray, T. R. Smith, Dorothy Hergesheimer, Noma Way, Anita Loos, Mrs. Talmadge (mother of the Talmadge sisters, met),[5] Blanche Knopf, Covarrubias. D'Alvarez sang Gershwin songs and Gershwin played the *Rhapsody in Blue* better than ever.

    1. Marie Louise de la Ramée, prolific nineteenth-century author of wildly romantic novels, often about the filthy rich (*Moths*) and once about the Foreign Legion (*Between Two Flags*), whose work CVV admired.
    2. Another unsatisfactory domestic, who lasted less than a week.
    3. Popular entertainers of the period attending Gershwin's musical comedy.
    4. American actress who had expressed interest to John Colton in playing in a dramatization of *The Tattooed Countess*.
    5. Constance and Norma Talmadge, silent film stars.

Wednesday, 10 December 1924

. . . Hunter [Stagg] comes in before lunch [in Richmond, Virginia]. Priscilla with Ballard comes in & drives me out to Dunbarton Grange for lunch with [James Branch] Cabell. After & before James & I have a long talk in his room. . . . Dinner at Ellen Glasgow's at 7. We have an old-fashioned Southern supper. Miss Bennett there, and talk until 10.30 when we go to a dance given by the Branches at the Woman's Club for Miss Glasgow of London (Ellen's niece). I meet the Branches, see Richard Crane who again invites me to Westover, etc.[1] Home at midnight & sleep badly.

1. A former American ambassador to Czechoslovakia, Crane had purchased and refurbished an antebellum plantation. His wife was a cousin of David Bruce.

Saturday, 13 December 1924

Hunter Stagg comes in & takes me to the train at 11 o'clock. Reading Proust's *Sodome et Gomorrhe*. Arrive in New York at 9 P.M. Find Marinoff & Edwin Knopf in the apartment. Go to Edwin's for a party. Mary Ellis, George Gershwin, & two other men. I give George hell about not orchestrating his songs. He leaves for Boston at one o'clock. Marinoff & I put Edwin to bed & talk till 3.20. I find proofs of *Firecrackers* here.

Friday, 26 December 1924

Bright, clear, cold day. Talked with Alfred & Blanche in the morning & agreed to do an introduction for the Alastair book.[1] Lunch in with Marinoff. At 2 o'clock George Gershwin comes in & talks to me about his life, in preparation for my paper for *Vanity Fair*.[2] He plays the themes of his prospective *Harlem Serenade*[3] for me, and also his "Yankee Doodle Blues." Dinner in, Marinoff cooking. . . . To bed early.

1. *Fifty Drawings by Alastair,* pen name for Hans Henning Voight, German fantasist. The book includes illustrations for CVV's *The Blind Bow-Boy* (1925).
2. "George Gershwin, A Notable Composer Who Is Writing Music in the Jazz Idiom," *Vanity Fair,* March 1925.
3. As a full-length composition this seems never to have been completed, although a number under this title was included in *Tiptoes,* a musical play, in 1929.

Saturday, 27 December 1924

Up a little after 7. Cloudy, cold day. Went out for a walk & to bank. Returned & wrote first draught of my paper on George Gershwin. . . . In the afternoon Marinoff goes to Best-Maugard's studio[1] & I go up to Edwin Knopf's. Mary Ellis comes in after matinee. Dinner with Donald Angus at Lily's. Then to Lucile Harper's where Edwin joins us. . . . At midnight, Edwin, Donald & I go back to his apartment, where we find Mary Ellis & George Gershwin. George plays many new things, including a new theme for the *Harlem Serenade*. Home at 4.00 A.M.

1. The Mexican artist Adolfo Best-Maugard was painting Marinoff's portrait.

Wednesday, 31 December 1924

Warm, semi-bright day, up at 8. Went out in morning to Knopf office, . . . bank, etc. Came home to lunch (Marinoff cooking) & read three chapters more of proofs of *Firecrackers*. Marinoff went to the matinee & returned with Rita Romilly. We dined with Reg Wallace at Lily's. At 9 o'clock Donald Angus came & we go to a party at Mary Ellis's. . . . George Gershwin, Jascha Heifetz, Covarrubias, [Vladimir] Golschmann (visiting conductor of the N.Y. Symphony, met), . . . Blanche & Alfred Knopf, Mildred Oppenheimer,[1] Edwin & Mary, Edgar Selwyn & his new girl.

1. Mrs. George Oppenheimer.

1925

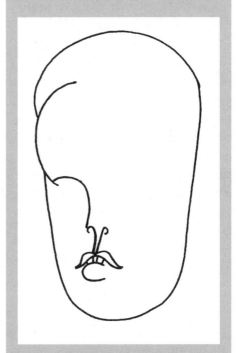

"Smalls, Philadelphia Jimmie's, The Nest, & Vaudeville Comedy Club. Home at 6.30 & didn't go to bed."

In 1925, Van Vechten's enthusiasm for African Americana inspired a number of articles for the influential white magazine *Vanity Fair* on blues, spirituals, the need for a "Negro Theatre," singers, and poets. Because of the black and white guest lists at the Van Vechtens' parties, Walter White dubbed their apartment "the downtown office of the N.A.A.C.P." Van Vechten regularly made forays to the vaudeville shows in Harlem, followed by all-night benders there in its cabarets. Also, he began to write *Nigger Heaven,* a serious novel that reflected a cross-section of Harlem life: its intellectual soirees, its pimps and whores, its economics, its young lovers, and the anguish of its inhabitants over an invidious American apartheid, dividing black New York from white New York at 125th Street.

Friday, 2 January 1925

Up at 8. Took Wallace Berkey's *Carnival* to Knopf.[1] Went to bank, etc. Terrific snow storm. . . . Eric Walrond and Donald Angus came in in the evening. Marinoff goes to see *Greed* (a moving picture after *McTeague*)[2] with Donald MacDonald.[3] They return at 11, & we go up to Mary Ellis's apartment. George Gershwin, Vladimir Golschmann, & Edwin Knopf. . . .

    1. Berkey had translated *Carnival*, a play by Hungarian writer Ferenc Molnar.

    2. Frank Norris's 1906 novel had been filmed a decade earlier, starring Fania Marinoff and Holbrook Blinn as *Life's Whirlpool*, of which no known print has survived.

    3. English actor, first in musical revues (sometimes in kilts because of his name), later in serious plays.

Saturday, 3 January 1925

. . . Snow piled high & melting. Finished second reading of *Firecrackers* proofs. Lunch in, Ella cooking.[1] Wrote most of third draught of George Gershwin paper. At 5 Ford Tarpley[2] of Ashville, N.C., comes in. Marinoff & I dine with Sam Hoffenstein at Leone's. Party at Walter White's Jan 3. James Weldon Johnson & Grace Johnson, Paul Robeson (met)[3] who sang Spirituals & his wife, Rosamond Johnson, Gladys White, Marinoff, Covarrubias, George Gershwin (who played his *Rhapsody*), Julius Bledsoe,[4] who sang. Party chez Mary Ellis. Marinoff went to a party at Lenore Ulric's.[5] . . . Home at 5.30. Marinoff gets in at the same hour.

    1. Ella Lee, yet another new domestic.

    2. A CVV collector, otherwise unremarked.

    3. African American actor and singer in the twenties and a powerful political activist thereafter. He and his wife, Essie, became immediate friends with the Van Vechtens and others in their circle.

    4. African American actor and singer, best known for his role in the Jerome Kern–Oscar Hammerstein II musical version of Edna Ferber's novel *Showboat*.

    5. White actress who played the lead in *Lulu Belle* in blackface.

Monday, 5 January 1925

. . . The new French maid, Alice [Monnier], arrives. She gets lunch for us. First review of *Red*, very favorable, in *NEA Review*. . . . Reading [Gerald] Heard's *Narcissus*. Dinner at Virginia Hammond's. Ann Andrews (met),[1] Marie Doro, Marinoff & I. Virginia (playing with Lenore Ulric) left for the theatre at 7.30. We came home. Marinoff goes to theatre with Edwin Knopf & Eric Walrond comes down to see me. He shows me the sketches he has written for *Vanity Fair*.

1. Popular American actress of the period who became an instant good friend of CVV because of their mutual affection for cats, of which she kept half a dozen at a time.

Thursday, 8 January 1925

. . . During the day I went nearly through 4 chapters of *Firecrackers* on a fourth reading. Went to Alice Thursby's to pick up Mabel Luhan.[1] Went with her to look at objects for sale. Then Mabel came to the house to lunch with Marinoff & me, Alice M[onnier] cooking. Philip Moeller came to dinner. At 10.30 he & I joined George Gershwin & E[dwin] Knopf in the latter's apartment. Mary Ellis arrived at 11.30. George played a new tune. George & Edwin just back from Stravinsky's first concert with the Philharmonic & talked about it. Two nights before George had played for Stravinsky . . . with only Laurette Taylor[2] present. Stravinsky cold.[3]

1. Alice Brisbane Thursby, social and arts patron, the daughter of social philosopher Arthur Brisbane and sister of editor Arthur Brisbane Jr.
2. Popular American actress from 1914 in *Peg O' My Heart,* by her English husband, J. Hartley Manners, to 1945 in *The Glass Menagerie,* by Tennessee Williams.
3. CVV was this Russian composer's earliest American champion, publishing accounts of the first performances of *The Rite of Spring* and other then avant-garde compositions.

Friday, 9 January 1925

. . . I go to the 2nd Stravinsky concert with Mary Ellis at Carnegie Hall. *Chant de Rossignol* & *Oiseau de Feu,*[1] marvellous. Mary comes home with me for a [*word*]. Dinner at home, Alice cooking. Then went to a party at Ettie Stettheimer's studio. Florine, Edna Kenton, Charles Demuth.[2] . . . Demuth has to take injections of insulin every two hours to keep alive. He has diabetes.

1. *Song of the Nightingale* and *The Firebird.*
2. American artist, best known for his exquisite watercolors of fruits and flowers and his "poster portraits" of artists Georgia O'Keeffe, Arthur Dove, and John Marin and poets William Carlos Williams and Wallace Stevens, among others.

Saturday, 10 January 1925

. . . Reading proofs on *Firecrackers.* Spud Johnson[1] & several others call up. Lunch at Marguerite D'Alvarez's. Then to Brentano's, then home. Mabel Dodge Luhan sends Marinoff a Persian miniature. Avery Hopwood, back from Chicago, comes in. Marie Doro comes to dinner & goes with Marinoff to Stravinsky concert. Donald Angus comes in. After concert Mary Ellis &

Edwin Knopf, Marinoff. I get drunk & get rough with Marinoff & she goes upstairs to sleep in Knopf apartment.[2] I went to bed at 3. Stravinsky's concert, 7.30, didn't go.

1. Willard Johnson, variously called "Spud" and Gipsy," edited *Laughing Horse*, a Taos, New Mexico publication. He had come East to write for *The New Yorker*.

2. This is CVV's first direct admission that he could be verbally and physically abusive when he had drunk too much, sometimes to friends, sometimes to strangers, sometimes to his wife. Regina Wallace later averred that on several occasions in the twenties, he "playfully" struck Marinoff—harmless little cuffs, he thought, but Marinoff was occasionally obliged to seek shelter with a friend overnight, although usually in anticipation of his behavior rather than in response to it.

Saturday, 17 January 1925

. . . Percy and Florence Hammond dined with us. Alice [Monnier] has her husband [Leon] help after dinner. Party, Adele Astaire (met),[1] she danced & sang; Mary Ellis & Edwin Knopf, Mary sang; D'Alvarez who sang Gershwin songs, 7 Negroes, Mr. & Mrs. James Weldon Johnson, Mr. & Mrs. Walter White, Mr. & Mrs. Paul Robeson. He sang Spirituals, & Jules Bledsoe who sang, danced & played. George Gershwin played the *Rhapsody*. Mercedes de Acosta & Marie Doro, Otto Kahn,[2] Blanche & Alfred Knopf, Covarrubias, Donald Angus, Mary Kennedy & Deems Taylor, Henry & Dorothy Harvey, Donald MacDonald, Frances Seligman.[3]

1. Sister and dancing partner of Fred Astaire.

2. Wealthy investment banker, progressive chair of the board of the Metropolitan Opera House, and influential theatrical producer.

3. Hugo Seligman's wife. The Seligmans were friends through the Stettheimers.

Friday, 23 January 1925

In all day working on papers and cleaning out closets. Lunch in, Marinoff cooking. At 4 o'clock Marie Doro came in & stayed to supper. Marinoff goes to Florine Stettheimer's to tea, but returns to get supper for us. Marinoff and I go to a box party given by Mary Ellis at Stravinsky concert (chamber music at Aeolian Hall), first performance of Stravinsky's *Ragtime*. Florence Reed[1] & Philip Moeller, Edwin Knopf. . . . This box party, to which Max Ewing was added, came to our apartment for supper.

1. Actress best remembered as Mother Goddam in John Colton's play *The Shanghai Gesture*.

Monday, 26 January 1925

... Lunch with Alfred Knopf at the St. Regis. We talked over plans for publication of *Firecrackers*. . . . Come home at 4.30. Willard Johnson comes in. Later Ettie Stettheimer arrives with a manuscript which she wants me to read. Still later Regina Wallace, Marinoff from an Equity meeting, Carrie Stettheimer. Gipsy Johnson & I go to dinner in Harlem with Countee Cullen & Eric Walrond. Then to the James Weldon Johnsons'. Walrond brings three girls in, including the wonderful Louella Tucker[1] who dances the Charleston more wonderfully than I've ever seen it danced.

> 1. With librarian Regina Anderson and Ethel Rae Nance, secretary to Charles S. Johnson of the Urban League, Louella Tucker maintained Harlem's version of several downtown salons and opened their apartment to young aspiring African American writers and artists in the twenties.

Friday, 30 January 1925

Sun, the roofs white with snow. My royalty reports, the largest I have ever received, arrive. There seem to be some errors & I call . . . at the office to correct them. . . . Lunch at home with Marinoff. Worked on M. P. Shiel and Fuller papers for *Excavations*. Read . . . *Firecrackers* for corrections on galley proofs. Claire [Burke Schermerhorn] & Sam Hoffenstein to dinner at 6.30. We have bouillabaisse. At 10 they go & Marie Doro comes for us & we go to the James Weldon Johnsons' for supper & a party. . . . Rosamond Johnson, Mrs. Rosamond (met), the Walter Whites, Mary Ellis & Edwin Knopf. We go to the wonderful midnight show [of] *Club Alabama* at Lafayette Theatre. Eddie Rector, Johnnie Hudgins, Al Moore, etc.[1] Begins at 1.30, over at 4.30. See Mr. & Mrs. Paul Robeson, Julius Bledsoe, Witter Bynner. In bed about 5.

> 1. Three African American entertainers. Al Moore later became one of CVV's early photographic subjects.

Monday, 2 February 1925

Cloudy day. Streets full of dirty snow. Cablegram from Alastair, thanking me for doing his preface. . . . At 5 Willard Johnson came in for half an hour. Dinner home with Marinoff. We went to see Emil Jannings in *The Last Laugh* at the Rialto, the best picture I have ever seen & the first moving picture without titles that I have seen. Marinoff goes home & I go to see Lewis Baer who has the dummy of the Negro number of the *Survey Graphic*.[1] Home at 11.30.

> 1. Spurred on by the Civic Club Dinner, 21 March 1924, that introduced young black writers to a number of white publishers, the *Survey Graphic* devoted its March issue to African American arts and letters.

Tuesday, 3 February 1925

. . . Drew $2,000 from Knopf & went on a spree, signing cheques & visiting shops for necessaries. . . . At 5 o'clock I meet Gipsy Johnson at the Algonquin. We go to Jack Harper's for a drink & then to Lily's. Closed. So we go to Leone's for dinner. He comes home with me for evening. Marinoff goes to theatre. She comes home at 11.15 & goes to spend night with R[egina] Wallace. I join Lewis Baer, Gordon Nielsen, Dick Barnett & Ted Arlen (met) & we go to Harlem. Small's, Leroy's (Pedro the waiter), & Log Cabin (Mabel Harris & Ivy Madison, the dancers). Gordon leaves early. The rest of us go to Lewis Baer's. He goes to bed at 7.30. Ted Arlen, Dick Barnett & I

Wednesday, 4 February 1925

come down to my apartment & get breakfast. After [*bathing?*] they leave about 9. None of us has been to bed at all. Marinoff gets home about 11.30. Lunch in & I sleep all the afternoon. At 6 Avery Hopwood comes in & takes me to Fornio's, a Spanish place, for dinner. Then we join John Floyd & go to Jack & Lucile Harper's. I leave them drinking champagne at 11. Home & to bed. Marinoff out to dinner with a milkman named Elwell.

Friday, 6 February 1925

Still bilious, but up and reading papers. . . . At 2.30 Donald Angus comes for me & we go to Harlem. Eric Walrond meets us at 135 Street Station & introduces us to Harold Jackman.[1] Then we go to a benefit for Negro Y.M.C.A. at Fletcher Henderson's.[2] Paul Robeson, Carroll Clark, a new [singer], & John Nail[3] made a speech. Talked with Robeson, the James Weldon Johnsons, etc. . . . (Marinoff goes to dinner at Lenore Ulric's house at 3.30.) Jackman, Angus, Eric and I go to the Petersons[4] in Brooklyn for a party. . . . Then the three boys come home with me & stay till 11.30.

1. Harlem school teacher, the physical model for the protagonist in CVV's novel *Nigger Heaven,* Countee Cullen's lover, and occasionally sexual partner for others, black as well as white, although CVV was not among them.

2. The leading African American bandleader of the period.

3. James Weldon Johnson's brother-in-law, Nail was largely responsible for the beginnings of black colonization in Harlem, circa 1905, when he persuaded a white landlord to rent empty apartments on Striver's Row (137th Street) to African Americans.

4. James Bowers Peterson, his daughter Dorothy, and his son Sidney, a medical doctor. Dorothy became one of CVV's intimate friends. He claimed that she alone served as physical model for the heroine of *Nigger Heaven.* Also present at this party was Nella Larsen Imes, whose novels CVV placed with Knopf.

Wednesday, 11 February 1925

. . . I feel a little better but have a powerful hangover. Our new couch comes, clean out & cover my literature boxes. Lunch in with Marinoff. Reading Pershing's *H. L. Mencken*, and *Those Barren Leaves* [by Aldous Huxley]. Dinner in with Marinoff. She goes with Irene McIver to see the film of *The Man Without a Country*. Eric Walrond & Jean Toomer (met)[1] come in after dinner. Also Countee Cullen (who does the Charleston), Harold Jackman, Gipsy Johnson, Donald Angus. Marinoff, who doesn't like the picture, returns at 10. I sleep in my room for the first time, as the bed is moved out of the living room.

1. The earliest of the young African American writers, whose *Cane* may be said to mark the beginning of the literary branch of the Harlem Renaissance. CVV had not yet read it.

Friday, 13 February 1925

. . . Write Machen chapter for *Excavations*. Lunch in alone as Marinoff is called out on a prospect of a job. Jack Harper comes in with liquor. Mahala Douglas & T. R. Smith come to dinner. After dinner John Emerson, Anita Loos, Florence Reed, Virginia Hammond, Percy & Florence Hammond, Edwin Knopf, Gerald and Mrs. Kelley, Donald Angus, and the following blacks: Mr. & Mrs. James Weldon Johnson, Mr. & Mrs. Paul Robeson, Louella Tucker, Eric Walrond, Walter & Gladys White, . . . Harold Jackman, Sol Johnson,[1] Julius Bledsoe.

1. Solomon Johnson was an African American journalist and political activist.

Saturday, 28 February 1925

. . . Worked on Albéniz paper.[1] Lunch in. Mabel Luhan sent me up her Duse paper & as much as is written of the "Memoires Intimes."[2] Avery Hopwood comes in at 4 & stays till six. Gispy Johnson at 6.30, for dinner. Leaves at 11, when I join Avery at the Ritz. Beach Cooke[3] is there. We go to Harlem, first Small's, then to The Nest where I met Mary & Jazzo. . . . Then to the Comedy-Vaudeville Club. Home at 7.30.

1. An essay about Spanish composer Isaac Albéniz from *In the Garret* (1919) that CVV was revising for *Excavations*.
2. In *European Experiences*, the second volume of Luhan's four-volume "Intimate Memories" (the French title seems to have been CVV's affectation) published a decade later, there is a twenty-page chapter about the Italian actress Eleanora Duse.
3. One of CVV's two regular bootleggers. The other was Jack Harper.

Wednesday, 4 March 1925

. . . In the afternoon Gipsy Johnson comes in at 5, followed shortly by Avery Hopwood & Clintock King (met).[1] Later, Horace Liveright, Regina Wallace. Gipsy & Reg stay to dinner. After dinner Bernardine Szold & Marinoff go to dress rehearsal of *Mandragola* at the Princess. Donald Angus arrives. He, Gipsy & I go to Plaza where we meet Mabel and Tony Luhan. Mabel drives us to Lafayette Theatre where I am excluded because of bottle of gin I carry. I hang around until the intermission when I go backstage to see Rosamond Johnson & he takes care of it for me, & then Tony, Gipsy, Donald & I go to Small's, where we are joined by Marinoff, Bernardine Szold, Lewis Baer, Witter Bynner, Dick Barnett, Harry Block, Walrond. Best-Maugard[2] comes in with another party. [*Not home?*] until 5 o'clock. Tony dances.

    1. Another of Hopwood's casual liaisons.

    2. The Mexican artist and teacher was an influence on Florine Stettheimer's paintings.

Friday, 6 March 1925

. . . Went to office, saw cover design for *Firecrackers*. Marinoff & I have dinner with Mary Ellis. She is having an affair with Basil Sidney.[1] Party at Walter White's turns out to be a party at Julius Bedsoe's. Gladys & Walter White, Marinoff, Donald Angus, Covarrubias, . . . Percy Hammond, Paul, Essie Robeson. We leave about 3.

    1. American actor who succeeded Gershwin, who had succeeded Edwin Knopf, on Ellis's roster.

Monday, 9 March 1925

. . . Slept badly last night & woke up with sort of cold. Feeling rotten all day. Lunch in. I worked on "A Note on Dedications."[1] Late in the afternoon Clintock King happened in without being announced, bringing Mark Mooring[2] with him. King was so drunk that I got rid of them quickly. Bernardine Szold came to dinner, Marinoff cooking. After dinner, about 10, we go to bed. But Tallulah Bankhead telephones & we go over to the Gotham to drink champagne with her & her maid, Mrs. Locke.

    1. Another paper being revised for *Excavations*. It had been published in *Bookman*, July 1923.

    2. Fashion designer and costumer for several editions of the *Greenwich Village Follies*.

Tuesday, 10 March 1925

. . . Cocktails with Somerset Maugham, 6 o'clock. Gerald Haxton,[1] Sherrill Schell, Jack Colton, Chamberlain Dodds & a Spanish doctor.[2] Everybody left but Gerald, Jack Colton, & I. We had dinner with Maugham at the Gotham. Donald Angus joins us & then spends the evening with me. Jack, Donald & I meet Maugham & Gerald after the theatre. . . . & go to Harlem, to Cecil Fields', 246 W. 136.[3] Maugham & Haxton go home about 2, & Jack disappears. Donald and I go to Small's, the Nest, Leroy's, and the Comedy Vaudeville Club . . . until 7.30. Donald comes home with me.

> 1. Maugham's longtime companion, secretary, and lover.
> 2. Donald Angus recalled this as a typical homosocial evening in the twenties, in which sexual activity played no role.
> 3. According to Angus this was a "buffet flat" or male brothel to which Colton escorted them, depositing them in a private room furnished with chairs, a table, and a bed. Colton then abandoned them, saying he would return but did not. Maugham then proposed, "Why don't you boys do something together and amuse us?" Haxton and Angus demurred. When Colton did not reappear after a lengthy time, they went their separate ways.

Wednesday, 11 March 1925

Donald wakes me up about 10.30. Ella brings me coffee in. He goes to work. I have some soup & go back to bed. In the afternoon Mahala Douglas, John Floyd, Tallulah Bankhead, Katharine Cornell,[1] Bernardine Szold, Witter Bynner, Gipsy Johnson . . . come in. Everybody stays till nearly eight. Then Marinoff & I go to Leone's to dine. . . . Home & to bed at 9 o'clock. . . .

> 1. Popular and respected actress whom CVV did not admire. Her husband, director Guthrie McClintic, made much of her dark glamour and husky voice in many plays, but her greater success came later as Elizabeth in *The Barretts of Wimpole Street.*

Friday, 13 March 1925

. . . Finished front matter of *Excavations*. . . . Napped in the afternoon & work, feeling worse. Went to dinner at Mary Ellis's. Basil Sidney there. He left before dinner. Mary repeats how happy she is without Edwin [Knopf]. After dinner Mary goes to the theatre. Marinoff goes to bed & I join Countee Cullen, Harold Jackman, & Donald Angus at the Alhambra Theatre to see the Charleston contest. Come home immediately thereafter. . . . Sleep very badly. Rain. Countee tells me that Harpers are to publish his book of poems, *Colour*, in the fall, and he has been made a member of Phi Beta Kappa.

Thursday, 19 March 1925

... Sent manuscript of "Overture in the Form of a Funeral March" (3 drafts) to Scott Cunningham.[1] Working on papers, etc. Marinoff sick. The poo is sick.[2] We send for Dr. Walters. Constipation & hairballs. . . . Prefacing my biography for *The American Encyclopedia of Biography*. . . . Late in the afternoon Irene McIver, who stayed to dine with Marinoff, Witter Bynner, Best-Maugard, who brings Marinoff's picture which he is doing, Avery Hopwood. Dinner with Virginia Hammond, 6, called off because Marinoff is sick. Went to dinner with Avery at Colony. Then to Irene Bordoni's (met).[3] Now that I recall it I had been introduced to her years before. . . . Then to 135 St. subway where we picked up Eric Walrond. We go to Louella Tucker's where there are a lot of girls, [&] Winold Reiss (met).[4] . . . We go to Mrs. Walker's (met),[5] more people but no drinks. Then Avery & I go to The Nest, where . . . I also dance & talk with Margy & Fleau, entertainers, & Johnny Corey & Mal Frazier. At 4 I leave to join Eric at Small's & then go home. . . .

1. A foreword to the bibliography of CVV's work that Cunningham had prepared for the Centaur Press.

2. "Poo" was the common sobriquet that Marinoff and CVV bestowed on all of their cats. This one was Scheherazade.

3. Popular French musical comedy actress, currently appearing in a Hopwood play.

4. German painter and teacher, responsible for many portraits of literary figures in the Harlem Renaissance, now in the National Portrait Gallery of the Smithsonian.

5. A'Lelia Walker, daughter of Madam C. J. Walker, who had become the first black millionaire through the sale of her hair and skin products for African American women. Madam Walker built a limestone mansion in Harlem and an American version of Versailles at Irvington on the Hudson, in both of which her daughter entertained lavishly through the twenties.

Friday, 20 March 1925

... Marinoff's birthday. Up at a quarter of ten. Give Marinoff $150 for clothes & she has flowers from Donald Angus & Covarrubias. Wrote part of second draft of Covarrubias preface.[1] . . . Before lunch John Floyd arrives, scarred, his arm in sling, deserted (temporarily by Avery), his funds cut off, penniless, thrown out of the Roosevelt [Hotel], hungry, he slept last night on a park bench. We give him some soup & I go down to the bank after lunch. Return & try to nap. Gipsy Johnson comes in at 3. Later Miguel Covarrubias with Gershwin caricature & Montgomery Evans. After they leave we go to dinner with D'Alvarez, 7.30, Hugo & Frances Seligman. We return home to find telegram from Mabel Dodge [Luhan] calling after Sunday party. Poo has begun to evacuate blood. We call Dr. Walters in to see her. He says she is better. I read in *The Autobiography of an Ex-Coloured Man* [by James Weldon Johnson] for a time & then go to bed.

    1. For *The Prince of Wales and Other Famous Americans*, a book of caricatures (Knopf, 1925).

Monday, 23 March 1925

. . . Wrote 3rd draft of Covarrubias paper & second and last drafts of Irving Berlin review for the *Tribune*.[1] . . . Also read the April [*American*] *Mercury* & the interminable *The Counterplot* [by Hope Mirrlees]. Best-Maugard comes in & finishes Marinoff's portrait, & Bernardine Szold who goes to dinner with her at Wittgenstein's. I go to dinner with Harry Block, 7 o'clock. . . . Lewis Baer takes me home in his car & we stop off at Buddie Baker's[2] where we find boys named Stuart & McCready.

    1. A review of *Dean of Jazz: The Story of Irving Berlin* by Alexander Woollcott.
    2. A speakeasy catering to homosexual trade.

Friday, 27 March 1925

. . . In the afternoon I went to see Arthur Ficke who has just had his tonsils removed. Dinner with Mary Ellis, Marinoff, Basil Sidney, George Gershwin. George played several new numbers from his new opera, *My Fair Lady,* which opens next week. Some kind of party in Harlem (Grace Johnson). Dance at the N.A.A.C.P. Manhattan Casino. With James Weldon Johnson we go up at 11, & stay until 3. Very large crowd. Eric Walrond, Countee Cullen, Louella Tucker, Mrs. Walker & her Harlem lover (Ja Brian [i.e., Krishna Sobrian]), Alain Locke (met),[1] . . . John Nail, Jean Toomer, Mrs. Rosamond Johnson, Rose McClendon,[2] Fletcher Henderson (his orchestra played), Sol Johnson & Catherine [Mrs. Solomon] Johnson, Harold Jackman, Mal Frazier, Walter White, Gladys White, . . . Miss [Dorothy] Peterson, Jim & Dorothy Harris,[3] Paul Robeson, Essie Robeson, & Lawrence Brown (met).[4]

    1. Howard University professor of literature, editor of *The New Negro*, often credited for helping to establish the Harlem Renaissance.
    2. African American actress who appeared on Broadway in several plays by white writers with black casts.
    3. African American painter and his wife, residents of Greenwich Village.
    4. African American pianist and composer/arranger, Paul Robeson's accompanist.

Friday, 3 April 1925

. . . Cat still ill. I am feeling well. Wrote third draught of Countee Cullen paper[1] & first draught of review of Ernest Newman's *A Musical Critic's Holiday*. Lunch in with Marinoff. . . . Jack Harper came up. Read Arthur Machen paper for *Excavations*. To dinner with Mary Ellis. Romney Brent[2] was there. After dinner Marinoff went with Johnnie Floyd to see his play[3] at the Yorkville Theatre. Donald Angus comes to see me & about midnight we go to Harlem. Small's first, where we met Jean Toomer, Harold Jackman, & Eric Walrond with a large party. Then to The Nest, where we talk with Johnnie Corey (Cobb, or Harper are other aliases), Margy & Mal Frazier. Home at 5.

   1. A biographical note and an assessment of his poetry for *Vanity Fair*, written to accompany a selection of the poet's work.
   2. American actor and musical comedy performer.
   3. Avery Hopwood's much younger lover and longtime companion had hoped for a career in the theater, but he seems to have performed in only one play (and that one by Hopwood); his own play, *The Wooden Kimono*, ran for at least several months on Broadway.

Saturday, 4 April 1925

Up at 10, with a hangover & remorse.[1] Bright, sunny warm day. The poo still has general trouble & drops of blood everywhere. Revising Ronald Firbank paper for *Excavations*. . . . Sent Countee Cullen blurb off to *Vanity Fair*. Lunch in with Marinoff. Also dinner. At 8 o'clock went to sleep after reading first chapters of [Ernst] Krehbiel's *Afro-American Folksongs*.

   1. The word "remorse" occurs with increasing regularity, always after a night of heavy drinking, although the context often suggests some other activity for which remorse might have been inevitable.

Sunday, 5 April 1925

. . . Paul & Essie Robeson, Lawrence Brown for dinner. After dinner Brown & Robeson sang all the evening. Anita Loos & John Emerson, Bernardine Szold, Rita Romilly, Theodore Dreiser, Eva Gauthier, Alfred & Blanche Knopf, Donald Angus came in. In bed at 2.

Tuesday, 7 April 1925

. . . Poo still flowing. Lunch in with Marinoff. Finished reading Henry Liscomb's *The Prince of Washington Square*.[1] Went to Stern's to buy covering for chairs and sofa. Then Marinoff & I walked up the avenue & I went to see Alfred & Blanche [Knopf]. They have taken Best-Maugard's book. Dinner in alone. Marinoff dines & goes to theatre with John Emerson. Countee Cullen & Henry Liscomb come up in the evening. The author of *The Prince of Washington Square* turns out to be a shy youth who scarcely speaks & refuses to dance the Charleston.

    1. A little-known early Harlem Renaissance novel.

Monday, 13 April 1925

. . . Mary Ellis calls up to say that Edwin left her last night, at her request. Revising *Excavations*. Send off state income tax. Lunch at Algonquin with Marinoff & Edwin Knopf. (Ella does not turn up so we have to go out for meals.) Home and reading plate proofs. I go up to see Mary (who is determined that Edwin will commit suicide). Later Edwin comes into see me. Basil Sidney at Macy's & he telephones me while Edwin is here. Marinoff & I dine at Lindy's, where we see Hess[1] & later go to opening of George Gershwin's *Tell Me More* at the Gaiety. . . . We go behind after the play to see Geo. He introduces us to Lou Holtz & Phyllis Cleveland (new prima donna) & others, & we go to the Trocadero with him, [and] his sister (met),[2] . . . Adele & Fred Astaire dancing at Trocadero. We go back to see them. Met Mrs. Astaire.

    1. Perhaps (but unlikely, given the circumstances) the English pianist Myra Hess, whom they had heard play two evenings earlier at a Knopf party.

    2. Frances Gershwin, a professional dancer and singer, later Mrs. Leopold Godowsky Jr.

Tuesday, 14 April 1925

. . . Poo is much better. Photographed by Nickolas Muray. Lunch in with Marinoff. Finished correcting proof of Alastair paper. Alfred Knopf, 3 o'clock. Took him the mss. of *Excavations* & the proofs of Alastair preface. Went over the Covarrubias drawings, & took out a few, not to be used in book.[1] . . . Edwin Knopf comes in at 6, and stays for dinner. He talked about Mary & leaves with his trunk about nine. . . .

    1. The Knopfs often relied on CVV's assessments, often of African American materials but not exclusively so.

Wednesday, 15 April 1925

. . . Wrote review of Scott Fitzgerald's *The Great Gatsby*. Read plate proofs of *Firecrackers*. 4 o'clock, Rose McClendon came in & I took her to see John

Emerson & Anita Loos in connection with a job. Home for dinner. Donald Angus dines here. After dinner I go to see Mary Ellis. Basil Sidney there. At 10 o'clock Marinoff, Donald & I go to party at Horace Liveright's office. T. R. Smith, Horace & Lucile Liveright, Edgar Lee Masters,[1] Ben Hecht, Anita Loos, John Emerson, Burton & Hazel Rascoe, etc. At midnight Donald & I go to Harlem to Small's. . . .

1. Lawyer and prolific writer of novels, biographies, and many volumes of poetry, largely remembered only for a series of poetic monologues, *Spoon River Anthology.*

Sunday, 19 April 1925

Up early. The telephone bell rings all night. The poo is about completely cured & I am not feeling so well. Reading papers, working on papers & bookcases. Zoë Akins came in in afternoon. Paul Robeson & Lawrence Brown at the Greenwich Village Theatre. Arthur Ficke, Louis Bromfield & Mrs. Lawrence Langner, Armina Marshall, etc. We went with Ann Andrews & Virginia Hammond. The event was a great success. Donald Angus party. James Weldon & Grace Johnson, Robeson & Lawrence Brown, Walter & Gladys White, . . . Nik Muray, . . . Marinoff, . . . Bernardine Szold, etc.

Tuesday, 28 April 1925

. . . At 5 we go to Nickolas Muray's studio to see proofs of Paul Robeson, nude. Meet Gladys Axman on Fifth Avenue. . . . Dinner at Lindy's. Then we went to see *The Princess Ida* [by Gilbert and Sullivan], first time I had seen it. I was disappointed. Home for baggage & found a remarkable piece of brocade (burned) somebody had left here, apparently as a joke. Then took Marinoff down to the boat (*Aquitania*) . . . & left my blessed Baby on the deck. To Lucile Harper's for a few drinks. Then home.

Wednesday, 29 April 1925

Up at 8. Feeling very desolate & nervous. Worked in morning. Ella and I cleaned Marinoff's closet. Then I began work on my paper on Negro Spirituals. . . . Donald Angus comes to dinner. At 11, Nils Nelson[1] joins us & we go to Harlem, meeting Eric Walrond by appointment at Leroy's. Then to Philadelphia Jimmie's, Connie's & The Nest. Home at 5.

1. Donald Angus's latest inamorato.

Friday, 1 May 1925

. . . At 5.30 Lawrence Langner appears. After he goes Eric Walrond & Rita Romilly appear & we go to *Opportunity*[1] Dinner where prizes are awarded to Negro writers. We sit at table with Louella Tucker, Robert H. Davis,[2] Fannie Hurst,[3] . . . Tom Smith. Talk with Grace & James Weldon Johnson, Robesons, . . . Rose McClendon, Winold Reiss, Jessie Fauset,[4] Countee Cullen, Langston Hughes,[5] Harold Jackman, etc. Met Charles S. Johnson.[6] Eric, Rita and I go to Mrs. Walker's at 11.30. . . . Then to Y.M.C.A. dance at Manhattan Casino, where I see numerous other people. . . . Then Rita, Eric & I join a crowd including Jim & Dorothy Harris at Bamville (cut time). At 4.30 we go to the Vaudeville Comedy Club where a wonderful party is going on . . . until 7.30 when Rita & I drive home through the sunlit park. John is sorting the mail as I come in.

1. The monthly publication of the Urban League.
2. Chicago poet.
3. Popular novelist and a longtime CVV acquaintance.
4. African American novelist whose first book, *There Is Confusion*, joined Walter White's *The Fire in the Flint* in sparking the intellectual element of the Harlem Renaissance, although CVV had already endorsed Countee Cullen's poems for publication in *Vanity Fair*.
5. Hughes had read some of his poems on this occasion, which motivated CVV's offer to recommend them to Alfred A. Knopf for publication. CVV's intellectual interest in the Harlem Renaissance does not seem to have commenced in any measurable way until this *Opportunity* dinner, after which he was inspired, he later reflected.
6. Head of the Urban League and publisher of its magazine, *Opportunity*.

Saturday, 2 May 1925

Man comes to tune the piano at 9, just [as] I am drinking coffee. At 11.30 I retire for a nap until 2. We put up summer curtains. Langston Hughes comes in at 5 & stays for an hour, bringing his book of poems[1] which I read after he has gone. . . . Rhea Wells[2] comes in at 8, with the prints of my Alastair drawings coloured & shows me some of his own flower drawings. In bed by 9.30.

1. The manuscript for *The Weary Blues* (Knopf, 1926).
2. Graphic artist, a friend of CVV's since 1910.

Sunday, 3 May 1925

. . . At 3 Langston Hughes comes in for an hour on his way to Washington. I give him back his poems with a few suggestions. Dinner alone. Then met Donald Angus & he and I attended Paul Robeson & Lawrence Brown's second concert at Greenwich Village Theatre.[1] Saw a great number of people & afterwards went to a party at Winold Reiss's. . . . Jessie Fauset, Walter White, Miller of Miller & Lyles (met),[2] Rita Romilly, . . . Dorothy & Jim Harris, Harold Jackman, Harrison Smith,[3] Carl & Irita Van Doren, Eric Walrond, Miss Hurston,[4] Nora (who danced nude),[5] etc., Nik Muray. Came home, at 1, to sleep badly. I have indigestion & a cold. Tossed with nightmares.

1. Although CVV does not say so here, he financed this second recital in addition to supplying a program note for it.

2. Flournoy Miller, playwright and popular blackface comedian in tandem with Aubrey Lyles, who had come to popularity with white audiences when they appeared in blackface makeup in *Shuffle Along* in 1921.

3. Publisher who merged with Bennett Cerf and Donald Klopfer in 1927 at Random House and its subsidiary Modern Library, which Cerf had recently acquired from Horace Liveright.

4. Zora Neale Hurston, African American anthropologist and writer and soon an intimate friend of CVV.

5. Nora Holt Ray, scandalous demimondaine of the Harlem Renaissance and nightclub singer; also, as Nora Holt, with a master's degree in music, a composer and later an influential musical critic in African American newspapers. She was five times married and between husbands the inamorata of communist lawyer William Patterson. She was the model for CVV's "Lasca Sartoris" in *Nigger Heaven*. She and CVV remained intimate friends until his death.

Thursday, 7 May 1925

. . . Lunch alone at Lindy's. . . . Went to Eric Walrond's room where I met Chick [*name*] of a Cuban baseball team. Then Eric and I go to Young's bookshop home to look at old books. Stop on 7th Ave. at a beauty parlor to see Mrs. Bernia Austin. Her husband comes in.[1] Also stop to see Zora Neale Hurston, Sol Johnson, but both are out. Then back to Eric's room. He makes another engagement. Not very pleased I go home. To Algonquin for dinner at 8 o'clock where I run into Bertha & Frank Case. Talk with them till 10.30. Stop at Lucile Harper's to pay a bill. . . . Home & to bed after a couple of bottles of beer.

1. In addition to her beauty parlor, Mrs. Austin chaired the Harlem Cooperating Committee on Relief and Unemployment. Her husband, Harry Austin, was at the Trinity Church of Pittsburgh.

Friday, 8 May 1925

. . . Eric calls up to apologize. Sent my Spirituals article to *Vanity Fair*.[1] Lunch in alone. Wrote first draught of paper on Paul Robeson. Grace Johnson's at 3. First meeting to discuss the Harlem Negro Theatre. Ridgely Torrence,[2]

W. E. B. Du Bois, Arthur Spingarn (met),[3] James Weldon Johnson & Rosamond Johnson, John Nail, Walter White. Walter White, Lawrence Brown & Paul Robeson come in for cocktails before the Civic Club Dinner, 9 P.M., for Robeson & Brown. I sit next to James Weldon Johnson & Dr. Du Bois. Frank Miller, Imes,[4] Harry Austin, Lester Walton[5] & others there. I met Lena Wilson, the Blues singer, Paul & Lawrence entertained with Spirituals. James Weldon Johnson came home with me & stayed talking till 4.

1. "The Folksongs of the American Negro," *Vanity Fair,* July 1925.

2. White playwright whose 1914 *Granny Maumee,* about African Americans (with white actors), first motivated CVV to recommend in print the establishment of a Negro Theater in *Trend,* April 1914.

3. Long-time white supporter of the NAACP who served as the organization's lawyer until 1909.

4. Elmer Imes, a Ph.D. in physics, was in research for Burroughs Magnetic Equipment Company on Staten Island. Earlier he had taught at Fisk University in Nashville, Tennessee, and he returned there to teach in 1930. In between, he married novelist Nella Larsen.

5. African American journalist, editor of *New York World,* and influential contributor to many periodicals. He may be credited for having insisted that the word *Negro* stop being printed with a lowercase *n.*

Monday, 11 May 1925

. . . Claire Schermerhorn Hoffenstein comes in at 5 to tell me she is leaving Sam. They have been married three months. . . .

Tuesday, 12 May 1925

. . . Ella Lee has a fight with her husband, James Lee, on the telephone just before dinner. Ellen Glasgow and her sister for dinner, 7 o'clock, . . . Philip Moeller also. After dinner, Ettie & Carrie Stettheimer, Carl & Irita Van Doren, Edna Ferber, Rita Romilly. . . . I got terribly drunk.

Wednesday, 13 May 1925

Up at 8, with a hangover. . . . Langston Hughes's book [i.e., manuscript for], *The Weary Blues,* arrives & I give it to Alfred Knopf who comes to lunch at 1. After he has gone I visit the office & then go to Florine Stettheimer's studio. . . . On my way home I ran into Adele Astaire & Dick Barthelmess[1] & walk up 6 Ave. with them. Dinner home alone. Then go to bed until 10. Harlem party with Lawrence Langner & Armina Marshall.[2] We meet Eric Walrond and Louella Tucker by appointment at Small's. Later we go to The

Nest. Mrs. [Nora Holt] Ray is there. She introduces me to a Mr. Patterson.[3] . . . Home at 4.

1. Richard Barthelmess, matinee idol in silent films.

2. Langner had left his wife for Marshall, an actress, and later co-director of the Theatre Guild.

3. William Patterson, Nora Holt's current paramour, later the lawyer for the Scottsboro Boys and husband of political activist Louise Thompson after the death of her husband, Harlem Renaissance novelist and gadfly Wallace Thurman.

Friday, 15 May 1925

. . . Read Dr. Du Bois's *The Gift of Black Folk,* not a good book. Russell Doubleday's[1] tea for Ellen Glasgow, the Coffee House, 4.30, 54 W. 45 St. Carrie Stettheimer studio at 5. . . . Donald Angus came to dinner. At 12.30 we collected Gladys Unger & Charles Meredith[2] & went to Harlem. Small's, Philadelphia Jimmie's. The Nest, & Vaudeville Comedy Club. Home at 6.30 & didn't go to bed.

1. Glasgow's publisher.
2. Actor in silent films.

Saturday, 16 May 1925

Note from Blanche [Knopf] accepting Langston Hughes's poems. Donald [Angus] left at 10.30. I have a bath, get dressed again and go down town to lunch at Algonquin with Andrew Dasburg at a quarter of one. Come home and go to bed. Up at 5 & go to Elmer & Nella [Larsen] Imes: dinner, 8.15 in Jersey City. . . . Left about 11, dead for lack of sleep. Elmer Imes & Dorothy Harris drive me to the 42nd Street ferry. Home & dropped into bed.

Wednesday, 20 May 1925

. . . Called up Essie Robeson about Paul's records. Lunch in alone. After lunch I went to the bank & then up Madison Avenue to Bloomingdale's for records. . . . On 59th St. met Covarrubias. We went together to Marconi's for some Blues & he walked home with me. As I entered the door Joe Hergesheimer was going in. He stayed an hour. At ten Rita Romilly arrived to tell me that she is having trouble with her family because she knows Negroes. . . .

Thursday, 21 May 1925

. . . Made some transcriptions of the words of Blues from phonograph records. Went over to Knopfs' at 12—met Nathan and Mencken on the way—to talk with Blanche about Langston Hughes. . . . Algonquin for lunch. Then to Lucile Harper's. . . . At 10.30 went to Regina Anderson's birthday party. Louella Tucker, Eric Walrond, Ethel Ray. . . . Eric and I went on to The Nest for a few moments. . . . Home at 3.30.

Saturday, 23 May 1925

. . . W. C. Handy[1] (met) at 4 o'clock, came to talk to me about the Blues. A'Lelia Walker . . . & Rita Romilly, dinner at 7. Muk de Jari & Donald Angus come in after dinner & we all go to spring dansante at Mrs. Walker's studio for the benefit of Augusta Savage.[2] . . . A'Lelia wants us all to go over to her house, but I get sore because she asks me to buy her a bottle of whiskey. I leave her flat. Then Muk, Donald, Rita, . . . and I go to The Nest where we dance & drink till 4.30. . . . Donald & I come home at 5.30 & stays the night.

    1. William Christopher Handy, often called "Father of the Blues," composer of "The St. Louis Blues" and other early examples of the form in print.
    2. African American sculptor.

Wednesday, 27 May 1925

. . . Working on paper of breakfasts.[1] Lunch in with Donald Angus who leaves immediately after. At 4 o'clock Zora Neale Hurston comes in to talk [with] me, a bright, rangy, intelligent Negro personality. She stays till six. I have dinner alone. . . .

    1. "A Note on Breakfasts," subsequently published in *American Mercury.*

Thursday, 28 May 1925

. . . Proofs came for *Theatre Magazine* for my Robeson-Brown article. Lunch in alone. At 1.30 Paul & Essie Robeson come in & tell me about their troubles. We discuss Blues, etc. They stay all the afternoon. At 4.45 I go to keep an appointment [with] Max Ewing to hear him . . . play his new piece for Paul Whiteman. I am a moment late, but run into Joseph Hergesheimer who takes me to the Ambassador to meet Pola Negri.[1] . . .

    1. Polish silent screen actress who, later in 1925, starred in a film version of CVV's novel *The Tattooed Countess.*

Saturday, 30 May 1925

. . . Presents from Marinoff arrive, from London, 3 pairs of pyjamas, 4 shirts, 15 ties, many of them Liberty. Paul Whiteman, Lamb's Club, 12.30 Saturday.

Nino Ronchi (Milanese painter, met), Max Ewing, & Whiteman's secretary, Gillespie.[1] Home and took a nap. To Harlem with Al Golden. He comes to dinner. At 9, Frances Seligman, Zora Neale Hurston & Donald Angus came in. We [*stay?*] home until 11.45, when we go to Small's. Then to The Nest, Johnnie [Cobb], Muk [de Jari], Katie, Marjorie,[2] & the gorgeous new girl who is a marvellous dancer, does the Charleston in slow motion. To the Vaudeville Comedy club. Home at 6.30, Golden & Donald spend the night.

    1. Jimmie Gillespie controlled Whiteman's spendthrift behavior and was actually his business manager; previously he had been manager for orchestra leader Vincent Lopez.

    2. Marjorie Sipp, African American singer whom CVV and Angus admired. She made no recordings and appeared only at The Nest.

Sunday, 31 May 1925

I got up at noon. At 3 we woke up Golden, send him away. At 4 I take Donald to Florine Stettheimer's studio. Gerald Kelly, English painter there. Donald & I dine at Algonquin, come home & I dislocate my jaw. Dr. Watts comes in from neighborhood, puts it back. To bed at 9 o'clock. Donald spends the night with me as I am very nervous.

Friday, 5 June 1925

. . . Down to bank, then up to Knopfs' to say goodbye to Alfred & Blanche.[1] They had just returned from Blanche's mother's funeral. Tonight Alfred's father's birthday dinner. Mencken at 5. He brings the proofs of "A Note on Breakfasts" & we have a good talk about Knopf office, books, sexual intercourse, etc. He leaves at 6.30 & I go to Al Golden's for dinner. Home & in bed at 10.30. In the afternoon I send "The Black Blues" to *Vanity Fair.*

    1. The Knopfs were sailing for Europe the next day.

Monday, 8 June 1925

. . . Edwin Knopf and Rita Romilly come in. Beach Cooke comes in with gin. Dinner with Sinclair Lewis at Great Northern Hotel. He is too drunk to speak. . . . Donald Angus makes his stage debut in *Caesar & Cleopatra* with the Theatre Guild.[1]

    1. Angus had a supernumerary's role in Shaw's play, arranged through his friend Helen Westley, who played Ftatateetah in the production; he acted only intermittently through the twenties.

Tuesday, 9 June 1925

... Feeling very shaky & nervous. Reading Mrs. Schindel's mss. novel, *Heat*.[1]
Went to bank in morning. Lunch in alone. Reading proofs on *Excavations*.
Donald Angus came in for an hour during the afternoon. Rita Romilly comes
to dinner & after dinner we go to The Palace where Fay Templeton[2] has returned for one week. Immense in size, over sixty, she is still a great artist. . . .
Fay breaks down & cries on the stage after her act. Rita comes home with me,
sits around until about one o'clock.

> 1. Isa Glenn Schindel wrote eight novels in as many years, under her maiden
> name, and then disappeared. In addition to *Heat*, CVV titled *Little Pitchers* and
> *Southern Charm* and was responsible for Knopf's publishing her books.
> 2. A popular musical comedy performer at the turn of the century.

Wednesday, 10 June 1925

... During the day I finished reading *Heat* and took it in the afternoon to
Harry Block. We discussed it & I took it back to Isa [Glenn] Schindel who
agreed to write the last part over. She agreed to dedicate it to me. Lunch &
dinner in alone. Stopped for Rita Romilly & we went to Countee Cullen's
party, 8.30, at his father's house & the church.[1] Harold Jackman, Zora Neale
Hurston, Harry Liscomb, Charles S. & Mrs. Johnson, Paul Robeson, Lawrence
Brown (who sang), Essie Robeson, Gladys & Walter White, etc. . . .

> 1. Cullen's adoptive father was the Reverend Frederick Asbury Cullen, pastor of
> the Salem Methodist Church in Harlem.

Saturday, 13 June 1925

Clear cool day. I got up at 8.30, had coffee & woke Scott [Cunningham] at 9.
Go marketing & to the bank. Run into Algonquin at 12.45 to meet Scott and
run into Ralph [Van Vechten]. He, Fannie, & Duane arrived from Italy today on the *Dinlio*. We all had lunch together. Then Scott & I come home. I
sleep during afternoon. At 6, Donald [Angus] comes to dine with us. He goes
to the theatre. Then Zora Hurston comes in. At 12 Donald returns & we go
to Small's. Then to Leroy's, then to The Nest. . . . Johnnie [Cobb] shares half
a bottle of gin. Stuffy dances the slow motion Charleston. Home at 7, Donald
& Scott & me. Find the poo with leukemia again.

Sunday, 14 June 1925

I get up at 11. Donald & Scott at 1. We lie around & read papers, etc. All have
dinner here. In the evening, a party. Paul Robeson & Larry Brown, who sing

several times, Marie Cahill[1] & D. V. Arthur[2] & Marion Cook,[3] Rosamond Johnson & his wife. Marie Cahill sings *Under the Bamboo Tree*[4] & several other songs of Rosamond Johnson. Cissie Loftus who imitates Bert Williams[5] & Fay Templeton.[6] Rosamond Johnson plays several of the new Spirituals he has discovered. Isa [Glenn] Schindel, Zora Neale Hurston, Harold & Mrs. Guinzberg,[7] George Oppenheimer, Donald Angus, Nils Nelson, . . . Rita Romilly, . . . & Harry Block who stays all night.

1. Musical comedy actress from the turn of the century.
2. Daniel V. Arthur, playwright and director.
3. Will Marion Cook, African American composer.
4. By James Weldon and J. Rosamond Johnson, from their turn-of-the-century musical play *In Dahomey.*
5. Greatly beloved (by both races) black comedian whose partnership with singer and dancer George Walker dominated African American entertainments at the turn of the century. After Walker's death, Williams drifted into the *Ziegfeld Follies* for several seasons, still performing in blackface makeup until his death in 1922.
6. White entertainers Cahill and Loftus were therefore imitating black entertainers for a racially mixed audience.
7. Musical entrepreneur and producer.

Wednesday, 24 June 1925

. . . I think my indigestion is better but I have a hangover. Worked on proofs. Donald [Angus] comes in from a rehearsal for lunch. Then we go for a walk & he comes back. Alain Locke comes in to see me at 4 & stays till six. We talk about Langston Hughes, Eric Walrond, Spirituals & other matters. Carrie Stettheimer comes to dinner & after dinner Emily Clark, Frances Newman & her young man Fanell Trotti (?),[1] Isa [Glenn] Schindel & her son Bayard[2] come in. They all clear out shortly after eleven & I go to bed.

1. Middle-aged librarian and novelist, best known for *The Hard-Boiled Virgin,* and her much younger lover.
2. Precocious novelist, drawing on the same Far Eastern background material that informed some of his mother's books.

Friday, 26 June 1925

. . . Hunter [Stagg] and I have breakfast. Hunter goes out . . . & I have lunch alone and work on proofs of *Excavations.* He comes back about 5. Montgomery Evans comes to dinner. A wild party after dinner. Bayard and Isa Schindel, Miguel Covarrubias & Rose Rolanda,[1] Harry Block, Donald Angus, Julius Bledsoe, Jim & Dorothy Harris, Nora [Holt] Ray, Zora Hurston, Dorothy Peterson, E. J. Morgan.[2] Party over about 5. Hunter & I then retired. Also read proofs for my Blues paper in *Vanity Fair*. Covarrubias brings me a drawing of a naked Negro girl.

1. Scottish Mexican dancer and, later, photographer, shortly to marry Miguel Covarrubias and collaborate on anthropological studies of the arts of Bali, Mexico, and Native Americans.
2. Turn-of-the-century actor.

Tuesday, 30 June 1925

... Went to office. . . . Then to bank, then home. Reading *Sodom et Gomorrhe* [by Marcel Proust], Mrs. Saltus's life of Edgar in the new *Harper's Bazar*, etc. Lunch in. Donald [Angus] comes in after lunch & we go to Harlem after records. I leave my telephone off the hook in the morning and as a consequence the phone is out of order all day. Donald comes back for dinner & leaves after dinner to go to the theatre. I go up to the Paul Robesons' where I meet Mrs. Goode (Essie's mother), one of her brothers, Paul's sister. Betty & Tony Salemne[1] come in & we went to a midnight benefit up at the Lafayette Theatre. Miller & Lyles, Sissle & Blake, Alberta Hunter, Florence Mills, Bill Robinson, . . . and others in the show. . . . Met Minnie Patterson with whose husband Nora [Holt] Ray is having an affair.

1. Italian American sculptor, noted at the time for his heads of African American performers, and his wife.

Saturday, 4 July 1925

... George Gershwin came to dinner & plays one of the themes for his New York concerto which he is writing for N.Y. Symphony. He has had some of these tunes for months as he originally intended to use them in *Black Belt*,[1] but many of them are new. The middle section, according to present plans, is to be a Blues. George started to write the concerto two days ago & has already written five pages. Went to bed about 12, & slept badly. Neighbors, etc. George is engaged to play this concerto with [Walter] Damrosch on Dec. 3–4 at Carnegie Hall. Before it is written!

1. The opera about Harlem that he had contemplated writing with CVV.

Sunday, 12 July 1925

... Rita Romilly came to supper. We telephoned A'Lelia Walker and after dinner took a train to Irvington & visited Lelia at the Villa Lewaro.[1] . . . Henry Miller[2] came in later & motored us home. I stopped at Rita's studio on 69th

St. for a sandwich & some Malaga brandy. Feeling sick. This is one of the hottest days of the year.

    1. The impressive estate that A'Lelia Walker's mother, Madam C. J. Walker, had built at Irvington on Hudson.

    2. Theatrical producer and actor.

Tuesday, 14 July 1925

. . . Edwin Knopf comes in & insists upon talking about Mary [Ellis], with whom he is still apparently very much in love. She left the cast of *Rose Marie* last night, as she has lost her voice. I got Edwin to shave his moustache, which he has had for about a month. Dine in alone & then go to see *Artists & Models* at the Winter Garden. An extraordinarily good show. . . . The poo has been very affectionate all day.

Saturday, 18 July 1925

. . . At 4 o'clock Caroline [Dudley] Reagan came in to talk over her proposed Paris Negro Vaudeville act.[1] After 5, Edwin Knopf came in & later Isa Schindel. Still later Donald Angus. Donald & Isa stay to dinner. After Donald goes to the theatre. Edwin Knopf comes back with George Gershwin who plays themes from his N.Y. concerto & other pieces. . . . George goes home & Donald returns from theatre at midnight . . . [to] go cabareting. Small's (girl sings "My Daddy Rocks Me"), Leroy's, The Nest, . . . Bamville. Home at 7, & breakfast chez moi. Donald stays here & we go to bed at 8.

    1. Reagan created the *Revue Nègre*, starring Josephine Baker and a company of twenty African American entertainers for Paris.

Monday, 20 July 1925

. . . Wrote first draft of "What's Wrong with the Negro Theatre.[1] . . . Paul & Essie Robeson at Rita Romilly's studio. They have a remarkable conversation in which Essie reiterates her desire to completely possess Paul & Paul expresses his resentment of this. They left about 1, and I stayed till 1.30. Home & to bed.

    1. Published as "Prescription for a Negro Theatre" in *Vanity Fair,* October 1925.

Tuesday, 21 July 1925

. . . Lunch in alone. Then went down to Tony Salemne's studio where I watched Tony work on colossal (life-sized) statue of Paul Robeson, who was tense posing nude. I stayed all the afternoon & at 5 Caroline [Dudley] Reagan came in to see Paul. Came home & dined alone. At 9, Mrs. Reagan came after me & we went to Lafayette Theatre where we heard & <u>met</u> Clara Smith, who sang "Nobody knows the way I feel dis mornin'" because I requested it & three other songs. . . .

Monday, 27 July 1925

. . . I work on third draught of paper on Negro Theatre. Donald Angus lunches at the Crillon. . . . I go to bank, then to Algonquin, where I see Ralph V.V. (Just in), Frank, Margaret . . . Case, Clifton Webb & his mother.[1] . . . To post office where I secured Hugh Walpole's *Crystal Box,* and then home. Johnnie [i.e., Jack] Harper came in with six quarts of gin. Edwin Knopf came in, and later Ralph [Van Vechten] who took us to dinner on 54th St. After dinner I give an impromptu party for him. Nella [Larsen] & Elmer Imes, Nora Holt Ray, . . . Edwin Knopf, Donald Angus, Percy & Florence Hammond, Isa Schindel. After the others have gone, Percy stayed & talked about me till 5 o'clock.

    1. The redoubtable Maybelle Webb, from whom her son was inseparable.

Sunday, 2 August 1925

. . . Lunch in with Marinoff . . . & at 4 Rudolph Fisher (met)[1] came to see me. I liked him enormously. Essie and Paul Robeson come for a cold supper which Marinoff gets. They have another quarrel while they are here. Paul's patience is about ready to break. There is now a question as to whether she will go to London with him. They leave at 10.30 & we go to bed.

    1. African American medical radiologist and author of *The Walls of Jericho* (containing a thinly disguised CVV as "Conrad White"), a novel about the Harlem Renaissance.

Friday, 7 August 1925

. . . Rita Romilly came in at 7. We went to a dinner, cooked by artist Sofo, that Jim Harris gave for A'Lelia Walker, who arrived an hour & 3/4 late, soused & promptly passed out. Elmer & Nella Imes . . . drove us home at midnight. . . .

Monday, 10 August 1925

. . . Found a letter from Langston Hughes suggesting minor changes in introduction to his book [*The Weary Blues*]. I rewrote introduction. Lunch in with Marinoff. Sam Knopf telephones that Famous Players wants a month's option on *Tattooed Countess,* at $12,500. This is anniversary![1] Hot, very hot, undressed all afternoon. . . . Caroline Reagan comes in for half an hour to tell me of the lack of progress she is making with the Negro show she is taking to Paris. . . .

    1. Marinoff and CVV met for the second time on this day in 1912.

Wednesday, 12 August 1925

. . . At 5 o'clock Ettie & Florine Stettheimer come in. Nora [Holt] Ray & Irita Van Doren come to dinner. After dinner Donald Angus, Clifford Savery,[1] Ralph Barton (who came in unexpectedly & uninvited), . . . Gladys & Walter White. At 4 they go home. Marinoff goes to spend the night with Reg, as I am soused.

    1. Angus's latest inamorato.

Friday, 14 August 1925

. . . *Firecrackers* is published today. . . . Avery Hopwood arrives on the *Aquitania* & comes in for cocktails. Later Donald Angus & Regina Wallace. Reg & Marinoff go to dinner. . . . Avery goes. Donald & I dine at 154 W. 54 St. & then go to the nine o'clock announcements of the *Crisis* Prizes at Renaissance Casino.[1] Dancing after the exercises. Saw Walter White, Rudolph Fisher, Louella Tucker, Eric Walrond, Jim Harris, . . . Langston Hughes & Richard Nugent (Riccardo, met),[2] Dr. Du Bois, Jessie Fauset, Bernia Austin, Countee Cullen, etc. Donald and I leave at 12 & go to The Nest, where we see Mal Frazier & John Corey [Cobb]. Avery [Hopwood] then arrives. Home immediately & to bed. Title of "Nigger Heaven" comes to me today.

    1. The journal of the NAACP began recognizing young black talent with cash prizes.
    2. African American artist and writer who built his reputation as a homosexual dandy with outrageous apparel and behavior.

Saturday, 15 August 1925

. . . At 5 Caroline Reagan comes in to tell me of her troubles with her Negro vaudeville act. She goes. At 6 Langston Hughes comes for dinner. At 9 Richard Bruce Nugent (Riccardo) arrives. The boys stay till midnight.

Sunday, 16 August 1925

Up at 7.30. Reading papers, washing dishes, boiling soup, writing letters, cleaning out kitchen, etc. Ella left us for good (?) last night. Marinoff got lunch. . . .

Reg Wallace came in for a few minutes before dinner & later Avery Hopwood who takes us to dinner at Leone's. . . . We come back to the house after dinner & at midnight Nora [Holt] Ray comes down. She stays till 4. I get very drunk, & drink six cups of very black coffee. Go nearly mad with nerves.

Wednesday, 26 August 1925

. . . In the afternoon went to Harlem with Mrs. Reagan to see the rehearsal of her Negro show. . . . Watched rehearsal at Harlem Casino & suggested again to her that she engage Donald Angus to manage show for her. She is to meet him tomorrow.[1] When I got home Edwin Knopf was here. Marian Anderson[2] at the Stadium. Didn't go. . . .

1. Angus accompanied the Revue Nègre company as its regisseur, found housing for the performers, doled out their salaries, and got them to rehearsals on time. Later he hired Sidney Bechet to join the orchestra.

2. African American contralto, later a cause célèbre when the Daughters of the American Revolution refused to approve of her singing in Constitution Hall. As a result, First Lady Eleanor Roosevelt resigned from the organization and invited Anderson to sing on the steps of the Lincoln Memorial.

Thursday, 27 August 1925

. . . Reading proofs all the afternoon. At 5 Regina Wallace, Phil Moeller, Edwin Knopf, Glenn Hunter[1] come in for cocktails. Phil stayed for dinner. After he had gone we went over to Edwin Knopf's. George Gershwin, George Oppenheimer, Noel Coward,[2] Mrs. Calthrope (met),[3] Edgar Selwyn & the girls. Coward sang several of his songs, including the inimitable "He Never Did That to Me," & "Poor Little Rich Girl," & George played a lot of his tunes, the *Rhapsody* (with cuts) & a long passage from the first movement [of] his new concerto. He came home with us for a copy of *Firecrackers*. . . .

1. Actor, Regina Wallace's current beau.

2. English composer and playwright, in New York to perform in his play *The Vortex*.

3. Gladys Calthrop, Coward's manager and assistant.

Wednesday, 2 September 1925

. . . Ellen Glasgow comes for tea. Later Ettie Stettheimer. Later Noel Coward & Gladys Calthrop for cocktails. I got my own dinner & went to Hippodrome. Heard Howard Panella play *Rhapsody in Blue* with Paul Whiteman. Edgar Selwyn's, at 11. Marinoff & Regina Wallace, . . . Charlie Chaplin (met), Ann Pennington,[1] Noel Coward, Gladys Calthrop, Lenore Ulric, Gilbert Miller,

Walter Wanger,[2] Francis de Croissart,[3] Jo Davidson,[4] . . . Condé Nast,[5] George Gershwin, Bessie Love,[6] Percy Hammond. In bed at 3.30.

1. Broadway dancing star.
2. Nephew of the Stettheimer sisters, later a film director and producer.
3. Prewar French playwright.
4. American sculptor based in Paris.
5. Publisher of *Vanity Fair*.
6. Silent film actress.

Sunday, 6 September 1925

. . . Breakfast and lunch with Walter White, 9.30–10, & Gladys. Also met Jane, the daughter.[1] Walter takes us to Abyssian Baptist Church where we hear Dr. [Adam Clayton] Powell. We walk down 7th Ave. to the park where we take a bus home. In front of the Lafayette Theatre we run into Trent, the musician who has been with Mrs. Reagan's show. . . . To dinner with Marinoff at Leone's. . . . Home & to bed by 9.30. Slept badly. Up and reading in the night.

1. Later Jane White became a highly respected African American actress in Euripides and Shakespeare and in commercial theater.

Monday, 7 September 1925

Rain. Cold better. Wrote blurb for *Excavations*. Reading Pierre-Quint's *Marcel Proust*. 12.30, George Gershwin, to hear his new concerto with Bill Daly at second piano, he played just two movements. Ira Gershwin there, George's younger brother, whom I met. I left about 2 & got lunch round the corner. . . . [To] dance at A'Lelia Walker's in Irvington, 4–10. . . . We get home at 11.30. To bed.

Wednesday, 9 September 1925

. . . Dinner home with Marinoff, after which I go to rehearsal of *Hotsy-Totsy* at Harlem Casino, taking Walter White. Caroline Reagan, Dorothy & Harry Harvey . . . are there. I meet Spencer Williams, one of the authors of "Everybody Loves My Baby." Caroline & Donald [Angus] drive me home at 12.

Thursday, 10 September 1925

. . . Florine Stettheimer came to dinner & I gave her (paid in full) $150.00 for her big picture of flowers which hangs in our living-room. In the evening Florine & I visit the Chinese Theatre at the Thalia, while Marinoff goes to bed. Sleep badly, cough, etc. A <u>hot</u> sticky night.

Friday, 11 September 1925

. . . Marinoff has a talk with Meda[1] who threatens to leave. Maybe she will. Lunch in with Marinoff. Meda changes her mind. In the meantime I write first draught of "Things in the Weary Plains," probably for *The Mercury.*[2] Read *The Venetian Glass Nephew* [by Elinor Wylie]. Meda asks to get off early & Marinoff gets dinner about 9.30. Edna Kenton strolls in & stays till one.

    1. Meda Frye, the latest and longest lasting—well over three years—in the Van Vechtens' series of domestics. All had been African American with the exception of Alice Monnier, the Frenchwoman who stayed briefly.

    2. Published as "Mutations among Americans" in *American Mercury,* December 1925.

Saturday, 12 September 1925

. . . Met Jack Colton on Sixth Ave. on my way home. Wrote letters, looked over proofs of Langston Hughes preface, etc. Lunch in alone. Wrote first draught of review of *The Venetian Glass Nephew.* . . . Claire Burke Schermerhorn Hoffenstein comes for dinner. She says she has left Sam & is going back to Schermie. At 10.30 we went to Stella Block's.[1] She danced for us. . . . Stella is living with a photographer, Mortimer Offner.[2]

    1. Originally Estelle Blouch, choreographer for *Garrick Gaieties, Intimate Revue,* and other Broadway shows.

    2. In 1927 Offner supplied several photographs for an illustrated edition of *Peter Whiffle.*

Monday, 14 September 1925

. . . Joined Avery Hopwood. We went to the Elysée & had cocktails, joined by Rose Rolanda, Ralph Glover, & a boy named Banks. Avery came home for dinner with us. After dinner Zoë Akins came in with George O'Neil (met). They stayed till about 3 and Avery stayed till four, telling me now he had given John [Floyd] syphilis.

Wednesday, 16 September 1925

. . . Marinoff & I attend the American first night of *The Vortex*[1] at Henry Miller Theatre, a brilliant night. . . . Then we went to Algonquin where we met Ben Ray Redman & Frieda Inescort.[2] Finally to party at the Embassy given by [Noel] Coward. Everybody there, but including Michael Arlen[3] whom I did not meet, Phil Moeller, Mercedes de Acosta, Eva Le Gallienne,[4] Lynn Fontanne, Alfred Lunt, June Walker,[5] Arthur Richman, Dwight Frye, . . . Glenn Hunter, Fred & Adele Astaire. . . .[6]

1. By Noel Coward, a play considered sensational at the time because it dealt with drugs, loose morals, and emotional incest, starring Lillian Braithwaite and Coward.

2. Actress, wife of Ben Ray Redman.

3. CVV was reading Arlen's "trashy book," *Mayfair*, at the time.

4. Actress who favored European plays and revivals of older works.

5. Actress who played Loreli Lee in the dramatization of Anita Loos's *Gentlemen Prefer Blondes*.

6. Le Gallienne through the Astaires: all popular performers of the period.

Thursday, 17 September 1925

Got home last night about 4, went to sleep about 5, & woke up at 8. Went out to get papers about *The Vortex*. Marinoff sick from too much champagne when she woke up. . . . Ralph [Van Vechten] came for dinner at 6.30, Regina Wallace also. With Marinoff we went to see *The Grand Street Follies*. Home & dressed & at midnight went to . . . "small party" for Lady Diana Manners[1] at Condé Nast's. Everybody there, including Michael Arlen whom again I did not meet, Lady Diana (met). . . .

1. Visiting minor English nobility who set fashions in dress at the time.

Saturday, 19 September 1925

. . . Party for Noel Coward in the evening. It did not "gell": James Weldon and Grace Johnson, Walter & Gladys White, Noel Coward, Lawrence Brown, Gladys Calthrop, Eva LeGallienne, Mercedes de Acosta, Muriel Draper, Edward Selwyn, . . . Regina Wallace, Percy & Florence Hammond, Ralph Van Vechten, Isa Schindel, Lenore Ulric, Sidney Blackmer, Jack Colton & two men, Mr. Mundy & Mr. Hill, Harry Block, John Emerson. Percy stayed & talked till 5 o'clock.

Tuesday, 29 September 1925

6.30, dinner with R[alph] Barton & Carlotta Monterey. Marinoff goes to theatre. I stay there & after the Bartons have talked for 3 hours about whether they will live together any more they take off their clothes & give a remarkable performance. Ralph goes down on Carlotta. She masturbates & expires in ecstasy. They do 69, etc. I leave about 12.30.

Sunday, 4 October 1925

We both have terrible colds. Lunch in. Working all day on papers, etc. At 4.30 Eugene & Boonie Goossens[1] come in. Later Marie Doro, Grace Moore (met),[2] and Vincent Youmans (met) who plays "Tea for Two" & some of his other tunes. Later Reg Wallace who stays for dinner. Dress rehearsal, *Hay Fever*.[3] . . . Afterwards party at Noel Coward's. He has taken Mae Murray's[4] apartment at 1 W. 67. . . . We went home at 3. Took Reg & Virginia Hammond home. George Gershwin tells me he has finished all but 2 pages of his concerto.

 1. English orchestra conductor and his wife.
 2. Metropolitan opera soprano.
 3. A popular comedy by Noel Coward, quickly assembled on the strength of the success of *The Vortex*.
 4. Silent movie actress, notable for her bee-stung lips in *The Merry Widow* and films by Eric von Stroheim.

Tuesday, 6 October 1925

. . . We dine alone & then go out to Clara Smith's. She sings for us. There are a lot of colored & vaudeville entertainers there. Home at 10. . . .

Wednesday, 7 October 1925

. . . After dinner Taylor Gordon[1] & Rosamond Johnson came in to sing Spirituals. Harold Guinzberg & his wife, George Oppenheimer, Fannie Hurst, . . . Grace & James Weldon Johnson, Rose Rolanda & Covarrubias. Harold Guinzberg decides to give a concert for Johnson & Gordon. This was their first appearance before a group. I took Boonie Goossens home at 3.30. Home and to bed.

 1. African American countertenor.

Sunday, 11 October 1925

Up at 6.30. Still have a cold. In fact it is worse. Poo is still flowing. . . . In the afternoon A'Lelia Walker telephones & I go up to her Harlem apartment where I find Mamie White,[1] open a bottle of champagne. A'Lelia tells me she is going to marry again. . . . Home & find Zena Naylor[2] & Marie Doro here. Zena spills the story of her affair with Goossens. Marie stays to dinner, which Marinoff cooks. I go to bed with several hot whiskeys.

 1. Walker's close friend, later manager of her literary salon, "The Dark Tower," when it became a speakeasy at the same address.
 2. CVV modeled "Noma Ridge," a character in his 1930 novel *Parties*, after Naylor: "A young English girl with dimpled, rosy cheeks who did not drink or smoke, but who atoned for the lack of these semi-precious vices by describing in an endless monotone the various forms of her amorous transports, and the characters of the persons with whom she enjoyed them."

Saturday, 17 October 1925

. . . Marinoff & I dine together & then go to Julius Bledsoe concert, at Town Hall, with James Weldon & Grace Johnson in their new car. The concert is a sham. Bledsoe is too refined. . . . After the concert J.W.J., Grace, Marinoff, & I go to Rosamond Johnson's to hear him sing with Taylor Gordon. Nora [Holt] Ray, Arthur & Mrs. Spingarn, . . . Gladys & Walter White. Home at 3. A.M.

Wednesday, 21 October 1925

. . . Poo is still flowing. Took a nap after lunch. While Marinoff went to the matinee, Covarrubias came in bringing his design for Langston Hughes jacket & several other drawings. Jack Harper comes in & brings 6 bottles of Scotch. I pay him. Dinner at a quarter of 8, Fannie Hurst & Joseph Hergesheimer. This is our eleventh wedding anniversary. After dinner Regina Wallace, Ralph Barton, Carlotta Monterey, Robert [Morss] Lovett, . . . Carl & Irita Van Doren, Edmund Wilson, Nora [Holt] Ray, Covarrubias, Rosamond Johnson & Taylor Gordon who sing. . . .

Saturday, 31 October 1925

. . . I read Mabel Luhan's "Intimate Memoirs" until 3, when Alain Locke comes in. He stays till six, talking about the collection of African sculpture in Bermuda, and then he discusses the character of Langston Hughes at some length, telling me extraordinary things about Countee Cullen (adopted by the Rev. Cullen at the age of 12), about Claude McKay,[1] etc. I liked him much better than I ever have before. . . .

    1. Although born in Jamaica and domiciled in London, Russia, and Germany until circa 1923, this poet and novelist was closely identified with the Harlem Renaissance.

Tuesday, 3 November 1925

Up at 8.15. Cloudy & cool. I still have indigestion. I walk to East River and back in the morning. . . . On my return I begin work on *Nigger Heaven* and write most of the first chapter before lunch. . . . At 5 o'clock Avery Hopwood comes in. Later John Floyd. Later Regina Wallace who stays to dinner. . . .

Friday, 6 November 1925

Mabel Luhan, lunch at 1, Brevoort. Mr. & Mrs. [Robert] Flaherty (met). He made the movies *Nanook of the North* & *Moana of the South Seas.* Will Irwin[1]

& Everett Marcy (met).[2] . . . Bertha & Frank Case come to dine with us at 6.45. They stayed till 10.30 and then we went to bed.

1. A recent Knopf author, earlier a journalist and war correspondent.

2. Mabel Dodge Luhan's ambiguous companion at the time. He is not mentioned in any of her voluminous autobiographies, but at this time he was a patient of Dr. A. A. Brill, Luhan's psychiatrist.

Saturday, 7 November 1925

. . . Wrote Chapter III of *Nigger Heaven* and then met Mabel Luhan at the Lido. She is at her most beguiling & dangerous. I think she wants me to have a "thing" with the beau Everett Marcy. Came home. Read her chapter on [Eleanora] Duse, etc. Max Ewing came in for a few moments. Dinner in with Marinoff. Edna Kenton at 8 o'clock. . . . She left at 11.30 & I went to bed.

Monday, 9 November 1925

Wrote for several copyright assignments. Wrote paper about Negroes sticking to their own material.[1] Lunch in with Marinoff. Went to Carnegie Hall, Dime Savings, Drake's, Harrison Nat'l, Holliday's & home. Took a nap. . . . Dined in with Marinoff & went to Lyceum Theatre to see first night of Irene Bordoni in Avery Hopwood's *Naughty Cinderella*. Saw the usual first night Hopwood crowd. . . . Home at midnight. . . .

1. This developed into CVV's own response to the questionnaire he prepared at Jessie Fauset's invitation for *The Crisis*: "The Negro in Art: How Shall He Be Portrayed?" This symposium ran for several issues, beginning in February 1926.

Tuesday, 17 November 1925

. . . My phlebitis going rapidly; nevertheless I spend an hour with my leg bandaged. Emily Clark Balch[1] comes to lunch. I copy my review of *Gentlemen Prefer Blondes*. . . . Later Covarrubias with his designs for *Androcles* [*and the Lion*] & Lewis Baer who wants to do a book of Negro Jazz. Dinner with Mabel Luhan & Dr. Brill, at Frank's.[2] Dr. Brill talks about Negroes. Later Everett Marcy comes in & takes Mabel to the movies. She acts so badly that I begin to know that she is having an affair with this callow youth. Dr. Brill says there is no doubt about it. I take Dr. Brill to Jack Harper's. He leaves early. I stay & talk to Lucile until 2. Then home & to bed. Marinoff stays all night at Reg Wallace's.

1. The editor of *The Reviewer* had married Edwin Swift Balch, an immensely wealthy, elderly Philadelphia lawyer more than twice her age, who retired to devote himself to supporting the arts.

2. A popular Harlem restaurant.

Monday, 23 November 1925

. . . Wrote Chapter VII of *Nigger Heaven*. . . . We meet Mary Ellis in hall & she drives us to Arthur Spingarn's, 8.30, where we spend evening looking at Negro books & African sculpture. Party for Covarrubias at Lee Simonson's. We got there about 12.30. Lynn Fontanne, Alfred Lunt, Phil Moeller, Louis & Jean Starr Untermeyer, June Walker, Tom Powers, Helen Westley, Gladys & Clarence Axman, . . . Romney Brent,[1] Teresa Helburn, Maurice & Mrs. Wertheim, Lawrence & Armina Marshall.

    1. Musical comedy performer in *Garrick Gaieties* and *The Little Show*, later a leading man in straight plays.

Wednesday, 25 November 1925

Up at 8.45. Hangover. . . . Addressed envelopes for Rosamond Johnson circulars & fooled around. Wrote Chapter IX (such as it is) of *Nigger Heaven*. Last night I told a few people about this title. Dinner with Marinoff who was tired & went to bed. I go along to Knopf party. . . . I spring my title [i.e., *Nigger Heaven*] on Grace Johnson, etc. She says it will be hated. Miguel [Covarrubias] & Harry Block drive me home. In bed at 1.30.

Thursday, 26 November 1925

. . . Wrote Chapter I of Book II of *Nigger Heaven*. . . . After lunch went on a walk with Marinoff in the park & fed pigeons. Then home. Reading [Charles W.] Chesnutt's *The Colonel's Dream*. Spingarns come for dinner, 6.45. Afterwards, Harry Block. We go to see Bessie Smith at Orpheum Theatre in Newark. Mr. [Leigh] Whipper, manager. . . . Then to Dietz's for beer. Home at 1.30.

Friday, 27 November 1925

. . . Read *The Marrow of Tradition* by Chesnutt. Wrote a paper about Bessie Smith. Countee Cullen comes in & we talk about my title *Nigger Heaven*. He turns white with hurt & I talk to him. Dinner in with Marinoff. Roland Hayes,[1] evening, heard him for the first time. Carnegie Hall was crowded, went with Marinoff. Saw Rudolph Fisher, Muriel Draper & Max Ewing. . . . Then we went to Rosamond Johnson's where we met Harry Block. All of us went to midnight performance of *Plantation Review* at Lafayette. Ethel Waters,[2] Eddie Rector. Afterward saw Bill Robinson, Taylor Gordon, Muriel [Draper] & Max [Ewing], etc., & met Ethel Waters. Home at 3.30.

1. African American tenor. His lieder recitals were always formal, but he concluded them with a group of spirituals. White critics were slow to acknowledge him, apparently only because of his color.

2. "Sweet Mama Stringbean," as the singer was then called, soon became one of CVV's closest friend and later a formidable actress in serious drama and in films.

Saturday, 28 November 1925

. . . Reading *The New Negro,*[1] writing letters, etc. Lunch in with Marinoff. At 3 o'clock Countee Cullen came in & we had another long argument about the sensitiveness of Negroes. He leaves at 5.30 & returns to Harvard tomorrow. Rita Romilly comes in. Marinoff & I dine in. At 8, Edna Kenton comes in & stays till 10. Then go to bed.

1. Alain Locke's anthology based on the March 1925 issue of *Survey Graphic* that had been devoted in its entirety to African American arts and letters.

Tuesday, 1 December 1925

. . . Worked all the morning on review of *The New Negro.* Walter White for lunch at 1 P.M. I told him about *Nigger Heaven.* "My only regret," he said, "is that I didn't think of it first so that I could use it." He spent the afternoon here. Langston Hughes for dinner with me & Marinoff. Party for him afterwards. Arthur B. & Mrs. Spingarn, Rose Rolanda & Covarrubias, Taylor Gordon & Rosamond Johnson who sang, Lady [Sibyl] Colefax, Irita Van Doren, Harry Block, . . . Florence Hammond, Marie Doro, Marjorie Siefert (who told wonderful character studies by palms), Louis & Jean Starr Untermeyer, Alfred & Blanche Knopf, Nora [Mrs. Rosamond] Johnson. In bed at 5.

Wednesday, 2 December 1925

Awakened by telephone at 9.30. Cloudy. In a bad way all day. Lunch in with Marinoff. Slept all the afternoon. At 5, Langston Hughes came in. At 6, Harry Block. Dinner with John Emerson & Anita Loos, 7.30, 109 W. 55. Spent evening there. Home & in bed by 11.

Friday, 11 December 1925

. . . Up at 5.00. Wrote most of Chapter IV of *Nigger Heaven* (Part II). Lunch in. Then went to corner with Marinoff, where I traded my two gold cigarette cases for Christmas presents for the Stettheimers & the Knopfs. Home, reading proofs on "Uncle Tom's Mansion" sent to me by Irita Van Doren.[1]

Mss of *Excavations* arrives. Rita Romilly came to take Marinoff to Charleston class. . . .

> 1. A review of *The New Negro* for the *New York Tribune*, where Van Doren was book editor.

Tuesday, 15 December 1925

Up at 8 am, with a kind of hangover. Meda [Frye] doesn't come & the house is all upset when I go out. . . . to Rivoli Theatre where my name is on the front in electric lights.[1] Then home for a nap. At 5 I had my first Charleston lesson. . . .

> 1. The film version of *The Tattooed Countess*, modernized and vamped almost beyond recognition as *A Woman of the World*, starring Pola Negri, was playing, an unqualified catastrophe in CVV's opinion.

Tuesday, 22 December 1925

. . . Robesons arriving on the *Majestic*. Wrote final chapter of first draught of *Nigger Heaven*. . . . Reg Wallace comes in with Marinoff from Charleston class. Dinner at Knopfs', 7.30. Alfred gives me first copy of *Borzoi 1925*.[1] Marian Anderson (met), . . . Larry Brown, Grace & James Weldon Johnson, Countee Cullen, Julius Bledsoe, Ruth Hale, Heywood Broun, . . . etc. Left for home at 1.00.

> 1. A volume of appreciations of Knopf authors by other Knopf authors, to commemorate the fifteenth anniversary of the founding of his Borzoi Books.

Wednesday, 23 December 1925

. . . Up at 7.45. Bright, cold day. Cleaned out my closet. Wrapped presents, etc. Not feeling so good. Lunch in alone. Went out to buy flowers, came back. Essie Robeson came in to borrow $25.00. Later Jack Harper. I slept for an hour & feel better. Party for Countee Cullen. Paul & Essie Robeson, Lawrence Brown. They sang. Carl & Irita Van Doren, Ralph Barton, Ruth Goldbeck,[1] William Rose Benét & Elinor Wylie, Louis Untermeyer & Jean Starr & son (met), Harry Block, Covarrubias, Donald Freeman,[2] Donald Angus, Ashley Pettis (met), a young piano instructor at Rochester brought by Boonie Goossens, Anita Loos & John Emerson, Emily Clark Balch, . . . Rita Romilly.

> 1. Barton's current inamorata, over whom Carlotta Monterey had left him.
> 2. Editor at *Vanity Fair*.

Monday, 28 December 1925

... Reg Wallace comes to dinner & we went to first night of George Gershwin's *Tip Toes.* . . . Then to N.A.A.C.P. cabaret at Bamboo Inn as guests of the James Weldon Johnsons. Ruth Hale, Donald Angus, Arthur Spingarn, at our table. Dorothy Peterson, Nora [Holt] Ray (who sang), Jessie Fauset, A'Lelia Walker, . . . Tom Smith, Sol Johnson, Jim Harris, Essie Robeson, Edna Thomas,[1] Bernia Austin, John Nail & wife. A brilliant party.

    1. African American actress Edna Lewis, married to restaurateur Lloyd Thomas.

Thursday, 31 December 1925

... Paul Robeson's new records released. We are invited to Stella Block's, Heywood Broun's, Dorothy Peterson's, and Knopfs' parties tonight. Also to a party for Jane Cowl, also Muriel Draper's. Up at 8. Worked on papers and letters in the morning. . . . Dinner in with Marinoff & she goes to bed, still sick. I go after Ettie Stettheimer & take her to party at Knopfs'. Storm Jameson (met),[1] Pinks (English agent), . . . Isa Glenn [Schindel], James Weldon & Grace Johnson, Rosamond & Nora Johnson, Taylor Gordon (sang), Paul Robeson, Larry Brown (sang), Essie Robeson, Witter Bynner, . . . Walter & Gladys White, Lady Colefax, . . . Mr. & Mrs. Sam Knopf, Emily Clark, Aaron Copland,[2] Louis Untermeyer, Jean Starr Untermeyer, Eugene & Boonie Goossens. Walter & Gladys White & I go to Muriel Draper's where we find . . . all [the guests] intoxicated. Whites drive me home at 5, streets <u>crowded</u>.

    1. Another popular Knopf novelist in the twenties.

    2. American composer whose studies in France identified him with its modern movement but who returned to become arguably the most American of composers.

Fania Marinoff and Carl Van Vechten, 1923 (photograph by Nickolas Muray; Van Vechten Trust)

Ettie and Carrie Stettheimer, 1932 (photograph by Carl Van Vechten; Van Vechten Trust)

Florine Stettheimer, circa 1917 (photographer unknown; Yale Collection of American Literature, Beinecke Rare Book and Manuscript Library, Yale University)

Florence Embry Jones at Marshall's, 1915 (drawing by Robert Locher in *Rogue*, May 1915; Van Vechten Trust)

Fania Marinoff and Feathers, 1920 (photograph by Harriet V. Furness; Yale Collection of American Literature, Beinecke Rare Book and Manuscript Library, Yale University)

Carl Van Vechten and Feathers, 1920 (photograph by Harriet V. Furness; Van Vechten Trust)

Poesia ed amore, circa 1917 (drawing by Marcel Duchamp; courtesy of Francis
M. Nauman and the late Joseph Solomon)

Avery Hopwood, 1915 (photograph by Eillman[?], Carl Van Vechten Papers, Manuscripts and Archives Division, New York Public Library, Astor, Lenox and Tilden Foundations)

John Floyd, 1920 (photograph by E. Brenel[?]; courtesy of Jack Sharrar and the Chamberlain and Lyman Brown Collection, Billy Rose Theatre Collection, New York Public Library for the Performing Arts, Astor, Lenox and Tilden Foundations)

Regina Wallace, 1932 (photograph by Carl Van Vechten; Yale Collection of American Literature, Beinecke Rare Book and Manuscript Library, Yale University)

The Tattooed Countess, 1924 (dust jacket design by Ralph Barton; Yale Collection of American Literature, Beinecke Rare Book and Manuscript Library, Yale University)

Pola Negri as the Tattooed Countess in *A Woman of the World,* 1925 (film still; Van Vechten Trust)

Marguerite D'Alvarez, 1919
(photographer unknown;
Estate of Donald Angus)

George Gershwin, 1933
(photograph by Carl Van
Vechten; Yale Collection
of American Literature,
Beinecke Rare Book and
Manuscript Library, Yale
University)

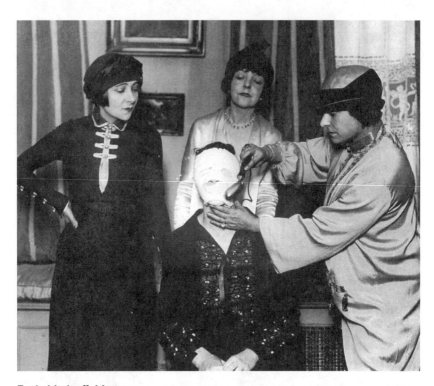

Fania Marinoff, Mary Young, Helena Rubinstein, and a client, circa 1925 (photographer unknown; Yale Collection of American Literature, Beinecke Rare Book and Manuscript Library, Yale University)

Henry Louis Mencken, 1932 (photograph by Carl Van Vechten; Van Vechten Trust)

1926

"I dream I am a Negro
being pursued."

By the time *Nigger Heaven* was published in August, Van Vechten had become a regular fixture in Harlem. His parties were automatically reported on in the society columns of the black press, he had become an unofficial envoy for white Manhattan to go slumming in black Harlem, and he had enlarged his circle of acquaintances in speakeasies and in cabarets there. However, 1926 must have been traumatic for Van Vechten: His father died, his wife threatened to leave him because of the abuse that his excessive drinking sometimes encouraged, he was served with a lawsuit over song lyrics he had quoted in his novel without permission, and he was not only astonished but crushed by a fierce backlash in the black press against *Nigger Heaven.* At the end of the year he headed West for Santa Fe and then Hollywood.

Monday, 4 January 1926

... Expected to hear from Ralph [Van Vechten] this morning, did not, finally telephoned him. He said Father was better and he expected to leave Cedar Rapids for Chicago. . . . A high-strung, nervous day which culminates in a telegram from Ralph arriving at a quarter of four telling me Father is worse. At 5 I am on the *Wolverine* bound for Chicago. I read *The Vatican Swindle* [by Andre Gide] & then got drunk on Scotch. So I sleep for the first time in my life in a sleeper.

Tuesday, 5 January 1926

... Arrive in Chicago at 2, met by Ralph's chauffeur with the car. He tells me Father died this morning at 7.30. At 3.30 I leave Chicago on the Rock Island, arrive in Cedar Rapids at 11.15. Ralph & Van Vechten Shaffer met me at the train. Came home, found Addie here & Angevine. Addie bearing up wonderfully. To bed about 12.30 & slept with the aid of remainder of whiskey. (Paul Robeson's concert, Town Hall.)

Saturday, 9 January 1926

... Read *Roughing It* [by Mark Twain] on the way to Chicago. Arrive Chicago about 9.30. Ralph's chauffeur meet[s] me & takes me to the Penn Station where I buy my ticket for N.Y. The Crown Prince of Greece is arriving & there is a tumultuous throng. To Ralph's house. He is in bed but Fannie receives me & sends me to Duane's room & dirty sheets! I have a sore throat & that & the sheets & the automobiles on the street keep me awake for some time. (Tea for Ellen Glasgow, 5 o'clock, at the Knopfs'.)

Sunday, 10 January 1926

... At 12.40 the family takes me to the Pennsylvania Station & I embark on the *Broadway Express*. Rotten hard bed but I sleep well & I dispose of a bottle of bourbon Ralph gave me. Talk in the smoker with Pullman porter.

Wednesday, 13 January 1926

Up at nine with a hangover. Nevertheless I worked all day over notes & magazines and music connected with *Nigger Heaven*. . . . Late in afternoon Claire Burke, again separated from Hoffenstein, came in, & later Duane Van Vechten who stayed to dinner. To bed at 9, but could not sleep.

Thursday, 14 January 1926

... At five Duane Van Vechten & Covarrubias came in. Donald Angus came to dinner & after dinner Harry Block. We all go to Hall Johnson's in Harlem, to hear a double mixed quartet sing Spirituals. They sing five or six I've never before heard, and then as I ask for them, one or another remembers the words of [*a*?] demanded Spiritual & then a [*word*] takes up the strain & harmonizes them. Thus Spirituals were born. Donald & I go to Harry Block's for an hour. Home about one.

Sunday, 24 January 1926

... Lunch at the Knopfs'. Eugene & Boonie Goossens, Polish ambassador & his wife. We drive Gene home to the Hotel Majestic & came home ourselves. Boonie came in for cocktails. Dinner at Lawrence & Armina Langner's. T. R. Smith, Witter Bynner. Marinoff goes with them to the Theatre Guild to see *The Goat Song* [by Franz Werfel]. I go to International Composer's Guild, with Rosamond Johnson. Goossens conducts. Respighi & his wife appear.[1] Florence Mills makes a sensation, singing four songs by Wm. Still.[2] Talk to Louise Varèse, Aaron Copland, Paul Rosenfeld, Carrie Stettheimer, etc. After the concert I brought Taylor Gordon & Rosamond Johnson home with me. They sang some new songs. Also Muriel Draper, Boonie & Gene Goossens, Alfred & Blanche Knopf, James Weldon & Grace Johnson, Walter White, Edward Wassermann,[3] Max Ewing, ... two other young men. Marinoff brings Harry Block & Donald Angus. In bed at 4. ...

    1. Italian composer Ottorino Respighi.
    2. William Grant Still, African American composer who studied with avant-garde French composer Edgar Varèse and academic American composer George Chadwick.
    3. Wassermann (who later changed his name to Waterman) was heir of the Seligman banking family and himself a Wall Street banker. Also, he was distantly related to the Stettheimers. A longtime CVV acquaintance, he became an intimate friend in the mid-twenties. Wassermann gave lavish dinner parties, and on occasion his apartment became privately notorious as a white version of a black buffet flat, where impromptu homosexual shows sometimes were staged, featuring mixed casts.

Thursday, 28 January 1926

Up at 4.30. ... Feeling fine. Wrote second draught of Chapter 1, Book II, of *Nigger Heaven*. Late in afternoon Duane Van Vechten, Tony & Mabel Luhan, Gipsy Johnson, Donald Angus, Elizabeth Sheffey Sergeant[1] with her Paul

Robeson article. Regina Wallace for dinner. Marinoff goes to theater & stays all night with her.[2]

1. A Knopf writer, biographer of her longtime companion, Willa Cather, and of Robert Frost.

2. By this point in time, CVV's drinking had got far out of control. Although he does not always indicate that he became abusive to Marinoff, he does so often enough to suggest the frequency by accounts of her spending the night with friends.

Wednesday, 3 February 1926

. . . Called Jack & Lucile Harper, learned that Avery [Hopwood] had been locked [in] his cabin on his recent voyage on the *Leviathan* because he was drunk & disorderly. . . .

Friday, 5 February 1926

. . . Went to Macy's with Marinoff & had a debauch buying Chinese boxes, etc. Home & wrote last chapter (second draught) of *Nigger Heaven*. Eddie Wassermann & Donald Angus came in. Donald stayed to dinner. Then to James Weldon Johnson's, where I meet Guy Johnson[1] of the University of North Carolina. Then to J. Rosamond Johnson's where Guy gave Rosamond Johnson several of the interesting Negro social songs he has collected. Taylor Gordon sang. Marinoff goes home at 12. Donald Angus joins us & we go to Connie's Inn. Saw review at Lafayette Theatre, also Nora Johnson, . . . Muriel Draper & Max Ewing (Taylor's party). A wonderful show! Home at 4.30.

1. Editor of books about African American folk songs, spirituals, and work songs.

Tuesday, 9 February 1926

. . . Spent the morning re-reading *The Autobiography of an Ex-Colored Man* [by James Weldon Johnson] and listening to Blues on the phonograph for phrases & instruments' effects. Looked over a great number of Paul Laurence Dunbar's books & read *The Sport of the Gods*.[1] Dinner in with Marinoff. Saw Jack Harper, came in with gin before dinner. Lenore Ulric opens in *Lulu Belle*.[2] . . . Backstage after. Saw Belasco.[3] Then to a party at Lenore Ulric's. . . . George Gershwin, Ann Andrews, Ruth Gordon,[4] . . . June Walker, Charles MacArthur, Neysa McMein,[5] Madge Kennedy,[6] Sidney Blackmer.[7] George played & we drove home in the snow at 4 A.M.

1. African American writer known to white readers largely through his verse in Negro dialect rather than through his serious poetry or novels such as *The Sport of the Gods,* about the plight of black New Yorkers at the turn of the century.

2. In this play by white writers about African Americans, Ulric played the lead in blackface, whereas much of the rest of the cast was black, none of whom seem to have been invited to her postperformance party, although most of the guests were connected with the theater.

3. David Belasco, a theatrical producer.

4. Actress and playwright.

5. Illustrator who supplied drawings of pretty girls for sixty *Saturday Evening Post* covers and, for fourteen years, every *McCall's* monthly magazine cover.

6. Popular actress in both ingenue and leading roles, notably with W. C. Fields in *Poppy*.

7. Actor at the outset of a long career on stage and in films.

Thursday, 11 February 1926

. . . Worked all day on Prologue to *Nigger Heaven*. . . . Eddie Wassermann comes in for cocktails. To dine chez D'Alvarez. Mrs. [Frank?] of the *Musical Leader* and her daughter Mrs. Smith—perfect asses—sneer at my argument on the Negro question. . . . Then a very funny party at Victor Wittgenstein's that was like a cheap serial. Everybody sang, including one of Clara Novello Davis's awful pupils. . . . Home at 1.30.

Sunday, 14 February 1926

. . . We go to Marie Doro's at 4. . . . Then to Ann Andrews' for cocktails. . . . Home & dressed & to Margaret Anglin's[1] for dinner (more row on Negro question), Rebecca West, Ralph Barton, whom we brought (on request). . . . At midnight to party at George Gershwin's: Ben Bernie's[2] apartment. Rube Goldberg,[3] F[ranklin] P. A[dams] & Esther Root imitated radio announcements. Queenie Smith[4] sang. Marc Connelly did a travelogue & illustrated song. Frank Harding's wife sang an air from *The Light for St. Agnes*. Katharine Cornell told me she is going to do a Negro play by Waldo Frank. Talked with Gershwin, Ethel Barrymore,[5] Zimbalist,[6] Lenore Ulric, June Walker, Sidney Blackmer, T. R. Smith, Ruth Goldbeck, Charlie MacArthur, John Emerson. . . .

1. Actress and producer whose Shakespeare productions CVV had lauded a decade earlier.

2. Popular comedian on stage and later in films.

3. Humorist who invented fantastic machines and contraptions and then illustrated them with cartoon drawings.

4. Musical comedy actress, white despite her name.

5. Leading actress since 1901 in *Captain Jinks of the Horse Marines*, sister of Lionel and John Barrymore.

6. Russian violinist Efrem Zimbalist.

Thursday, 18 February 1926

. . . Dinner at Eddie Wassermann's with Frances Seligman and Marinoff. He took us to Town Hall to hear Paul Robeson sing. Talked with Witter Bynner & Ruth Hale.[1] Then party for Paul at our house: Paul & Essie Robeson, Katharine Cornell, . . . Walter & Gladys White, Lenore Ulric & Sidney Blackmer, James Weldon & Grace Johnson, Frances Seligman & Eddie Wassermann, Rebecca West, Donald Angus, Harry Block, Covarrubias, Best-Maugard, Regina Wallace, Rita Romilly, Louis Calhern[2] & Ann Andrews. Last guests left at 4 A.M. I stayed sober. Rain.

1. Journalist, Mrs. Heywood Broun.
2. Avuncular American actor, married successively to writer Ilka Chase and sometime actress Julia Hoyt.

Monday, 1 March 1926

Bright, warm day. In all day. I finished typing *Nigger Heaven*. Hurray! Donald Angus came in at 5 for cocktails. Dinner in with Marinoff. . . . Then to bed at 9 o'clock. Slept badly. Wakened at 12 by Poo who begins to discharge again. I put her in the kitchen & read for an hour & a half. Then to bed again. Rain. Warm. I'm very restless.

Friday, 5 March 1926

Up at 8. Sunny & cold. Marinoff still sick. My cold is perhaps better. Went to the dentist's in the morning. Lunch in with Marinoff. . . . At 5 Kit Cornell came in & we talked about *Malva*.[1] 6.30 James Weldon Johnson & Grace Johnson, returning the mss. of *Nigger Heaven* with favorable comment. They stayed till midnight & we talked of many matters.

1. Waldo Frank's play with African American subject matter in which Katherine Cornell proposed to act.

Saturday, 6 March 1926

Up at 7. Worked all day revising *Nigger Heaven*. Lunch in with Marinoff. Harry Block came in late in afternoon bringing Covarrubias caricature of me as a Negro.[1] Marinoff & I go to Knopfs' for dinner. Then we go to Isa [Glenn] Schindel's party. Harry Block, Covarrubias, Mr. Nichols of the Nyack Cult stops his heart beat, does some card tricks, & finally pierces his tongue with a hat pin. We came home about 1.

1. Titled "A Prediction."

Tuesday, 9 March 1926

. . . My nose is still running. . . . After lunch I walked downtown, went to Hubert's Dime Museum on 42 Street & saw the flea circus. Then walked up Fifth Avenue to Brentano's & home. Eddie Wassermann came in at 4.30 with 2 bottles of absinthe. Donald Angus & James Weldon Johnson who comes to talk with me about *Malva*. Eddie stays to dinner & takes Marinoff to the Phila. Orchestra concert. I go to Lucile Harper's & talk to her until 10.30 when Eddie Wassermann comes in. Later he & I go to the Plantation (first time) to see Florence Mills. Later we go to The Owl, another downstairs supper club. . . . Then to Eddie's. . . . 4 o'clock.

Thursday, 11 March 1926

. . . I lunch at Marguery's with Emily Clark [Balch]. Then to Knopfs'. Alfred does not like *Nigger Heaven*. Talk with him & Blanche. Home. . . . Emily Balch, Isa [Glenn] Schindel, Harry Block. Isa brings *Heat* to me. James Weldon Johnson comes in to tell me that he doing a book for Knopf. Dinner with Harry & Best-Maugard at Fornio's. Later Harry & I go to Lucile's. . . . Home at 1.30. *Drunk*.

Tuesday, 16 March 1926

. . . We went to hear Hall Johnson's Harlem Jubilee Singers at International House. Sat with Rosamond & Mildred Johnson, Taylor Gordon, Gladys & Walter White, Paul & Essie Robeson. Went back to see the singers. . . . Garland Anderson,[1] Negro bus-boy, author of *Appearances*, made some offensive sounds. Home at 11.00.

    1. San Francisco bellhop whose play *Don't Judge by Appearances*, about a black man falsely accused of raping a white woman, raised money in a cross-country tour for the first African American full-length play to open on Broadway.

Wednesday, 17 March 1926

Up at 8.15. . . . At 4 I went to call on Fannie Hurst & stayed till six, talking mostly about Negroes & Zora Hurston in particular. Came home to find Waldo Frank here. We talked about his play. Dined in with Marinoff & then we go to see The Stagers' dress rehearsal of Conrad's *One Day More* & Strindberg's *Easter*, in which Blanche Barrymore (Michael Strange)[1] makes her debut as an actress. . . .

    1. American playwright and actress under a pseudonym.

Thursday, 18 March 1926

... Cleaned out Marinoff's closet. Then to office where I talk some more with Alfred about *Nigger Heaven* & we decide to send it to the printer. Then to Elmer Adler's[1] where I pass on title page of *Nigger Heaven* & go to lunch with him & three other men at Sardi's. ... Marinoff & I go to Cameo Theatre to see *Waxworks*, a new German film with Emil Jannings. Talked with Adolf Bolm,[2] Harry Block, Miguel Covarrubias, Best-Maugard, Alfred Kuttner, Mortimer Offner, Stella Block, etc. Home. Blanche Knopf calls for me & I went with her, Benno Moiseiwitsch[3] & Myra Hess. We went up to her house, had champagne, & later went to Small's & to The Nest. Home at 4.

> 1. American book designer who frequently worked for Knopf.
> 2. Russian dancer and choreographer, Anna Pavlova's early partner and subsequently *premier danseur* with the Diaghilev Russian Ballet Company on its first American tour.
> 3. Russian pianist whose reputation was strongly predicated on his playing Chopin's music.

Friday, 19 March 1926

... Spent the day going over my books & throwing them out. ... We join the Spingarns, Grace Johnson, Pierre Matisse (met),[1] Carl & Zelma Brandt.[2] Then to the N.A.A.C.P. dance at Manhattan Casino. The most brilliant affair I have yet attended in Harlem. A'Lelia Walker, Lloyd & Edna Thomas, Taylor Gordon, Paul & Essie Robeson, Dr. DuBois, John Nail & his wife, Dorothy Peterson, ... Eddie Wassermann, etc. Home after 4. ...

> 1. French art dealer, son of painter Henri Matisse.
> 2. Literary agent and his first wife. In partnership with his brother as Brandt & Brandt, his agency represented many successful writers.

Saturday, 20 March 1926

Up at 10, with a hangover. ... Cleaned out my closet. Marinoff's birthday. She gives me a silver flask & I give her some flowers. Lunch in with Marinoff. Late in the afternoon Donald Angus & Paul Robeson come in. Donald stays to dinner. About 9 we pick up Eddie Wassermann & go to a house warming at Jim & Dorothy Harris's own house at 13 Gay Street. A brilliant party. Paul & Essie Robeson, ... Covarrubias, Harry Block, Dudley Murphy,[1] Evelyn Preer[2] & Eddie Thompson, Edna & Lloyd Thomas, Elmer Imes, Vi Stoner,[3] A'Lelia Walker, ... Bernia Austin, ... Dorothy Peterson. I stand against a candle & burn a hole in my coat. Went home with Eddie at 5. Came home at 6.30.

1. American stage and film director, notably for *St. Louis Blues*, with Bessie Smith, 1928.

2. African American actress who appeared with the Ethiopian Art Players in Oscar Wilde's *Salome* on Broadway, also with the Lafayette Players in Harlem, and in many black films.

3. Vivian Stoner, a visiting friend of Nella Larsen Imes.

Wednesday, 24 March 1926

. . . Wrote first draft of review of Walter White's *Flight* & part of jacket for *Nigger Heaven*. . . . At 5 Blythe Daly & Donald Angus came in. Rebecca West gives a dinner at the Pullman Porters. Mrs. Somerset Maugham (met),[1] Marinoff, Walter & Gladys White. . . . Then we went to Whites' where we were joined by Taylor Gordon. Marinoff goes home. Gladys very morose. The rest of us go to Small's where we see Covarrubias & Blanche Knopf with a handsome young man, & take Mrs. Maugham & Rebecca to Lucile Harper's. She won't let us in. Chop suey at the Far East restaurant. Then home at 3.

1. English interior decorator Syrie Maugham.

Friday, 26 March 1926

. . . Marinoff has lunch with me & goes to radio rehearsal. . . . At 4.30 Marinoff & I go to Eddie Wassermann's. . . . Jim & Grace [Johnson], Boonie [Goossens], Marinoff, Eddie Wassermann, Dudley Murphy, Dorothy Harris & I go to the Constantinople Restaurant for supper. Back to Eddie's. Dudley, Dorothy, Boonie, Eddie & I go to Sardi's. . . . Then to The Nest. At 4.30 Eddie goes home & the rest of us stay till 6.30. Home in the sunlight.

Friday, 2 April 1926

Up at 8 with a hangover. Bright clear morning. Reading *Les faux-monnayeurs* of Andre Gide's.[1] . . . After lunch I went to Elmer Adler's to tell him about my jacket *(Nigger Heaven)*. Met Frank Case on the street on way to the bank. He & Bertha are sailing for Europe tomorrow with Douglas Fairbanks & Mary Pickford. Van Vechten & Angevine Shaffer came to dinner. After dinner a party. Victor Wittgenstein, William Rose Benét, James & Grace Johnson, Elinor Wylie, Ben Ray Redman, Frieda Inescort, Eddie Wassermann, Lawrence & Armina Langner, Carl & Zelma Brandt, Miguel Covarrubias, Harry Block, Dudley Murphy, Langston Hughes, Donald Angus, Moiseiwitsch, Waldo Frank, D'Alvarez & four men,[2] Phyllis Povah, Ann Andrews, Louis Calhern, George Cukor, Boonie Goossens, Blanche Knopf, Emily

[Clark] Balch, Margaret Freeman. Langston stayed till 4. I sent him home &
went to bed. A wild night.

    1. *The Counterfeiters.* CVV often referred to French novels by their French titles,
but he read most of them in English translation. His French was serviceable but
not fluent.

    2. Then, as now, women of a certain age who were cult figures—D'Alvarez of
her generation, Tallulah Bankhead of hers, for example—were frequently accompanied by one or more willing social gigolos.

Saturday, 3 April 1926

Up at 11. Lunch in with Marinoff. . . . Late in the afternoon Emily [Clark]
Balch, Bayard & Isa [Glenn] Schindel come in. Dinner with Marinoff. Then
to WEAF station where I hear her read Viola in *Twelfth Night* over the radio. . . . Home at 10.30. Go to bed. Nightmares. Can't sleep. I climb into
Marinoff's bed.

Monday, 5 April 1926

Up at 8, fairly clear & fairly warm. Still have indigestion. . . . Lunch in alone.
In the afternoon I have my hair cut. Home. Read some more. James Weldon
Johnson comes in. I witness his contract with Knopf for him. Langston
Hughes comes to dinner. He leaves at a quarter of nine & I go to bed. Slept
heavily with horrible dreams.

Thursday, 8 April 1926

. . . Proofs arrive (½ of *Nigger Heaven*) & I read them all. Went down to Elmer
Adler's to O.K. jacket for *Nigger Heaven*. . . . Dinner with Marinoff. Then I
went to see Florence Mills's show at the Alhambra. Saw [Noble] Sissle. Then
to party at Knopfs' for Mr. & Mrs. John Galsworthy (met),[1] Margaret Freeman, H. L. Mencken (just down from Boston after his successful encounter
with the Watch & Ward Society),[2] Mr. & Mrs. Sam Knopf, Mrs. Guggenheim,[3]
Fannie Hurst whom I took home, Paul & Essie Robeson. He sang unaccom-
panied. . . . In bed at 1.30. The poo is discharging again.

    1. Prolific English novelist and playwright.

    2. When *The American Mercury* was banned in Boston, Mencken (co-editor of
the magazine) deliberately bought a copy there so that he could be arrested to test
censorship.

    3. Minnie Guggenheim, philanthropic New York dowager.

Wednesday, 14 April 1926

Up at 8.30, finished third reading of *Nigger Heaven* proofs. . . . Angevine Shaffer & her sister Dolly Heyward came in for cocktails. Also Boonie & Gene Goossens, Eddie Wassermann, James Weldon Johnson. Marinoff goes chez D'Alvarez for dinner. Angevine & Dolly stay here. After dinner we go to see a private showing of Dudley Murphy's *Ballet Mechanique.* Julia Hoyt,[1] . . . Dudley Murphy, Dorothy Harris, Laurence Stallings, Theodore Dreiser, D'Alvarez, Paul Robeson, . . . Marinoff, Boonie & Gene Goossens, etc. A crowd of us attend Hubert's Museum & flea circus.

> 1. A rich New York flapper who occasionally acted in the late twenties.

Monday, 19 April 1926

. . . Took 9.15 train for Baltimore where Emily [Clark] Balch met me with her car & we motored to Richmond. We had a slight accident outside Washington, but go to Richmond before 8 o'clock. Dinner alone at the Jefferson [Hotel]. Hunter Stagg came in.

Friday, 23 April 1926

Woke about 6 & couldn't sleep any more, hot & windy. At a quarter of ten, Emily Clark [Balch], Mrs. Clark, & Hunter came for me & we motored to Hampton.[1] As we stepped out on the campus a band began to play & we discovered that we had stumbled in on the fifty-eighth anniversary of the founding of the school. I had been expected, as James Weldon Johnson had telegraphed. We had lunch at the president's, Dr. Gregg. . . . In the afternoon we heard commencement exercises & the school sang Spirituals. Motored home & at 8.30 went to see Alice Clark. . . . I insulted Mrs. Conquest[2] by saying I preferred colored people to white people, after a few drinks of corn whiskey.

> 1. Hampton Institute, African American college where Booker T. Washington studied.
> 2. Elise Conquest, a Southern dowager, one of several CVV met or renewed acquaintance with during this week in Richmond and Charlottesville.

Thursday, 29 April 1926

Up at 9. Clear day. Working on letters & papers all the morning. Lunch in with Marinoff. In the afternoon I went to post office, to Saks, to Knopf office where I talked with Blanche & Alfred, Harry Block. As we went out met Fannie Hurst & Ettie Stettheimer. Drove to Harlem for some new records. Dummy of *Nigger Heaven* arrives. Marinoff goes out to dinner with Victor

Wittgenstein. I go to Far East (walking up with D'Alvarez) for chop suey. Home. Edna Kenton comes in & bores me for four hours. What a fatuous, gossiping, futile old busybody she is. In bed at 12.

Friday, 30 April 1926

Up early. Worked on papers and letters. . . . Then Jack & Esther Marinoff for dinner. At 10.30 we dressed and went to Club Mirador . . . to party given by Theodore Dreiser (very dull). . . . At 1.30 we dashed to Manhattan Casino in Harlem to Fashion Show dance. . . . Later a crowd of us went to Small's & listened to "My Daddy Rocks Me."[1] Then we were found by Rose [Rolanda] & Covarrubias. In bed at 5.

> 1. "My Daddy Rocks Me with One Steady Roll," a scabrous song popularized by Nora Holt.

Saturday, 1 May 1926

Up at nine. Went to bank & Knopf office. . . . I went to *Opportunity* contest dinner. Met Amy Spingarn.[1] . . . Took Harry Block. Saw Jessie Fauset, Arthur Fauset,[2] Alain Locke, . . . Zora Hurston, Eric Waldron, Paul & Essie Robeson, Walter & Gladys White, Stuart Sherman,[3] Charles S. & Mrs. Johnson, Eddie Wassermann, Jim & Dorothy Harris, Dorothy Peterson, Dudley Murphy, Rudolph Fisher, Mrs. Fisher (met), Miss Fisher,[4] . . . Grace Johnson, . . . Louella Tucker, Regina Anderson, Nella & Elmer Imes, Marita Bonner (met),[5] Nathaniel Dett[6] & many more. Then to a party at Rudolph Fisher's where many of these re-gathered & finally to Small's with a crowd of about twenty. Home about 5.30 with Eddie & Harry.

> 1. Joel Spingarn's wife, who joined her husband in supporting the NAACP from its formative years. She later established awards for young black artists and writers.
> 2. Philadelphia-based African American poet, Jessie Fauset's brother.
> 3. American literary critic.
> 4. Pearl Fisher and her sister-in-law, June.
> 5. African American writer and educator.
> 6. Robert Nathaniel Dett, African American composer and founder of the Hampton Institute Choir, which toured the United States and Europe.

Sunday, 2 May 1926

. . . In the afternoon R. Nathaniel Dett, Alain Locke, Marie Doro come in. Later Harry Block who takes me to dinner at a Japanese restaurant on 58th Street. We come to the house for a while & then go to a party chez D'Alvarez. Marinoff, Donald Angus, Dudley Murphy, a man named Bailey, Hugo & Frances Seligman, etc. I get very drunk & abusive. Home at 2 o'clock.

Monday, 3 May 1926

... Went to bed after lunch. At 4.30 walked to bank to deposit royalties. Then to Eddie Wassermann's, where Harry Block & Taylor Gordon presently forgathered & we had dinner. Then to Lafayette Theatre to see Mamie Smith[1] for first time. A couple of wonderful comedians in the bill: Dusty Fletcher & Bob [*Bransuit?*]. . . .

> 1. When white entertainer Sophie Tucker was prevented by contract from recording with African American–owned Okeh records, Mamie Smith replaced her, thereby becoming the first African American to make solo recordings.

Saturday, 8 May 1926

... At 5 I go to see Julia Hoyt. Max Gordon[1] there. He drives me uptown. I get out at 52 & Broadway & run into Lynn Fontanne on her way to the Guild Theatre. She takes me to see Alfred Lunt. Victor Wittgenstein there. I dine alone at Fornio's. Then to Lucile Harper's. . . . Lucile & I go to Harlem at midnight, first to Small's Paradise, then The Nest. Saw Mal Frazier. A boy named Louis Simms danced the Charleston. Carl Brandt & Zelma there. Then we go to Royal Gardens. Met . . . Johnny Cobb again, Marjorie Sipp. Home at 4.30.

> 1. American theatrical producer.

Friday, 14 May 1926

Awake at 4. Poo begins to yowl. Thunder & rain. . . . Blanche & Alfred Knopf come to dinner. After dinner Dr. Rudolph Fisher, his wife, & sister come in to meet the Knopfs. Everybody leaves about 11 & Marinoff & I go to Muriel Draper's farewell party for Elinor Wylie who is sailing next week. She gets very drunk & sick. . . . A rotten party.

Sunday, 16 May 1926

Up at nine. Sick & discouraged about *Nigger Heaven*. I wish I could do it all over again. Cloudy. Reading papers, etc. Lunch at the Lawrence Langners' with Marinoff and the Dankenkos (Monsieur et Madame). He is director of the Moscow Art Theatre musical studio. She speaks English. Both are enchanting persons. Came home to meet Rudolph Fisher who brings back the mss. of *Nigger Heaven* with report that the end is a knockout. Beginning "To pro, hey so," he gives me many excellent suggestions.[1] Tea with Margaret Freeman for Emily Clark [Balch] at . . . 125 E. 70 St. Monte Evans & a Mr. Bagin, young Frenchman, Alfred & Blanche Knopf & four flappers, one of whom Charlestons beautifully. We take Emily & Margaret to dinner at the Japanese restaurant & brought them home. In bed at 11. Slept badly, worrying about my damn book. Poo discharging again.

1. For an appendix to the novel of African American slang and popular phrases.

Thursday, 20 May 1926

. . . Finished third reading of page proofs of *Nigger Heaven*. Lunch in. Then to the office with proofs. Saw Blanche & Alfred. Home. Rudolph Fisher came in. Then I go to Julia Hoyt for cocktails, a lot of men were there, including an actor named Robert Montgomery[1] whom I met. Then to 75 Washington Square to dinner with Elinor Wylie & Bill Benét. Aldous & Mrs. Huxley (met),[2] Mr. & Mrs. John Peale Bishop,[3] John Farrar & fiancée (met), F.P.A. & Esther Root. Afterwards some of us went to F.P.A.'s new house. Home about one.

1. At the outset of his career, later a popular film star and, still later, a television host.
2. English novelist and his first wife, Maria. CVV read all of Huxley's books as they were published but never passed judgment on any of them in the daybooks.
3. American poet and novelist and his wife.

Friday, 21 May 1926

. . . Dinner with Marinoff. Then we go to *The Great God Brown* [by Eugene O'Neill], which bores me to death. . . . Then to a party at the Coffee House given to celebrate the actors and the Greenwich Village Theatre. A terrible party & we stay about 15 minutes. . . .

Saturday, 22 May 1926

. . . Cocktails at 6. Madame Lachet (Marinoff's French teacher) & Eddie Wassermann for dinner. James Weldon Johnson drops in unexpectedly & stays too. Eddie, James, & I go to the Alhambra to see Bill Robinson's review. . . . Afterwards we go round to see Bill, who is one of the world's greatest dancers. His wife there. She drives us to Small's. We stay there till 12.30, go to pick up Grace [Nail Johnson] & on to the Royal Gardens, . . . Paris (The Green Cat) & Philadelphia Jimmie's across the street.[1] Bojangles (Bill R.) &

his wife appear & later 4 pink friends[2] of James Weldon. Later we go to Connie's Inn, where Bill does the most astonishing dance. Home at 5 o'clock.

1. All Harlem speakeasies, all within walking distance of each other.
2. African Americans used "pink" and "white" interchangeably to designate Caucasians.

Sunday, 23 May 1926

Up at 11. Bright day. Feeling all right. Read papers, eat lunch, take a nap, & loaf generally. . . . At 6 o'clock Marinoff & I go with Eddie Wassermann to Harlem where we pick up Zora Hurston & go to Craig's (for dinner where we see . . . Bill & Mrs. Robinson, Paul & Essie Robeson, Jim Harris, Eddie Thompson & many others). After dinner Zora takes us to a sanctified church in a real estate dealer's office, where there is shoutin', moanin', yelling during & praying hours on end to the music of a cornet & guitar & jumping & dancing. Exactly like the jungle. The guitar plunks a rhythm like a tom-tom. Afterwards we go to a speakeasy on 130 & Lenox for beer. Home at 11. It is a <u>cold</u> day.

Tuesday, 25 May 1926

Up at 9.30. Finished Blues paper & sent it off to Irita [Van Doren].[1] Wrote a long letter for a party we are [giving] on June 2. Claire Burke came to lunch. . . . Regina Wallace comes to dinner & she & Marinoff go to see Rahman Bey, the fakir. Rhea Wells—who is sailing—came in to see me. Later I join Marinoff at a party given . . . at Writers' Studio. An evening of some historical importance for six Negroes not only mingle with the 200 or so whites but <u>dance</u> with them also. Taylor Gordon & Rosamond Johnson who sang, James Weldon & Grace Johnson, Dorothy & Jim Harris. Also T. [R.] Smith, Blanche Barrymore i.e., Michael Strange, Eddie Wassermann, Dick Barnett, Otto Kahn, Rita Romilly, Mary Ellis, Violet Kemble Cooper,[2] Arthur Mayer,[3] etc. Some of us go down to Eddie Wassermann's for a couple of hours. Home at 3.

1. A review of W. C. Handy's *Blues* (1926), the first extensive study of the subject, text by Abbe Niles and music by Handy.
2. English actress, then appearing on the stage in New York.
3. Publicity director for Paramount Studios and the Rialto Theatre in New York, author of books about Hollywood: *Truly Colossal* and *The Movies*.

Thursday, 27 May 1926

Up early & at 10.30 Emily [Clark Balch], Alice [Clark] & I drive to Doylestown [Pennsylvania] to inspect the Bucks Co. Museum, a marvelous place, full of the tools & stage coaches & fire engines of earlier America. Then to . . . Dr. Henry Mercer, who built the museum. His house, called Fonthill Abbey, is a fantastic castle, created of concrete studded with tiles, full of winding staircases, strange rooms. At 3 we motored to Lincoln University where we saw Langston Hughes,[1] . . . & a lot of other boys. Had tea at Prof. Larabee's, met the acting president, Wright & his sister. Back to Philadelphia & dinner at 8. In bed at 2.00.

    1. Hughes was then enrolled as a full-time student at Lincoln. He graduated in 1929.

Friday, 28 May 1926

Up at 8.30. Took train for New York [from Philadelphia] at 10. Home for lunch with Marinoff. Alfred [Knopf] called me up to say that Mencken thinks *Nigger Heaven* is censorable. Paul Robeson comes in to tell us he is having an affair with a white girl. He has been faithful (apparently) up till now. . . . Eddie Wassermann & I dine at the Pullman Porters. Then to Lafayette Theatre. Abbie Mitchell[1] & others in *Black Alabam'* review. Then we walk up Seventh Avenue, run into Charlie Davis, Lloyd Thomas, & Charlie Craft. We go first to a bar, then to the re-opened Fifth Avenue Small's, now called The New World, & run by Dixie Bonds. A marvellous & thrilling evening. Ruth Trent, entertainer, sings new verses of "Shake That Thing," & a song called "Take Yo' Fingers Off It, Rastus Crump," a drummer does a marvellous stunt. Charlie Davis puts on a dance & the band plays "Mean Oh Slow Blues." Home at 4 A.M.

    1. African American musical entertainer, later a dramatic actress on Broadway.

Saturday, 29 May 1926

. . . Gladys & Walter White come in in the evening, and at midnight we go to Small's (The New World) where we are joined by Eddie Wassermann and practically everything happens that happened last night. Home at 5 o'clock.

Sunday, 30 May 1926

. . . We stay in all day with the poo, & somehow towards noon I know she is going to die. She is so weak, so pitiful. I call the doctor but he gives me no advice but to feed her quinine. At night, after dinner, we leave her. I really couldn't bear to see another cat die. We go to Zora Hurston's as she wants me to meet a Barnard professor.[1] Bruce Nugent is there. Then to Walter White's. . . . We come home at midnight, & found the poo died in an agonizing attitude on the floor in Marinoff's room.[2]

1. Probably the anthropologist Franz Boas, her advisor.
2. This cat was called Scheherazade, the last of a long list of cats CVV had had since 1908.

Monday, 31 May 1926

Up early, to dispose of the poo's body, & to put her pan & basket away, a dismal, rainy day. . . .

Wednesday, 2 June 1926

Up at 8.30. Bright, clear, & hot. Worked in my room in the morning. Paying bills, etc. Lunch in with Marinoff. Then took a nap. Then went to talk to Blanche Knopf about advertising for *Nigger Heaven*. . . . Emily [Clark] Balch and Alice Clark came to dinner. After dinner I gave a party for them. Taylor Gordon & Rosamond Johnson sang, George Gershwin . . . played. Stella Block danced & James Weldon Johnson recited "The Creation."[1] Eddie Wassermann, Victor Wittgenstein, Alfred & Blanche Knopf, Blanche Yurka,[2] Rudolph & Mrs. Fisher, Pearl Fisher, Theodore Dreiser, Nora Johnson, Grace Johnson, Dreiser's girl,[3] Florence Sternberger.[4] . . . In bed at 3.

1. One of Johnson's several sermons in verse based on Bible stories, from *God's Trombones*, written in the voice of a Southern Negro preacher.
2. American actress, later in films.
3. Helen Richardson, Dreiser's longtime mistress.
4. To this list of guests, Emily Clark adds Elinor Wylie and the Robesons, in her memoir, *Innocence Abroad* (1931).

Thursday, 3 June 1926

Up at 10. Got dressed & went down to see Ben Stern[1] about changes to meet the censor in *Nigger Heaven*. Home for lunch. . . . I go [to] office to talk to Alfred about *Nigger Heaven*. Then for Mrs. Clark & Emily. I take them to the flea circus, then to the house. Paul Robeson comes in & sings. Ralph Van Vechten comes in. I go to dinner at Eddie Wassermann's & then we go to the Urban League to hear some of the music of *Goophered*, an opera Hall Johnson wants to put on. It is no good. Paul, who got lit at my house, staggers in soused at midnight & we go to The New World. Paul, Walter White, Eddie & myself. Home at 4.

1. Legal counsel for Alfred A. Knopf.

Thursday, 10 June 1926

Up at 8, bright, warm day. Went out in the morning. Stationery shop, bank, Charles, which from being a fashionable grocery has become a sort of a delicatessen where clerks eat lunch. Home. Man came to clean typewriter. Lunch in with Marinoff. Writing letters. At 3.30 McEvoy[1] is supposed to appear to talk to me about some Negroes he wants for his new revue. He blabbers instead. At 4.30 George Stevens of the Knopf office arrives to talk about the advertising for *Nigger Heaven*. I find out he is a professional Southerner. He tells me the *Chicago Defender* has refused advertising on account of the title. Reg Wallace comes in. She & Stevens leave & Marinoff & I dine at the Arthur Spingarns' with two more people. I get very drunk. Home at midnight.

    1. J. P. McEvoy, *Chicago Tribune* writer who adapted some of his stories as *The Potters* for the stage. Also, he supplied the book for George Gershwin's *Show Girl*.

Friday, 11 June 1926

Up at 8.45. Bright, cool day. Have a hangover, but feeling rather well. . . . Marinoff left for Woodstock to spend the weekend with the Langners, at 5.20. Walter White & James Weldon Johnson came in & I give Walter the proofs of *Nigger Heaven* to read. Eddie Wassermann & Donald Angus come in & stay to supper. Later, Elmer & Nella [Larsen] Imes, Bud [i.e., Rudolph] Fisher, & Zora Hurston. We go to The New World & have fun. . . . Eric Walrond & party came in. The place closes at 2 according to new city ruling. We go to The Nest & try to get in. See Mal Frazier, Johnnie Corey, & Oscar Hammerstein [II], but The Nest is closed too, so we go home. Donald stays all night. In bed about 5.

Sunday, 13 June 1926

Up at 10. Donald gets up at 12 & we lunch at 1. The hottest day we've had this summer. In the afternoon Walter White comes down & raves about *Nigger Heaven*. He also identifies most of the characters[1] & predicts it will be a sensation in Harlem. Donald goes home after lunch & came back before Walter leaves. About 7 Donald & I go to Miyako's for dinner. Then to Harlem where we pick up Zora Hurston and . . . go to see *The Ring Shouters*. Then we drop in on Bessie Smith who is rip-roaring. . . . Home a little after one. Donald spends the night here.

    1. Nearly all characters in the novel are based on actual people, not always in a flattering light. Jessie and Arthur Fauset, A'Lelia Walker, and Mamie White are

somewhat caricatured, but Nora Holt, Harold Jackman, and Dorothy Peterson are given accurate physical approximations.

Friday, 18 June 1926

. . . Walter White's encomium [for *Nigger Heaven*] comes out in the *Pittsburgh Courier*. I call up Walter & he comes to lunch with us. . . . Went to have cocktails with Caroline [Dudley] Reagan, just back from Europe. Dorothy [Dudley] Harvey, Katherine Dudley, Donald Angus, Jack Oakman,[1] & another man. Home for dinner. Reg Wallace here. Marinoff leaves to spend the night with her. I take a nap. Invited to a party at Dorothy Peterson's & Jules Bledsoe's this evening. But Donald [Angus] came for me & we go to a party at Clara Smith's. She sings four tunes. . . .

1. Identified only as the second husband of Greta, formerly Mrs. Edward Everett Hale, J., whose face James A. Whistler, in a fit of pique about the amount of his commission, had painted over the face in his portrait of Sir William Eden's wife.

Tuesday, 22 June 1926

. . . Roscoe Conkling Bruce (met)[1] came to see me about the difficulties of the *Negro Who's Who*. Later Caroline Reagan, who wants to start another Negro show. She stayed to dinner & after dinner we went to the Palace Theatre & saw Bill Robinson. . . . Donald Angus with us. The three of us went to Harlem where we had a grand time. . . . Home at 3.

1. Harlem architect who constructed the Dunbar Apartments, one of Harlem's showplaces and home of several African American artists, writers, musicians, and activists.

Wednesday, 23 June 1926

. . . After dinner went to bed & sleep till 11, when we went to [a] . . . party for George Gershwin (sailing tomorrow), Mayor Jimmie Walker, Geo. [Jean] Nathan, . . . Helen Hayes, Al Jolson[1] (who sang "Swanee"), Lenore Ulric, Sidney Blackmer, Arthur Richman. . . . At 1 I left to attend a party given by Francis Wellman[2] for Elsie de Wolfe (met).[3] Frances Alda,[4] Vincent Youmans who played, Neysa McMein, Wm. Beebe.[5] . . . At 3.30 I left & went back to Edgar's party where we stayed till 6.

1. This popular Jewish entertainer sang and danced in blackface makeup.
2. Celebrated trial lawyer, one-time husband of opera singer Emma Juch, and author of several books about law.
3. Fashionable interior decorator, a regular guest at the Stettheimers' parties.

4. Metropolitan Opera House soprano from 1908 through the twenties.

5. Popularizer of scientific subjects through his nontechnical, accessible books.

Thursday, 24 June 1926

. . . Leonore Ulric & Sidney Blackmer came to dinner. After dinner they went to the theatre. Marinoff went to hear her swami & Donald [Angus] came in to see me. Late at night Donald, Marinoff, Lenore & Sidney & I went to The New World. Home at 4. I became abusive & Marinoff went out.

Friday, 25 June 1926

Up at 10. Hot, clear day. Marinoff does not return. Neither does she call up. I nearly go out of my mind. About 4 Donald [Angus] comes up. He telephones the Algonquin & finds she is there & I talk to her. She says she is through forever. If she is, what is there in life for me? I take a taxi down to the Algonquin but she has left. Then back to the house. Then to Reg Wallace's. The word is that she is not in. I wait there for an hour & then I keep my engagement with Bud [i.e., Rudolph] Fisher for dinner at his house. His wife, sister, & mother there. I am afraid I was a rather glum guest. At 9.30 I come home & find that Marinoff has been here, packed her bag & left. I walk the floor till 12.30 & finally manage a little sleep with hot milk & whiskey together.

Saturday, 26 June 1926

Up at 7. Still no word. I shall go mad. . . . At 11 I telephoned Reg & found that Marinoff had gone to the country. So I telephone Esther [Marinoff] & find she is there. Then I go to bank, to Consolidated Ticket Office. Then . . . at one I am off for Bergenfield [New Jersey] arriving slightly after 2. I go directly to the Marinoffs' house where I find Marinoff eating lunch with Esther. . . . We make up and after lunch take a long walk & pick daisies.[1] Jack [Marinoff] comes home for dinner. After dinner he drives us to the 42 St. Ferry. Home before 11, & in bed.

1. CVV seems finally to have learned his lesson, for a time at least. In her old age, Fania Marinoff averred that he had always been drunk at the time of the altercations and that after her threat to leave him, he was never abusive again. The daybooks call her memory into question at least once.

Tuesday, 29 June 1926

. . . Dinner in with Marinoff & then to see Mae West in *Sex* at 63rd Street Theatre. After we came home we made 8 quarts of raspberry brandy. In bed about one.

Thursday, 1 July 1926

. . . Went to Holliday Book Shop & the bank. Then met Marinoff at stage entrance of the New Amsterdam Theatre, where we saw Bill Robinson dance with his pupil, Linda, of the *Sunny* company. . . . Lunched at Algonquin with Marinoff . . . & Dudley Murphy. Then I went to see Lon Chaney in *The Trap* at the Colony Theatre. Home. Eddie Wassermann came in for cocktails. Dinner in with Marinoff. Then I met Dudley Murphy at Steinway Hall & . . . we go to Tony's on 49 St. for a drink. Dorothy Harris joins us. To the Park Lane Hotel to pick up Mal[colm] St. Clair.[1] He has gone to another place. We join him at Blumenthal's at 50 Central Park West. Lya de Putti[2] & her secretary there. Later Dudley, Dorothy, & I go to Mal's apartment at the Park Lane where we are found by Mrs. St. Clair and Jimmie, the chauffeur. Dudley plays roughly with Jimmie & butchers him. Mrs. & Mrs. St. Clair get sore. I go home at 3.

    1. Hollywood film director, responsible for *A Woman of the World*, based on *The Tattooed Countess*.
    2. Hollywood film star.

Friday, 2 July 1926

. . . In the afternoon Langston Hughes comes in & stays to dinner with us. In the evening Donald Angus. Marinoff goes out to read *Nubi in the Squall* for the author. At 11.30 Donald, Langston & I go to the *Paris* to join Bill Robinson's farewell party before he goes to London. . . . Alain Locke at the Paradise with a young white boy named Crown. Also Maxwell Bodenheim[1] & Norman Bel Geddes.[2] Place closes at 3 & we go home.

    1. Quintessential Greenwich Village writer, first a sardonic poet and later a proletariat novelist.
    2. Avant-garde stage designer.

Monday, 5 July 1926

Up at 8, after a fairly restless night. Clear & cool. Lunch in with Marinoff. Then we go to the zoo. Marinoff looks upon snakes with evident pleasure for the first time. Home & she gets dinner. We call up the Walter Whites & they came down. Sam Hoffenstein calls me & brings in Bud DeSylva[1] (met) and his wife. All of us, sans Marinoff, go to the New World where we meet Zora Hurston, Langston Hughes & John Davis (new literary editor of *The Crisis*) (met), go to Phila. Jimmie's for gin. . . . Home at 2.00 plastered. . . .

    1. B. G. DeSylva, prolific musical comedy lyricist.

Wednesday, 7 July 1926

Up at 8. Hot & clear. Rivetting: a 31 story hotel is being erected on the corner of 7th Ave. & 55 St. . . . Donald Angus comes in at 5, & stays to dinner. Then we go to a party at Nan Thurston's,[1] Corinne Barker's maid, at 145 W. 135th St. Miss Barker was there & a large company, mostly of cooks. Wonderful food, especially baked beans. . . . Sol Johnson, . . . Langston Hughes, Andrew Sissle,[2] Mrs. Eubie (Avis) Blake. Left about 3. . . .

    1. African American actress, popular in Harlem.
    2. The son of Noble Sissle, composer Eubie Blake's lyricist.

Saturday, 10 July 1926

Up at 8.30. Hot. The morning spent telephoning as to whether or not we shall go to West End to visit the Stettheimers & whether or not Marinoff is going to Rochester to play *Nubi in the Squall*.[1] Lunch in with Marinoff. She does not hear from the manager & so we take the Sandy Hook boat to Atlantic Highlands & the train to West End. She goes to the Stettheimers'. I stay with Frances Seligman. Eddie Wassermann (visiting the Stettheimers) on the porch when I arrive. . . . After dinner Marinoff comes over with Florine Stettheimer. . . . Frances & I motor back to the Stettheimers. In bed at 11. . . . A terrific storm.

    1. This play seems never to have been produced in New York.

Sunday, 11 July 1926

Up at nine. Breakfast in bed. Jack Sterner[1] & I motor to Asbury Park. Frances, Hugo [Seligman], Jack & I lunch at the Stettheimers'. In the afternoon we motor to Long Beach, Asbury Park, inspecting the Negro & white beach. . . .

    1. Marie and Albert Sterner had been connected with the Knoedler & Company Gallery, which had given Florine Stettheimer her first exhibition in 1916.

Monday, 12 July 1926

. . . Walked down to Eddie Wassermann's. Dinner there. Then we went to Lucky Roberts's musical show, *My Magnolia*, at the Mansfield. The place was crowded with people I know. . . . Eddie came home with me at beginning of second act (show was very bad) & stayed till 2.

Tuesday, 13 July 1926

. . . First bound copy of *Nigger Heaven*. I don't like the ink,[1] so I go to the office to consult Smith about a change. . . . Took a nap after lunch. Awakened by the arrival of Aaron Douglas[2] who came in to see his first published advertisements. At 5.30 Langston Hughes arrived. At 7.30 we go to Dorothy Harvey's for dinner. Caroline Reagan there. Langston reads some of his new poems. We come back to the house & everybody stays till 2.30.

    1. The ink used to stain the tops of the pages of the book, a common practice at the time.

    2. African American artist who designed the advertisements for *Nigger Heaven*.

Thursday, 15 July 1926

. . . This is the fourteenth anniversary of the night that Paul Thompson introduced me to Fania Marinoff. . . . In the afternoon went to *The Great Temptations* at the Winter Garden. Enjoyed Roseroy & Cappella, nude dancers, & Jack Benny, comedian. Lenore Ulric . . . came to dinner. Later Sidney Blackmer. After they had gone to the theatre we started out in the rain for *George White's Scandals*. Couldn't get in, so we went to see *Sunny*, with Marilyn Miller, Jack Donahoe, Clifton Webb, . . . etc. Although this has been running at the New Constantinople for a year the house was sold out & we were forced to buy tickets of a scalper for $13.20!

Tuesday, 20 July 1926

. . . Rita Romilly & Harry Block come for dinner & spend the evening. Marinoff goes to bed shortly before midnight & the rest of us go to The New World. See . . . a wonderful fat woman, Jeddie Peters, who sings "Go Back Where You Stayed Last Night." Ruth Trent sings "She's Got Good Bread." We go past The Royal Gardens to learn that Johnnie Cobb has left. Then to the Paradise. Then to a place for food. Home at 5.

Wednesday, 21 July 1926

Awakened by flies & heat at 9 o'clock. . . . At 4 I put on a shirt & a pair of trousers & went to see Eddie Wassermann who is in bed with a touch of flu. . . . Home for dinner. Lawrence Langner & Armina [Marshall]. Later Langston Hughes brought in Wallace Thurman[1] for me to meet. Rosamond

Johnson came in with a song of Langston's he has set to music & another song called "Bayou Moon." Also Taylor Gordon & Mrs. [J. Rosamond] Johnson. Everybody left before midnight & Marinoff & I went up to Lenore Ulric's—this is her birthday—and stayed till 4. Sidney Blackmer was there.

1. Arguably the most intellectual and perceptive of the young artists and writers of the Harlem Renaissance (a designation he mistrusted), editor of a notorious one-issue magazine, *Fire!!,* guaranteed to offend conservative black intellectuals, and author of two novels.

Thursday, 22 July 1926

Marinoff leaves for the country with the Langners. I have lunch alone & send Meda home. . . . Late in the afternoon Eddie Wassermann comes in. I call up Mal St. Clair & we go to his apartment at the Park Lane. . . . We . . . see a Russian soviet film, *Potemkin.* It is marvelous & cannot be released here. The March of the Cossacks shooting the crowd before them down a long staircase is especially fine. . . . We had dinner at the Maison Doria. Eddie & I go to Mal's. . . . Rudolph Valentino[1] there. . . . Eddie comes home with me & stays till 4.

1. Movie matinee idol.

Friday, 23 July 1926

Eddie Wassermann comes to dinner & after dinner we pick up Frances Seligman & go to a party given by Zora Hurston and Gertrude Bosley[1] at the latter's house, 404 St. Nicholas Ave. Wallace Thurman, Bruce Nugent, and John Davis, all drunk. Mrs. Randolph & Casca Bonds,[2] [Jules] Bledsoe, Harold Jackman, etc. [William] Patterson (Nora [Holt] Ray's friend) & Fred R. Moore, editor of the *N.Y. Age* (met). Home early.

1. Roberta Bosley, an African American model for sculptor Richmond Barthé, was later active in the James Weldon Johnson Literary Society.
2. An aspiring singer and one of A'Lelia Walker's minions.

Monday, 26 July 1926

. . . Langston Hughes dropped in at 5.30 to tell me that he had won the undergraduate prize of $150 offered by Witter Bynner. Dinner with Lawrence Langner at the Elysée. Then to opening of *Americana* at the Belmont. Talked with Geo. Gershwin & J. P. McEvoy. Then took Lawrence to Jack Harper's for a dinner & then home. He talks about himself & his two wives, Estelle & Armina. In bed about 2.

Wednesday, 28 July 1926

. . . I read Clement Wood's *Nigger*[1] & didn't think much of it.

> 1. This novel was published and reviewed a month before the release of *Nigger Heaven*, but there was no outcry in the black press over the title, nor over Ronald Firbank's *Prancing Nigger* in 1924.

Thursday, 29 July 1926

. . . We go to Miyako's for dinner. Then to see *Geo. White's Scandals* which bored me. Then we pick up Zora Hurston & go to The New World. Walter & Gladys White join us & of course Pedro, Ruth, Louise, etc.[1] J. P. McEvoy was there, came to our table, got interested in Zora, and went home with her. Helen Morgan[2] from *Americana* there (met), Gladys, Walter, & I go to The Nest for food, quiet.

> 1. Entertainers at The New World, which featured a variety floor show.
> 2. Cabaret singer best remembered as Julie in *Showboat*.

Wednesday, 4 August 1926

. . . Geo. Gershwin came for dinner & played some new tunes. He is anxious to write some more orchestral pieces, one an American dance rhapsody with Chabrier's *España* as a model, the other the adventures of an American in Paris. He left about 9, & I sat by myself & thought till 1.30. Fania goes to Great Neck to see Reg[ina] Wallace in *Love 'em, Cowboy,* an opening night with Reg.

Sunday, 8 August 1926

. . . Lunch in with Marinoff, after which we went to Rivoli to see Aileen Pringle[1] in *The Great Deception.* I had never seen her before. She looks old & is no shakes as an actress. The picture is pure bunk. Then dinner in & we retired early, I am reading back numbers of *The American Mercury.*

> 1. Silent movie star best known for her roles in films based on Elinor Glyn's overheated novels. She was considered the darling of the literati in the twenties. CVV knew her through Hergesheimer and the Knopfs. At that time she was involved in a long-distance love affair with H. L. Mencken. After 1953, when she retired to live in New York, she became CVV's intimate friend.

Monday, 16 August 1926

. . . Langston Hughes came in & later W. C. Handy. At 6.30 Marinoff & I start in a taxicab during a cloudburst for Harlem & Walter White's. After a drink there we all go to the New Symphony Club, 131 Street, for dinner—first time—place opened last Friday. Then to Alhambra to see Ethel Waters in *Miss Calico*. She sang "Dinah," Shake That Thing," "Heebie Jeebies," Blues, etc. In our box sat Booker T. Washington's son (met). Also in audience Langston Hughes & Wallace Thurman, Rosamond Johnson, Eddie Wassermann, . . . Butterbeans & Susie,[1] etc. Home at 11.30. We went back to see Ethel and have a long talk with her. . . .

    1. Husband-and-wife comedy act in African American vaudeville shows.

Tuesday, 17 August 1926

. . . Yesterday two more Negro papers, the *Pittsburgh Courier* & the *New York Amsterdam News*, refuse advertising of *Nigger Heaven* on account of the title. Walter White straightened out this situation & I go to . . . Knopf office this morning to tell . . . Sam Knopf who is disappointed by the advance sale. It's gone to about 9,000. Home for lunch alone. Paul & Essie Robeson came down in the afternoon to talk about my book & this affair. After they left at 4.30 I went to bed sick. Got up at 6.00 to receive Florine & Ettie Stettheimer who came to dinner with us. They left at 10.00, & we went to bed.

Thursday, 26 August 1926

. . . A flock of reviews, some good, some bad, all stupid. . . . I am fairly discouraged about *Nigger Heaven*. It's been out a week & I haven't heard a word about the second edition [i.e., printing]. Walter White comes to lunch. It is the second anniversary of our meeting. Later Rosamond Johnson & Langston Hughes come in. They want me to write a [musical] review with them. Donald Angus at 4.30. It is his birthday. Taylor Gordon sends me a review of *N.H.* from *Boston Transcript* (wonderful). . . . At 6 I call on Ellen Glasgow at the Chatham. She appears to be crazy about *Nigger Heaven* & we make a compact to review each other's books. Eddie Wassermann & Emily Stevens[1] come to dinner. In bed at 2.

    1. Actress whom CVV knew through Philip Moeller's play, *Sophie*, based on the life of eighteenth-century actress Sophie Arnould. She sought permission to have W. Somerset Maugham dramatize *The Tattooed Countess* for her.

Friday, 27 August 1926

. . . F[ranklin] P. A[dams] gives me a wonderful send-off in *The World*. . . . I have a hangover. Nora [Holt] Ray writes. Went to office, talked with Geo.

Stevens about the advertising & Sam Knopf about sales. About 12,500 sold. Second printing ordered today (5,000). Walked out with Geo. [Jean] Nathan who is crazy about the book. . . .

Thursday, 2 September 1926

. . . A lot of good reviews came, including Burton Rascoe's. . . . At 4.30 Langston Hughes who brought me an attack on *Nigger Heaven* in *N.Y. Age,* by Hubert Harrison.[1] Also Willard Johnson, & later Donald Angus. Donald & Willard stay to dinner. . . . Emily Stevens . . . call[s] up to tell me that Maugham cables that he hasn't time to dramatize *The* [*Tattooed*] *Countess.* At midnight Donald & I go to The Nest where Johnnie Corey, Mal Frazier, & Lizzie Miles[2] (met) sit at our table. . . .

> 1. Influential African American journalist and editor for the *Amsterdam News.*
> 2. African American New Orleans blues singer.

Friday, 3 September 1926

. . . Meda brings me more Negro papers, with more attacks. . . . While we are eating dinner Horace Liveright calls up & asks if he can bring Paul Robeson to dinner. It is arranged & they come. It seems they have been refused admittance at Ritz, Algonquin, & Italian Restaurant. . . .

Saturday, 4 September 1926[1]

Up at 8.15. Clear & cool. Wonderful letter from Arthur Spingarn anent *Nigger Heaven.* Finished reading *The Romantic Comedians* [by Ellen Glasgow]. Before lunch I went to the post office. Lunch in with Marinoff. I wrote first draft of review of Ellen's book, lie down for a while & then read *Smoke* [by Ivan Turgenev]. Victor Wittgenstein comes to take Marinoff out to dinner. Edna Kenton comes to dine with me. We talk about *Nigger Heaven* all the evening. She leaves at midnight. I go to bed about one & dream I am a Negro being chased in riots.

> 1. See facsimile on p. vi.

Wednesday, 8 September 1926

. . . I dream I am a Negro & being pursued.

Thursday, 9 September 1926

... A long letter from Charles Chesnutt on the use of "Negro" & "colored." Meda says there is a West Indian in Harlem sore at the use of the word monkey chaser in the book. ...

Saturday, 11 September 1926

... Alfred [Knopf] tells me that *Nigger Heaven* is selling better than *Show Boat* [by Edna Ferber] in N.Y. . . . . Richard Frye,[1] grown very tall, comes in. Meda finishes clearing & departs for a week's vacation. ...

    1. Teen-aged son of CVV's domestic, Meda Frye.

Tuesday, 14 September 1926

... Late in the afternoon Langston Hughes brought Gwendolyn Bennett[1] in. Later Donald Angus, Harry Block, Robert [Morss] Lovett. . . . Marinoff & I go to Eddie Wassermann's for dinner. After dinner Zora [Neale Hurston]. I get very drunk & abusive & finally pass out. Caroline Reagan & Langston come in later. Caroline, Langston, & Zora come home with us. In bed about 3.

    1. African American writer, painter, educator, and assistant editor for *Opportunity*.

Saturday, 18 September 1926

... In the afternoon Jack Harper arrived with a case of scotch. . . . At 7.30 we go to Zora Hurston's to dinner which she cooks. Caroline Reagan, Langston Hughes, Marinoff & [*a spiteful monster?*] named Johnson, Charlie Potts, Zora's cousin, & her brother Everett. Later Rosamond Johnson & a man named Grant. Marinoff left about 10 & I came home at 11. The elevator boy asks to borrow a book of mine. I give him something else. The proof of James Weldon Johnson's wonderful review [of *Nigger Heaven*] in *Opportunity* comes in.

Monday, 20 September 1926

... At 8.30 Caroline Reagan & Donald Angus stop for us & we go to the Lafayette . . . to see Ethel Waters's new review. The house is packed but chairs are placed in the aisle. Afterwards, with Earl Dancer,[1] we go back to see Ethel Waters. Then on to party at Small's, given by Langston Hughes & three other Lincoln boys to raise their tuition. Ethel Waters joins us & almost everybody in the colored world there & almost everybody talking about *Nigger Heaven.*

Saw Countee Cullen for the first time since he got back from abroad & met Clement Wood. (He introduced himself.) Home around 4.30.

    1. Ethel Waters's fiancé.

Wednesday, 22 September 1926

... At 4 Langston Hughes appears & later Jim Harris with a list of questions regarding *Nigger Heaven,* as apparently he is being pestered by people who say I have betrayed the race! All this upsets me as much as usual. Ellen Glasgow—a little more revolting than usual, "You say something about me & I'll say something about you"—came to dinner with Mrs. Carrie Duke of Richmond. They left at 9.30 & we retired but I slept badly on account of a rising temperature & Jim Harris's remarks and before dawn crept into Marinoff's bed.

Monday, 27 September 1926

... Read *Sea Fog* by J. S. Fletcher. Third printing of *Nigger Heaven* arrives. *Sea Fog* is interesting as a mystery story in which the criminals escape, and the mystery is never entirely solved. Dinner in with Marinoff. Then read a chapter of *The Blind Bow-Boy.* Then began to re-read *Bertram Cope's Year* [by Henry Blake Fuller], found it rather fussy. ...

Tuesday, 28 September 1926

... Finished *Bertram Cope's Year* before lunch & on many accounts admire it as much as (or more than) at the first reading.[1] ... At 3 o'clock Elmer Imes comes in to see me. He wants, I gather, money for his business. He asked for a letter to Lawrence Langner which I give him. We discuss *Nigger Heaven* & the Negro problem in general. He leaves about six & I dress for dinner. Ralph Barton & Rita Romilly here. Rita takes Marinoff & Ralph takes me to opening night of *Gentlemen Prefer Blondes.*[2] A host of compliments for *Nigger Heaven.* Zoë Akins tells me she thinks it is a very great book, that Edna Ferber agrees with her. Walter Wanger raves about it, George Gershwin says it's the talk of the town. ...

    1. CVV's 1922 assessment of Henry Blake Fuller's novel, reprinted in *Excavations* (1926), suggests that discretion had bade him to allude only elliptically to its homosexual subtext.

    2. Based on the novel by Anita Loos, which Barton had illustrated and CVV had favorably reviewed.

Wednesday, 29 September 1926

... A letter from Lewis Baer informs me that the management of Small's doesn't want me at W. C. Handy's party! Work over *Second Book of American Negro Spirituals.*[1] ... I am cross & distrait. ...

    1. CVV was preparing a review of James Weldon Johnson's book.

Friday, 1 October 1926

... Lunch in with Marinoff. Then I go for phonograph records, etc. To bank, to Algonquin where I see Edward Knoblauch who speaks of dramatizing *Nigger Heaven.* Home. ... Late in afternoon James Weldon Johnson & Walter White come in. Afterwards Helen Westley & Philip Moeller. Emily Clark Balch came to dinner & after dinner she expresses a desire to go to Harlem & as I have a desire to see if it is really true if I am banned from Small's Paradise, I decide to go up. We pick up Zora [Neale Hurston] & meet several people at her house. ... Then to Walter White's. Then to Small's Paradise where ... several ... greeted me with enthusiasm. Then to The Nest where I saw Johnnie Corey & Lizzie Miles. Had a wonderful time. Home about 3.

Sunday, 3 October 1926

... Donald Angus comes up & later Langston Hughes with a mss. copy of *Fine Clothes to the Jew,* his new book of poems, which he is dedicating to me. Marinoff is supposed to go to a big dinner at the Astor with Rita Romilly but Rita is so late that Marinoff refuses to go & she has dinner at home. Donald, Langston & I go to Miyako's. Then back to the house. Langston leaves about 11, Donald about 12. I sleep badly. There is a rising temperature & I toss & dream.

Thursday, 7 October 1926

... Marinoff in bed for the day with a bad cold. She is cross as hell & twice as aggravating. ... Late in the afternoon, Hugh Walpole, Gerald Haxton, Somerset Maugham, Miguel Covarrubias, Paul Robeson come in. Marinoff has dinner alone at home. I go to Knopfs. Mr. & Mrs. Frank Swinnerton,[1] Ralph Barton & Mencken. Ralph drives me home at midnight in his new car.

    1. Popular English satirical novelist and critic.

Friday, 8 October 1926

... To Gotham Hotel where I spent an amusing hour & a half with Somerset Maugham & Gerald Haxton. Home & dinner with Marinoff. After dinner Donald came in & we went to Harlem to see a very amusing fashion show at Harlem Casino. . . . About 3 Eddie Wassermann, Donald, Dorothy Harris & I go to Small's Paradise. Cherry the manager wants to give a banquet for me.

Thursday, 14 October 1926

... I read Willa Cather's *My Mortal Enemy*, with warm amazement for its uncanny perception. Then I join Somerset Maugham at the Gotham & Gerald Haxton. . . .

Tuesday, 19 October 1926

... At office I talk to Harry Block & then to Blanche Knopf who informs me that sixth printing (3,000) of *Nigger Heaven* has been ordered. This with the fifth printing (5,000) brings the number printed to 34,000. 25,500 have already been sold. To Ralph Barton's for lunch, 10 East 53 St. Then to see Fannie Hurst. Walked home, meeting Barney Gallant. Then went to see Eddie Wassermann. He is despondent & talks of suicide. . . .

Friday, 22 October 1926

... In a highly nervous state. I wish I could write. I looked at magazines, etc. . . . Grace Johnson comes in to take Marinoff to the Y.W.C.A. to see Queen Marie [of Romania]. Gwendolyn Bennett brings in Frank Horne (met).[1] Alfred & Blanche Knopf came to dinner. They seemed at dagger points. Marinoff left about 10 to go to a party at Nickolas Muray's. I go to bed about 12.

    1. African American poet, then unpublished.

Monday, 25 October 1926

... I take Langston's mss, *Fine Clothes to the Jew*, to Blanche Knopf. . . . Then to. . . . Aeolian Hall for records & home. Negotiations begin to get Taylor Gordon to sing Louis Gruenberg's version of "The Creation" [by James Weldon Johnson] at a League of Composers concert, conducted by [Serge] Koussevitzky. He refuses. . . . Taylor Gordon & Rosamond Johnson come in about 4.30. They sing for Somerset Maugham, who arrives later, also Gerald Haxton, Rudolph Fisher, Langston Hughes, & Donald Angus, later Reg Wallace who comes to dinner. She & Marinoff go to theatre together. Harry

Block & Donald Angus come to see me. At 10 we go to Ralph Barton's to see the films he has taken this summer.[1] Blanche Knopf there & Zena Naylor (Ralph's apparently latest), Captain Douglas,[2] later Alfred Knopf & Marinoff. Home about 1.30.

1. Barton was gathering footage of various people in the arts to turn into the home movie version of *Camille* he was making with Anita Loos. Its cast of characters drops as many names as CVV ever did in recording guest lists at parties.

2. Douglas and Naylor were father and illegitimate daughter, and they often traveled together. After Carlotta Monterey left Barton, having discovered him in flagrante delicto with Ruth Goldbeck, he had several minor affairs.

Tuesday, 26 October 1926

. . . Reading Ernest Boyd's *Maupassant* (finished it). It contains nothing new or startling and is not a very good book. . . . Read "The Blue Hotel," an amazing story by Stephen Crane. Alfred Knopf calls up to tell me that Shapiro Bernstein Co. is sueing for infringing on their copyrights of "Shake That Thing" & "If You Hadn't Gone Away" in *Nigger Heaven*.[1] The penalty, Alfred says, of success. Eddie Wassermann, extremely dull, comes in for cocktails. Marinoff & I dine alone & go to bed. I read most of my *Interpreters*[2] & a good deal of *Borzoi 1925* before I fell asleep.

1. CVV had innocently copied down the lyrics to these songs from phonograph recordings and inserted them—along with others—in *Nigger Heaven*.

2. CVV's collection of essays about a number of opera singers (1920).

Thursday, 28 October 1926

Up at 9. A telephone call from Alfred took me to the office. We spent the morning discussing copyright aspects of *Nigger Heaven* with Ben Stern,[1] Alfred & Sam Knopf. Lunch at the Ritz with Zena Naylor & Capt. Douglas. Home. Expect Alfred to call me after his father has seen Bernstein but I don't hear till late in the afternoon when Alfred calls up to say that Bernstein wants money. I get dressed & go up town . . . to meet Mrs. Mary McLeod Bethune, head of Dayton (Fla.) Industrial School. She is a remarkable woman & I have a remarkable hour with her. Saw Frank Horne's mother. He was there too. Then to dinner at Grace & James Weldon Johnson's, Marinoff too. Then to a party at Alfred Knopf's. Rosamond Johnson & Taylor Gordon sang, also Judith Gauthier (Eva's sister) sang Esquimaux songs. Mr. & Mrs. Sam Knopf, Rudolph, Pearl, & June Fisher, . . . Ralph Barton, Somerset Maugham, Gerald Haxton, Ettie Stettheimer. . . . Walter White, Benno Moisewitsch, George Gershwin, etc.

1. Legal counsel and lawyer for Alfred A. Knopf, Inc.

Friday, 29 October 1926

Up at 8 & at Knopf office at 9. Conference: . . . After a long & stormy talk dominated by Sam, losing his patience & yelling like a bull, we decided to pay Bernstein something to shut up & ask Langston Hughes to rewrite the songs in the book. I spend hours trying to get Langston on the phone at Lincoln [University]. Lunch in with Marinoff. Can't get Langston at Lincoln. I try Philadelphia. We dine at Fannie Hurst's. Phil Moeller, Edna Ferber (who on this occasion behaved surprisingly like a gentlewoman). . . .

Saturday, 30 October 1926

. . . Langston appears at 7 o'clock, & after dinner begins work immediately on the songs for *Nigger Heaven*. He has completed rough drafts of *all* the songs before we go to bed.[1] He stays with us.

> 1. Hughes wrote verses to fit, line for line, into the page plates of the novel so that sales need not be interrupted.

Sunday, 31 October 1926

. . . Langston works all day on songs for *Nigger Heaven* & about 5 o'clock he is done, & we go to a party at Frances Seligman's new apartment, 45 Park Avenue. Hugo & Susie Seligman, Eddie Wassermann, Florine & Ettie Stettheimer, Jack Sterner, Victor Wittgenstein, etc. Then to the Charles Nail Thomas's[1] for supper. Marinoff (who read *Twelfth Night* over the radio at 6 o'clock) joined us here. Rebecca West, Walter & Gladys White & a man. With the Whites & Langston we went about 9 to James Weldon Johnson's where I met Clarence Darrow.[2] Jack & Grayce Nail, & old Mr. Nail, Newman Levy,[3] etc. James Weldon read, Darrow read, & Langston read. Arthur Spingarn & Langston came home with us & Langston leaves for Lincoln.

> 1. Founder and proprietor of Underwood & Underwood, Photographers, a company responsible for many pictures of entertainers in the twenties.
>
> 2. Celebrated criminal lawyer, notably remembered because of his defense in the Tennessee Scopes trial over teaching evolution and in the Leopold and Loeb murder trial.
>
> 3. Writer of light verse and (with Edna Ferber) playwright, also a practicing lawyer and assistant district attorney for New York County.

Tuesday, 2 November 1926

Up at 7, a mood of anxiety. Cloudy, but later the sun comes out. Spent a worried morning. At 1.30 I call up Mr. Mills.[1] He hasn't seen Mr. Bernstein yet, promises to call me up later. Out for a walk, and up to the post office. Home, and cocktails! Paul Robeson drops in. Mills calls up to say lowest figure Mr. Bernstein will accept is $2,500. . . . Then George Gershwin comes in at my request but has no good advice. . . .

    1. E. C. Mills, head of ASCAP.

Wednesday, 3 November 1926

. . . See Mills at 10. He is very pleasant but says Mr. Bernstein unreasonably insists on his $2,500. I tell him I'll have to think about it & go back to office where another long conference ensues, this time including Ben Stern, the lawyer. Back to see Mills who thinks we can settle if I hand him a cheque for $1,500 to give to Bernstein. I return to the office for further discussion & send him the cheque. Then I come home & proceed to get drunk. . . .

Thursday, 4 November 1926

. . . Arranged Langston Hughes's inserts for printer & sent them over to Alfred. . . . Another day of horror & nightmare. E. C. Mills does not call me up. . . . Alain Locke comes in at 4.30 with some pieces of African sculpture. Robert [Morss] Lovett comes in. Paul Robeson & Fredi Washington,[1] Zena Naylor, Captain Douglas, Rita Romilly, Regina Wallace. I run over to the Gotham for five minutes to say goodbye [to Somerset Maugham]. Elmer & Nella [Larsen] Imes come for dinner. After dinner Rebecca West & Conrad Bercovici appear. Later Lawrence Langner & Armina & Mr. & Mrs. DuBose Heyward.[2] They leave about 2.

    1. African American actress who because of her pigmentation was unable to pursue a successful career. Except for a role in *Imitation of Life*, a film based on a Fannie Hurst novel, she was rejected as too light to play black characters, and she was denied the right to play white characters. Her sister Isabel Washington, also an entertainer, retired to marry Adam Clayton Powell.

    2. Authors of *Porgy* and other novels and plays with black subject matter.

Friday, 5 November 1926

. . . Up at 8. Marinoff gets up about 9 & is disagreeable as hell. I fuss with papers, etc. At 11.30 Mr. Mills telephones me he has my release from Shapiro Bernstein. I go to office first, talk to Blanche & Sam Knopf & then to Mills's office, get release, & take it back to Blanche. Home for lunch, a wreck. . . . Blanche tells me that Sam Knopf insists that Langston Hughes change the name of *Fine Clothes to the Jew*, a pretty piece of impertinence, this.

Saturday, 6 November 1926

. . . I went to Harlem for phonograph records, newspapers, & finally to see Clara Smith[1] just back from tour. She was wonderful & introduced me to her husband /?/ Charles Wesley, a baseball player on the Memphis colored team. . . . Dinner in with Marinoff. Then we went to Nik Muray's studio to see a private showing of *Greed,* the film after *McTeague.* . . . Afterwards went to Daniel Frohman's[2] apartment in the Lyceum . . . & left Marinoff & came home. In bed by 2.

    1. One of the three singers (with Bessie Smith and Ethel Waters) about whom CVV had published an appreciative essay on blues singers in *Vanity Fair* the previous year. He had known her for more than a year by this time.
    2. Theater director who had often featured Fania Marinoff in his productions.

Sunday, 7 November 1926

. . . Worked all day on papers, letters, etc. I'm a week behind on account of Bernstein case. . . . A'Lelia Walker called up endearingly.[1] At 4.30 Eddie Wassermann comes in. Later Donald Angus. Donald & I go to dinner at the Symphony Club on 131 St. & find this place, which only opened two months ago, closed. So we dine at Johnny Brent's on 7th Ave. Then we go over to Clara Smith's & spend a quiet evening at home with her & her husband, and a couple of others who drift in & out. Clara makes some extraordinarily sagacious remarks about *Nigger Heaven,* sings a bit to a player piano, talks seriously, etc. Clara crazy about children. Home at 11. Rain.

    1. In *Nigger Heaven,* "Adora Boniface" is based on A'Lelia Walker but not in an entirely flattering way.

Wednesday, 10 November 1926

. . . The Bernstein fiasco cost us $2,500: $1,500 to Bernstein, $400 to Allan Davis (lawyer), $500 to Ben Stern (lawyer), $100 to Langston Hughes.[1] Marinoff upset because she does not get a chance at a Fannie Hurst play. Edna Kenton & Mabel Reber drop in. Essie Robeson drops in. After they have gone I go to 42 St. for a haircut. Find English edition of *Nigger Heaven* when I get home. We dine at . . . Arthur M. Reis's[2] with Mr. & Mrs. Lawrence Langner & Mr. & Mrs. Walter White. Then we go to Mr. Eustace Seligman's[3] to hear Walter White give a talk on the New Negro before a crowd of intellectual rich Jews. I arranged this. Home at 11.30.

    1. To approximate the purchasing power of these figures in 2003, one must add at least an additional 0. Hughes's "honorarium" was worth more than $1,000.

2. Executive owner of A. Reis & Company, manufacturer of men's fashionable clothing.

3. American economist, a Stettheimer relative.

Sunday, 14 November 1926

. . . In the afternoon I went to the Colony Theatre to hear the Vitaphone & was really amazed to find out how good it is. To hear Al Jolson sing & to see him appear simultaneously on the screen is quite thrilling. Home. Langston Hughes comes to dinner, Marinoff cooking. Then I take him to Paul Robeson's concert at the Comedy. . . . Home at 1.30.

Tuesday, 16 November 1926

. . . I have a hangover. Read Susan Glaspell's really remarkable biography of Jig [i.e., George Cramden] Cook called *The Road to the Temple.* . . . Later Sartur Andrie,[1] a young Russian friend of Langston [Hughes]'s who wants to go on the stage, comes in to consult Marinoff. Rita Romilly here. At 7 Marinoff & I go to dine at Zora Hurston's where we find Annie Nathan Meyer![2] whom I have not seen in years & whom I hope never to see again. She has, it appears, through her endless loquacity, an inferiority complex about being a Jew. . . .

1. Sartur Andrzejewski, Hughes's best friend in high school in Cleveland, Ohio.

2. White author of an earnest play about African Americans, *Black Souls.*

Thursday, 18 November 1926

. . . James Weldon Johnson came in, to discuss <u>who</u> is to go in my place to talk about *Nigger Heaven* for the Twentieth Century Club in Boston.[1] Read Frances Newman's *[The] Hard-Boiled Virgin,* an exposé of a cheap, meretricious, small mean soul. . . .

1. A meeting called to discuss the novel, at which CVV himself was not welcome.

Saturday, 20 November 1926

. . . The sixth edition of *Nigger Heaven* arrives. Sam Knopf has inserted a few pages of Langston's corrections without consulting me. The result is rather messy. I go to the office & raise hell & am backed loyally by Alfred & Blanche. Also this morning arrives W. E. B. Du Bois's dirty attack on the book in *The Crisis.*[1] . . .

1. In *Crisis,* Du Bois recommended that his readers burn *Nigger Heaven.*

Wednesday, 24 November 1926

. . . Just before lunch the sheets of seventh printing of *Nigger Heaven* arrived and I examined it without finding any errors. Lunch in with Marinoff & then went to bed again. At 3 I got up & went to Landry's Phonograph Shop to order an electric winder for my phonograph. Then to bank, to Eastman Co. for pictures, for flowers & home. Had some cocktails & dinner in with Marinoff. Then we started for Harlem (stopping for Blanche Knopf) & Clara Smith's. When we got there, find her & her husband. Later Taylor Gordon, Paul Robeson, Germaine Tailleferre, Georges Lepape, Boutet de Monvel, Ralph Barton.[1] Later Porter Grainger (met) arrived & played for Clara to sing. She was marvellous. . . . Home at 3, *soused.*

    1. Fashion designers LePape and Boutet de Monvel had introduced French pianist-composer Tailleferre to Barton shortly before.

Tuesday, 30 November 1926

. . . A'Lelia [Walker] gives a party at her studio for 15 guests from the West who are staying with her at Irvington. It was a highly dicty[1] affair. Swell Harlem was there & a great many from down town. I ran into Dr. DuBois for the first time since his attack in *The Crisis* & we chatted amiably. Osbert Sitwell,[2] Ralph Barton & Germaine Tailleferre who announced they were to be married next Saturday, Geo. Lepape, Muriel Draper, . . . Boutet de Monvel, T. R. Smith, Harry Block, Julian Messner, Best-Maugard, James & Grace Johnson, Rosamond & Nora Johnson, Lloyd & Edna Thomas, Essie Robeson, Minnie Patterson, . . . Harold Jackman, Gladys & Walter White, Geraldyn Dismond, . . . Jim & Dorothy Harris. . . . Home at 4.30.

    1. Black slang for high-toned.
    2. Visiting English writer.

Wednesday, 1 December 1926

. . . Lunch in with Marinoff. Then we went shopping for Xmas presents. . . . Then to a party Eddie Wassermann gives for A'Lelia Walker & her fifteen honor guests from Cleveland. . . . Everybody got pie-eyed. . . .

Saturday, 4 December 1926

Up at 8.30. Rain. Hangover. . . . Then to Gershwin-D'Alvarez concert, at Hotel Roosevelt. D'Alvarez sings some of his songs & he plays for the first time his five preludes. Marinoff & I sit next to Rita Romilly & as they have quarrelled they don't speak. Both stay to see George & Marguerite. The latter I kiss for the first time since I insulted her. . . . Home. Nella [Larsen] Imes comes in to bring mss. of her novel, "Cloudy Amber"[1] (read this after dinner & find it in many ways remarkable), Dorothy Peterson with her. Dinner in with Marinoff. Then I go to a party at Arthur Spingarn's new house on 9 St. James & Grace Johnson, Donald Angus, . . . and a lot of others.

    1. Published as *Quicksand* (Knopf, 1928).

Monday, 6 December 1926

. . . Donald Angus came to dinner, chop suey! After dinner we played records a while & then went to Clara Smith's, very drunk, & then The Nest. . . . Clara wanted me to get Tootie (her husband) a new winter overcoat! Home about 3. Donald came up & we played more records, especially "I'm Coming, Virginia," which I bought today.

Friday, 10 December 1926

. . . Very depressed. Wondering if I can write again. . . . In the evening after finishing my detective story[1] I got an idea for a novel, of a colored girl in love with a white boy & her family forces her to marry a black. This seems good at 10 P.M. after some cocktails

    1. *The Missing Chancellor,* by J. S. Fletcher.

Saturday, 11 December 1926

but not so good today. Still snowy, dreary & slushy. . . . Read Maxwell Bodenheim's *Ninth Avenue* in which I am portrayed as Paul Vanderlin. Ben Hecht is Ben Helgin, & Bodenheim himself as Max Oppendorf. Not very convincing towards the end. . . .

Thursday, 16 December 1926

. . . At five James Weldon Johnson called to talk to me about the preface that I am to write for new edition of *The Autobiography of an Ex-Coloured Man.* A little later Edna Thomas came in with Dorothy West & Helene Johnson (met).[1] . . .

    1. Two young African American poets.

Monday, 20 December 1926

. . . In the afternoon I read *Little Pitchers* [by Isa Glenn], a great book. Robert [Morss] Lovett comes in for cocktails. At 7.30 we go to dinner at the Arthur

Richmans' with the Edouard Bourdets. Later we go to Small's Paradise. . . .
Home at 4 & have a scrap with Marinoff till five. Very drunk.

Friday, 24 December 1926

. . . Working on Christmas all day. Giving to the Boys, etc.[1] Sent telegrams &
flowers in the morning. Lunch in with Marinoff. Then down to the Knopfs
& Harlem with gifts. Paul Robeson comes in in the afternoon. He is, I'm
afraid, becoming insufferably conceited. Ziegfeld has offered him $1,500 to
appear in *Show Boat*. We dine at Frances Seligman's at 45 Park Avenue. . . .
Then we go to a party at the Stettheimers'. Stella Wanger,[2] Marcel Duchamp,
the Steichens, Alfred Seligsberg, Victor Wittgenstein, Muk de Jari, Philip
Moeller, Marie Sterner, Bobby & B[eatrice] Locher, Henry McBride, Best-
Maugard, etc. Home about 1.30.

> 1. Doormen and elevator staff at 150 West 55th Street.
> 2. Another Stettheimer sister, the mother of film producer Walter Wanger.

Saturday, 25 December 1926

Up at 10. Bright, clear, & warm. Busy with Christmas letters, telephone, etc.,
in the morning. Walter White arrives about 1.30 & talks for an hour. At 3,
Arthur & Madeline Richman, Ralph & Germaine [Tailleferre] Barton for
dinner. A suckling pig, champagne. Hannah Ellis[1] comes to help Meda &
Richard Frye comes to dinner. After dinner Edouard & Mrs. Bourdet, Georges
LePape, Blanche & Alfred Knopf, Lauritz & Mrs. Melchoir,[2] T. R. Smith,
Donald Angus, Mercedes de Acosta, Frances Seligman, Hugh Walpole and
probably others come in for cocktails. Later Jim & Dorothy Harris, who stay
till 10.30 when I take Eddie [Wassermann] to a party at John Nail's. Grace &
James Weldon Johnson. . . . When I leave with the Spingarns & Eddie it is
rainy & hard to get a taxi. So we go to Small's & pushed to get attention. . . .

> 1. Edward Wassermann's housekeeper and cook, hired for the evening.
> 2. Danish heldentenor at the Metropolitan Opera House.

Sunday, 26 December 1926

Up at 10, with a hangover & remorse. . . . In the afternoon Caroline Reagan
comes in & tells me she is having an affair with Marcel Duchamp. Paul Green,[1]
the South Carolinian, is supposed to call at 3. At 4 his wife telephones that
he can't make it. . . . We have supper at 7 & I am in bed at 8. Have horrible
nightmare & nearly freeze

> 1. Pulitzer Prize–winning white dramatist for *In Abraham's Bosom*, with an all-
> black cast.

Monday, 27 December 1926

but stay in bed till 8. It is very cold & snowy. Mabel Luhan calls up at 9 to make arrangements about my going to New Mexico with her. . . . About 11 I go to Algonquin to arrange about my passage.¹ . . . At 5 I go to join Blanche Knopf & told Alfred I didn't think I'd be having a novel in August. We talk about the possibility of an illustrated edition of *Nigger Heaven*. . . .

    1. CVV was going to Hollywood via Chicago and Santa Fe.

Wednesday, 29 December 1926

. . . Marinoff takes me to *Twentieth Century* & I leave for Chicago at 2.45, very depressed. Wrote a letter to Marinoff & then read William C. Bullitt's *It's Not Done*, a very bad book but with some moments & portraits of . . . Cavaliere,¹ & Bob Chanler. . . .

    1. Lina Cavalieri, a beautiful soprano who won notoriety for her naughty songs in Roman cabarets. Later she sang at the Metropolitan Opera House and with the Manhattan Opera Company.

Thursday, 30 December 1926

. . . Saw Ralph [Van Vechten] in Chicago. Called . . . at Marshall Fields where I signed a lot of books. . . . Ethel Waters is capturing the town. . . . Tried to get Ethel Waters on the phone but only got Earl Dancer's brother . . . and then went to Orpheus to call on Bill Robinson. They made me wait for him downstairs. Finally saw Bill for a few minutes. Then to Ralph's. . . . At 7.10 John drove me to *Santa Fe* Station & found Tony & Mabel Luhan on train. We left for West. I talked with them till 10. To bed about 11, slept badly & dreamed of . . . gardens.

Friday, 31 December 1926

. . . All day through long, lone, uninspired Kansas, the prairie. By western time I retired at 9.30. I woke at 1.30 . . . to see the new year in. Stars everywhere, and at 7 in the morning a pale new moon over my right shoulder. We are now in New Mexico.

1927

"Then to my house . . . where
we have a very gay party
& everybody takes off
their clothes."

Van Vechten stopped for two weeks in New Mexico, en route to California, to see his old friend Mabel Dodge Luhan in Taos, and newer ones in Santa Fe, before going to Hollywood for an extended stay. At the Ambassador Hotel, in film studios, and at parties in private homes, he was surrounded by movie stars in a world he found as fatuous as it was artificial, and he said so in four articles about the place for *Vanity Fair.* But he sealed a new friendship there, with the mascot of the literati, film actress Aileen Pringle. After suffering temporarily from writer's block as a result of the notoriety surrounding *Nigger Heaven,* Van Vechten began a new novel but with difficulty—about Hollywood—called *Spider Boy.* Also at this time, through the death of his brother, he inherited a million dollars in trust and was therefore absolved of ever having to write again.

Saturday, 1 January 1927

Awakened about 1.30 by puffing of engines—three—to pull the cars up the mountains. Looked out the window on bright stars, everywhere. Slept again to waken to see a frail new moon at 7 over my right shoulder—I wished Fania everything. . . . About 10 we landed in Lamy & sat in the sun for an hour looking at the snow capped mountains after inspecting the [Fred] Harvey Spanish Hotel. Then to Santa Fe. . . . Lunch there & then to Ida Rauh's, where I met her son & Andrew's. Saw Andrew Dasburg, Arthur [Davison] Ficke, Gladys Ficke, and Dorothy Harvey, called up Hal [i.e., Witter] Bynner. Then we motored up the Rio Grande, 75 miles to Taos. Met Miss Brett ([D. H.] Lawrence's ex-secretary)[1] and Loren Mozley of Albuquerque.[2] Dinner at the house, then to my room.[3] Mozley & I talked till 12, then went out. Bitter cold—slept under rugs as well as blankets. . . .

1. English painter and writer, Honorable Dorothy Brett, initially a member of the D. H. Lawrence entourage in Taos who stayed on after Lawrence and his wife, Frieda, moved to Italy.
2. Taos and Albuquerque painter and lithographer.
3. Mabel Dodge Luhan's house in Taos.

Sunday, 2 January 1927

About 8.15 Manuel came in to make a fire in my room. Bright sunny outside, snow on the ground & cold, breakfast with Tony [Luhan] & Mozley. . . . Mabel [Dodge Luhan] has done her adobe house in the luxury & beauty that she always continues to invest her houses in, a great bank of a plateau surrounded by mountains. After lunch we drive out to Tony's Pueblo & I get a superb view & introduces me to his relatives. We come home. I work a little on the revisions of *The Tattooed Countess* for the cheap edition.[1] Then we go to the Taos Inn for dinner—the servants going out—and to an awful movie: Barthelmess in *Ransom's Folly*. Home, build a fire in my room and retire by 10, all the windows closed.

1. Gosset & Dunlap had purchased the rights to reprint CVV's novel. The word *cheap* did not carry automatically pejorative overtones in the twenties; Knopf used it openly in his advertisements for inexpensive reprints of books. A "cheap" person, on the other hand, was miserly or vulgar.

Monday, 3 January 1927

. . . Sunny & cold but warm out in the sun. Later drive to town with Tony, go to post office, drug store, etc., & all have lunch at the Inn because the cook is sick & doesn't appear . . . but as we leave . . . we walk into Dr. Martin[1] who invites us to drive with him to Arroyo Secco, seven miles away, where he has to see a patient. We go, Mrs. Martin driving through mud & slush, to this dirty little Mexican town. Back to have tequila at the doctor's, then home. Conchia the cook is ill. Mabel is ill. Tony has gone to a wedding feast in Ranchos. Just as Brett & I start walking to the Inn, Indians appear in the courtyard. They have come to dance. . . . We have an hour of dance & song & then go to bed.

> 1. The first Taos resident that Mabel Dodge Sterne (not yet Luhan) met, called only "Doc," apparently an eccentric general practitioner who ministered to the Taos Pueblo. He assisted the Sternes in finding local property to rent and then purchase.

Thursday, 6 January 1927

. . . After lunch we drove out to the Pueblo & saw the Buffalo Dance, principally remarkable for the surroundings. The brilliant shawls & blankets, the groupings on the pueblo roofs, etc. Home. Mabel has a thing & does not want to go to dinner with us at the Inn—the cook is still away—because Tony goes back to the Pueblo for dinner & the evening. The evening is very entertaining, Mabel in a tantrum. She suggests that Ida [Rauh Dasburg] & Hal [Bynner] go home. Hal, Andrew [Dasburg], Ida & I have a talk in Hal's room. Tony, it "appears," is jealous of guests & misbehaving!

Friday, 7 January 1927

. . . Lunch with Mabel & Tony at . . . a bad Mexican Hotel, chile con carne. In the afternoon I return to my room, Ida gives Mabel a good talking to, & Mabel becomes more agreeable. Brett keeps a bottle of moonshine & we have a party before supper at the Inn. After supper a big Indian dance at the studio. . . . After the party a drunk at Ken Adams's[1] studio—Victor Higgins,[2] Robert McAlmon,[3] Andrew, Hal, and Everett Marcy. I got very drunk & Loren again begins to scream. In bed at 3.

> 1. New Mexico artist located in Taos.
> 2. Texas artist located in Taos.
> 3. American editor and writer, married to English novelist "Bryher," Winifred Ellermann.

Monday, 10 January 1927

Awakened at 7.30 by Everett Marcy who wanted to build my fire. I told him to let Manuel do it. This "discombobulating" (maid's word) youth, conceited enough to want to call butterflies to himself all the time, goes away to N.Y. this morning. . . .

Tuesday, 11 January 1927

. . . Mabel sends for me to tell me that she is going through a change of life. Possibly this is true, but it sounds like a Tenth Day explanation of her moodiness. Breakfast in the kitchen—a busy one—with Brett and Andrew writing letters, etc. . . . Telegram from Blanche [Knopf] about trip to Hollywood. A solemn dinner: Mabel is ill. Loren Mozley appears & takes Andrew & me to a meeting of the Taos Association Club. . . . Met . . . Miss Arnold, the U.S. gov. nurse at the Pueblo who tells us about syphilis, meningitis, etc. Then Andrew & I stop in at Ken Adams's for a drink. Victor Higgins appears. Andrew descends into the cellar under my room for a quart of Brett's moonshine. . . .

Wednesday, 12 January 1927

. . . Nine telegrams from Blanche. Mabel is still in bed. . . . Andrew seeks more moonshine in Brett's several kegs under the floor in my room. In bed about 11.

Thursday, 13 January 1927

Andrew & I get up very early, say goodbye to everybody and are off. . . . A beautiful drive across the frozen mesa in the fog—cold, sharp. I shall not soon forget an encounter with a grand flock of sheep on the table-land, in the snow layers & mist on the blue mountains. We had a blow-out on the Grand Canyon of the Rio Grande but arrived, at La Fonda, in Santa Fe where I am stopping, at 1 o'clock. Andrew lunched with me. I bought my ticket for Hollywood. . . . Cocktails at Dorothy Harvey's adobe. Home at 6. To Hal Bynner's for dinner. . . . Home at 4 A.M.

Monday, 17 January 1927

Up at 7 to catch the [Fred] Harvey Bus at Lamey at 8.40. Then the train, through New Mexican desert all day. . . . As usual on a train I do not talk to a soul. I go to bed at 7 & am asleep by 7.30.

Tuesday, 18 January 1927

. . . Until noon we passed through desert country; after San Bernadino a succession of orange groves. Los Angeles at 2.15. Then began my two hour drive to the hotel[1] & I was introduced to Los Angeles distances. . . . Presently, while I am unpacking, Scott & Zelda Fitzgerald call on me. He is here working. As soon as I am dressed I go to see them & have a drink. At 7 I start on the fifteen mile taxi drive (the fare is $5.10!) to Aileen Pringle's at Santa Monica where I dine with her & Blanche Knopf & Adrian Grahame.[2] He takes me home at 11.30.

1. The Ambassador, where CVV stayed in La Replea, one of the small cottages there.

2. As "Adrian," Grahame had designed costumes for the annual *Greenwich Village Follies.*

Wednesday, 19 January 1927

...At 7 I start off for Joseph Schildkraut's, passing through Hollywood, where I dine, and after dinner he asked me to go with him to Los Angeles opening of *An American Tragedy.*[1] At the door an astonishing sight: Kleig lights & megaphones, announcing the arrivals & taking their pictures. I see a great many people I know & meet Pauline Starke[2] & Patsy [Ruth] Miller.[3] Pepe [i.e., Schildkraut] & I go to a party at Eddie Mayer's in a lovely villa on top of this wooded hill, with views in every direction....

1. Film based on Theodore Dreiser's novel of the same title.

2. A silent film star whom CVV later described to Marinoff as "a moron but very picturesque and very nice," 1 June 1927.

3. Another silent film star. Nearly everyone CVV met was connected to moviemaking in one way or another; only those of more than passing interest are individually identified.

Thursday, 20 January 1927

Up at 8.30. Rain. Breakfast in room and dress rapidly. At 10.30 Joseph Schildkraut comes for me in his car to take me to the Cecil [B.] De Mille studios to see the filming of the earthquake scene of *The King of Kings.* ... The scene with the falling rocks & dirt, the wind, the cleft earth, etc., very thrilling.[1] Then ... to Metro-Goldwyn studios where we look in vain for Aileen [Pringle], but ... we meet Pauline Starke with Donald Freeman.[2] Rain in torrents. Home. Eddie [Mayer] & I start drinking. Scott Fitzgerald arrives with a boy named [Christopher] Gray, who later disappears. Aileen arrives from the studio in makeup with Cedric[3] & Blanche [Knopf] & we all have dinner in my room. When the gals go we cross the yard to Carmel Myers' apartment in Siesta,[4] & with her mother carry on till late, Carmel singing. She had come in in the afternoon (met). When I go home Scott comes with me & calls up bellboys for information about Hollywood night life. None is vouchsafed.

1. A silent film version of the life and death of Jesus Christ, seasoned with De Mille's blend of the sexy and the sacred, soon to become his trademark in later films.

2. The editor from *Vanity Fair* was visiting Hollywood, Pauline Starke's beau.

3. Cedric Gibbons, set designer.

4. Silent film star, living in another cottage at the Ambassador Hotel, near CVV's.

Sunday, 23 January 1927

... Went to see Scott & Zelda [Fitzgerald] who started off for Long Beach in a car—with a hangover. Then . . . Aileen Pringle & Cedric Gibbons arrived to take me to a party at Lois Moran's[1] where I met Lillian Gish, Jim Tully[2] & wife, etc. Also there, Scott & Zelda, Joan Crawford,[3] Pasty Ruth Miller, Carmel Myers, & Donald Freeman. Then to a party of Billy Haines (met):[4] King Vidor & Elinor Boardman,[5] . . . Patsy Miller again, Carmel Myers again. Then we drove to Marion Davies's Tudor home at Beverly Hills for dinner. Max Reinhardt,[6] Morris Gest, William Randolph Hearst (met),[7] Marion Davies (met), Mrs. Glyn,[8] Pola Negri. . . .

1. Hollywood starlet who aspired to appear in a film version of CVV's *The Blind Bow-Boy.*

2. Popular and prolific novelist.

3. Only another Hollywood starlet at the time.

4. Openly homosexual actor, later an interior decorator for other film stars.

5. Film director and his actress wife.

6. German film director.

7. Newspaper magnate and, circa 1903–06, CVV's titular employer on the *Chicago American*, from which he was fired for "lowering the tone of the Hearst syndicate." Silent film star Marion Davies was his mistress.

8. Elinor Glyn, author of steamy novels written in purple prose, whom CVV had interviewed in Paris in 1908. She considered Aileen Pringle her reincarnation in a film based on her novel, *Three Weeks.*

Monday, 24 January 1927

Up at 9. A beautiful clear day. Bertha Case, who has just arrived, telephones. I sat in the sunny garden & read in the morning. Lois Moran, her mother & Donald Freeman lunch with me at one. Then Lois & her mother drive me to the Famous Players Studios where we go to Mrs. Glyn's set. The picture is *Ritzy.* . . . Later we go to Florence Vidor's set & I see Jocelyn Lee, the girl who had an affair with H. B. Warner, almost broke up the Christ picture. . . . Lois needs a leading man. I suggest Scott <u>Fitzgerald.</u>

Saturday, 29 January 1927

Up early to get ready to go to Tia Juana. Beautiful day. We (Pauline Starke whose car Donald Freeman drives) do not get started till nearly noon. Lunch at Santa Ana, a terrible Presbyterian-looking place at Saint Ann's Inn about 1.30. Then we drive on & I get my first view of the Pacific. In San Diego, a picturesque town & a naval base, the plaza full of sailors & marines, the harbors full of warships, about 5.30, too late to go to Tia Juana as the border closes at 6. Instead we go to . . . the Hotel del Coronado, a vast wooden Victorian structure, with a great bar. The juveniles of Coronado inside the grill (including H. B. Warner—Christus[1]) & upstairs old age plays cards, etc. . . .

    1. Playing Jesus Christ in De Mille's *King of Kings*.

Sunday, 30 January 1927

Up at 9, & met Pauline & Donald downstairs at 10.30. She has a toothache. We started for Tia Juana on a beautiful day . . . there. Lunch at Caesar's Bar. I drank & gambled all day. Everybody drunk, prostitutes, cockfights, etc. At 5 we started to get over the border which shuts at 6. Miles of cars in four lines waiting to pass the customs. . . . Home about 1 o'clock, at the Ambassador. Saw H. B. Warner, the Christ of *The King of Kings* at Tia Juana.

Monday, 31 January 1927

. . . Gladys Moran[1] . . . drives me to Famous Players in her car. We go to see Lois in her dressing-room. At 12.30 I join Mr. [Jesse] Lasky, . . . Zabelle Hitchcock, the Cases, & met Eddie Cantor & we have lunch. . . . Mr. Lasky escorts us about the lot, to see Roy Pomeroy's (met) wonderful miniature dept., to see James Cruze (met) take an aero scene with Wallace Beery (met) in *Louis XIV*. Met Clara Bow[2] & talked about *Blind Bow-Boy*. . . . Met Emil Jannings[3] & had my picture taken with him. . . . To Lois Moran's set & talked with her & Roland Lee, her director. Bertha [Case] took some moving pictures. Then Bertha & Frank & Zabelle drove me home. Gilmore Millen[4] comes in, and later Scott Fitzgerald & Brown of the *Herald* who gets very drunk & objectionable. At night went to see *The Miracle* opening with Jeannie Macpherson's party. . . . Supper at Cocoanut Grove. . . .

    1. Lois Moran's mother.
    2. The "It" girl, who, like Lois Moran, also aspired to play "Zimbule O'Grady" in a film version of CVV's novel.
    3. German actor, making a film in Hollywood.

4. White American novelist whose *Sweetman* (1930) perpetuated some racial stereotypes with a black pimp as protagonist. CVV persuaded George Oppenheimer at Viking to publish it.

Wednesday, 2 February 1927

...After lunch Pauline [Starke] drives me to Metro-Goldwyn Studios where I watch King Vidor for an hour or two directing a scene & have a talk with him about *Nigger Heaven*. Then to Aileen Pringle's set. Miraculously she gets through shortly after five & after seeing some of the rushes with her & Conrad Nagle I go home with her for dinner, also her mother, Mrs. Bisbee (met) & Cedric Gibbons who takes me home drunk. I get Scott Fitzgerald out of bed & drag him down.

Monday, 7 February 1927

Up at 9. Packing. A beautiful day. At 12.30 I drive out to Cecil De Mille Studio where I have visit with him. . . . We talk about possibilities of doing *Nigger Heaven*. At 3 I rush over to Metro Goldwyn to say goodbye to Aileen [Pringle] & Pauline [Starke]. Neither is there. . . . Take a car home to Ambassador. . . . Expect the Morans to take me to the train, but they get stuck at the studio. Bertha & Frank Case officiate instead & on the train . . . I retire immediately after dinner & sleep badly.

Friday, 11 February 1927

Arrived in New York at 10 o'clock. Home. Found piles of letters, papers, stocks, etc. to straighten out. Lunch in with Marinoff. Late in afternoon Donald Angus comes in, also Eddie Wassermann. Dinner in with Marinoff. Then I called on Ralph Barton, & spent the evening with him & Germaine [Tailleferre]. Saw his moving pictures, etc. At home at one o'clock.

Saturday, 12 February 1927

. . . Late in afternoon Blanche & Alfred Knopf come in & later Langston Hughes. Eddie Wassermann comes to dinner & we go to a party at his house for me: . . . Donald Angus, Muriel Draper, Everett Marcy, Jacob Wassermann (met),[1] . . . A'Lelia Walker, James Weldon & Grace Johnson, Nora & Rosamond Johnson, . . . Dorothy Harris, D'Alvarez, John Floyd who very drunk insulted everybody, . . . Alain Locke, Harry Block, Langston Hughes, T. R. Smith, Covarrubias, etc., Best-Maugard. Home about 4.

1. Jakob Wasserman was a prolific German writer whose novels regularly appeared in translation in the twenties. CVV spells his name Jacob; this person might be only a relative of Eddie Wassermann.

Wednesday, 16 February 1927

Up at 9 o'clock. Cloudy. Working on letters & papers all the morning. Gladys Brown [Ficke] comes to lunch with me. Then Jack Marinoff appeared & finally Paul Robeson. It was 3 o'clock before I could get back to work. Just before five o'clock Langston Hughes came in & drove with us in the rain . . . to A'Lelia Walker's in Irvington [on Hudson] for dinner. . . . We arrived two hours late but dinner was marvellous. . . . On the way home about 1.30 I was dropped off at a party at Ralph Barton's. . . . I talked with Charlie Chaplin till 5 o'clock & he drove me home.

Thursday, 24 February 1927

. . . At last I get to work & write most of an article about Hollywood for *Vanity Fair*.[1] . . . At 5 we go to Louise Hellström's for cocktails & stay for supper. Lizzie Miles sings & Cliff Jackman plays for her. Lawrence & Armina Marshall, Bob Chanler, Emerson Whithorn, Jane Heap, Marcel Duchamp, . . . William C. Bullitt,[2] . . . Max Ewing and many others, inc. Robert McAlmon. About 9 we move on to Lawrence's where we find Rita Romilly, Ernest Boyd, Arthur & Madeleine Richman,[3] and later Madeleine Boyd & Stuart & Mrs. Rose. Home & change & go to a party at Lenore Ulric's: Harry Richman,[4] Ethel Barrymore with whom I talked most of the evening, . . . Jeanne Eagels, Ruth Chatterton, Beatrice Lillie (met), Gertrude Lawrence (met).[5] . . . Home at 4.

1. CVV wrote four articles about Hollywood for *Vanity Fair* that ran during the summer of 1927, arguably the first serious assessment of the film capital, its stars, and its denizens.
2. Socially prominent diplomat, writer, and third husband of Louise Bryant, widow of Greenwich Village poet and anarchist John Reed.
3. Playwright and his wife.
4. Musical comedy performer and singer in early films.
5. American (Eagels, Chatterton) and English (Lillie, Lawrence) actresses appearing on stage in New York at the time.

Saturday, 26 February 1927

. . . Worked all the morning on another movie article for *Vanity Fair*. . . . Langston Hughes interrupted me just before lunch but I sent him away. . . . Dinner in with Marinoff & then to my room. Langston Hughes came & spent the evening. I went to bed about 11.30. Invited to a party at Sam Hoffenstein's & to Harlem with Mercedes de Acosta but didn't go.

Sunday, 27 February 1927

Up about 10 after horrible nightmare. . . . Read & straightened out papers all morning. Lunch at Stettheimers'. Home & to work again at 3.30. Then to Donald Angus's with Marinoff for cocktails. . . . Then to dinner with Rebecca West at the Wellington. Elinor Wylie & Bill Benét. . . . Got very drunk & Marinoff went out when we returned at 12.

Thursday, 10 March 1927

Up at 8.30. . . . Wrote third draft of "Hollywood Parties" for *Vanity Fair*. Marinoff gives a supper party.[1] Hannah [Ellis] to help: Armina Marshall & Lawrence [Langner]'s sister, Elinor Wylie, Ruth Chatterton & her mother, Peggy O'Neill,[2] Regina Wallace, Isa Glenn, D'Alvarez, Virginia Hammond, Rita Romilly Madeleine Richman. . . . I stayed and made cocktails. Later Horace Liveright & Bill Benét arrived. In bed about 1.30.

> 1. This all-women's party, with its strange games and no menu, was later memorialized in Isa Glenn's novel *East of Eden* (1932).
> 2. Actress, usually in comedienne's roles.

Tuesday, 15 March 1927

. . . In the afternoon a cocktail party: Ethel Campau,[1] Ettie & Carrie Stettheimer, Gladys Moran, Deems Taylor & Mary Kennedy, Regina Wallace, Charles G. Norris,[2] Fannie Hurst, . . . Fannie Butcher,[3] . . . Tom Smith, Edwin Knopf. Went to dinner in Mulberry Street with Tom Smith where we picked up Theodore Dreiser, Helen Richardson, . . . Ernest Boyd, Dorothy & Tony de Sanchez. Later went up to Dreiser's new apartment. Home about 4.

> 1. Wife of Francis Denis Campau, CVV's most intimate companion in their youth and at the University of Chicago.
> 2. Sociological novelist, husband of novelist Kathleen Norris.
> 3. Chicago book reviewer who had endorsed all of CVV's novels.

Wednesday, 16 March 1927

. . . Bright day & I have a hangover. . . . Dorothy Hergesheimer & Noma Way came to dinner. After dinner a party: Nella & Elmer Imes, Henrietta Metcalf & Nik Muray, William C. Bullitt & Louise Bryant,[1] . . . Virginia Hammond, Gladys Moran, Donald Freeman, Elinor Wylie & Bill Benét, James & Grace

Johnson, Lawrence & Armina Langner, Rita Romilly, . . . Benno Moiseiwitsch, Blanche Knopf, Arthur Richman, Donald Angus & Nora Holt Ray (who sang), Jack & Grayce Nail, Georges Lepape, Crystal Bird.[2] In bed about 4.

1. American socialist, identified before World War I as one of the "New Women." Her affairs with Eugene O'Neill and poet-anarchist John Reed were common knowledge in Greenwich Village circles. Later she married Reed, and after his death she married Bullitt.

2. African American social and political activist but "perfectly terrible, not at all Negroid, of course, and a very bad singer," CVV wrote to Marinoff. Bird attempted to sue African American lieder singer Roland Hayes for breach of promise, then later married poet Arthur Huff Fauset.

Friday, 18 March 1927

. . . Marinoff goes to *Götterdammerung* with Regina Wallace, who comes to lunch. I write rough draft of fourth Hollywood article for *Vanity Fair*. Paul Robeson comes in & tells me that Essie is going to have a baby. I go to dinner at Arthur Richman's. . . . Dramatization of *Nigger Heaven* is broached. Then to Mabel Reber's. Neil [Reber] there. Edna Kenton, Fannie Butcher, Philip Moeller, Andrew Dasburg. Home at 2 o'clock.

Saturday, 19 March 1927

Up at 8.15. Cloudy. I have a hangover. . . . We dine at the William & Louise Bullitt's. . . . Home about midnight.

Sunday, 20 March 1927

. . . Party at Rita Romilly's in honor of Marinoff's birthday: Sigmund Spaeth (met),[1] Jean Gorman,[2] Donald Angus, T. R. Smith, Nella & Elmer Imes, Covarrubias, Best-Maugard, Juliette Crosby,[3] Arthur Richman, Harry Block, Armina Langner, etc. Home about 3. . . .

1. Composer and musicologist, also author of popular texts about music.
2. Wife of writer Herbert Gorman.
3. Actress then appearing in George M. Cohan's *The Show-Off*.

Wednesday, 23 March 1927

. . . Marinoff & Rita Romilly go to theatre. They stop for us & we all go to the Ralph Bartons' where see M. and M. Morand,[1] Geo. Lepape & Charlie Chaplin. After half an hour we go to Harlem. The Sugar Cane,[2] Small's Paradise, & finally The Nest. . . . Home at 4.30.

1. French writer Paul Morand and his wife. He wrote *New York* (1930), a collection of essays about various aspects of the city, including Harlem and CVV.

2. Few whites and fewer educated blacks went slumming at this raunchy speakeasy on the fringe of Harlem's actual slums. It was patronized largely by black pimps, prostitutes, and petty gamblers.

Monday, 28 March 1927

. . . Preparations for Marinoff going away, etc. Her passport doesn't come & I have a hangover. . . . Late in the afternoon Scott Fitzgerald appears—soused—and later Zelda. They stay to dinner. Also Regina Wallace. Marinoff goes to bed directly after dinner. I go to bed at 11.

Tuesday, 29 March 1927

. . . At 1.30 Mr. [*Lavalley?*] brings Marinoff's passport, just when we had all given up hope of getting it. . . . Later Lenore Ulric stops for us & takes us to Eddie Wassermann's for dinner: Paul Morand, Scott Fitzgerald, T. R. Smith, Donald Angus, Rita Romilly, Lawrence & Armina Langner, Kathleen Kerrigan.[1] Later party at the Langners'. All of the above are there. Sigmund Spaeth (he sang), . . . Nora Holt (who sang), Nella [Larsen] Imes, Walter White, Dorothy & Jim Harris, Gladys Moran & Donald Freeman, Zelda Fitzgerald, Rebecca West, Ruth Chatterton, Virginia Hammond, Ettie & Carrie Stettheimer, Jim & Grace Johnson, Percy & Florence Hammond, Helen Westley, Philip Moeller, etc. Home about four. Bob Chanler, Louise Hellström, Bill Bullitt & Louise Bryant.

1. Actress in silent films since 1914.

Wednesday, 30 March 1927

Up at 8 & went to Hoboken with Marinoff to see her off on *President Harding*. Regina Wallace was there & we had champagne. Then Reg came home with me for lunch. . . . Dinner in alone and lonely. After dinner I . . . went on to Rebecca West's party at Fannie Hurst's: James Weldon & Grace Johnson, Walter White, Earl Carroll,[1] Dorothy Knopf (meet). She is going to jail on Monday.[2] . . . Elinor Wylie & Bill Benét, Ruth Hammond & Donald MacDonald, Ruth Hale & Heywood Broun, etc. Home about two. . . .

1. Producer responsible for an annual musical revue, *Earl Carroll's Vanities*.

2. The *New York Times* does not account for this intriguing reference.

Friday, 1 April 1927

. . . I take Eddie [Wassermann] to Bob Chanler's for dinner. . . . . Later Donald [Angus] takes me on to another party: chorus gals & college men, somewhere on Barrow St., where I talk to a moron named Marian Gillen. Home at 3.

Tuesday, 5 April 1927

. . . About 10.30 I go to a party at Bob Chanler's. Everyone very soused. . . . A Spanish boy named Eli . . . dances. John Canon punches him & he punches John & Bob Chanler. John & I go home with Lawrence & Armina Langner & finally to my own home at 3 o'clock.

Wednesday, 6 April 1927

. . . Dinner with the James Weldon Johnsons. Rita Romilly there. Then to Jimmie Harris's dance at Renaissance Casino. . . . A brilliant party, a great many young white boys in drag. A'Lelia Walker, . . . Paul Robeson, Nella & Elmer Imes, Walter White, Catherine [Mrs. Solomon] Johnson, Binga & Geraldyn Dismond,[1] Donald Angus, . . . Edna & Lloyd Thomas, Rudolph, Pearl, & June Fisher. . . . [Floyd] Snelson of *The [Chicago] Defender.*[2] . . . Home at 4.

> 1. An influential gossip columnist in Harlem under the pen name "Gerry Major," and her husband.
> 2. *The Chicago Defender* was founded in 1915, the first black newspaper with a national readership. It was in part responsible for spurring the Great Migration of African Americans from the South to Chicago and other Midwestern industrialized cities and to New York during World War I.

Friday, 10 April 1927

Up at 10 o'clock. Read papers and waste time on this gorgeous sunny day. Late in the afternoon Eddie Wassermann comes in with Rougier, a Haitian hotel keeper, also Nora Holt. I take Eddie to dinner at Leone's where we see . . . Arthur Richman with a dame. Then we go to the George Anthiel concert at Carnegie Hall. I loved the din & everybody in New York was there. Afterwards Donald Friede[1] gives a ball & supper at the Club Deauville, & nearly everybody was there, including Nora Holt, A'Lelia Walker, . . . the Robesons, . . . Pauline Starke, Muriel Draper, . . . etc. Then a crowd of us go to Tom Smith's where I meet Lewis Galantiere & his wife.[2] Home at 5. <u>W. C. Handy conducts orchestra at the club. I talk with Anthiel.</u>

> 1. Partner in Covici-Friede Publishers.
> 2. Multilingual intellectual who lived with his wife at the Algonquin Hotel.

Thursday, 14 April 1927

. . . Rita Romilly's tea for A'Lelia Walker: Donald Angus, Bernia Austin, Grace & Jim Johnson, Lloyd & Edna Thomas, T. R. Smith, . . . Eddie Wassermann, Florence Sternberger,[1] . . . Geraldyn Dismond, . . . Donald Freeman. Then to dinner at Louise Hellström's: Armina & Lawrence Langner, Eva Gauthier, Alexander Smallens,[2] Bob Chanler, etc. After dinner [*word*] Eva sang, & Eli, the Spanish boy, who danced. Bill & Louise Bullitt. E. E. Cummings.[3] (He broke glass.) Bob strangled him. Louis Bouché, Jean & Herbert Gorman,[4] Esther Murphy,[5] . . . & Mrs. Ann Barton (Ralph's second wife, met).[6] Home and in bed about 5.

    1. A social acquaintance of Edward Wassermann.
    2. Russian American conductor with several opera companies and symphony orchestras.
    3. Poet who espoused organic prosodies rather than free verse.
    4. Prolific writer of poetry, novels, and biographies, and his wife.
    5. Visiting English minor writer.
    6. Ann Minnerly Barton was then having an affair with E. E. Cummings. They married two years later.

Friday, 15 April 1927

Up at 10. No hot water. Fooled with papers, etc. Hugh Walpole came to lunch. After lunch Langston Hughes came in. . . . Late in the afternoon Spud Johnson who is leaving for Santa Fe next week. Nora Holt in a Poiret gown. Rita Romilly & Eddie Wassermann for dinner. Then to a party at Rita Romilly's: Florence Eldridge,[1] Zelma Brackett,[2] Nils Nelson, Donald Angus, Aaron Copland, Lawrence & Armina Langner, Grayce & John Nail, Grace & Jim Johnson, Larry Brown & Sadie Jackson, Langston Hughes, etc. Sadie Jackson sang & so did Nora [Holt] Ray. Home about 4. I invited Dick the night elevator boy in for a drink. He stayed an hour.

    1. Actress, long married to actor Frederic March, with whom she often appeared on stage and in films.
    2. First wife of screenwriter and novelist Charles Brackett.

Saturday, 16 April 1927

Up at noon. . . . Hangover. . . . Late in the afternoon Gwendolyn Bennett came in. To dinner at Eddie Wassermann's with Nora Holt, Donald Angus, . . . Rita Romilly. Later we went up to Lloyd & Edna Thomas's. . . . Donald came back to spend the night.

Sunday, 17 April 1927

... To lunch with Duane [Van Vechten] at the Algonquin. Home after lunch. I am very much shaken,[1] and after reading papers I lie down for an hour. Read in the evening. To bed at 8.

> 1. There is no definite identification of what had "shaken" CVV nor what in the entries that follow had left him "shattered." Donald Angus observed that from time to time, when CVV's drinking overtook him, he experienced the equivalent of mild delirium tremens and gave up liquor temporarily.

Monday, 18 April 1927

... Still shattered. ... I telephone Donald [Angus] & take him to lunch at the Crillon. Then he walks me to Bloomingdale's & home. ... At 4 o'clock Langston Hughes & Harry Salpeter arrive, the latter to interview the first. I take Donald to dinner at Leone's & then to the circus, where ... the great new star is the Spanish tightrope dancer, Callerno. Donald comes home with me & learns about me. I sleep fitfully. Nervous. I haven't touched alcohol in two days.

Tuesday, 19 April 1927

Up at a quarter of nine. No longer shattered. ... Langston Hughes appears. ... Nella & Elmer Imes & Dorothy Peterson come in at 5. Later Donald Angus who stays for dinner & till one o'clock watching me drink hot whiskey. I fall asleep as soon as he departs.

Wednesday, 20 April 1927

... Langston Hughes comes in in the morning & stays to lunch. ... Late in the afternoon Reg Wallace comes in with flowers. Dinner alone. Colin McPhee[1] calls. Lenore Ulric calls up asking me to join a box party at the Palace. ... Colin & I stay for a couple of acts & then come home. He stays all night. Ethel Waters sends a note to me in the box at the Palace. I go back & see Earl Dancer.[2] Today is the hottest April 20! 88 Fahrenheit.

> 1. A young American composer and student of Edgar Varèse. He was writing music for a ballet scenario by CVV.
> 2. Waters's manager, current lover, and later husband.

Thursday, 21 April 1927

Up at 8. Hot still. Colin [McPhee] plays for me & beautifully. Stays to lunch. ... Still shattered. At 4 Grace Johnson, Bertha Randolph,[1] Lola Wilson ...

come in. Lola Wilson sings & plays sufficiently badly. I am <u>shattered.</u> Wish devoutly Marinoff were here. Dine at the Stettheimers': [Alfred] Stieglitz & [Georgia] O'Keeffe, Phil Moeller, Edna Kenton, . . . [Carl] Sprinchorn.[2] Home at 11. Slept badly.

    1. Wife of African American labor leader A. Phillips Randolph.
    2. Artist, a regular member of the Stettheimer circle.

Friday, 22 April 1927

. . . Earl Dancer comes in to protest against coming to dinner. He is endlessly alarmed, but I persuade him.[1] In the days past I have found Mary Hutchins (Ralph Barton's maid)[2] a job with Jack Harper, my bootlegger. . . . I write a letter of protest to Benjamin Brawley about his article of "The Negro Literary Renaissance" in the *Southern Workman*.[3] Ethel Waters, Earl Dancer, & Duane Van Vechten come to dinner. After dinner Rita Romilly, Eddie Wassermann, Nils Nelson, Donald Angus, Harry Block, Colin McPhee. . . . Ethel who tells us she is a bastard.

    1. Encounters in theaters and speakeasies did not trouble Dancer, but he was hesitant to dine privately with white people.
    2. Barton and his fourth wife, Germaine Tailleferre, had moved to Paris.
    3. Brawley, an African American academic journalist and reviewer, had contended that CVV's influence had corrupted Langston Hughes's poetry in *The Weary Blues*. CVV pointed out that the contents of that book had been completed before he had met Hughes.

Sunday, 24 April 1927

. . . About 3.30 I went with Colin [McPhee] to his room on Third Street, where he played me some of his compositions. Then we went to the Knopfs' for dinner. . . . After dinner Colin played. We came home about 12 & Colin stayed all night.

Tuesday, 26 April 1927

. . . D'Alvarez & Colin McPhee for lunch. Colin plays for Marguerite. He stays on till nearly four. . . . At 6.30 I go to Algonquin where are gathered Blanche Knopf . . . & Alfred Knopf in Mencken's room. Frank Case comes in for a moment to receive my congratulations on Margaret Case Morgan's baby, born today. Then we go to Hoboken to the Haufbrau for dinner. Home about midnight. Dick [the elevator operator] not here, thank God.

Saturday, 30 April 1927

. . . Donald Angus (who goes to Baltimore on Monday to play with Edwin Knopf's company) comes to dinner & spends the evening. About 12 o'clock Arthur & Rose Wheeler[1] arrive. All leave about 1.30. In the meantime I get gloriously drunk. To bed. 12 edition *Nigger Heaven* ordered.

    1. A stockbroker and his "perfectly enchanting" wife.

Saturday, 7 May 1927

. . . Emily Clark [Balch], in widow's weeds, for lunch. After lunch James Weldon Johnson, bearing a first copy of *God's Trombones*[1] for me, & Walter White, who is going to Arkansas to investigate another lynching, came in and later Jack Stephens[2] of Indianapolis, who outstays them. Still later Blanche Knopf & Duane Van Vechten. I get up about 4, dress in evening clothes & depart with Elmer Imes for Dorothy Peterson's in Brooklyn. Cocktail party. Dorothy Harris, Sidney Peterson, Dorothy's father, Bruce Nugent, Nella [Larsen] Imes, Harry Block, etc. We go to the *Opportunity* Dinner at Fifth Ave Pub where I see *everybody*. . . . Met Georgia Douglas Johnson,[3] Alice Dunbar Nelson,[4] Arna Bontemps.[5] Nella, Elmer & Grace Valentine[6] go home with me, at midnight. Jack Stephens arrives & stays the night.

    1. Johnson's poems on biblical subjects, written in the vernacular of an old-time Negro minister.
    2. Indiana, Ohio, and Kentucky (successively) librarian and bibliophile.
    3. African American poet who conducted a salon in her Washington, D.C. home.
    4. Widow of African American poet Paul Laurence Dunbar. She described CVV in her memoirs as looking like a "white slug."
    5. African American poet, novelist, educator.
    6. Administrator at the Bordentown School for Negro Youth in New Jersey, for which CVV established a scholarship.

Tuesday, 10 May 1927

. . . Ruth Snyder & Judd Gray[1] convicted of first degree murder, according to morning papers. If capital punishment is justice this judgment is just. . . . I am invited to join Ethel Waters at a midnight banquet for Mississippi Floor Sufferers at Lafayette but did not go.

    1. A Queens housewife and her corset salesman lover had bludgeoned her husband to death, then adopted fashionable Freudian defenses that commanded more attention in the newspaper than the coverage of the Sacco & Vanzetti Case. Snyder and Gray were executed a year later.

Monday, 16 May 1927

... Home reading *The Magic Mountain*[1] and napping. Then to dinner with Alfred & Blanche Knopf. Henry Mencken there & Margaret Freeman, & Geo. Jean Nathan. Henry & I play piano duets. At ten we go to the pier (sans Geo.) to see Alfred off on the *Columbus,* a beautiful new North German Floyd boat. His mother & father there. Then Henry, Margaret, & Blanche come home with me for an hour. I get an idea for a film & try to get [Herman] Mankiewicz[2] in Hollywood on the telephone. Finally I go to bed.

    1. Novel by Thomas Mann, published by Knopf.
    2. Film producer CVV had met in Hollywood.

Wednesday, 18 May 1927

... At 4 o'clock took a taxi, stopped for Emily Clark, & then to a cocktail party at the Langners': Eugene O'Neill, Taylor Gordon, Rosamond Johnson, Rita Romilly, Romney Brent, Eleanor Boardman, Hortense Alden,[1] Ernest Boyd, Virginia Hammond, . . . Mr. & Mrs. Joseph Wood Krutch,[2] Lee Simonson, Alma & Maurice Wertheim, Terry Helburn, etc. Home at 6.45. Colin McPhee came to dinner we went to *The Circus Princess.*[3] Colin came home with me & stayed the night. In bed about one. I slept badly.

    1. Actress noted for her performances in two plays in the twenties, *The Firebrand* and *Grand Hotel.*
    2. Influential critic and essayist, author of Poe and Johnson biographies and, in 1929, *The Modern Temper,* an insightful literary obituary of the pointless inanity of the twenties, even before the decade was over.
    3. *Die Zirkusprinzen,* a German musical comedy by Emerich Kalman and Henry B. Smith, notable not for its story and music but for its variety of circus acts.

Thursday, 19 May 1927

... At 5 to a cocktail party at Eddie Wassermann's. Farewell for Taylor Gordon & Rosamond Johnson.[1] Esther Murphy, Max Ewing, Grace & Jim Johnson, . . . Florine Stettheimer, Muriel Draper, . . . Gilbert & Mrs. Seldes, etc. Nella [Larsen] Imes, Elmer Imes, Duane Van Vechten, Harry Block, Dorothy Peterson, Louise Hellström, Taylor Gordon. Eddie & I go to dinner at Constantinople. They refuse to serve us, so we go to Fornio's. Then to my house (all but Eddie & Louise Hellström) where we have a very gay party & everybody takes off their clothes.[2] In bed about 3.

    1. Johnson and Gordon were about to embark on a European tour.
    2. CVV's punctuation makes it impossible to determine who went to dinner and who attended the "very gay party." The word *gay* should not be read as "homo-

sexual." Gertrude Stein seems to have been first to use the word as a euphemism for homosexual, in 1911 when she wrote "Miss Furr and Miss Skeene," but that story was not published until 1922, in her *Geography and Plays*. A year later, when the fashionable and influential *Vanity Fair* reprinted "Miss Furr and Miss Skeene," *gay* was slowly taken up by homosexual readers of the magazine and used increasingly as a code word thereafter. Heterosexuals were unlikely to have caught the double entendre in popular song lyrics of the period by homosexuals Noel Coward, Cole Porter, and Lorenz Hart. The wider use of the word has been in heterosexual currency only since circa 1980.

Saturday, 21 May 1927

. . . Lunch in and at 2.05 off on the train with Lois & Gladys Moran for Wilmington [Delaware]. Ernest Boyd also on the train but asleep in a compartment. We all tumble off at Wilmington to be met by Scott Fitzgerald in his new Buick, with Charlie MacArthur. Then we drove to Scott's place in the country on the Potomac River. A divine old yellow plaster Victorian House with iron balconies, endless space, etc. Presently Zelda [Fitzgerald] & Jed Chandler appear & after endless cocktails we have a gay dinner. After dinner, more cocktails & a very bad Negro band. Dancing by guests & retainers, Estella the waitress & her daughter Pearl, expressly unfriendly. John Biggs, author of *Demi-Gods*, Christopher Ward, son of the parodist.[1] Jed gets very sick & Ernest very drunk. The Fitzgeralds pass out. I go to bed about 4. Charles Lindbergh arrives in Paris today in 33 hours from N.Y. in his aircraft.

      1. American journalist who sometimes wrote parodies of the books he reviewed, including "The Tittattooed Countess" and "The Blind Booby by Carl Far Fechten."

Sunday, 22 May 1927

Woke up about 9 & had breakfast about 10 with Scott & Lois [Moran]. Others appeared gradually in dressing gowns & later, bathing suits. About 12 we start off to get John Biggs. I climb in his car & he escorts us twenty-five miles to the pool . . . of a chilly chateau near West Chester where all but me bathe. Home for lunch about 2 & very hungry. An uneventful afternoon. After supper everybody leaves for N.Y. at nine, and I go to Baltimore a few minutes earlier. . . . Donald Angus comes in for supper & leaves about 2.

Saturday, 4 June 1927

. . . A letter from Duane informs me that Ralph [Van Vechten] may have a cancer. After lunch alone I went to the Paramount to see Lois Moran (lovely) in a horrible film called *The Whirlpool of Youth* and then to hear Paul Whiteman murder the *Rhapsody in Blue*. Then to a cocktail party at Blanche Knopf's. . . . Jim & Grace Johnson, Paul Robeson, Margaret Freeman, King Vidor, Eddie Wassermann. I take Colin McPhee & later we go to dinner at Virginia Hammond's. Ann Andrews & Arthur and Madeleine Richman. Colin & I go back with the Richmans for a drink & then pick up King & Blanche & go to the Sugar Cane. . . . Later to Small's. . . . Home at 4.

Sunday, 5 June 1927

Colin stays the night. Up at 10. We have lunch at the Stettheimers' & go for a walk & wind up at Blanche Knopf's. Pat [Alfred A. Knopf, Jr.] is there & I arrange for him to take lessons of Colin. Home at 6.30 & to Leone's for dinner. After dinner I come home & go to bed. Colin awakens me at 10.30 when Blanche Knopf arrives. Colin plays. Later Regina Wallace arrives & gets very drunk, but I manage to get her out at 1.30. Then we go to bed.

Tuesday, 7 June 1927

. . . Take a nap after lunch & read Geo W[ashington] Cable's *The Silent South*, a book written to protest against the lack of civil rights of the Negro, as true today as when published in 1885. I wish I might get started on a book. . . . Read Charles Pettit's *Son of the Grand Eunuch*, & enjoyed it more than any other book I have read in months. . . . At midnight I went to a party. Tailors & ambitious people & cheap kikes. . . . In bed at 3.

Wednesday, 8 June 1927

. . . Ralph [Van Vechten] is not expected to live & I quickly make my plans to go out there, on Saturday. Then I go to Blanche Knopf's for dinner. . . . I have two or three good cries (alone). Eddie [Wassermann] comes home with me. I am very drunk. Poor old Ralph!

Sunday, 12 June 1927

. . . After a long talk about Ralph's condition we went to see him in Duane's studio on the roof of the North Park Hotel. He was very weak & pathetic & as thin as I am & he insisted he is going to die. Back to the house for lunch. Then again to see Ralph. This time he was more cheerful . . . & he laughed as we talked of prohibition, Indians, etc. . . . Then I got in touch with Nora Holt. Called for her. We went to The Sunset where she sang. . . . Later to the Café de Paris, a marvellous black & tan place. Home at 4.30.

Monday, 13 June 1927

. . . I asked him if he would like to hear Nora Holt sing & he immediately became excited, and began to plan a cocktail party for tomorrow, which developed as the day wore on. . . . This cheered Ralph enormously. . . . Later . . . Ralph . . . discusses the party, decides on the food & drink & guests, & then begins giving orders and getting querulous. Fannie says it is his best day in a week. . . .

Tuesday, 14 June 1927

. . . John [the Van Vechten chauffeur] comes for me . . . & we get Nora Holt & take her to sing for Ralph. A large crowd of people come. . . . After dinner Nora sings enchantingly. . . .

Wednesday, 15 June 1927

. . . Van Vechten [Shaffer] and I talked till eleven when we went up to see Ralph & found he had had a hemorrhage & had taken morphine. . . . Then out to Nora Holt's . . . & we go to the Café de Paris where we run into Noble Sissle. Home about 7.30.

Friday, 17 June 1927

Home on the *20th Century,* about 11.30. . . . A cablegram from Marinoff announces that she will return on the 25th. . . . Supper at 7, joint birthday party [for] Pat Knopf, James Weldon Johnson, & me. Grace Johnson, Jack & Grayce Nail, Frances Seligman, Colin McPhee, Eddie Wassermann, Blanche Knopf. Colin stays the night.

Thursday, 23 June 1927

. . . In the morning I make a tentative attempt at writing. . . . It's something to have done that. . . . At 6.15 Earl Dancer comes for me in the car & we motor to Ethel Waters. She cooks dinner for me. Her mother & her aunt there. . . . Later Nella Imes whom we call up. We stay till about midnight when Ethel, Earl, Nella, & I motor to my home, where they stay till 1.30. Ethel in grand form. She said: "I would go to a fancy dress ball as September Morn if my hand was big enough. . . ."

Friday, 24 June 1927

... Colin calls up in excitement. He has seen the ballet master at the Roxy & that one says there is a great chance of getting a ballet done. He comes up to talk it over & reads my scenario. . . . Dinner at Eddie Wassermann's with Blanche Knopf. After dinner Ethel Waters (who danced) & her husband Earl Dancer, . . . & Rita Romilly. I did not drink a drop & was interested to see how silly people are when they are not drunk. Home at 12.

Saturday, 25 June 1927

... To lunch with Eddie Wassermann at the Ritz. After lunch we go to the Roxy Theatre. When I get back around 4 I find a telegram . . . saying Ralph is so weak he is not expected to live over the weekend. . . .

Tuesday, 28 June 1927

... In the morning, Van [Vechten Shaffer] & I met Emma [Van Vechten] Shaffer at *20th Century.* Ralph's illness entirely new to her & a great shock. We took her to the studio but Ralph does not recognize her. . . . He died peacefully at 11.40. . . .

Thursday, 30 June 1927

... Funeral at 3. . . . Then we came back . . . & go to . . . office to have the will read. The will already is a surprise. Fannie is the executrix & the estate is kept together for perpetuity.[1] . . . I go to South Side to see Nora Holt, Café de Paris, & Sunset. Home at 3. I fall hard off the wagon for the first time in a week.

> 1. After a number of specific bequests, Ralph Van Vechten's will left his estate of $6,000,000 in trust to his wife; on her death a few months later, two thirds of this amount went to his foster daughter, Duane—whose real name was Censolina Halper—in trust; the other third was divided equally, also in trust, between CVV and Van Vechten Shaffer.

Sunday, 3 July 1927

... In the afternoon James Allen, the Negro photographer, comes to see me. Then I go to Walter White's to see for the first time Carl Darrow White.[1] . . . Later to Nella Imes's for dinner. After dinner Harry Block comes in. We go to Clara Smith's. She sings & is marvellous. . . . I go home about 12, & have nightmare.

> 1. The Whites' newborn son was named for CVV and lawyer Clarence Darrow; later he became a professional tenor.

Monday, 4 July 1927

. . . Regina Wallace comes for me at a quarter of nine & we go to French line pier to meet Marinoff who gets in about 10. . . . She has trunks full of dresses & presents. Home, unpacking. . . . I adore having Marinoff back. She is the only satisfactory person alive. . . .

Tuesday, 5 July 1927

. . . I am worried about my condition. . . . Dr. Livingston . . . finds my prostate gland inflamed & my bladder affected. . . . I call up Blanche to protest against the excisions planned for the French *Nigger Heaven*. . . . Marinoff & I dine at Eddie Wassermann's with Blanche Knopf. After dinner we go to 63rd Street Theatre to see a rehearsal of Ethel Waters's *Africana*. Talk to Earl . . . Dancer, Donald Heywood,[1] Geraldyn Dismond, etc., & finally Ethel arrives & tells us a marvellous story of how she found Earl naked with a woman & chastized him. She sang "Smiles" on the stage with the chorus. . . .

    1. African American composer for musical revues.

Monday, 11 July 1927

. . . It is hot, but not too hot. Altogether a splendid & amusing summer. Muriel Draper & Eddie Wassermann come to dinner, & we go to see Ethel Waters in *Africana* at the 63rd Street Theatre, a great show. . . . We all go back & find Ethel in tears & Earl sad because Ethel didn't get dressed in time to appear in the finale. . . .

Sunday, 17 July 1927

. . . At 3.30 Olga Hilliard's[1] car comes for us & drives us to the Claremont where we find Eddie Wassermann . . . & James Corrigan of London and Cleveland (who had the foresight to buy the wine cellar of the Ritz when prohibition was declared. 1840 cognac stands on the tables, but I am not drinking.) Then Olga, Eddie, . . . Marinoff & I proceed up the Hudson in Olga's Rolls-Royce. We stop at A'Lelia Walker's in Irvington. Paul & Essie Robeson there, Minnie Patterson, Mrs. Goode, Stinnett,[2] Manchester,[3] etc. Then on to Lenore Ulric's to supper. . . . There is a fine collection of morons about. . . . Lenore's lover is being sued for divorce by his wife, naming Lenore as correspondent. . . . In fact an air of melodrama hangs over the house & Olga & I enjoy ourselves. . . .

    1. A wealthy social acquaintance of Edward Wassermann's.

2. McCleary "Mac" Stinnett, dancer, model, A'Lelia Walker's bootlegger, and on occasion a performer at Edward Wassermann's parties.

3. Eddie Manchester, Harlem denizen and, at one time, Ethel Waters's lover.

Tuesday, 19 July 1927

. . . Regina Wallace & Witter Bynner for dinner. Hal tells how Otto Kahn took him to *Africana* last night & how he thinks he has got Otto to finance the show. After dinner we go to *Africana* & find the show enormously improved, whipped up, & the new comedians. Ethel stops the show with her specialty. . . .

Thursday, 21 July 1927

. . . Paul Robeson came in about 3. He has practically decided to go abroad. . . . Then Earl Dancer who tells me that Kahn gave him $5,000 yesterday, $8,000 today, & promised him $20,000 in two weeks if the show should improve. Earl wanted either Covarrubias or Aaron Douglas to do the sets, I got Douglas for him. . . .

Friday, 22 July 1927

. . . Jack Dempsey won the fight last night with a knockout over Jack Sharkey. This is not surprising, considering the fact that a [Gene] Tunney-Dempsey fight was the stronger draw for Tex Ricard than a Tunney-Sharkey fight. . . . I am drinking again. Hal [Bynner] & I go to 63 Street Theatre at 11.15, pick up Earl, Ethel, & Louis Douglas.[1] Earl drives us in his car to Johnnie Brent's[2] for supper. Eddie Thompson[3] & Evelyn Preer[4] are there. About 2, Earl drives Hal & me home.

1. Musician with *Africana*, later prominent in jazz groups.

2. Harlem restaurant on Seventh Avenue.

3. African American actor and Evelyn Preer's husband.

4. African American actress in serious plays with the Lafayette Players and in black musical revues or in white plays calling for black performers on Broadway. She appeared in many films in the twenties.

Thursday, 28 July 1927

. . . Eddie [Wassermann] & Marinoff go to see Cecil De Mille's cinema, *The King of Kings,* while I stay home, arranging bindings, etc. An idea I derived from Paul Morand's *Bonda & Her Vivant:* the indifference of this generation has given me the idea for a novel which is germinating. . . .

Tuesday, 2 August 1927.

. . . At 3.30 Aaron Douglas comes in & I talk to him about the possibility of painting [a mural in] our bathroom. He seems to be shy about talking business. At any rate he refuses to set a price. . . .

Saturday, 6 August 1927

. . . We take a train for Croton & a house party at George Biddle's,[1] who has taken Gloria Swanson's[2] house. Jane Biddle, Francis Biddle,[3] Mrs. Harrison Smith, Floyd Dell, Louis Bouché, Mrs. W. B. Seabrook,[4] Louise Hellström, Max Eastman, Louise Bryant & Bill Bullitt. We get home before midnight & Earl Dancer calls me & I join him & his party at Small's Paradise. . . . We go to a party at Castro's. . . . Pick up Geraldyn Dismond & take her with us to The Nest. . . . About 4.30, the party goes to a rent party[5] at Hall Johnson's,[6] & I disappear. Home & in bed.

1. Realist painter and collector.
2. Silent (primarily) film star.
3. A financier and his wife who were art patrons.
4. Katie Seabrook, wife of William Seabrook, travel writer and candid autobiographer.
5. Rent parties were common in Harlem. Minimal admission was charged to attend parties in private residences at which the tenants were attempting to raise money to pay the rent. In return there was live music, dancing, and soul food.
6. African American choral director and composer.

Monday, 8 August 1927

. . . At 2, Aaron Douglas comes to paint the bathroom & brings a marvellous design.[1] . . . At 5.15 Robert Chisholm, the Australian baritone who is to sing in Arthur Hammerstein's opera, *Golden Dawn,* came in to meet Edna Thomas who is to teach him a Negro dialect. Regina Wallace came to dinner & she & Marinoff go to see Ethel Barrymore in *The Constant Wife* while I stay home & get drunk. In bed about 1.

1. The only evidence of the mural appears in the background in CVV's photographs of the artist. Conceivably, Douglas's work still lies under many coats of paint at 150 West 55th Street.

Wednesday, 10 August 1927

. . . Aaron Douglas <u>paints</u> the bathroom. Marinoff & I have dinner together & then go to the Roxy. There is a Russian song & dance number & a terrible film, *Don Juan,* in which Jack Barrymore struts & poses ridiculously. In bed at 10.30.

Friday, 12 August 1927

. . . Wrote second chapter of new novel.[1] Lunch in with Marinoff. Aaron Douglas at two comes to continue painting the bathroom. . . . Ann Andrews & Mark Mooring for dinner. . . . Hal Bynner comes in with Tom Smith & a gal. Ann and I go after Ethel Waters, Earl Dancer & Geraldyn Dismond & bring them down to the house. The party lasts till 3.30.

    1. *Spider Boy* (Knopf, 1928), as yet untitled.

Monday, 15 August 1927

. . . I make final version of my ballet, *The Princess Without a Heart.*[1] . . . Later we visit Tony & Betty Salemme,[2] hoping Ethel Waters will come & pose. I saw her head, started in clay, but she did not appear, but the head of the trustees of Rutgers College comes in to look at Tony's statue of Paul Robeson which might be bought for Rutgers College. Have dinner with Eddie Wassermann here. I am bored & irritable, tired of all these people, looking for something fresh. If only novel would work! In bed at 10.30.

    1. Neither McPhee's score nor CVV's scenario seems to have survived except in notes for the latter.
    2. Italian-born American sculptor and his wife.

Thursday, 18 August 1927

Up at 8. Rain. Still have a cough, and feeling bilious but put the bathroom in order & start Chapter III. Lunch in with Marinoff. Aaron Douglas comes in to put an extra touch on. . . .

Saturday, 20 August 1927

. . . Up at a quarter of eight. Cool & cloudy. After a while I got to work & produced what may be Chapter IV, but God knows if it is. If I am writing anything I am certainly doing it subconsciously. I doubt very much if I <u>am</u> writing anything. . . . Harry Block comes in for cocktails. Jimmie [i.e., James] Allen brings my photographs & Colin McPhee goes with us to dinner at Nella Imes'. All Harlem is gay with flags for the Elks convention next week. . . .

Monday, 22 August 1927

. . . We take the 3.14 to East Hampton, L.I., to Florence & Percy Hammond. Arrive at 6 & drive to his charming 18th century farm house which Florence has furnished beautifully in early American. We dine & talk till quite late.

Tuesday, 23 August 1927

... Channing & Anna & Helen Pollock[1] & Dwight Taylor[2] for dinner. We dine at the Country Club. Dwight comes home with us & stays till late. I get quite stewed.

    1. Prolific playwright Channing Pollock was a friend from CVV's early newspaper days in Chicago; Anna Marble Pollock, his second wife, was one of CVV's most intimate friends; Helen Channing Pollock was her daughter from her first marriage. Even this family's black domestics named themselves Pollock.

    2. Film writer and memoirist, son of actress Laurette Taylor.

Friday, 26 August 1927

... Meda doesn't come & so Marinoff gets lunch & I make the beds. . . . Later Harry Block with first copy of illustrated *Peter Whiffle*. We celebrate. Then Marinoff & I go to Eddie Wassermann's. Ethel [Waters] & Earl [Dancer] there & Donald Angus for whom there is a cake with one candle in honor of his birthday. Then to the Caviar Restaurant for dinner. Marinoff & Donald have a fight but make it up later at my house. In bed about 2, soused.

Saturday, 27 August 1927

... Left at 12 o'clock for Northampton, Mass, with Colin McPhee. We are met at Northampton by Bill Bullitt who drives us to his beautiful farm in the Berkshires.

Sunday, 28 August 1927

... Bill takes me for a long drive & I find a farm, want to buy: the Lavant Gray place, all rolling meadows, a friendly prospect. Home for lunch, with Louise Bryant Bullitt, Colin [McPhee] & Bill [Bullitt] & Rogique Bey, their Turkish protégé. . . . Then on another drive to the Gray farm . . . and finally to Ashfield to the MacLeishes'[1] for dinner. . . .

    1. American poet Archibald MacLeish and his wife.

Monday, 29 August 1927

... Archie MacLeish had told us that the Gray farm was available, cheap. We pick up Mina Curtiss[1] & drive there & find it is not for sale at all.

    1. American writer and editor, on the faculty at Northampton College, ballet impresario Lincoln Kirstein's sister.

Wednesday, 31 August 1927

. . . A hot, sticky day & cloudy, but I feel pretty well & Marinoff doesn't. . . . Met in the street Bertha & Frank Case & Zabelle Hitchcock. Also Samson de Breer! The boy who has been writing me for two years. He informs me that he is the re-incarnation of Shelley.[1] To *Vanity Fair* office to see Donald Freeman. Henriette Metcalf is there. Home. Isa Schindel comes in to talk about her novel.[2] Later Dorothy Hergesheimer. . . . Eddie Wassermann & Reg Wallace for dinner. They spend the evening here but we retire before midnight.

    1. This young man is never again referred to in the daybooks. Elinor Wylie made this same claim about herself—in apparent seriousness—to CVV.
    2. CVV had just read Isa Glenn's *Southern Charm* in manuscript.

Thursday, 1 September 1927

. . . Write letters, etc., particularly to Philipe Soupault refusing permission to Kra to publish *Nigger Heaven* with the proposed cuts.[1] Lunch in. After lunch I had intended to go out but the rain continued to beat down so savagely that I stayed in & read *Death Comes for the Archbishop* [by Willa Cather] instead, a book which is very beautiful in its majestic simplicity. Marinoff goes out to dinner & theatre with Eddie Wassermann & I dine at home with Donald Angus. We spent the evening here & when Eddie & Marinoff come in we go to the midnight show of *Africana*. Saw Ethel [Waters] & Earl & Johnnie Dancer, Geraldyn Dismond, Muriel Draper & E. E. Cummings & Louis Bromfield. Home for supper about 3.

    1. Soupault, an established French novelist, had translated CVV's novel, deleting nearly one-third of the text by cutting passages that dealt with social, political, and economic conditions in Harlem. What remained were two love stories, one salacious and one anemic, and scenes in speakeasies. Despite CVV's objections, the translation appeared in print in 1927.

Sunday, 4 September 1927

. . . Avery Hopwood arrives from Europe & came to lunch. About 3 he goes to his hotel (the Barclay) for a rest & returns at 5, when Zora Hurston & her husband [Herbert] Sheen (met) are here. Later Lenore Ulric. They stay to supper. Later . . . Ethel Waters & Earl Dancer. Colin McPhee was here for a while in the afternoon but became restless, because Sheen was playing the piano, & went home.

Tuesday, 6 September 1927

. . . Dinner at Eddie Wassermann's: Boonie Goossens, Ethel Waters, Earl Dancer. After dinner Donald Angus & Sidney Peterson, Nella & Elmer Imes, Harry Block, Zora Hurston & her husband Sheen (who played), Langston Hughes. About 1 o'clock I was giving an imitation of the communicants at the Sanctified Church & screaming right lustily. The windows came open & a crowd collected. Then a man from the Home Protection Agency appeared & later 3 policemen, also the District Attorney & this [*word*] appeared. Nella & Elmer drive me & Boonie home.

Thursday, 8 September 1927

. . . Painters put second coat of paint on my room. The house is hellish. It takes us three hours to get the orange red I wanted but we get it. The room is really thrilling when done with its blue woodwork & canary yellow ceiling. . . .

Thursday, 15 September 1927

. . . Locatelli sends in a bill which infuriates me & we hear an exchange of compliments over the telephone. Then I settle down to scrap books, etc. I am more & more determined not to write until I have something to write about. . . .

Friday, 16 September 1927

. . . Mercedes de Acosta, Donald Angus, Louise Bryant [Bullitt] for dinner. Marinoff dines at Eddie Wassermann's, & comes in with Johnnie Floyd about midnight. Earl Dancer & Eddie Wassermann arrive to take Louise Bryant & me to Harlem, first to a marvelous buffet flat, & then to a box party at a midnight show of Butterbeans & Susie at the Lafayette. . . . Home about 4.30.

Sunday, 18 September 1927

. . . House is in perfect condition and I haven't even a desk to clean out. I'm afraid I'll have to start writing! . . . I read in *The Grandmothers* [by Glenway Wescott] & find it a wonderful book. I begin to talk about getting a car.[1]

  1. CVV never bought a car; moreover, he never learned to drive.

Tuesday, 20 September 1927

. . . Reading over mss. In an effort to interest myself once again in writing. Irita Van Doren for lunch. Marinoff goes out. After Irita goes I get dressed and go to see Ethel Waters at the Palace. I find her in a rage . . . in her dressing room because she has made such a success that no one will follow her & she has been given last place on the bill. But I stay to see her succeed in this spot. Then to a cocktail party Louise Bryant [Bullitt] gives in her tiny apartment on Patchin Place. . . . Then to Edna Kenton's (for the first time in over 3 years) for dinner. It is now very sordid at 240 W. 15. Garbage pails & squalling babies everywhere. . . .

Friday, 23 September 1927

. . . Wrote on Chapter V of *Spider Boy* which seems to be moving. . . . James Weldon Johnson comes in. Later Avery Hopwood who takes Marinoff & me to dinner at Leone's. After dinner we go to A'Lelia Walker's. . . . Later we go to look at A'Lelia's studio. . . . Still later A'Lelia, Avery, Marinoff & I go to Harry Glynn's bootlegging place on Lower Sixth Avenue. Home about 3.

Thursday, 29 September 1927

. . . Finish Chapter VII and write Chapter VIII of *Spider Boy*. Getting more & more enthusiastic. It ought to be an amusing book & turnabout satire. . . . Home to receive Nella Imes & Dorothy Peterson. Marinoff & Nella exchange dresses. James Weldon Johnson, Donald Angus, & Avery Hopwood for dinner. The latter two stay till 1.30 when I go to bed.

Saturday, 1 October 1927

. . . Louise [Bryant Bullitt], Marinoff, Alice de la Mar[1] (driving) & I go out to look at houses.[2] Marinoff sees the stone house & likes it. Then home for lunch. In the afternoon we drive to Deerfield & lose Pip Pip, Anne Bullitt's little Scotch terrier. Also Louise, in pointing, takes a piece out of Marinoff's eye. Later for cocktails at the Curtiss's & meet Rosamond Lehmann.[3] Home for dinner & a wild evening. Lewis Galantiere, very quiet. Millie Morris very drunk & noisy. In bed about 11.

    1. Wealthy lesbian patron of the arts whose houses in Connecticut and Florida often hosted artists and writers.

    2. CVV and Marinoff were again searching for a country house to purchase, although no two people were less likely candidates for a successful tenure out of the city.

    3. English novelist.

Sunday, 2 October 1927

. . . Alice de la Mar promised to give [me] an automobile driving lesson but all the cars are out. So we fool around the terrace till 11, when Jim [i.e., James Weldon] Johnson drives up & takes us off across country, through Lenox & Stockbridge to his place at Great Barrington. We have lunch at his place with Grace . . . & then look at houses. Home on the train with . . . Jim—in compartment—at 6.58, arriving at 10. Hubert, Jim's chauffeur, makes a miscalculation after we leave Ashfield & we drive past a house with a for sale sign that I like enormously. It has a marvelous view.

Wednesday, 5 October 1927

. . . Finished Chapter IX of novel & wrote Chapter X. Marinoff goes . . . for another eye treatment. . . . Avery Hopwood, Donald Angus & Armina Marshall [Langner] for dinner. Armina & Marinoff go to theatre. Nella & Elmer Imes come down. At 11 we are joined by Marinoff with Eddie Wassermann & Olga Hilliard & we go to the opening of Lloyd Thomas & Gardner Pinckett's cabaret: The Club Ebony, decorated by Aaron Douglas. Lizzie Miles is one of the entertainers & I give her the first tip. Saw the Seabrooks, Flournoy Miller,[1] Ethel Waters & Earl Dancer, A'Lelia Walker, Geraldyn & Benga Dismond, Tom Smith, . . . Evelyn Preer, . . . Jim & Dorothy Harris, Jimmie Allen, etc. Home at 4.30.

    1. African American comedian, stage partner in writing and performing of Aubrey Lyles.

Monday, 10 October 1927

Up at 9. Cool & sunny. Meda brought me the *Pittsburgh Courier* which contains Lyles's (of Miller & Lyles) attack on me. Finished Chapter XII of *Spider Boy.*

Thursday, 13 October 1927

. . . Avery Hopwood, going to Cleveland, comes in to say goodbye. Then I go to a farewell party at Rita Romilly's for Paul Robeson, who sails tomorrow for a concert tour of Europe. Paul, accompanied by Larry Brown sings magnificently. . . . Marinoff & I & Donald [Angus] go to a bad place on 96 St. for dinner & then to the Riverside to see Barbette,[1] who is really wonderful. Donald comes home with us & stays a while. In bed by midnight. Avery tells me he has written a long novel.[2]

    1. Female impersonator.

2. Hopwood's roman à clef, *The Grand Bordel*, in which CVV appears as "Amory Van Dusen," has never been published.

Saturday, 15 October 1927

. . . I have a slight hangover but I feel pretty good. I write on Chapter XVI of *Spider Boy*. Lunch in alone . . . and then to the Roxy . . . to hear Hall Johnson's chorus sing spirituals. He is no showman & the effect was pretty tame. The Dark Tower, A'Lelia Walker's new tearoom,[1] opens tonight. We cannot go, but I send her a telegram & flowers. . . . At 10 o'clock we go to a party at Maurice & Alma Wertheim's for Dorothy and DuBose Heyward.[2] Constance Collier,[3] Mamoulian,[4] Jim & Grace Johnson, Richard Hammond,[5] Marion Bauer,[6] Elizabeth Sheffey Sergeant, Aaron Copland, Lee Simonson, Armina & Lawrence Langner, Georgette Harvey (who sang),[7] Elmer Rice,[8] John & Mrs. Farrar,[9] Johnnie Weaver,[10] etc. Home before one.

1. *Tearoom* was a widely recognized euphemism for *speakeasy*.
2. The Heywards' dramatization of *Porgy* had just opened, very successfully, with an all African American cast.
3. English actress of the old school of performing in the grand manner.
4. Rouben Mamoulion, theater director and designer.
5. English composer of a ballet, *Fiesta*, and other works.
6. American composer and piano composition teacher.
7. African American entertainer, with an international reputation based on her performances during a decade in Russia, who returned to the United States to act in many black revues and in white plays calling for black casts.
8. Social realist (*Street Scene*) and expressionist (*The Adding Machine*) playwright.
9. American playwright and his wife, also co-author of plays with American poet Stephen Vincent Benét.
10. Light versist John V. A. Weaver, also co-author with playwright George Abbott of *Love 'Em and Leave 'Em*.

Sunday, 16 October 1927

. . . Home at 4 to find Nella Imes here. She & Marinoff have been making over a dress. They go to a party at Tom Smith's. I stay home from this and also a party at Jack Stern's[1] for Frances Seligman. Marinoff & Nella come home & cook supper for Eddie Wassermann & me. Later in the evening Armina & Lawrence Langner come in on their way to a party at Nik Muray's. (This also I am invited to, but I have sworn to cut out parties for a while.) Eddie Wassermann is extremely drunk & obnoxious & I insult him as much as possible. Everybody goes about midnight & we go to bed.

1. Editor and publisher of the *Underwear and Hosiery Review*.

Tuesday, 18 October 1927

. . . I spend the morning & part of the afternoon going over my note-book in search of ideas for *Spider Boy.* I find very little. . . . I read Mary White Ovington's *Portraits in Color.* The book is too lush in tone & too badly written to be effective. None of the portraits seem real because they are so lacking in criticism of the subjects. . . .

Monday, 24 October 1927

. . . Worked a little on *Spider Boy.* . . . Then Marinoff & I went to the Capitol to see Marion Davies in *The Fair Co-ed,* a rotten film, and then to Gimbel's to inspect their antique department. Then to Ovington's new shop & home. Eddie Wassermann and Emily Clark. Eddie was drunk & again objectionable, talking about the Bullitts' (whom he doesn't know) social position in Philadelphia. They went home about midnight. I got very drunk & (I hope) insulted everybody.

Friday, 28 October 1927

Up at 6.30. My teeth do not seem to improve.[1] Spend most of the day writing Chapter IV of *Spider Boy.* . . . Late in the afternoon I take a short walk & call on Blanche Knopf. . . . Home. Telegram from Aileen Pringle gives me leave to entertain her on Tuesday. So I begin calling up her friends. . . .

> 1. CVV's buck teeth were an easy mark for amusement because they were large and ugly, like shards of thick crockery, and his widely spaced upper front teeth jutted out, inspiring plenty of similes. He was variously described as "a friendly werewolf," "a walrus," and "a wild boar." He suffered all his life with serious dental problems but was never embarrassed by his appalling teeth. In old age, when one of the front buck teeth ulcerated, he had it replaced with a duplicate because, he averred, so many people identified him with them.

Sunday, 30 October 1927

. . . Gums are a little better. Reading papers, writing letters, etc., in the morning and until late in the afternoon when I call on Aileen Pringle at the Park Chambers Hotel. She has just arrived from Hollywood. Henry Mencken comes in. Home at 6.30. A'Lelia Walker, Avery Hopwood, Arthur Spingarn, Rita Romilly, Donald Angus, Capt. Douglas & Zena Naylor for supper. They stay quite late & I got soused.

Monday, 31 October 1927

Up at 8. Hangover. Essie telephones that Paul's first concert on Saturday in Paris was a sell-out. I do some feeble work on Chapter VI of my novel, which is a mess. Then have lunch in & go to . . . have all my teeth X-rayed & find another has to be pulled. . . .

Tuesday, 1 November 1927

. . . Ethel Waters calls up at 8 o'clock to tell me that Florence Mills is dead.[1] Then I worked for a while on Chapter VI. . . . At 5, party for Aileen Pringle: Irene Mayer[2] & her sister, Mrs. Lloyd Osborne, . . . Carmel Myers, Mamoulian, Armina Langner, Charlie Shaw,[3] Mary McKinnon,[4] Regina Wallace, Julia Hoyt, . . . T. R. Smith, Donald Freeman, Jimmie Reynolds,[5] Louis Calhern, . . . Olga Hilliard, Rita Romilly, Edward Wassermann, Bernard Boutet de Monvel,[6] Ralph Barton, Irita & Carl Van Doren, . . . Eva Gauthier, Steichen, etc.[7] After that cocktail party six of us go to Blanche Knopf's for supper. Home about 11 & to bed. Slept badly. It is very hot.

1. The most popular African American entertainer of the twenties had died of peritonitis at the age of 26.
2. Actress, later married to David O. Selznick.
3. American humorist writer.
4. American portrait painter currently doing a portrait of Fania Marinoff.
5. American set and costume designer of Broadway plays.
6. French painter and designer.
7. This is the first of several CVV parties since 1925 that included no African Americans on its guest list. Pringle had deep-seated racial prejudices from her years in the Bahamas, when she was married to John Pringle, son of the governor there. CVV gradually broke down her resistance over a period of time by introducing her slowly to his black friends. In her old age, Pringle spoke openly and admiringly about his ability to free other people as well as herself from the stigma of racial prejudice.

Wednesday, 2 November 1927

. . . At 4.30 I go to . . . have another tooth pulled. Weary of a sore gum. It comes out in many pieces. Home at 6. Avery Hopwood takes me to dinner at the Coffee House with Constance Collier. Then we take her to rehearsal & go to Harry Glynn's place.[1] . . . In bed about 12 o'clock. The doctor used wedges, drills, etc., on my teeth & I was in the chair nearly an hour. My nerves are shattered.

1. This speakeasy operated by a bootlegger was patronized largely by homosexuals.

Thursday, 3 November 1927

. . . Woke up with a swollen jaw that is sore but no pain. At 11 went . . . for a treatment. Rain all day. Home & lying down. . . . Avery came in to see me and stayed most of the afternoon & for dinner. In the evening Marinoff goes to theatre with Regina Wallace. I go with Avery to Harry Glynn's . . . place. Avery gets very drunk & insults everybody & breaks a lot of dishes. Michael Goring, a pale London youth of his acquaintance appears, & I slip out. Home around 12 & to bed alone. Marinoff stays with Reg. Outside the speakeasy my pocket is deftly picked. I lose my beautiful Viennese leather purse & 25 dollars.

Friday, 4 November 1927

. . . I worked on the horribly unsatisfactory Chapter VI of *Spider Boy*. . . . My tooth begins to throb. To bed with an ice-bag. . . . Blanche Knopf came to see me & tells me Donald [Angus] is doing very well.[1] Donald came to dinner with me & spends the evening here while Marinoff (in my place) goes to see Philip Barry's play, *John*, with Avery Hopwood. I have a bad night. It turns cold.

> 1. Angus had been hired as a copy editor and fact checker at Alfred A. Knopf, Inc.

Sunday, 6 November 1927

. . . Pain in my gum seems to be worse than ever. I take more aspirin & it makes me sick. Besides I have a pain in my groin. Wanted to go to Florence Mills's funeral but not feeling up to it. . . . Marinoff goes to concert with Carlotta Monterey, but I stay home. . . . Go to bed at 8 & sleep till 12 when I toss in pain till 5. In anguish I take two grains of aspirin & sleep till 8.30.

Monday, 7 November 1927

. . . The aspirin is beginning to wear off. I get dressed & go to Dr. Van Saun who treats my gum & puts novocaine in it. This very painful. Pass a miserable day, writing. . . . Some hours free from pain in the afternoon during which time I read Julian Green's *Mont Cinere* at one sitting & find it so splendid that I start his *Adrienne Mesurat*. . . . Towards night the pain recommences & I . . . am up four times in the night & take aspirin & codeine & a new drug. Up definitely before 7.

Tuesday, 8 November 1927

In the morning the pain is so excruciating that I try dropping novocaine in the cavity. This makes it worse. So I live on aspirin & codeine during the day. . . . I finish *Adrienne Mersault* during the day, in its way as remarkable as *Mont Cinere* but not as organized a book. I have discovered Green's formula. It is the Cinderella story turned inside out. The drudge who never discovers Prince Charming. His characters seem inspired by an extraordinary fate, . . . impelled toward . . . disaster by some kink in their character. To the dentist at 3.30. He drops iodine & peroxide into the cavity to relieve the excruciating pain. Home. . . .

Saturday, 12 November 1927

Up at seven. It is much warmer. I dress and walk to Holliday Book Shop, to the bank, to Schirmer's to get George Gershwin's *Concerto in F,* to Landay's for records & home in time for lunch. After lunch I play records & rest. At 5 Aileen Pringle comes in. . . . I dine with Avery Hopwood & Bob Montgomery. . . . Later Avery comes home with me to talk about the mishaps in his life. Paul Lane[1] & Donald Angus come after us & we go to Harry Glynn's: a very amusing cunt[2] called "Madge" Kennedy entertains us & I meet a mulatto named Tom Johnson. He & Harry Glynn go with us to Harlem, first to The Dark Tower, which we leave immediately when we find A'Lelia is not there. Then to Club Ebony where I saw . . . Lizzie Miles. We stay till place closes & then go to The Nest. . . . We have a gay time till 5 & go to Johnnie Brent's to eat. Home about 6.30.

    1. Another of Angus's brief liaisons.
    2. In the homosexual slang of the period, this word stood for drag queens and transvestites.

Monday, 14 November 1927

. . . Late in the afternoon Charles S. Johnson comes to talk to me about my award to *Opportunity* authors[1] & Lucile Harper comes in with a bottle of absinthe. Dinner alone with Marinoff. After dinner I put [Wilhelm] Kemper in the Mendelssohn concerto on the phonograph, do some more work & then go to bed about 10. A horrible night: my nerves are shattered by last week's experiences. I sleep badly & when I fall asleep I have horrible nightmares.

    1. CVV established an annual $200 literary award for the best writing published in *Opportunity,* the magazine of the Urban League.

Thursday, 17 November 1927

. . . The weather is horrible. Feeling some better. Working on *Spider Boy.* Upton Sinclair's ridiculous book, *Money Writes,* arrived and I find a chapter devoted to me.[1] Aileen Pringle & Arthur Richman come to lunch & Aileen stays all the afternoon, meeting Emily Clark at 4. They like each other. Aileen leaves at 6.30. At 7 Constance Collier, Avery Hopwood, Carmel Myers (in place of Mildred Knopf[2] who is ill) & Edwin Knopf come for dinner. Edwin is starting a new stock company in Baltimore & wants Marinoff to play in it. . . .

    1. Sinclair eviscerated *The Tattooed Countess* as a novel calculated from its inception to make money by pandering to its readers.

    2. American writer of cookbooks.

Thursday, 24 November 1927

Thanksgiving. Up at 8.30. Cloudy & warm. Working all morning on Chapter XII of *Spider Boy* & started Chapter XIII. At two we give a dinner: Constance Collier & Donald Angus. Later Einar Norman & his wife (Danish caricaturist brought here by Eva Gauthier), . . . Nella & Elmer Imes, Avery Hopwood, Paul Bern,[1] Juliet & Arthur Hornblow, Noel Murphy.[2] Donald stays on. About 11—very drunk—I go to a party at Alfred & Blanche Knopf's where I insult Emily Clark. . . . [Josef] Lhevinne, pianist (met), Main Bocher,[3] Adele Astaire, Eddie Wassermann, Margaret Freeman, Irita Van Doren, Aaron Copland, Koussevitzky & Mme., Geo. Gershwin (who played), etc.

    1. Head of production at Metro Goldwyn Mayer.

    2. Mrs. Frederic Murphy, who lived abroad, primarily in Paris.

    3. Some time later, as Mainbocher, a celebrated clothes designer.

Monday, 28 November 1927

. . . I was awake an hour in the night coughing & my cold seems just the same. Writing on Chapter XV of *Spider Boy*. It seems to be terrible. . . . I feel miserable. Late in the afternoon I go over to the Elysée to see Avery [Hopwood]. He, his mother, Bob Montgomery I find in Carmel Myers's room. . . . Later Avery, Bob, his mother & I have dinner in Avery's room. A. gets very drunk & goes out when I do, taking me to Florence Embry Jones's where I stay till 5 o'clock. Harry Glynn comes in. Florence sits with us. She has been in Paris for years & I have not seen her since she used to sing at Marshall's.[1] Home about 5.

    1. Marshall's, a well-known black hotel on West 53rd Street, in the heart of what was called "Black Bohemia," from the turn of the century until the end of World War I, featured a basement restaurant where African American intellectuals gathered and several white patrons were regulars, notably the artist Charles Demuth and CVV. The floor show featured Florence Embry and her accompanist husband, Palmer Jones. After the war, they moved to Paris and opened their own bistro, Le Grand Duc. She returned to the United States in 1927 to sing in various clubs and died in poverty a few years later.

Monday, 5 December 1927

. . . Clear, cold. Snow on the roofs. My cold is looser. My lungs are full of phlegm. But I work on Chapter XV & clean up generally around the place. . . . Dinner in with Marinoff. She goes to the theatre & Avery Hopwood comes to see me. He tells me that N.Y. at present is wilder than any European city. . . .

Friday, 9 December 1927

. . . God knows how I feel. I get more & more depressed as morning wears on. Lunch in with Marinoff. She called the doctor who arrives at 2.30, gives me more medicine & sends me outdoors. It is <u>very</u> cold. . . .

Tuesday, 13 December 1927

. . . I write part of Chapter XVII of *Spider Boy*. . . . Feel rotten after lunch & clean out my desk, reading with scant pleasure the letters concerning Father's will and Addie's dower rights. . . . Rains all day & I continue to feel rotten. Regina Wallace & Eddie Wassermann for dinner. After dinner Reg & Marinoff go to the theatre & Eddie goes to a party. So I sit & drink whiskey & get drunk. In bed after midnight.

Friday, 16 December 1927

. . . Help Marinoff finish packing.[1] . . . We dine with the Langners: Tom Smith, Mercedes de Acosta, Alma & Maurice Wertheim, Philip Moeller. Later Rosamond Johnson & Taylor Gordon, Jim & Grace Johnson, Rita Romilly, Horace Liveright, etc. We leave at 11 & go to a party at Edwin Knopf's. . . . Home around 2.30.

  1. Fania Marinoff had been engaged to join Edwin Knopf's stock company in Baltimore, playing first in *He Who Gets Slapped*.

Saturday, 17 December 1927

. . . Marinoff leaves for Baltimore at 12. I go to train & see Edwin Knopf, Helen Chandler, Robert & Dolly Randall, Julie Ruben, Gilbert Douglas & Robert Montgomery[1] on the special train. Then I . . . buy Marinoff a pair of 1820 Russian sapphire & gold bracelets. Then to Wanamaker's to buy ice bowl. Then to bank, then to Algonquin where I have lunch with Burton Rascoe & Lewis Galantiere. . . . I go upstairs to see Bertha Case & Persian kitten I gave her. I meet Margaret [Case] downstairs. Home. It is very cold & my cold is no better. . . . At 4.30 Beverly Nichols[2] comes to see me & we meet. He goes about six & Main Bocher & Donald Angus stop for me to go to dine with Nella & Elmer Imes. Dorothy Peterson for dinner. . . . At 11.30, Main, Donald & I go to Club Ebony & met Beverly. From there to Lulu Belle's, a remarkable dive. Then to Sugar Cane. Home about 4. Donald spends the night.

    1. Members of Knopf's stock company for the Baltimore season.
    2. Prolific English essayist.

Sunday, 18 December 1927

For some curious reason I feel better this morning. . . . Donald takes me to the train & we have lunch in Pennsylvania Station. Train departs at 2.40 for Atlantic City. I . . . arrive at 5.45, very depressed & register at Ritz. I dine alone in the great dining salle. . . . Then take a short walk on the boardwalk. Then to my room for reading Isadora Duncan's story [*My Life*], & to bed about 9.30. Slept fairly well, except awakened occasionally by the cold.

Monday, 19 December 1927

Up at 8.30. Very cold but my room, with an ocean view and southern exposure, is very attractive. Breakfast in my room & wrote letters. Later I finish Isadora Duncan's book, go for a walk around the hotel & a little outside—it is too cold to stay long. Back for lunch. Then to my room where I read Isa Glenn's *Southern Charm*. For a short walk before dinner & dinner in my room. Also play solitaire occasionally. I am no more bored than I should be on a railroad train. My cold, however, persists. After dinner I read Oppenheimer's *A Double Traitor* till about 10.30 when I turn in. The wind howls & rattles the casements, but I sleep well.

Wednesday, 21 December 1927

Up at 7.30. Warmer & clear. I am better, but more nervous. Last night I about decided to go home today & I think I shall. Took a walk—warmer—sent some telegrams, came back, ordered my tickets. Then played solitaire till lunch time. Lunch at the Ambassador. Feeling rather sicker & don't eat much lunch. Back to get my bags. Meet Edna Ferber in the lobby & catch 1.55 train arriving in N.Y. around six. So endeth another lesson in folly.[1] Drank some orange juice. Avery Hopwood came in to spend evening. In bed around 11, & slept fairly well.

    1. CVV does not record that he went to Atlantic City, determined to give up smoking and drinking. Later he embellished this story by declaring that he had had himself locked in his room by the hotel staff for seventy-two hours to break these habits. He never smoked again.

Thursday, 22 December 1927

. . . As usual I have no idea how I feel. But no worse, apparently. . . . At 4.30
I . . . go to a cocktail party at Rita Romilly's, but I am not drinking or smok-
ing. Taylor Gordon, Rosamond Johnson, Armina Langner, Jean & Herbert
Gorman, Jacob & Mme. Epstein,[1] Joseph [Wood] Krutch, Charles Sheeler,[2]
Mercedes de Acosta, T. R. Smith, Sigmund Spaeth, etc. Home at 5.30. . . .

    1. English sculptor and his wife.
    2. American Precisionist painter.

Friday, 23 December 1927

Up at 6.30. Feeling infinitely better. . . . At a quarter of eleven I start out with
Christmas packages. . . . Home for lunch, then out on another pilgrimage for
Xmas. Then home again, writing letters, etc. Late in the afternoon Langston
Hughes came to see me. About 7 I leave for Virginia Hammond's with gifts
& see her palatial house, which looks as though she was very well kept. Then
to the Knopfs' for dinner. Tom Beer, who is more boorish than usual, Margalo
Gilmore, Main Bocher, Benno Moiseiwitsch, Myra Hess,[1] & Edna Chase,
editor of *Vogue*. Alfred shows moving pictures, etc. Main sails. Then home
by eleven & in bed soon after. . . .

    1. English concert pianist.

Sunday, 25 December 1927

. . . It is sunny, bright, & cold, a beautiful Christmas. I call Marinoff up in
Baltimore, & she is feeling nervous & rotten. Lots of telephones, lots of telegrams, but somehow the spirit of Christmas is elusive. Donald Angus, Eddie
Wassermann, Rita Romilly for dinner at 2. We had suckling pig. Later Blanche
came in, earlier Elmer Imes. Donald stayed on after the others had left till
about seven when I went to Blanche Knopf's for buffet. Alfred was there &
Myra Hess, later Benno Moiseiwitsch. Blanche talks about herself & her
troubles & I went home to bed about 11.30.

Monday, 26 December 1927

. . . I haven't had a drink or a cigarette since a week ago Saturday. I work on
Chapter 17 of *Spider Boy*, get my own lunch & then go to A'Lelia Walker's. . . .
About 4.30 I go over to Nella Imes's, & stay to dinner with her & Elmer. Elmer
drives me home about nine & I go to bed about 10. . . . My cold is almost gone.
My tongue is clear & I am looking better than I have looked in months.

Tuesday, 27 December 1927

. . . Worked on Chapter XVIII of *Spider Boy*. At 5 Mina & Harry Curtiss of Northampton, Ettie Stettheimer, Robert [Morss] Lovett, Nella & Elmer Imes, Eddie Wassermann. Ettie invites everybody to a party but Nella Imes, & I call her up later to chide her. "Are you teaching me manners?" she demands & hangs up the receiver. Colin McPhee for dinner & I spend the evening here. In bed about 12.

Thursday, 29 December 1927

. . . Early in the afternoon, Countee Cullen comes in, bringing the name of the winner of the *Opportunity* award. I gave him a check of $200, made out to the National Urban League, to be awarded to the winner. Later Taylor Gordon comes in & tells me how he has whored it in London, etc., & borrows $50. Rhea Wells comes to dinner & spends the evening here. He goes at 11 & I go to bed.

Friday, 30 December 1927

. . . I feel lacking in nervousness as I haven't smoked a cigarette for two weeks. . . . At 5 o'clock Blanche Knopf comes in. I have dinner alone & then call on Paul & Mme. Morand at the Ambassador. They have been in town 3 days & are sailing tonight. . . . Then I go to a party chez Donald Angus for Noel Sullivan.[1] . . . Home around midnight & to bed. No drinks or smokes.

    1. Wealthy West Coast patron of young artists and writers, notably Langston Hughes a few years later.

Saturday, 31 December 1927

Up at 7.15 and packing. Rainy & warm. I feel a little stuffy. I leave New York at 1.10 for Baltimore, . . . go directly to the Stafford Hotel. . . . Marinoff & I have dinner together & then I go to see her play Zenida in *He Who Gets Slapped* with Edwin Knopf's Stock Co. A pretty weak performance. She was fair & so was John Ruben. After the theatre we go to a New Year's party with Edwin. Home about 1.30 & to bed. It has been rainy all day but it turns cold at night. I take a slight drink at midnight, the first in two weeks.

Alfred A. Knopf, 1935 (photograph by Carl Van Vechten; Yale Collection of American Literature, Beinecke Rare Book and Manuscript Library, Yale University)

Blanche Knopf, 1932 (photograph by Carl Van Vechten; Yale Collection of American Literature, Beinecke Rare Book and Manuscript Library, Yale University)

Nigger Heaven advertisement, 1926 (illustration by Aaron Douglas; Van Vechten Trust)

Carl Van Vechten's "Famous Beauties of the XXth Century" (photographers unknown; Estate of Donald Angus and the Van Vechten Trust; clockwise from top left): Donald Angus, circa 1919; Max Ewing, circa 1923; Edward Wassermann, circa 1917; and Tom Mabry, 1923

Fania Marinoff, circa 1921 (photograph by Nickolas Muray; Estate of Donald Angus)

Zora Neale Hurston, 1934 (photograph by Carl Van Vechten; Millersville University, Helen A. Ganser Library, Special Collections and University Archives)

Langston Hughes, circa 1922 (photographer unknown; Yale Collection of American Literature, Beinecke Rare Book and Manuscript Library, Yale University)

Nella Larsen Imes, 1934 (photograph by Carl Van Vechten; Yale Collection of American Literature, Beinecke Rare Book and Manuscript Library, Yale University)

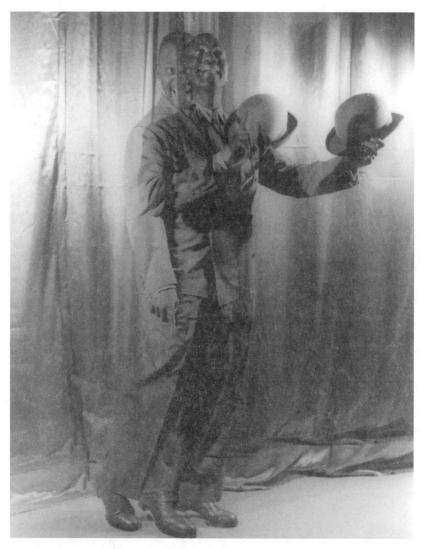

Bill Robinson and Bojangles Robinson, 1941 (composition photograph by Carl Van Vechten; Yale Collection of American Literature, Beinecke Rare Book and Manuscript Library, Yale University)

Ethel Waters, 1938 (photograph by Carl Van Vechten; Yale Collection of American Literature, Beinecke Rare Book and Manuscript Library, Yale University)

Clara Smith, circa 1925 (photographer unknown; Millersville University, Helen A. Ganser Library, Special Collections and University Archives)

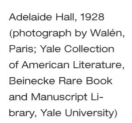

Adelaide Hall, 1928 (photograph by Walén, Paris; Yale Collection of American Literature, Beinecke Rare Book and Manuscript Library, Yale University)

The Mad Whirl of the Dance (ink and wash drawing by Ralph Barton; editor's collection)

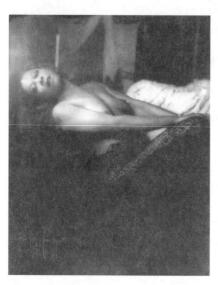

Nora Holt, circa 1920 (photograph by James Hargis Connelly; Yale Collection of American Literature, Beinecke Rare Book and Manuscript Library, Yale University)

A'Lelia Walker, circa 1925 (photographer unknown; courtesy of A'Lelia Bundles and Millersville University, Helen A. Ganser Library, Department of Special Collections and University Archives)

Paul Robeson, 1932 (photograph by Carl Van Vechten; Yale Collection of American Literature, Beinecke Rare Book and Manuscript Library, Yale University)

1928

"Probably if I don't stop
drinking I'll blow up."

After pausing en route for the funeral of his brother's wife in Chicago, Van Vechten returned to Hollywood for a second visit, then cut it short on finding the place more impossible than it had seemed the year before. After a stopover in New Mexico, without seeing Mabel Dodge Luhan, he returned to New York to see *Spider Boy* published to mixed reviews and to plunge again into Harlem's night life. By 1928 Van Vechten had grown heavy from too much food and alcohol. Meanwhile, Fania Marinoff was on a holiday in Europe when Van Vechten's best friend, playwright Avery Hopwood, died there in August. Van Vechten joined his wife in September and hired a chauffeured automobile for a tour that included Munich, Prague, Vienna, Budapest, and several places in Italy. He suffered strange maladies in Paris and London, then returned to the United States before the end of the year.

Sunday, 1 January 1928

Baltimore at the Stafford Hotel. . . . About one everybody leaves for the theatre & a dress-rehearsal of *Spring Cleaning*. . . . About six Marinoff back from rehearsal. Mencken arrives & takes us to dinner in a private room at Marconi's. Sarah Haardt (met).[1] . . . I drink but don't smoke.

    1. Southern writer, later Mrs. H. L. Mencken.

Tuesday, 3 January 1928

. . . Goodbye to Sweet Mama Marinoff & 11 o'clock train for New York. Read [Norman] Douglas's *In the Beginning*, a rotten book, on the train. . . . Avery [Hopwood] called up almost immediately. To dinner with him & Donald Angus at Leone's & then to Harry Glynn's. Johnnie Floyd . . . fights with Avery. Later Jack & Lucile Harper, & we all go to Chez Florence,[1] also an English boy Avery picks up. Dagmar Godowsky, Richard Watts, Jr.,[2] Percy Hammond & others turn up at Florence's. I am there till dawn.

    1. A Harlem speakeasy where Florence Embry Jones entertained.

    2. Film critic for the *Herald Tribune;* later drama critic there and, still later, for the *New York Post.*

Thursday, 5 January 1928

Up at 9, cold & clear, with a hangover. . . . After lunch . . . went to the bank & to see Avery at the Elysée. Found him with a cockney lad called Tom Measor[1] & later George Brandt & Pepito.[2] I left them at 5 & came home. Avery eventually arrived for dinner here. Then we went to Harry Glynn's. . . .

    1. Another of Hopwood's casual liaisons.

    2. Hopwood's long-time secretary and his pet monkey, Pipi-squeak or Pepe-squeak, alternately called Pepito by CVV.

Sunday, 8 January 1928

. . . Called on Avery in the afternoon & discovered him in bed with a new boy, named Dick Lockwood. Telephoned for Donald. We went from there to Jack Harper's. Then to Harry Glynn's. . . . Then to Guild Theatre (after dinner at my house) to see *Marco Millions* [by Eugene O'Neill]. Met Lawrence & Armina Langner at box office. Seats were so bad, I left Donald there & went back to Lucile's, continue to drink till 10.30. Feeling terrible, home & to bed. Didn't go to afternoon party chez D'Alvarez or evening party for Molnar[1] chez Condé Nast.[2]

    1. Hungarian playwright Ferenc Molnar.
    2. Publisher of *Vanity Fair* magazine.

Saturday, 14 January 1928

Up at 8.30. Cloudy & warm. Wrote Chapter V of *Spider Boy*, finishing, as usual, about 4. Man comes to tune the piano. After lunch I walk to the bank, to grocer's, etc. . . . Late in afternoon Jack Barker[1] & Kay Kenney[2] came in & we got plastered. Then I went to dinner at Blanche Knopf's. . . . Later to Sugar Cane in Harlem with Donald Angus, Jack Barker, Kay Kenney, Avery Hopwood, Eddie Wassermann, Charlotte Ives,[3] Blanche Knopf. Some of us go to the Lulu Belle, but there is a fight on & we can't get in. To Ebony. . . . Home around 4.

    1. Actor in musical comedies and revues, including the Marx Brothers' *The Cocoanuts.*
    2. An aspiring American playwright, two of whose scripts were produced in the thirties.
    3. Minor American actress.

Sunday, 15 January 1928

. . . Late in the afternoon Kay Kenney, Jack Barker, . . . & Avery Hopwood arrive & drinking begins again. Harry Block here. At 7 I drive everybody off but Harry & we go to dinner at Fornio's. Then back home. I send Harry away at 9.30 & go to bed. Sleep pretty well. Telephone rings at 3, but I don't answer.

Monday, 16 January 1928

. . . A Mrs. Webster calls me up at 9 o'clock to ask me where Jack Barker is, as if I should know, and in the evening she calls up three more times. Jack in the meantime calls up to say he is with Kay Kenney. Donald Angus for dinner & here for the evening. We play records. In bed about 11 & slept well.

Thursday, 19 January 1928

. . . In the afternoon it rains. So I stay in & re-read Neith Boyce's *Harry.* It seems to me now that Neith creates in her own mind a figure that did not exist, but she is so truthful that a rather dull, slow-witted, obstinate boy emerges.[1] . . .

    1. Neith Boyce [Mrs. Hutchins Hapgood] wrote her son's biography after his early death.

Friday, 20 January 1928

Up at 8.30. Colder & sunny. Wrote Chapter X of *Spider Boy*. Lunch in. Then I made a cover for *Spider Boy* & corrected 2nd draught of Chapter II. Wrote most of Chapter XI. Then Marinoff & I go to Vantine's sale where I buy . . . some shirts, to Crichton's to look at some earrings. Then to a cocktail party at Frank & Bertha Case's where Sara [Victor][1] gets me very drunk. Neysa McMein, . . . Hendrik Van Loon,[2] Gene Markey,[3] Ina Claire,[4] Madeleine & Ernest Boyd, Judith Anderson, Jesse Lasky, Margaret Morgan,[5] Taylor Holmes,[6] Marc Connelly, etc. Home to dress & then to Langners' dinner: Louis & Mrs. Bromfield, Lois Long & Peter Arno (met),[7] . . . & Eddie Wassermann. After dinner Bob Chanler. I get very drunk & misbehave frightfully & forget everything I've done next day.

1. The Cases' cook.
2. Dutch American author and illustrator of historical and cultural subjects prepared for a popular readership.
3. Writer and caricaturist, later a film actor.
4. Popular American stage actress.
5. Margaret Case.
6. American actor, primarily in comedies.
7. *New Yorker* cartoonist and his wife, the dramatic critic for *Vanity Fair* and, as "Lipstick," the nightclub columnist for *The New Yorker*.

Monday, 23 January 1928

. . . Lunch in alone. Marinoff lunches with Carlotta Monterey who is planning to elope with Eugene O'Neill. After lunch I walk to bank & back & then work on Chapter XIV. At 5 Leon Goossens[1] comes to see me & stays till Marinoff & I are picked up by Blanche Knopf to go to Isa Glenn's for dinner. Alfred there, Bayard[2] whom I lecture. What a tiresome boy! Home around midnight & eat a lot. I have a tremendous appetite these days.

1. English oboist, brother of Eugene Goossens.
2. Bayard Schindel published his first novel, *Golden Passage,* at age 21, a year later.

Saturday, 28 January 1928

. . . At 5 we go to see dress rehearsal of Eugene O'Neill's play, *Strange Interlude* (produced by Theatre Guild) at John Golden Theatre. After 5 acts we dine at the Stettheimers'. . . . Then back to see last 4 acts. All over at 11.20. On the whole a terrible play but interesting in spots. To bed about 12.

Thursday, 2 February 1928

. . . Lunch at Algonquin. Marinoff, Rita Romilly & D'Alvarez. . . . Home around 3. Jack Harper brings case of scotch and case of gin. Around 4 Avery Hopwood & Covarrubias (just back from Paris) appear, then James Weldon Johnson, Hunter Stagg, . . . Paul & Essie Robeson, Bob Montgomery & friend, Boonie Goosens (alone) just back from Paris. After they go Marinoff & I get dressed, have dinner & go to Alfred's box at the Boston Symphony. . . . Home & in bed before 11. . . .

Friday, 3 February 1928

. . . Went to Jack Auer's gymnasium with Avery Hopwood, & was banged around and rubbed for an hour. . . . I have Hunter Stagg & Tom Rutherford[1] for dinner. Then we go to Nella Imes'. Elmer [Imes] arrives. Then to Sugar Cane, Ebony Club (closed), Lulu Belle, & finally to Nest. Hunter got nasty & they drove me home at dawn (5.30).

    1. An aspiring actor, eventually in Leonard Sillman's *New Faces of 1936* and in regional productions of Shakespeare but in 1928 only another of CVV's *jeunes gens assortis.*

Saturday, 4 February 1928

Up at 10.30. . . . Dressed & walked to Sardi's where we had lunch with Bob Chanler & Louise Hellström. . . . I had a dreadful hangover & was very amusing. After lunch I went to see Hunter Stagg. I forgave him for misbehaving last night, but he is a very lucky person. Home & lie down. Miriam Wolff[1] came in & Langston Hughes, Eddie Wassermann, Sara Allgood[2] & a man. After dinner Philip Moeller, Helen Westley. . . .

    1. A Marinoff relative.
    2. Irish actress in New York appearing in Sean O'Casey's *The Plough and the Stars.*

Sunday, 5 February 1928

. . . After lunch Carlotta Monterey comes in to say goodbye. She is eloping with Eugene O'Neill on Friday. Then we taxied to the new Rockefeller Apartments on 150th Street, to see Paul & Essie Robeson & their baby. Made plans for Paul & Marinoff to appear in *Othello* together. Called up an enthusiastic Basil Rathbone.[1]

    1. The English actor was invited to play the role of Iago in this production. Nothing came of the plan, although it was still under consideration two years later when the Van Vechtens visited the Robesons in London.

Monday, 6 February 1928

Up at 8 o'clock after not so good a night. My muscles are torn & shaken by my exercises at Jack Auer's. . . . Hunter Stagg for lunch. He was held up in a speakeasy on Saturday night. . . . At 6 Marinoff & I have dinner & then go to the Rivoli to see Gloria Swanson in *Sadie Thompson,* a screen version of "Rain" & a great performance.[1] We had an engagement later in the evening to accompany the Robesons to Basil Rathbone's to discuss *Othello* but got a message that this was called off.

    1. John Colton's dramatization of W. Somerset Maugham's short story "Miss Thompson," earlier a stage play with Jeanne Eagels.

Tuesday, 7 February 1928

. . . Avery [Hopwood] calls up & I join him. Dick Lockwood[1] is there & occasionally his mother & Avery is drunk. Jack Harper comes in with booze & drives me home. Miriam Wolff comes in with gefüllte fish & stays to dinner in room with Marinoff. Hunter Stagg for dinner. After dinner Tom Rutherford. We go to A'Lelia Walker's. Several people there. We leave at 11. I take the boys to Harry Glynn's, see Eddie. . . . Home at 1.00.

    1. A prostitute whom Hopwood had engaged. "His mother" presumably refers to Jule Hopwood.

Thursday, 9 February 1928

. . . Looked over the French translation [of *Nigger Heaven*] & found some amusing & very silly mistakes. We dine at Mercedes d'Acosta's. . . . Later Boonie [Goosens], Marinoff, & I go to Chez Florence. Avery there, pie-eyed with a roughneck. . . . Home about 3.

Friday, 10 February 1928

. . . Blanche Knopf operated on for appendicitis & a tumor. I telephone hospital & learn she is all right. Then I go to Goldfarb's to order flowers for her, for E. Wassermann: it's his birthday tomorrow, & to Carlotta Monterey who sails tonight on the *Berengaria* with Eugene O'Neill. Home for lunch. Joe Hergesheimer telephones & asks me to buy flowers for Blanche. I do so & then go to bed for an hour. Donald Angus comes in to talk over jacket for *Spider Boy.*[1] Marinoff has a cold & decides not to go out so Reg Wallace comes to dine with her. I go to Eddie Wassermann's for dinner. Olga Hilliard, Bob Chanler, & Louise Hellström who fight. Avery Hopwood who brings Lucile

Harper and a male whore named Dick Lockwood, Harry Glynn who comes with gin, Nella & Elmes Imes, Boonie Goosens, Taylor Gordon. Joined later by Tom Rutherford. We all go to N.A.A.C.P. dance at Manhattan Cabaret, a very brilliant affair. Drive Tom home at 3 o'clock.

> 1. Angus had arranged for a friend of his, Ronald MacRae, to design the dust jacket for *Spider Boy*.

Saturday, 11 February 1928

... Tom Rutherford telephones he can't keep our engagement so I trek over to Avery's where he is drunk ... & his mother. Later Jack Barker. I come home & have dinner with Donald Angus & Marinoff. After dinner I call up. ... Harry Block to come over & we all join Avery & go to Harry Glynn's, which is a riot. Stay there till 2.30. Then home.

Sunday, 12 February 1928

... After eleven we drive to a party at A'Lelia [Walker]'s studio in Harlem for Florence [Embry] & Palmer Jones. ... I have a fight with A'Lelia & leave about 4. ... To bed at 5.

Monday, 13 February 1928

Up at 10. Bright & cool. I am feeling a little wild. The world calls up. Colin McPhee comes for lunch. I take him over to Avery's where we find Tom Measor. Jack Barker is supposed to come for me but he does not turn up so Colin & I go to a cocktail party at Jim Harris's. ... Rita Romilly drives me home. We dine at Sardi's because Meda is sick. Then to see Lawrence Langner's new play, *These Modern Women*. I am very soused & one act is enough for me. ...

Wednesday, 15 February 1928

... Marinoff & I walk to Algonquin, she to take Virginia Hammond & Armina Langner to lunch, me to lunch with Joseph & Dorothy Hergesheimer. He is beginning to grate on me, but we talk for two hours. ... Blanche Knopf calls up in tears. Benno Moisiwitsch has just left her in the hospital to be gone a year on a concert tour. ...

Thursday, 16 February 1928

... Home to find a telegram that Fannie Van Vechten died this morning. Eddie Wassermann leaves with Marinoff for dinner. ... Donald & I got plastered.

I have a fight with Marinoff & one with Florence [Embry Jones]. Home, in bed at 3.

Saturday, 18 February 1928

Up at nine o'clock & a little later we arrive in Chicago. . . . Then to bank & then to house where I see Duane, not too overcome. . . . Then to crematory where so lately I saw Ralph put away. . . . Van Vechten & Angevine Shaffer & Nora Holt for dinner. After the Shaffers have gone . . . Nora takes me to . . . the After Dark. . . . Home around 5.

Sunday, 19 February 1928

. . . More dead than alive proceed to Nora Holt's. She dresses & we go to . . . Dinner. Dr. Chesnutt,[1] Charles Waddell's son there. A pleasant & splendid dinner. After dinner some ladies come in but I am about dead. I go home at 9.30, stopping to see Jack Stephens on the way. In bed by eleven.

  1. Chesnutt was arguably the best of the early modern African American novelists who began publishing their work at the end of the nineteenth century.

Monday, 20 February 1928

. . . We go to Duane's for dinner, an extraordinary meal in which this little bitch Duane flies her true colors. Later Leah, Kirk, & Henry Storm come in. Duane refuses to give the Maynards the things that belong to them.[1] I see Nora at 11.30 & we go to the Apex. . . . Stay till 5. Then home & to bed.

  1. Fannie Maynard Van Vechten was the older sister of Leah, CVV's childhood friend, who married Henry Storm. Ralph Van Vechten's will had provided bequests to the Storms, who in 1924 had adopted a child born circa 1918. Duane Van Vechten, the foster child of Ralph and Fannie Van Vechten, had no legal claim to the residuary estate. However, she received two-thirds of it in trust; CVV and Van Vechten Shaffer each received one-half of the remaining third in trust. CVV and Fania Marinoff therefore inherited the annual interest on about $1 million until their deaths, at which time the principal—about $4 million—reverted to the estate.

Tuesday, 21 February 1928

. . . The probate court accepts the petition to have the State Bank executor of the will. . . . I leave [at] 7 to catch the Chief & start for Los Angeles at 8. . . .

Wednesday, 22 February 1928

. . . Telegrams from Lois Moran & Aileen Pringle, offering to meet me, etc. Started cocktails late in afternoon. Dinner in my room & got two porters drunk. . . .

Friday, 24 February 1928

Arrived in Los Angeles 9 in the morning. Aileen Pringle, bless her, met train & drove me to Ambassador where everybody was wonderful & sent me to a sitting room in Huerta 19. Some dumb reporters (4) call . . . to interview me. . . . Lois Moran pops in at 6 to drive me out to her house for dinner. . . . [A] marvelous colored girl named Mabel . . . is Lois's personal maid. . . . Then Gladys [Moran] drives me back to hotel. On the [*porch?*] we encounter Pauline Starke who is too inebriated to introduce her husband.

Saturday, 25 February 1928

Up at seven and read two rotten interviews in the papers. . . . At 12.30 Carmel Myers comes for me & we go to Montmartre for luncheon. I ran into Dudley Murphy (who lunches with us), Jack Gilbert (met),[1] . . . Charlie Chaplin, Constance Talmadge, Jack Colton, etc. . . . After lunch Carmel drives me to Metro Goldwyn studio where I . . . meet Aileen. Aileen drives me to her place in Santa Monica . . . to dinner at Aileen's with Mrs. Bisbee, Matt Moore,[2] Cedric Gibbons, Jack Gilbert, and Greta Garbo (met) & Juliet & Arthur Hornblow. Aileen wants me to stay but sends me home at 3 o'clock.

    1. A leading matinee idol, often with Greta Garbo in silent films.
    2. Silent film actor in *Coquette* and *Rain* and close friend of Aileen Pringle.

Sunday, 26 February 1928

. . . Having breakfast when Mabel Luhan appears with Everett Marcy & Spud Johnson. . . . Aileen's chauffeur . . . drives me to Santa Monica. Aileen & I lunch at one of the beach clubs & then join Cedric Gibbons & Matt Moore at the latter's house. . . . We listen to Aimee Semple McPherson[1] preach on the radio for an hour. She is a marvel. Save for short musical interruptions she talks all day Sunday. . . .

    1. Hugely popular evangelist whose public and private lives were tangled in scandal.

Thursday, 1 March 1928

. . . Aileen & Mrs. Bisbee call for me at 2.30. We drive to Metro-Goldwyn studio where I met Ralph Wheelright who arranged the Aimee McPherson dinner. Home around 4 with Aileen. We order dinner—herself as host. At 6 Aimee Semple McPherson, Ralph Jordan & wife (her manager), her daughter appear. . . . After dinner we go to Angeles Temple to hear her preach & see her baptize. Afterwards with Frank & Bertha Case . . . who have joined us we go all over the temple escorted by Aimee. A wonderful night.

Saturday, 3 March 1928

. . . At 1 Phil Bartholomae arrives with Robert Hunt, son of Myron Hunt, the architect, & George Kennedy (met), two of the most charming & amusing boys I have ever seen.[1] They spend the afternoon here. We drive . . . to Gilbert [Clark]'s and he drives me to Marion Davies's house in Santa Monica. . . . Geo. & Bob came for me about 11 & drive me to their hotel. . . . Bebe Daniels & Mabel Normand[2] call up.

> 1. Hunt and Kennedy were about twenty-one years old, new additions to CVV's list of *jeunes gens assortis*. Kennedy was employed at the time at Metro Goldwyn Mayer; Hunt was later Witter Bynner's longtime companion.
> 2. Popular movie queens of the silent screen.

Sunday, 4 March 1928

. . . Bob Hunt & George Kennedy come in for a couple of hours. Then Aileen comes for me & drives me to Adela Rogers St. John's[1] place in Whittier. . . . We drive home about 11 & Aileen tells me she is in love with Mencken and wants to marry him, but she won't live with his sister or in Baltimore.

> 1. Writer of popular fiction and film columns.

Monday, 5 March 1928

. . . I am beginning to loathe everything about this place except Aileen, Hugh,[1] Bob, & George. Well, that's enough! . . .

> 1. Los Angeles decorator at Zimmerman & (Hugh) Brackenridge Studios.

Tuesday, 6 March 1928

Up at 7. Sun comes out & I feel better. But my revulsion towards the picture world & all it connotes is complete. Got my tickets for Santa Fe, meeting a couple of slimy reporters in the lobby. . . . Bob Hunt & Geo. Kennedy come early to see me. . . . At 4 Adrian comes to see me with his drawings & stays for two hours during which we get well acquainted. A little after six Aileen arrives from the studio, dresses here & we have dinner in the room & go to see Mary Garden[1] in *Resurrection*. Afterwards go back to see Mary, the same as ever, looking more marvelous. . . .

> 1. Opera diva in the early twentieth century; CVV was her strongest supporter, praising her interpretations at the expense of vocal purity in reviews and essays.

Sunday, 11 March 1928

. . . Andrew Dasburg comes for me & takes me . . . to the Teseque Pueblo which I see for the first time. The men are clearing out the plaza and the women sit huddled against the fence giggling. Then I go home with Andrew & sleep for an hour. Then to the Fickes where I find Hal Bynner. . . .

Tuesday, 13 March 1928

Up at 7. The noise & light of this place are bad but the view is wonderful looking across towards the cathedral towers, the silver crosses on the convents & the sun-capped mountains. Met Andrew [Dasburg] for breakfast at La Fonda and he tells me all about his troubles with Ida [Rauh]. She has, it appears, no continuity. Caroline Reagan drifts in, having had two hours sleep. I go to Santa Fe Trading Co. to buy some tin & silver. Andrew meets me there & we drive to Santa Domingo (where I buy my first Chimayo blanket) & then to San Felipe which I visit for the first time. Both have adorable churches. . . .

Thursday, 15 March 1928

. . . Colorado & Kansas, cold & snow. Writing letters, etc. Blizzard all day across the plains of Kansas. Train very late. All my drinks are gone. In a compartment.

Saturday, 17 March 1928

. . . In the afternoon I go with Jim Burke, Pullman porter, into a drawing room & we drink scotch & get acquainted. Every porter in the country seems to know the author of *Nigger Heaven*. . . .

Sunday, 18 March 1928

. . . At 4 o'clock Charles Waddell Chesnutt, a remarkable old gentleman (met), came to see me. Later, . . . to Knopfs' for dinner. Later we go to Virginia

Hammond's. Marinoff is there with Lenore Ulric & Sidney Blackmer. Home around midnight, very drunk.

Friday, 23 March 1928

. . . To Eddie Wassermann's for dinner. Boonie Goosens (who tells me she is divorcing Gene), Val & Bibi Dudensing.[1] After dinner. . . . [we] go to Lucile's, to Harry Glynn's (Tom Measor & Lockwood & Harry there). Then to a drag at the Savoy & to a dance given by Jimmie Harris. Drag is very brilliant. I see hundreds of people I know. . . . Eddie drives me home around 4 o'clock.

    1. Art dealer Valentine Dudensing and his wife.

Saturday, 24 March 1928

. . . Finish *Mr. Hazard & Mr. Hodge* & write Elinor how much I admire it.[1] Join Avery at the Elysée. He is in bed with a boy named Davenport. Kay Kenney comes in. I lunch with Tom Rutherford at Sardi's. He goes . . . with me to Holiday Book Shop, to Goldfarb's, & then to a restaurant where we join Avery, Davenport, & Kay. . . . We drink all the afternoon. At 5 we come home & I am interviewed . . . for some German paper.[2] Tom goes home & I have dinner, very soused. . . .

    1. *Mr. Hodge and Mr. Hazard* was Elinor Wylie's fourth and final novel.
    2. *Nigger Heaven* in German translation had been running serially in the newspaper *Frankfurter Zeitung.*

Monday, 26 March 1928

. . . Marinoff goes to Baltimore at 4.50. I take her to the train. Tom Rutherford comes at 6 to dine with me. He gets a job with *Her Unborn Child* and so cannot go to *Porgy*[1] with me as we had planned & after all I find Phil[lip Moeller] has forgotten to leave seats for *Porgy.* So I come home & finish *Home to Harlem,* no great shakes, except as regards dialogue.[2] At 11 Tom appears. He stays till two & we play music.

    1. Highly successful dramatization of the novel by DuBose Heyward and his wife, Dorothy, with an all-black cast.
    2. W. E. B. Du Bois condemned Claude McKay's novel even more vitriolically than he had *Nigger Heaven* for its exposé of Harlem low life.

Tuesday, 27 March 1928

. . . I go to . . . have my new false teeth (2 of 'em, count 'em) adjusted. Then go to Savings Bank . . . so that I can send Taylor Gordon some money, etc.

After lunch I read proofs of *Spider Boy* for two hours. Taylor Gordon comes in to borrow money & stays for a couple of hours. Then Donald Angus comes to dinner, Boonie Goosens (who is sailing tomorrow) & Dan Reagan[1] drop in on way to a concert & come back later. Paul Robeson came in, very drunk, & sings Blues. Everybody goes before 1.30 and I retire.

> 1. Caroline Dudley's first husband, an officer in military service; subsequently she married French writer Joseph Delteil, and Reagan became Boonie Goosens's companion.

Saturday, 31 March 1928

. . . My gums hurt & I removed my teeth. Reading Mercedes de Acosta's really vile book [*Unto the Daybreak*]. Donald Angus comes to dinner & after dinner we go to Val & Bibi Dudensing. Avery [Hopwood] was there, Eddie Wassermann, Louise Hellström & a couple of others. A vile drunken party. . . .

Sunday, 1 April 1928

Up at 9 o'clock, feeling terribly depressed. My gums feel as though I had trench mouth. . . . At one o'clock I called for Andrew Dasburg (here in New York to arrange a reconciliation [with Ida Rauh] with the assistance of Dr. Brill & took him to lunch at the Crillon. Then home for a while. Again he proposes that he paint me. When he goes I finish Mercedes de Acosta's incredible book. I <u>can't</u> write her about it. . . .

Tuesday, 3 April 1928

. . . I have a hangover and some remorse. . . . Taylor Gordon comes in with a lady from Montana. Later Colin McPhee comes for me. He plays a little. I see tears in his eyes. Later we leave about six to go to Elysée to say goodby to Avery and Mrs. Hopwood. . . . At 7.30 I take Colin to dinner at Leone's. About 8.30 he comes home with me & breaks down & tells me his life is a failure & cries & cries. I send him home about 10—with 30 dollars.

Thursday, 5 April 1928

A letter from Colin which somewhat relieved my mind, in spite of its sadness. Poor Colin has to give up his piano & his room. . . . After lunch Paul Robeson, sailing tomorrow to London to play *Show Boat,* comes in to say goodbye. I read Nella [Larsen] Imes's *Quicksand* with growing enthusiasm. . . .

Friday, 6 April 1928

. . . Tom Rutherford comes to lunch & after lunch we go to Bob Chanler's for me to pose.[1] Louise Hellström just leaving. . . . My picture coming fine. Later Esther Murphy who relates a ridiculous fight the Scott Fitzgeralds had in The Jungle the night before. . . . Tom & I go to Hotel Seymour to see J. Stuart & Virginia Reynolds & their daughter. Mrs. Reynolds has just been putting Mrs. Arthur Jones, hysterical from drink and drugs, to bed.[2] After this I say goodbye to Tom & go to dinner at the Knopfs', . . . then to a party at Langners'. Dreiser is there, Helena Rubinstein. Tom Smith, . . . Max Eastman, etc. At two, . . . [p]icking up a taxi with Rita [Romilly] on Fifth Avenue, I come upon a bicycle & ride up & down the block. . . .

    1. Chanler was painting a portrait of CVV in a fireman's red shirt, with his mouth closed and his preposterous teeth therefore hidden.

    2. The actors in this remarkable playlet are otherwise unmentioned and unidentified in the daybooks.

Saturday, 7 April 1928

. . . Donald Angus comes at 11.30 & we leave for Philadelphia on the noon train. Emily Clark [Balch] (with her chauffeur Charles) meets us at West Philadelphia & we start off. Stop at Lincoln University for a few minutes. Then on again to Baltimore, arriving at 5.30. Dinner in room, Emily, Donald, & Sara Haardt. Then to theatre (with Sara) to see Marinoff play Anna Valeska in *Captain Applegate*. She is splendid & beautiful. . . .

Sunday, 8 April 1928

Up at 8.30. Breakfast in my room with Donald. In Emily's car, Charles driving, we leave Marinoff, Emily, etc., at noon, arriving at Wilmington for lunch at the Fitzgeralds' (Zelda & Scott) at 2. Then about 4 we motor through West Chester to see Joe [Hergesheimer]'s house and on to Philadelphia dinner at Emily's: Mr. & Mrs. Adolphe Borie (met),[1] . . . & Charles Demuth . . . We all get very drunk. Go to bed about 2.30. Emily carries an open bottle of aromatic spirits of ammonia in her pocket, ruins Marinoff's dress, hat, and underwear.

    1. Philadelphia socialites; also, he was a Sunday painter.

Wednesday, 11 April 1928

. . . In the afternoon Dorothy Peterson comes over to tell me about starting a Negro theatre & Tom Rutherford comes in. . . . Theodore Dreiser, Helen Richardson, James Weldon Johnson & D'Alvarez for dinner. After dinner

Andrew Dasburg, Phil Moeller, Lawrence Langner, Cathleen Nesbitt,[1] Regina Wallace, Virginia Hammond, . . . a lovely old party. In bed about 1.30.

> 1. English actress whose early romance with poet Rupert Brooke was cut short by his death during World War I. She went on to a distinguished career on stage (T. S. Eliot's *The Cocktail Party* and Lerner and Lowe's *My Fair Lady*).

Thursday, 12 April 1928

. . . I have quite a lovely old hangover. I go to lunch at Bob Chanler's. Esther Murphy is there, . . . & Eva Sikelmann, a hideous woman with bare legs & a drab dress who wants to revive the Delphic festivals. After lunch Bob paints me some more & finishes my portrait. Home for dinner. Donald Angus & Eddie Wassermann who goes to Boston Symphony with Marinoff. Later party for Bessie Smith who came (soused) with Porter Grainger[1] & who sang three times. Walter White, just returned from Europe, Tom Rutherford, Jim Johnson, Constance Collier, Cathleen Nesbitt, . . . Alice de la Mar, . . . D'Alvarez, Harry Block, Covarrubias, Regina Wallace, . . . Blanche Knopf, etc. David Marion helped in the kitchen & made hot dogs. In bed at 2.30. Finished reading *Debonair* [by G. B. Stern].

> 1. African American playwright, actor, and on this occasion accompanist. He had coerced the blues singer to attend the party, at CVV's urging. Smith arrived drunk, drank more, performed, and on departing felled Fania Marinoff (who had tried to kiss her goodbye) in pushing her away. The incident, laced with verbal obscenities, was elaborated on and passed around in Harlem until it took on mythic proportions, thereafter sometimes reported inaccurately.

Monday, 16 April 1928

. . . I read proofs all the morning. Lunch in, Marinoff cooking. Then I lie down for an hour. I seem to have the sleeping sickness. . . . Alfred telephoned that *Nigger Heaven* is to be done in Polish. . . . Read *Rainbow Round My Shoulder* [by Howard Odum], which is good but not as good as one calls it. Too— for one thing—padded. Then with Marinoff to Fornio's for dinner. . . . Then to see Mae West in *Diamond Lil* which I adored. Miss West is marvelous. Saw Edna Ferber between acts. Home about 11 & to bed.

Thursday, 19 April 1928

Up early. Finish reading proofs of *Spider Boy* in the morning. Andrew Dasburg & Ida Rauh for lunch. . . . Kirk Askew[1] comes to dinner. Then we go to see Mae West in *Diamond Lil,* sitting in front row. I like it even better than before. . . .

1. One of the Harvard modernists, a group of graduates instrumental in founding the Harvard Atheneum Museum; later Askew was director of an art gallery in
New York and with his wife, Constance, held a regular salon.

Monday, 23 April 1928

. . . I wire Cedar Rapids Woman's Club that I'll give them $500 towards con-
verting Uncle Giles [Van Vechten]'s house into club house. Marinoff has a
grand blow-up—one of her worst. . . . Read [Luc] Durtain's *Hollywood
Depasse* till I get too bored to continue. . . .

Tuesday, 24 April 1928

. . . Marinoff still nagging. Tom Rutherford for lunch. After lunch Tom & I
go to see Marion Davies in *The Patsy*, an enormously amusing picture. Home
& have another fight with Marinoff. She is in a terribly nervous state. . . .

Wednesday, 25 April 1928

. . . A lot of turquoise has come from the West for Blanche & I take it over to
her. When I get back I find Marinoff getting my lunch. She flies into another
unreasonable rage. She goes out to lunch with Mary McKinnon[1] & stays all
the afternoon. Late in the afternoon D'Alvarez calls for me & takes me to Billy
Pearce's coloured dancing studio where I meet Buddy Bradley & Leonard
Sillman[2] & watch them dance. Home for dinner & then to see *Our Betters*
with Donald. Enjoyed it extremely. Constance Collier & Ina Claire both superb. Went back to see Constance after. Cathleen Nesbitt there with a copy
of the play, *Tampico*.[3] Walked home & in bed before 12.

> 1. American fashion illustrator who had been painting Marinoff's portrait in
> which she is wearing Nella Larsen Imes's Poirot gown.
> 2. A musical comedy juvenile who later became a successful producer of Broad-
> way reviews.
> 3. This was presumably based on Joseph Hergesheimer's novel.

Friday, 27 April 1928

Up at 8.30. I feel very bloated. Probably if I don't stop drinking I'll blow up.
Nevertheless I go out & run a few errands. . . . Later called Dr. Livingston who
said I had alcoholic gastritis & proscribed a high enema. So I had that & went
to bed. Not going to the Stettheimers' for dinner, & not going to W. C.
Handy's concert at Carnegie where I had a box. To sleep at 9.

Wednesday, 9 May 1928

. . . Had a bad headache & stayed in bed all day on a diet of oatmeal & bouillion. . . . After dinner felt well enough to drive & see *Blackbirds of 1928*, with Adelaide Hall, Aida Ward, Tom Moore, & Bill Robinson. Then we picked up Constance Collier & went to a very nondescript party at Leonard Sillman's at Billy Pearce's dancing studio, at which Clara Smith sang beautifully. Sillman tried to but was too drunk. . . . I was not eating or drinking. At home at 3 o'clock. . . .

Tuesday, 15 May 1928

. . . After lunch I go to see Alfred about advertising of *Spider Boy*. Also see Donald who is about to separate from Nils [Nelson]. . . . Home & continue with letters, etc. Jackets for *Spider Boy* arrive. Marinoff & I dine with Jack & Esther Marinoff at Mrs. Beerman's Yiddish place on Third St. A perfectly marvellous restaurant. Fania goes home with Jack & Esther & hears all Jack's troubles. I go to see Donald Angus. Leonard Sillman is there. Home at 10 & find Marinoff very emotional about Jack. We talk till midnight.

Thursday, 17 May 1928

. . . Fania goes out to get her ticket on the *France* & her French visa. . . . Late in the afternoon Essie Robeson came to see us. She is sailing tomorrow to join Paul in London. Marinoff & I dine in alone. Donald comes in in the evening. Nils [Nelson] is leaving & he is in a bad way. He leaves about midnight.

Saturday, 19 May 1928

. . . First cheque received from Ralph's estate. . . . My belly hurts again & after lunch of oatmeal I go to Dr. Livingston for a treatment. Also stop at Park Century Shop to have my big flask marked "Woof! Woof! Woojums!"[1] . . . Dinner at Algonquin with Donald Angus. Then spend the evening at home with him & Jackie Barker. Geo. Muldur's [speakeasy] is raided & closed. In bed about 12. Marinoff out to dinner, theatre, & Mayfair dance with Eddie Wassermann. Finished Frances Newman's extremely silly *Dead Lovers Are Faithful Lovers*.

1. It was CVV's habit to "bark" in enthusiasm (and on occasion to accompany the barking with biting): "Woof! Woof!" *Woojums* was a word he invented to apply to a cocktail in his 1930 novel *Parties*: "five parts gin, one part bacardi, a dash of bitters, a dash of absinthe, a teaspoonful of lemon juice, and a little grenadine."

Later he occasionally applied the word to people of whom he was inordinately fond: Aileen Pringle, Gertrude Stein (Baby Woojums), Alice Toklas (Mama Woojums), Langston Hughes, and ballet dancer Hugh Laing.

Monday, 21 May 1928

... Marinoff very aggravating & my stomach very squeamish.... Haven't had a drink of booze for two weeks. Went out after a meagre lunch of oatmeal....

Tuesday, 22 May 1928

... Dinner with Marinoff—we go to *Showboat* but she is so disagreeable that I leave after the first act & come home to have awful cramps. She goes to a party at Constance Collier's. I am in bed by 11.

Friday, 25 May 1928

I worry because Marinoff got home so late & slept fitfully between 6 & 7. Then at last finding she was in I went to sleep & slept till 10.... Then read D. H. Lawrence's *The Woman Who Ran Away* with great satisfaction.... We have dinner together & about a quarter of ten head for the boat. Marinoff sails on the *France*. I give her a sapphire necklace. Donald Angus, Jackie Barker, Leonard Sillman, Taylor Gordon, Regina Wallace came to see her off & we drink 3 quarts of champagne before the boat sails....

Sunday, 27 May 1928

... Donald & I lunch at the Ritz. In the afternoon Leonard Sillman came in. Dinner with Donald at the Plaza. Back to the house. Max Ewing came in. Donald & I go to bed before midnight.

Tuesday, 29 May 1928

... Nella Imes came in about 5 & stayed to dinner. Also Tom Rutherford, drunker than ever, came to dinner, left to go to *Blackbirds* after Nella & I go to a party at Max Ewing's. I forget my keys but fortunately have left Marinoff's in the vault at the Algonquin & I get these. Max Ewing's party I am quite too drunk to remember.

Wednesday, 30 May 1928

Up at 7.30, with a hangover.... Donald came in for cocktails & presently Jack Barker. We go to dinner at Leone's. Later Sidney Peterson & Louis Cole.[1] We all get drunk & go down to a party at Bob Chanler's. I take my portrait back. In bed about 1. Donald & Jackie spend the night here.

    1. African American dancer in New York and Paris nightclubs, sometimes in drag.

Saturday, 2 June 1928

. . . Saw Donald off to work & then writing cheques, etc. At 10.30 I started off sending a cablegram to Marinoff, dropping off my too small pyjamas at Long Sang Ti's & to Jac Auer's to work out & am massaged by Nelson. Home with flowers. . . . Did marketing for party tomorrow after lunch. I feel surprisingly good, considering how new exercise is to me. Colin McPhee comes in for a couple of hours. Then I sign large paper & vellum sheets for *Spider Boy*.[1] Donald Angus for dinner & we go to Joe Cook in *Rain or Shine*. Home & in bed by 12.

    1. It was Alfred A. Knopf's habit to issue limited editions for collectors of the books of his best-selling authors. For *Spider Boy*, for example, there were 220 copies on rag paper with combed blue paper-covered boards and 75 copies on Japanese Inomachi bound in red vellum, both versions slipcased.

Sunday, 3 June 1928

. . . A little low but not very. Donald gets up about 11. Reading papers, etc. We lunch at the Ritz. Home & fool around for an hour or two till people begin arriving for a party: Meda cooks & David [Marion] helps her. Cocktail party for Arthur and Gladys Ficke & supper after: Nella & Elmer Imes, Florine & Carrie Stettheimer, Arthur & Madeleine Richman, Dorothy Peterson, Albert Carroll,[1] Elizabeth Shaffer,[2] . . . Bill Benét, Ruth Hammond & Donald MacDonald, Muriel Draper, Max Ewing. . . . Over at 2. David stays the night.

    1. American musical comedy actor.
    2. CVV's sister's daughter, later married to Edwin Hull.

Tuesday, 5 June 1928

Up at 8. Rain. Donald [Angus] off for business. At 10.30 I go to gymnasium, feeling pretty good. An hour's hard work tires me, altho I find the movements easier than before. . . . Lunch in alone, a nap & then Langston Hughes, just arrived in town, calls up & comes up. Then I read [W. E. B. Du Bois's] *Dark Princess* for an hour or two—it grows steadily worse—have dinner alone, & go to one of the Guild performances of *Volpone* which is superb. Engaged a taxi and collect Constance Collier at the Henry Miller Theatre, over to her house for a party. . . . Feel rather dismal as I am not drinking. Home at 2.

Wednesday, 6 June 1928

. . . Donald Angus for dinner & we go to see the new *Grand Street Follies* which is pretty poor save for a little of Albert Carroll & <u>all</u> of Dorothy Sands[1] who is brilliant. Meet Max Ewing & bring him home with us. He stays a while & then leaves. Donald stays all night & we are in bed by 12.30. Meet Agnes de Mille[2] at theatre. I am <u>not</u> drinking.

    1. American monologist.
    2. American ballet dancer and, later, choreographer.

Thursday, 7 June 1928

. . . Finish Dr. Du Bois's asinine book, *Dark Princess,* & also some papers.

Wednesday, 13 June 1928

. . . Nora Holt arrives from Philadelphia for party for herself. Arthur & Madeleine Richman, Nella [Larsen] & Donald Angus with her here for dinner. After dinner Elizabeth Schaffer with a male dumbbell, Harry Block, Miguel Covarrubias, Rose Rolanda, Edna Kenton, Harry Harvey, . . . Katherine Dudley & a boy named Gaston (Rosamond Pincot's[1] husband), Irita Van Doren, Jack Barker, Albert Carroll, Constance Collier, & a boy named Todd, . . . Ina Claire, Gene Markey, Bill Bullitt, Mr. & Mrs. Bill Robinson. Bill danced, Nora sang. In bed about 4. Donald stayed the night.

    1. English actress who played "The Nun" in Max Reinhardt's *The Miracle.*

Sunday, 17 June 1928

My 48th birthday is cool & bright. I wake up at 7.30 feeling fine. A cake with a spider web (in honor of *Spider Boy*) from the Stettheimers & lots of telegrams. At noon I take the train for White Plains where I have lunch with Alfred & Pat Knopf and their guests.[1] Stay till 4.49 & then take train home. There is a fire in our block as I approach & the street is full of fire engines. Donald & Jackie Barker came in around six for cocktails. Jackie leaves & around 8 Donald & I go to . . . Manhattan Casino to see the beginning of the Endurance Dancing Contest. We go home early & we are in bed before midnight.

1. CVV, Alfred A. Knopf, Jr., called Pat, and James Weldon Johnson often celebrated their June 17 birthdays together.

Friday, 22 June 1928

... Esther Marinoff comes in to tell me what a bad time Jack is having ... & wants me to help him out. I have already given Donald 75 dollars today. I am getting a little tired of these touches from all the world. Arranging phonograph records, books, etc. Donald Angus came to dinner & we went to see *Blackbirds of 1928.* Enjoyed it hugely and after it was over went back to see Bill Robinson. Met Adelaide Hall,[1] Aida Ward. ...

1. Because of limited opportunities in New York, this singer emigrated to London and there made a career as successful as it was lengthy.

Monday, 25 June 1928

... I pack for Ashfield. Take the 12 o'clock train. . . . Louise Bullitt meets me at Springfield & drives me out to their place where I see Bill [Bullitt] & Marsden Hartley[1] who is painting & writing here. After dinner we drive over to see the Sullivan estate which I am thinking of buying. The view is still very beautiful in the twilight mist. ...

1. American Abstract Expressionist painter, one of Alfred Stieglitz's protégés.

Wednesday, 27 June 1928

... Feeling none too good. I do not find I want a country house. Bill takes Marsden & me on a long jaunt through the wood which he owns, later over climbing fences, stumbling about in marshes, even fording a brook. We get home at lunch time very hungry & I am feeling better. ...

Saturday, 30 June 1928

Up at 7.30. <u>Hot!!</u> Writing letters, etc., all the morning, Lunch in alone. . . . Later Tom Rutherford comes in to say goodbye to me before he leaves for Maine & a tool company. Later I go to Harlem with Donald Angus & Jack Barker, to Small's where I meet Paul Meeres[1] & then to the Lenox Club where we see Louis Cole. Home about 5.

1. Exotic dancer in several Harlem nightspots, later a model for CVV's photography.

Sunday, 1 July 1928

. . . At 1 Donald [Angus] & Jack [Barker] appear. We drink some absinthe & have some champagne cocktails, lunch at the Ritz. They come back in the afternoon & leave about 4.30, all having a gay time. I lie down for a while and at 7 Jack Stephens appears. We have some more champagne cocktails & go to the Plaza for dinner. Home again. Jack leaves about 11. A little later the phone rings. It is the *N.Y. Times* to inform me that Avery Hopwood has been drowned at Nice.[1] I call up Donald immediately & he comes up to stay with me but I lie awake all night.

    1. Hopwood suffered a heart attack, standing in ocean surf at Juan les Pins in France.

Monday, 2 July 1928

Up at 6.30. The news is in the morning papers. Darling Avery. He has been closer to me than anyone else almost, except Fania & Donald. Hot. I am a wreck. . . . After lunch in alone I keep an appointment with Alfred Knopf but break down & cry, so I come home & go to bed. No news of Mrs. Hopwood & no more news of what happened to Avery. What a horrible day & night. I can't get it into my head that I shall never see him again. Jack Stephens arrives about 6.30 & we go to the Crillon for dinner. . . . Back to the house & get drunk enough to go to bed & go to sleep by 11.

Wednesday, 4 July 1928

. . . A cablegram from Marinoff indicates she is in Nuremberg & had not yet received my cable about Avery. . . .

Thursday, 5 July 1928

. . . *Tribune* says Mrs. Hopwood, unwarned, arrived in Nice yesterday. [Jacob] Schwebel, Avery's lawyer, calls me to let me know he has heard from Mrs. Hopwood. . . . Rudolph Fisher comes in & I give him my old evening clothes, a blue suit & a pair of trousers. Louis Cole (his birthday) & Donald come to dinner. Louis leaves at midnight. Donald stays all night. I have another crying spell.

Saturday, 7 July 1928

. . . No word from Fania yet. A little later a cablegram comes & a telephone message from John Floyd who arrived last night on the Aquitania. . . . Lunch with Donald at the Plaza. Then we come to house & wait for John Floyd, who appears apparently only looking for sympathy. He is very sweet & nice. He stays for an hour. He was nearly the last person to be with Avery, leaving Juan les Pins only ten days before Avery's death. . . . Donald & Jack Barker come in & I take them to dinner at Fornio's. Donald comes home with me. We had a crying jag till 3.30. He stays the night. <u>Hot!</u>

Sunday, 8 July 1928

. . . I go to have lunch with the three Stettheimer girls, bursting into tears the moment I meet them at thought of Avery. We have a lovely time together. . . . This is the hottest day of the year.

Tuesday, 10 July 1928

. . . I am still depressed & curiously lacking in initiative. I feel lost with Ralph & Avery dead. Well, a few minutes later I develop initiative & call up a lot of people. . . .

Wednesday, 11 July 1928

. . . A letter from Marie Doro offers me her Pierce-Arrow! A dubious gift. Dinner alone at Fornio's where they speak of Avery & I drink a bottle of white wine & then go to see a very bad talking picture, *The Lights of New York*. . . . Donald comes in about 11 & spends the night.

Friday, 13 July 1928

. . . John Floyd makes his daily telephone call. Donald Angus comes for dinner & spends the evening. . . . At midnight we go to Harlem. Just to Small's Paradise where we see many old friends, waiters, & performers. . . . Then to Lenox Ave. Club where we see Louis Cole. Home at 3 o'clock. Donald stays the night.

Saturday, 14 July 1928

. . . Man calls from Cunard Line. . . . Cabled Marinoff that I will sail. A tragic letter from Constance Collier about Avery. Donald Angus, Nils Nelson, Max Ewing for dinner at Fornio's. Then back to the house. Louis Cole comes over. At midnight to the Lenox Ave. Club & stay there all night. Donald . . . goes home about 2.

Thursday, 19 July 1928

. . . I . . . order a spray of white lilacs for Avery's funeral (next Monday). Then to. . . . leave my watch, . . . then to have enlargements made of Mary Garden films Alfred took, & finally to Hotel Chatham to see Julie Hopwood. We talked all day, had lunch together & she told me that Avery died instantly of heart failure in two feet of water. Several people came in, including Jack Harper, & there was plenty to drink. So when I got to the Stettheimers' for dinner . . . I was plenty lit. . . .

Sunday, 22 July 1928

. . . To the Ritz to see a picture with Ramon Novarro & Renée Adorée & home in the rain to write more letters. Donald & I dine at Fornio's & have a real gazpacho. It pours with rain & the proprietor drives us home. In all the evening. Donald is a woe-begone object, terribly upset about Nils leaving him. I send him home at 2.

Monday, 23 July 1928

<u>Hot.</u> Up at 8, and clearing books out of the hall for the painters who arrive tomorrow. Avery Hopwood is buried today. . . . Then to see Alfred Knopf who tells me over 12,000 *Spider Boys* have been sold & book has gone into its second printing of 5,000. Alfred tells me that Donald is a complete flop in the office. . . .

Tuesday, 24 July 1928

The painters arrive shortly after eight & it takes the whole morning to arrive at the Chinese pink I have decided upon for the ceiling. When we get it I go to the post office. Back in the afternoon & there is more trouble about the green.[1]

    1. The foyer and drawing room at 150 West 55th Street were painted bright pink, pale purple, and bright turquoise, the colors later employed by "Famous Beauty of the XXth Century" Prentiss Taylor in the dust jacket for CVV's last book, *Sacred and Profane Memories* (1932).

Wednesday, 25 July 1928

Up at 6 o'clock. I clean up room for the painters, who arrive at 8 to paint living room. . . . Spent the entire day in but at night, the big room done, I took Donald & Nils Nelson to Fornio's for dinner. It was pathetic to see Donald try to get Nils back, it being too late.[1] They come up & spend the evening here, & leave about 1.30 when I go to bed.

1. Angus's long affair with Nelson had undergone several separations of varying length before this final split.

Friday, 27 July 1928

...A letter from Sara Haardt about *Spider Boy* (the first), another from Arthur Ficke. . . . Donald Angus, Max Ewing, Harry Block for dinner. We all go to Lafayette Theatre to see Louis Cole in a terrible revue. Met Earl Dancer (now living with Cora Green[1]) on the sidewalk. . . .

1. African American musical performer and speakeasy singer.

Saturday, 28 July 1928

...Packing for the country at 7.30. Hot. Isa Glenn called up about *Spider Boy.* Donald is very sad & I am worried about him. What is to become of him when he pulls himself together. He takes me to the train. . . . Leave N.Y. at noon. Reading Alfred Neumann's stirring book, *The Devil.* Arrived Springfield at 3.30. Nobody at the station, but . . . the porter takes care of me & presently . . . I greet Bill, Louise & Ann Bullitt on their farm shortly after 5. I go to bed at 11.

Sunday, 29 July 1928

... Everybody gets up by eleven & we go to see the Bennet farm which is for sale & the most possible place I have seen out here. . . .

Monday, 30 July 1928

Up early. Reading *The Devil* with increasing fascination. Lawrence Langner drives off for Worcester & about 11 Louise, ill, Armina & I start off for New Hampshire, stopping at Greenfield for lunch, . . . on to the Hapgood farm where we find Neith the same as ever, Myriam & Beatrix.[1] The house & the country are tumble-down, sad & broken. . . .

1. The daughters of Neith Boyce and Hutchins Hapgood.

Tuesday, 31 July 1928

... We start off at 10.30, Bill driving the Marmon, Louise, Armina, & me, through Pittsfield, Lenox, Stockbridge. At Grace Johnson's for lunch at Great Barrington at 1. . . . Then . . . we motor to Edna St. Vincent Millay's at Austerlitz & have a drink with her & Gene Boissevain.[1] Then at 4.15 Armina

& I in the Langner car (which Lawrence has sent back) out across country to Hartford where we meet Lawrence at 7.30. . . . They drive me to New Haven where I take the N.Y. train, arriving about 1.

    1. American poet and her husband.

Wednesday, 1 August 1928

Up at 7. Read a few letters about *Spider Boy*. . . . Nora Holt comes in, & we go to *Blackbirds* together. Afterwards go back to see Adelaide Hall, Aida Ward & Bill Robinson (whose valet is following him around with a palm leaf fan), meet Lew Leslie.[1] Nora comes back to dinner, also Donald Angus & Max Ewing. After dinner Nora sings & Porter Grainger comes to hear her. . . . Nora leaves for Philadelphia on the 11 o'clock train.

    1. White producer who staged annual installments of *Blackbirds*.

Sunday, 5 August 1928

Up at 8.30. I have a terrific hangover & it's the hottest day I've ever seen so I don't do much but lie around. . . . By dint of absinthe & will I get up, pack, & make a train for Alfred Knopf's house at White Plains. . . . To bed early.

Saturday, 11 August 1928

. . . I go out to send a cablegram to Fan & to try on two suits at Benham's. Home for lunch. I still feel gas pains & have only oatmeal. Reading a mss. of Baron Corvo's *The Desire & Pursuit of the Whole,* an amazing autobiography of Corvo's last days in Venice. . . . Donald Angus comes to dinner & we dine at the Algonquin. . . . Then to Tony's, a speakeasy on 49 St. . . . I do not drink.

Sunday, 12 August 1928

. . . My indigestion seems to be better. In fact I seem to be all right when I don't drink. Lunch at the Plaza. Then to see Greta Garbo in *The Mysterious Lady* at the Capital. She is quite extraordinary. . . .

Monday, 13 August 1928

I had some drinks last night, but no gin & seem to feel all right today. . . . Read Robert Nathan's *The Bishop's Wife,* very frail but charming, and start [Theodore] Canot's *Adventures of an African Slaver*—a thrilling book—which after dinner alone I read into the night. . . .

Wednesday, 15 August 1928

I drank nothing but rye, cognac, & sauterne last night, & feel better than usual this morning. Up at 7, hot & clear. *Spider Boy* is published today. More letters & telegrams & a stupid review by Harry Salpeter in *The World.* . . . . Elmer Imes comes in—trouble—for dinner. . . .

Friday, 17 August 1928.

. . . Nella Imes comes in to see me.[1] To Mahala Douglas's (Hotel Plaza) for cocktails. She is here for the day, sailing tonight on *Ile de France.* Jack Colton there. . . . To Fornio's, for dinner alone. After dinner Jack Colton joins me. We sit around till nearly 11.30 when Donald Angus calls us up to come down to a party. Angelo Romano, Billy Commander, Jack Fulear, Joe Acker, Billy Kruger, Monroe Schoen, & ten or twenty more.[2] A highly amusing time. . . .

1. Nella Larsen and Elmer Imes were experiencing financial difficulties.
2. The guest list seems to be composed of Angus's own *jeunes gens assortis,* most of whom turned up sooner or later at all-male parties given by Edward Wassermann, Lewis Baer, or Harry Glynn.

Saturday, 18 August 1928

. . . Out to lunch . . . with Donald. He comes home with me. Jack Colton comes in. We drink for a couple of hours. Later I get hold of Nora Holt, take her to Tony's for a drink, to St. Regis roof for dinner, back to house where we talk & play records. On to Harlem, to Small's Paradise where we see the review. I meet Johnnie & Mildred Hudgins.[1] To Lenox Ave. Club where I see Louis Cole who takes us over to the reopened Lulu Belle (now upstairs) & as sinister as ever. Home about 4.

1. African American speakeasy entertainers.

Monday, 20 August 1928

. . . Feeling rather exhausted with a hangover. Gets hotter as day goes on. Ethel Waters comes to lunch & talks to me about leaving Earl [Dancer] & her plans. . . . Louis Cole comes in. Later Monroe Schoen & a couple of people & Donald Angus. Everybody out about one & I go to bed. A canary flies in the window & can't get out. Stays the night.

Tuesday, 21 August 1928

Up at 7. . . . I have quite a hangover. . . . Joe Acker comes to dinner & I take him to see Edwin Knopf's production of *The Big Pond,* a rotten show. . . .

Then I take Joe to Tony's where I met Harry Block with two girls & a guy & take them home with me. When they leave I go to sleep with my clothes on and all the lights on.

Thursday, 23 August 1928

Up at 7.30. Still nervous & shaken. It is cold & wet. I go to Dr. Livingston & he finds my blood pressure is 180. He advises me to cut out liquor. Walking up from his office I meet a young man I haven't seen in years & that upsets me more. . . . My nerves improve as the day goes on, but my gums ache terribly. I lie down, read [Isadore] Lhevinne's *The Safer Ship*, extremely interesting, & try, without success, to read Djuna Barnes's *Ryder*.[1] Jack Colton, . . . Nora Holt, & Louis Cole come to dinner & we all go to *Diamond Lil*. Jack writes a note to Mae West, we all go back to meet her. She is marvellous. Then to Pod's & Jerry's, to Sugar Cane, to Lulu Belle, all equally marvellous. Home about 4.

1. CVV had employed Djuna Barnes to supply illustrations for his Sunday feature articles in the *New York Press*, 1913–14. At the time CVV first met Donald Angus, Angus was a close friend of Barnes and served as the model for two of her drawings in her first published work, *A Book*. Angus never knew that Barnes and CVV had known each other.

Tuesday, 28 August 1928

. . . Nella Imes comes in. She wants to go to Viking Press. I dissuade her. Essie Robeson calls up to tell me she is going to defy Equity & break contract with Caroline.[1]

1. Caroline Reagan, who was responsible for the *Revue Nègre*, had hoped to mount a second all-black stage show in Paris, for which she had engaged Paul Robeson.

Friday, 31 August 1928

. . . I feel rotten & I go to the dentist & feel worse as he fills the canal of my big front tooth & it hurts like hell. . . . After lunch I go to the doctor's, who again paints my throat. Home for an hour. Then to Jack Stephens at Knickerbocher. Then to Al Jones's office where we talk with Geo. Kauffman about possibility of making a play out of *Spider Boy*. Home for dinner with Jack Stephens. Feeling rotten & go to bed before 11.

Wednesday, 5 September 1928

Up at 8. Cloudy. The day begins in a whirl of activity & Sidney Peterson appears at 10. I pack all the morning, lunch in. Donald [Angus] comes over.

Finish packing early in the afternoon but cannot lock trunk, so call in man from Saks. To Jack Stephens for an hour. Back & play Parcheesi with Sidney. I win eight games & he one! We put out all the lights, close the apartment, & Meda, Sidney, & I start off for the *Mauritania* at 8 o'clock. (Last time I sailed on this boat it was 2nd class with Marinoff & we <u>loved</u> it.[1]) This time . . . I have the dining saloon (with beds) of one of the royal suites. Everything is comfortable & easy. There are six quarts of champagne & many come to say goodbye: Donald Angus, Nora Holt, Arthur Richman (whose play *Heavy Traffic* opens tonight), Jack Colton, . . . Namara[2] & Mildred Lord,[3] Harry Block, Muriel Draper, Eddie Wassermann & Hannah [Ellis] who talks to Meda, George Hoy and Nils Nelson, Dorothy Peterson, Nella & Elmer Imes, etc. They leave at 11 & I go to bed.

> 1. In June 1914, four months before their marriage, Marinoff and CVV went abroad together to England, France, and Austria.
> 2. Sometime opera diva Marguerite Namara, primarily in Chicago, who was shortly to marry George Hoy, with whom Donald Angus had an affair after he broke with Nelson, who then was having an affair of his own with Hoy.
> 3. English minor writer.

Saturday, 8 September 1928

. . . Feeling rotten, but after breakfast & a bath and a good walk on the upper deck I feel better. . . . Towards lunch time I feel worse & so I eat sardines & spaghetti & almost recover. There is amusing boxing on the sundeck in the afternoon. . . . I drink six cocktails before dinner, have barsac for dinner, a big dinner, & half a dozen cognacs after dinner with the result that I retire quite squiffy.

Sunday, 9 September 1928

. . . Gastritis is much better, but feeling depressed. . . . Take a long walk around upper deck, finished *The Well of Loneliness* [by Radclyffe Hall]. Had a good lunch, came down to write some letters, including one to Harry Block on *The Well of Loneliness:* "The Lesbian's Black Beauty." Then packed a little. Dinner, a cognac or two & to bed early.

Monday, 10 September 1928

. . . We drew into Cherbourg harbour around 12.30 & were off for Paris on the boat train at a quarter of two. . . . Met by Boonie [Goosens] & Marinoff. Off to Hotel Carlton, where I was interviewed by *N.Y. Herald* & *Chicago Tribune* (Paris edition). Then to Dan Reagan's for dinner. . . . Then to the Salbert

& the Rotonde, . . . & finally to Montmartre where I met Bricktop.[1] Marinoff & I lose the party, have a row & finally get home in a terrible fight around 4.

1. Ada Smith du Conge, called "Bricktop" because of her red hair, an African American entertainer who operated *Le Grand Duc,* a nightclub popular with American tourists.

Tuesday, 11 September 1928

Paris is divine. After breakfast & a slow dressing we walk out in the cool October [*sic*] air about 1 o'clock. Then to the Café d'Harcourt for lunch but they no longer serve lunch, and so to Foyot's. Then to the Luxembourg Gardens, through the Mousée. Taxi to . . . Ralph Barton's house in Passy,[1] a charming affair. . . . Home at 6 . . . Have a champagne cocktail in the bar— 5 francs (which is 20 cents). . . .

1. Barton and his fourth wife, Germaine Tailleferre, had decided to live permanently in France and had transformed their house into a showplace featured widely in American magazines.

Wednesday, 12 September 1928

. . . Scott Fitzgerald, Dan Reagan & Boonie Goosens come for cocktails. Scott passes out. . . . Marinoff & I drive to Ralph Barton's where we have a magnificent dinner. Then Germaine [Tailleferre] & I play duets & we see moving pictures. Ralph takes movies of me. Home about 2.

Sunday, 16 September 1928

Up at 8 o'clock, with a hangover & sick. Finish packing, etc. We leave for Strasbourg at noon, and arrive about 7 at night. . . .

Monday, 17 September 1928

. . . After breakfast we go out & walk in the quaint streets, and ascend to the spire of the cathedral, an extraordinary climb & view. After this we discover pâté de fois gras, a very bad restaurant called La Marne, take a train at 2.10, travelling first & getting a carriage all to ourselves by tipping a bit. We pass through Baden-Baden where we certainly should have stopped, had I known. Then on to Munich arriving at 9.30.

Thursday, 20 September 1928

. . . It is sunny & bright & I am feeling much better. A cocktail or two in the foyer where I lost my new fountain pen. Then with Marinoff to the Preysing

Palais for lunch, . . . to the Neuer Gallery . . . & found a marvellous Van Gogh (sunflowers) & a fine Cezanne (still life). . . . After a very bad dinner at the Hoftheater Restaurant we come home & have a good row. In bed about 10.30.

Saturday, 22 September 1928

. . . At 10.57 we take the train for Prague. Have a wonderful lunch on board. Trip is adorable, the broad green fields, fir trees, etc., past stacks of sugar beets & poles on which hops grow. We pull in to Prague, rainy & cold, about 3 & drive to the Hotel Esplanade. After a bath we go for a walk, and see some of the old part of Prague, besides finding a Jewish restaurant where we eat. . . . In spite of fact we have two rooms, Marinoff cannot sleep because she hears the elevator. I change rooms with her.

Sunday, 23 September 1928

. . . Walked along the river, down to the picturesque Karlsbrauch, with the cathedral & palaces mounting on the other side of the river, back to the square . . . for lunch, not very good but we were so hungry it didn't matter. . . . To the National Theatre to hear sensational *Prodana Nevesta* [by Bedrich Smetana], a very characteristic performance before a crowded house. To the Jewish quarter, saw the exterior of the old synagogue, & on the night before Yom Kippur. . . .

Wednesday, 26 September 1928

Up at 6.15, and off in the cold & fog, for Buda-Pesth at 8. . . . Our room overlooks the Danube, fall gardens, the recommended head waiter is splendid & a gipsy band headed by Magyary Isma plays occasional music.

Thursday, 27 September 1928

. . . Private motors are difficult to get by the hour & so for the first time in my life I get in a rubber neck wagon[1] we drive to St. John's Hill, from which many excellent views. Coffee at 6, Handel's *Xerxes* & Strauss's ballet *Schlagobers* at the opera. Supper at 11 & in bed.

    1. Twenties slang for tourist bus.

Friday, 28 September 1928

. . . In the big wagon we go to the public market, the palace, the ballroom . . . and the coronation church. In the afternoon in the same manner we visit parliament & the island in the middle of the Danube. Lunch & supper in the hotel, under the tutelage of the divine Graber, who gives us splendid dishes & good wine. Magyary Isma, the gipsy, plays. Coffee at 6 in the hotel. We hear *The Gipsy Baron* [by Johann Strauss] at the opera and "The Rackoszy March" at the end of the second act incites the house to great enthusiasm.

Sunday, 30 September 1928

. . . Packing. Walked out on the Danube, a beautiful warm day & this scene a popular thing to do on Sunday morning. Then to the bar where I consume lots of cognacs. The bill is extremely reasonable. We leave Buda-Pesth at 1.15. Another grand meal at the wagon-lit & off for Wien. Arrive at 6. . . . Rooms are so noisy & no evening water that we have a fight at once. We go to the Theatre An der Wien to see a stupid operetta, *Das Kergogan von Chicago* and afterwards go to the hofspiel to look for rooms. Arrive & eat supper. To bed at 12.30.

Tuesday, 2 October 1928

. . . After lunch in the Stefansflaty we pick up Otto, a chauffeur, whom we keep all the afternoon for about $3.00! He drives us to Schönbrunn. What a palace! Through the Prater & back to the hotel. We have dinner in the bar & go to bed early.

Wednesday, 3 October 1928

Otto comes for us at 10, takes us to the Belvedere, a lovely old palace where we see lots of pictures, to Schubert's birthplace, now a museum, to the old Rathaus, etc. . . . Dinner in the Bristol Bar, & to the opera: a very ugly theatre where we see Stravinsky's *Oedipus Rex* (very dull) & *Der Goldino Kranz,* a silly songspiel. . . . After the opera Franzl Von Poklair (met)[1] joins us & we go to Schroeder's for supper.

    1. This passing acquaintance gave CVV the physical appearance and personality of the Gräfin Adele von Pulmernl und Stilzernl in his 1930 novel *Parties.*

Thursday, 4 October 1928

. . . Otto comes for us at 10. We drive to the Lichtenstein Gallery, see many lovely pictures. Then to the new Rathaus, finally to the Albertinea where many of the most exquisite Dürers are. Then to Cook's & farewell to Otto. . . . From 4 to 6 we lie down. Then to Franzl Van Poklair's [for] a marvellous supper &

to the Johann Strauss Theatre for a jazz operetta called *Spectator.* We have an amusing time and enough cognac. . . .

Friday, 5 October 1928

Marinoff has a terrible cold. She goes out with Franzl to see a doctor about her breasts which pain her & I stay in to write letters, etc. . . . Marinoff returns about noon with good news. The doctor says her breasts hurt because she menstruates so little. We lunch at Schoner's, then have a shopping debauch in the Marianhilfenstrasse. Later to Cook's, & home. Marinoff to the hairdresser's. With Franzl we drive to Rockenbauer's where we have a debauch on new wine. She buys the supper. Home at 10.

Saturday, 6 October 1928

. . . Off in every state of flurry & catch the . . . train for Salzburg. I am hungry by 3.30 & eat a wiener schnitzel, potatoes, cheese, coffee, a bottle [of] wine & 4 cognacs. At Salzburg at 7.30, a lovely room in the Hotel de l'Europa & a garden. . . .

Wednesday, 10 October 1928

. . . On station platform I renew my acquaintance with Orvieto[1] . . . & am quite lit when we arrive at 7.30 in Milan at the Palace Hotel. . . .

    1. An Italian white wine.

Friday, 12 October 1928

Up early to see the church, the piazza, the old walls, & the 2 towers of Siena. . . . An amusing encounter with the director of museum at San Vitale, as funny as any caricature of a foreigner on the stage. At 3 we drive through Rivoli to mountain republic San Masino. Back to Ravenna for dinner & night at the Aquila d'Oro.

Sunday, 14 October 1928

. . . Romolo appeared at 2 o'clock & drove us to the Villa Curonia where we found the gardener Pietro who took us all over the villa. How beautiful it is & how sad I am to see it again.[1] . . .

    1. During the summers of 1913 and 1914, CVV had visited Mabel Dodge's Florentine villa. It has been memorialized in her own memoirs, in CVV's *Peter Whiffle,* and in Muriel Draper's *Music at Midnight.*

Monday, 15 October 1928

. . . A marvellous day. We wandered down the Lungarno & have a debauch on china. Then to the Bargallo to see my Donatello's *David*. . . . Wonderful San Gimignano in the afternoon. Siena at night, the Hotel Continental. I am very depressed & it is very cold. . . .

Saturday, 20 October 1928

. . . We stopped at the Credite Italiano, no mail, & at the office to telegraph to Naples for reservations on the boat. Then started for Naples. . . . A peep at the gardens of Caserta, a remembrance of a restaurant in New York, & in Taormina, & then to wild wishes, always picturesque & amusing & dirty, & on the *Argentina* for Sicily. A good dinner & a fair sleep. A calm voyage.

Wednesday, 24 October 1928

. . . As it is so dismal & Marinoff has been sick, I decide at once to return to Palermo & Rome. Romolo is discontented but we get off. The road is horrible but we reach Palermo before 3 & get Marinoff aboard ship by 4. At 6 she is taken violently ill. Romolo finds unknown doctor aboard who provides laudanum. The steward is marvellous. I get seasick when the boat starts—it is rough—but fall asleep when I learn Marinoff is better. Bad dreams.

Thursday, 25 October 1928

Marinoff is better in the morning. The day is clear. I woke up at 6 & shortly Capri looms in view from the porthole. To Rome at 9 o'clock. A beautiful hot day. . . .

Sunday, 28 October 1928

Up about 7 after a good sleep on my first night on a wagon-lit. We pass through the Alps, snow on the ground. All day in the train. Floods everywhere in the south of France. Arrived Paris about 5 o'clock. To the Carlton where we were ushered to our apartment. . . .

Monday, 29 October 1928

. . . Marinoff gone to the hairdresser. I have a champagne cocktail in the bar, have my hair trimmed, drive to the bank for mail. Walk to the Castiglione Bar where I drink a cocktail & read my mail. Meet Marinoff at the Brasserie Universelle. . . . Back to the hotel. Then stop for Gertrude

Stein[1] & Alice Toklas[2] & take them to dinner at Boilevan's. A boy named
Georges[3] there. . . .

    1. Expatriate American experimental writer whose work CVV had continued to
champion since 1913, when they met.

    2. Stein's longtime companion, secretary, and persistent advocator.

    3. French poet George Hugnet, whose sequence of poems *Efances* Stein approxi-
mated in English as *Before the Flowers of Friendship Faded Friendship Faded* in 1931.

Tuesday, 30 October 1928

Up early with a hangover. Feeling shaky. Rain. . . . A drink or two. Then lunch
at Larue's after a walk in the rain with Germaine [Tailleferre] Barton. Saw
Madeleine Boyd & the Bromfields there. Germaine motors us home. Marie
Doro—bless her!—comes to see me at 4 & stays two hours. We have a grand
time. . . .

Thursday, 1 November 1928

. . . Lunch at Brasserie Universelle where I have some wonderful snails. Then
we meet Germaine Barton at the Salle Maraivaux & see a very wonderful
French picture, *La Passion de Jeanne d'Arc* with Falconetti & Sylvain. Cocktails at Castiglione Bar. Then I drive Germaine home, meet her & Ralph's
second daughter (Diana).[1]

    1. Diana was the daughter of Ralph Barton's second wife, Ann Minnerly; Barton
had left Paris for New York in October.

Saturday, 3 November 1928

A sunny day but I am in bed all day & quite sick. Eat nothing. . . . Paul Morand
was giving a lunch for me. Julian Green,[1] André Maurois,[2] etc. I could not
go. He comes to call. Fan sees him. We were to dine at Gertrude Stein's, go
to the Bal Coloniale & meet Les Juives. Could not go. Germaine Barton. Marie
Doro's mother telephones.

    1. American-born French writer whose novels CVV had read and admired.

    2. French biographer, critic, and novelist.

Sunday, 4 November 1928

In bed all day and all my meals in bed. . . . In the afternoon Gertrude Stein
comes to see me. . . .

Monday, 5 November 1928

. . . Feel some better. . . . Lunch in with Marinoff who has been out & goes out again. . . . Gertrude Stein & Alice Toklas come in late afternoon. Dinner with Marinoff & bed about nine.

Wednesday, 7 November 1928

. . . Apparently I am destined to be sick in Paris. [Herbert] Hoover is elected president. I am neither surprised nor sorry. The country usually thrives on stupid republican presidents. . . . In all day. Marinoff out & lunches with Dagmar Godowsky. Germaine Barton comes to see me in the afternoon. They have sold their house.[1] To bed early after dinner.

    1. Ralph Barton moved manically, this time from the jewel he and Germaine Tailleferre had made in the rue Nicolo to a large estate in the South of France.

Thursday, 8 November 1928

. . . To Gertrude Stein's for dinner. Guevara (met),[1] after dinner Kristians Tonny (Dutch painter), George Hugnet, Natalie Barney[2] (who drives us home), Tristan Tzara,[3] & Virgil Thomson.[4] . . .

    1. Méraude Guevara, a Parisian friend of Stein and Toklas.

    2. Natalie Clifford Barney, American-born expatriate hostess and writer whose literary salon catered to lesbians in the arts.

    3. Romanian Sami Rosenstock, who changed his name and founded the Dadaist school of arts and letters.

    4. American composer studying in Paris who had set some of Gertrude Stein's texts to music, including an opera, *Four Saints in Three Acts.*

Saturday, 10 November 1928

. . . Julian Green has lunch with me & we have a charming time. Then I meet Virgil Thomson & go to Tristan Tzara's to see his Negro things. Then to the Bal Champs-Elysées. Marinoff & I . . . see Yvette Guilbert[1] who makes a sensation in her chansons in Hotel de Les Vertes. We go back to see her after Act I & she is darling. Then home.

    1. Aging French diseuse CVV had admired since his early days in Paris, 1907.

Sunday, 11 November 1928

. . . Watched the Armistice Day parade, including the lame & the halt & the blind on the Champs-Elysées. Couldn't cross the street & missed Gertrude Stein & Alice Toklas who called on us. We call on them immediately, but they are not at home. . . . Then to Bal Coloniale which is becoming white & dull, but saw Countee Cullen and Andre [*name?*] & Jacques. Jacques being kept I suspect.

Tuesday, 13 November 1928

. . . We leave on the *Golden Arrow* at noon & arrive in Paris [i.e., London] at 7.30. . . . To the Carleton where we are stowed temporarily in a bedroom. Alfred Knopf we heard has just arrived on *Mauritania* & I go downstairs to see him. In bed before midnight.

Wednesday, 14 November 1928

. . . Off to see Hugh Walpole at 11.30. He has a charming apartment on Piccadilly & has bought [Jacob] Epstein's head of Paul [Robeson]. . . . Home & move into a two-room apartment. . . .

Thursday, 15 November 1928

. . . Marinoff is ill—after champagne—and stays in bed. I unpack some clothes & then go to see Alfred Knopf at his office. He introduces me to the London Staff. . . . Cocktails at Zena Naylor's at 6, where there are quantities of handsome young men. Back to the Carlton. Dress & dinner in our rooms. Then to the Globe Theatre to see *The Truth Game*. After met Ivor Novello[1] in his noisy & dirty flat. Home at midnight.

    1. English composer of popular songs and operettas.

Friday, 16 November 1928

. . . Drive off with Tallulah [Bankhead] in her new Rolls-Royce & watched her try on gowns at Worth's. . . . Back home, invaded by the English press, about Miss Dyars & Alfred Knopf.[1] Then to Rebecca West's for dinner where I met Evelyn Waugh[2] & his wife, . . . & Vyvyan Holland, Oscar Wilde's son. Home about 2, feeling rotten.

    1. The *London Times* makes no mention of this alliance.
    2. English novelist whose early books were sometimes identified with those of Aldous Huxley, Ronald Firbank, and CVV.

Tuesday, 20 November 1928

. . . Dr. Carly . . . gave me an injection & sent me home to bed. So I broke all engagements including supper with Ivor Novello & stayed in bed. . . . Toward evening Emilie Grigsby[1] appeared. Then Constance Collier, Hugh Walpole, then Tallulah Bankhead & Anthony de Boshari[2] (whose engagement is announced in the evening papers), then Alfred Knopf with Ernest Newman & friendly David Garnett[3] who stayed to dinner—a wicked night. . . .

    1. An English friend of Edward Wassermann.

    2. An Italian count briefly engaged to Tallulah Bankhead while he was still married to improve his monetary credit rating on the strength of her celebrity.

    3. English writer, all of whose novels CVV had read and admired.

Thursday, 22 November 1928

. . . 2 vaccinations & home to bed again. Rain. In bed all day. After lunch Constance Collier comes to see me & at 4 Arthur Machen who is enchanting. He talks about London fogs & old Wales & many other subjects with a delightful wit & humor. . . .

Monday, 26 November 1928

Up at a quarter of eight & off to the doctor's. He says I may go out tonight! Hurrah! It is [a] crisp sunny day. Unseasonably good November weather. I stay in bed in the morning & then Fania & I go to Hugh Walpole's for lunch. . . . Home & in bed again. Alfred Knopf comes in. Dinner at home. Then to Drury Lane to see Paul Robeson in *Show Boat*. Then (with Constance Collier in her car) to a party given for me in his house in St. John's Wood by Paul Robeson: Lord Beaverbrook,[1] . . . Layton & Johnson,[2] Leslie Hutchinson,[3] Delsia,[4] Mrs. Pat Campbell,[5] Alberta Hunter, . . . Hugh Walpole, Fred & Adele Astaire, Cathleen Nesbitt, . . . etc. Everybody gay. An amazing party. Home at 3.

    1. English press lord, who controlled a "white list" to prevent nonwhite entertainers from appearing at command performances.

    2. Turner Layton and James P. Johnson, African American musicians and entertainers.

    3. As "Hutch," this Grenadian—of mixed ancestry but identified as a Negro—was the most popular café pianist and singer in England for nearly thirty years.

    4. Alice Delsia, English singing actress.

    5. The leading English actress of the period, noted for her roles in plays by George Bernard Shaw and, later, for their long correspondence.

Tuesday, 27 November 1928

. . . Last night I heard some very nasty things about Aldo Castellani[1] but it behooves me to pay him attention. . . .

    1. The medical doctor who was treating CVV for various mysterious ailments.

Wednesday, 28 November 1928

... I go to Castellani for treatment & then return. . . . David Garnett comes to lunch & tells me of his scheme of invading America, incognito in a motor. After he has gone ... Mrs. Ernest Newman calls but we were unable to have her up. . . .

Thursday, 29 November 1928

... I go to see Castellani as usual. Then to Harrod's where I order quantities of phonograph records sent to America. . . . Rebecca West comes in after lunch. Then Marinoff to the opening of Max Beerbohm's[1] exposition at the Leicester Galleries. . . . Late in the afternoon Alfred Knopf comes in. . . .

    1. English writer and caricaturist.

Friday, 30 November 1928

Up at a quarter of eight & to doctor's as usual. Then home & with Emilie Grigsby & Marinoff to the Caledonian market where we bought a lot of things. . . .

Saturday, 1 December 1928

Up at a quarter of eight to go to Dr. Castellani. . . . I am tired of this—<u>very.</u>
. . .

Wednesday, 5 December 1928

Up early & dressed & to the doctor's where I wait for him for an hour in a freezing room & when I see him he is vague & more unsatisfactory than ever. I come away in a rage, forget my foot paint, but Marinoff goes after it & vamps the formula from his assistant. From the hotel I go out with John Van Druten[1] to see the fat boy at Pie Corner.[2] Then we go to Old Bailey (where I see a trial) & Lincoln's Inn. Then we meet Cathleen Nesbitt & Marinoff at Savroni's & lunch there. . . .

    1. English novelist and playwright.
    2. A tourist attraction: a gilded figure at the corner of Giltspun Street and Cock Lane opposite St. Bartholomew's Hospital, the site where the Great Fire of 1666 burned out.

Sunday, 9 December 1928

Up and packing. . . . After lunch Marinoff & I visit the National Portrait Gallery. Then return to hotel & receive visitors: . . . John Van Druten, Paul & Essie Robeson, Rebecca West, Elsie Janis,[1] & finally Alfred Knopf who stays to dinner & takes us to the boat train at 9.50, Paddington Station. We go to bed. I sleep till the train reaches Plymouth about 3.

    1. American musical comedy actress.

Wednesday, 12 December 1928

Up very early. The sea is nearly calm & I think I am feeling better. . . . In the afternoon see Gilda Gray.[1] . . . To sleep about 9.30. . . . How we do pitch!

    1. American dancer claiming to have invented or at least to have popularized the Shimmy, a dance named, she averred, for "shaking my chemise."

Friday, 14 December 1928

Up at 8. Packing trunk, straightening out customs, etc. . . . I have a cold. . . . Dinner with Gilda Gray & her boy friend & then to the ship concert which was a riot. In bed about 2. I fell off the wagon & got drunk on cognac.

Sunday, 16 December 1928

Boat docks at 9.30 of a cloudy morning. Regina Wallace, Donald Angus, Eddie Wassermann at the dock to meet us. Later Bertha Case. Sidney Peterson arrives too late to find us. We are on the dock for 2 hours because we have 25 pieces of baggage, most of which has to be opened. . . . Home & find Meda. The house full of telegrams & flowers. Everybody, apparently, has thought of us. . . . Later we go to a cocktail party & supper at Eddie's: Muriel Draper, D'Alvarez, Colin McPhee, Louise Hellström, Aaron Copland, Olga Hilliard, Arthur Richman, Donald, Reg, Harry Block, Frances Seligman, Emily Clark, Blanche Knopf, etc. Home early. I have a slight cold. No drinking.

Saturday, 29 December 1928

Up fairly early. . . . To post office, to Holliday's, to Drake's, & to Saks Fifth Ave. where I buy some ties for my boy friends.[1] Then lunch with Beverly Nichols at the Algonquin. Bertha Case introduces us to Dorothy Gish.[2] After lunch I walk most of the way home. . . .

    1. The phrase "boy friend" should not be construed to refer automatically to lovers or sexual partners. In the twenties and well into the thirties, "boy friend"

referred only to a male social companion. Misreading the phrase has led more than one writer to make false assumptions.

2. Silent film actress whose sister Lillian had a much longer and more celebrated career.

Monday, 31 December 1928

Up at 8 o'clock. Bright & cool. Spent the morning cleaning out my desk, etc. To bank to start "thrift account," deposited $5,000, and to Robert's to have lunch with Ralph Barton, who has separated from Germaine Tailleferre & is living in New York again. . . . Home at 2. Miriam Wolff is there. We go to see Mrs. [Edgar] Saltus & Elsie Saltus[1] . . . on Park Ave. A dreadfully funny tea. To dinner at D'Alvarez's: Donald Angus, Harry Block, Louise Hellström. Then to New Year's party at Muriel Draper's: Julia Hoyt, Cecil Beaton, Raymond Mortimer,[2] Mabel Luhan, [Honorable Dorothy] Brett, Bobby & Beatrice Locher, John Colton, . . . Esther Murphy, Blythe Daly, Charlie Brackett, Lewis Galantiere, Alice de la Mar. At home around 1.30.

1. Edgar Saltus was an American novelist whose lapsed career CVV labored to resuscitate through essays and reviews.

2. English book reviewer for the *London Times.*

1929

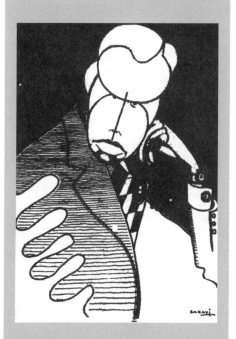

"Feeling rather bouleverse by
the season & the number of
people I am seeing. I think it
would be wise for me to withdraw from life for a while."

The Van Vechtens passed 1929 largely in the manner of the idle rich, spending their sudden wealth extravagantly on decor, clothing, and objets d'art, giving and attending an endless round of parties, always going somewhere and getting nowhere but to boredom. In May they sailed for London and spent nearly a month there, again giving and going to parties, with a minor diversion when Van Vechten visited Hugh Walpole in Scotland while Marinoff toured the cathedral cities. Then they spent a month in Paris, with side trips to several cities in Spain and to visit Eugene O'Neill and Carlotta Monterey at their French château. In August they returned to the United States suddenly, bored again. Two weeks into the long hangover that followed the stock market crash at the end of October, Van Vechten began to write his final novel, *Parties*.

Tuesday, 15 January 1929

Blanche [Knopf] telegraphs me that they have fired Donald [Angus]. Donald telephones later. He is apparently lacking in any qualities which will make him get on. Sara Haardt comes to lunch. After lunch I go to . . . try on my clothes. Back home, then to Blanche Knopf's for tea. Ralph Barton, Witter Bynner, Richard Ordynske.[1] Home for dinner. Edna Kenton came & spent the evening. . . . Later I go to Harlem with . . . Dick Barthelmess . . . & Clifton Webb. To the Cotton Club. Then to the Sugar Cane & finally Lenox Hill Club. . . . Meet Bill George who has just married a white woman. Clifton Webb drives me home about 5.

    1. American stage actor.

Saturday, 19 January 1929

. . . Lunch at Henri's with Donald Angus. He tells me Sam Knopf is trying to get him a job at Jay Thorpe [Clothing Store]. I am not so sorry for him as I might be if he showed more sense. I leave him to go to Goldfarb's to order flowers for Anna Pollock. Then home to dinner at the Pollocks'. Channing is more of a moron than usual. . . . We leave at midnight & go to a party at Muk de Jari's. . . . Home about 1.30.

Monday, 21 January 1929

. . . Cleaned out old receipts & cheques & read Muriel Draper's *Music at Midnight*. . . . I finished reading *Amimas*. Both Walter Park's and Muriel's books suffer because neither knows how to write. In bed about 11.

Thursday, 24 January 1929

. . . Bertha Case has lunch with me chez nous & goes with me to the Philharmonic Concert which is dull. She has changed very much from the demure Bertha of yesteryear who could not be separated from Frank. . . . Home to dress & to dinner chez D'Alvarez. Blanche Knopf, Eddie Wassermann, Louise [Hellström], Paul Morand, Bibi & Val Dudensing. A lewd party & I get sore & drag Marinoff away to a party at Theodore Dreiser's. . . . Home about one.

Friday, 25 January 1929

. . . Meda comes with the news that Richard, her son, has run away from Bordentown. Lunch with Mabel Luhan, Muriel Draper. . . . Home around 3. At 5 I go to Fannie Hurst's for tea (rotten coffee). . . . Dinner with Marinoff (who appeared for the Actor's Fund in afternoon) at Langners' with Horace Liveright, Ina Claire, Gene Markey, D'Alvarez. After dinner & later Alfred Lunt & Lynn Fontanne, Massine (met),[1] Jonathan Cape,[2] Peggy Wood,[3] Helen Flint,[4] Dudley Murphy, Caroline Dudley [Reagan], Mercedes de Acosta, Eddie Wassermann, Helen Westley, etc. Some Africans with drums do some native music. Home about 1.30.

    1. Leonid Massine, Russian dancer and choreographer.
    2. English publisher.
    3. English musical actress.
    4. Minor American actress.

Sunday, 27 January 1929

. . . Marinoff & I took Constance Collier to dinner at Robert's & to Bledsoe's concert at the Globe Theatre. Bledsoe has improved enormously. The audience represented a thrilling part of Harlem: Jim & Grace Johnson (with Alma Wertheim), Jack & Grayce Nail, Bernia & Harry Austin, Geraldyn Dismond, . . . Gladys & Walter White, Edna Thomas, Arthur & Marion Spingarn, etc. We were not invited to a party given after, so we took Constance home & went to bed. I have pain in my belly all night. Bledsoe was announced to sing "The Creation"[1] with the composer conducting, but [Harold] Guinzberg did not arrive in N.Y. in time for a rehearsal & it was dropped.

    1. Based on one of the sermons in verse in James Weldon Johnson's *God's Trombones*.

Monday, 28 January 1929

. . . Meda comes late. Richard is not yet found. To . . . lunch with Mabel Luhan, Neith Boyce, & Edna Kenton. After lunch I go with Mabel & Neith to the American Art Galleries [i.e., American Place] to see . . . Stieglitz and some of O'Keeffe's paintings. . . . I learn that Florence Hammond has been ill three months with heart trouble, & I call her up. To see Max Ewing's "exhibition."[1] Gilda Gray, C. D. Krepps,[2] Lawrence & Armina Langner for dinner. . . . Later: Lenore Ulric, Sidney Blackmer, L[ouis] Calhern, Julia Hoyt, Virginia Hammond, Regina Wallace, Blanche & Alfred Knopf, Donald Angus, Jack Colton, Dudley Murphy, T. R. Smith, Val & Bibi Dudensing, D'Alvarez, Rita Romilly, Cecil Beaton,[3] Mercedes de Acosta, Richard Ordynske, Eddie Wassermann, Hal Bynner.

    1. Ewing had created an art gallery in part of his apartment, completely covering the walls with photographs and reproductions of them, from newspapers and magazines, of a broad cross-section of people connected with the arts.

2. C. David Krepps, an associate with the Zurich Casualty Company.

3. English portrait and fashion photographer.

Saturday, 2 February 1929

... A letter from Elisabeth Marbury[1] submitting terms for dramatization of *Nigger Heaven*. This upsets me & so does everything & indigestion develops. . . . To lunch with Donald [Angus], & then to a show at the Roxy. Home & Marinoff nags me into a furious temper. Dinner with Charles Norris.[2] He has ten men & "music." . . .

1. Literary and theatrical agent.

2. Literary and film editor, husband of novelist Kathleen Norris.

Monday, 4 February 1929

... Spent the morning finishing *Prima Donna,* a very ordinary piece of work, written by a <u>writer</u> & a <u>musician,</u> but not by a creator of character.[1] The post office where I get English pocket book edition of *The Blind Bow-Boy,* . . . a telegram to Hugh [Walpole] on his birthday & flowers to Margaret Freeman in hospital in Richmond. Then to Algonquin for lunch with Marinoff. . . . Then to exhibition of Russian work in Grand Central Palace. Then to discuss Marbury['s proposal to dramatize *Nigger Heaven*] with Alfred Knopf. Then to see Marbury. . . . Dinner alone with Marinoff. I am very depressed. Read . . . *The Blacker the Berry*[2] by Wallace Thurman, a good book but lacking in tenderness.

1. *Prima Donna: A Novel of the Opera* (two volumes, 1929) by John Pitts Sanborn, CVV's longtime friend and occasional rival earlier in the century, when both men were music critics.

2. A novel about the Harlem Renaissance in which CVV appears as "Campbell Kitchen."

Tuesday, 5 February 1929

... Alfred [Knopf] telephones that Jakob[1] is a crook & a bigamist & I telephone Marbury that negotiations are off. In arranging for seats for *Whoopee* tomorrow night we find that [we] can get them from an agent for 15 dollars apiece! Lunch in alone. Then I go to Dr. Diamond's & have two more teeth out. No unpleasant effects, but I come home & stay. To bed about 10.

1. Otherwise unidentified, "Jakob" aspired to dramatize *Nigger Heaven.*

Wednesday, 6 February 1929

Up at 8.30, cold & rainy. I have a sore throat. I get dressed & go . . . to have my hair cut. Then to Macy's, then to Algonquin where I visit Bertha Case & her cat. Then meet Marinoff, Mabel Luhan & her son's wife, Mrs. John Evans, & we have a very stiff lunch. Home. To Dr. Diamond's for a short examination & home again. Donald telephones that he is working at Jay Thorpe's.[1] . . . Tom Smith & Emilie Grigsby come to dinner & we take them to *Whoopee,* where we see Mercedes [de Acosta] & I meet George M. Cohan.[2] From *Whoopee* we go to Muriel [Draper]'s party . . . & stay ten minutes. . . . We get home at 12.30 & go to bed. Rain!

> 1. Angus eventually became chief window decorator at Jay Thorpe's for more than thirty years, until this fashionable store closed.
> 2. American composer, librettist, director, and actor in musical comedies.

Monday, 11 February 1929

. . . To a party at Bertha Case's. Mencken, Rita Wellman,[1] Thyra Sampter Winslow,[2] Gene Markey, Constance Collier, Madge Kennedy, Margaret Morgan, Ernest & Madeleine Boyd, etc. Marinoff got very drunk & when we went to Eddie Wassermann's for dinner—his birthday—flopped. Eddie, Blanche & I went to *Follow Thru,* a fairly amusing musical show. Picked up Fania after the show & took her home.

> 1. Philadelphia art critic and painter.
> 2. American short story writer and novelist published by Knopf.

Tuesday, 12 February 1929

. . . Marinoff is sick with a bad hangover. I work on preface to catalogue for Bob [Chanler] & also on income tax returns. . . . Then I take Eddie Wassermann to see Ruth Draper,[1] at the Comedy Theatre, first time, & then to Sam Hoffenstein's for cocktails. . . . Home quite lit for dinner & to bed before 9.

> 1. Monologist, Muriel Draper's sister-in-law.

Thursday, 14 February 1929

. . . Finished *The True Heart*[1] not with too great enthusiasm & read a shilling shocker called *Red Harvest* which is immense.[2] . . . To the Chatham to see Mrs. Hopwood. I leave Marinoff there & go to Deems Taylor & Mary Kennedy. She gives me a play to read. Home at 6.30. Virginia Hammond for dinner & she & Marinoff go to the theatre. I go to a party at Zoë Akins and Jobyna Howland's,[3] 121 Madison Ave. . . . Marinoff comes for me at 11.30 & we go home.

1. By Sylvia Townsend Warner, whose earlier novels, *Lolly Willows* and *Mr. Fortune's Maggot*, CVV had reviewed enthusiastically.

2. Knopf had just published the first of Dashiell Hammett's detective novels. CVV was an immediate enthusiast and supplied subsequent dust jacket encomiums.

3. Actress in musical plays and revues.

Friday, 15 February 1929

... To lunch with Arthur Davison Ficke at Robert's. See Constance Collier & meet Natasha Rambova.[1] ... Read Mary Kennedy's not very good play, *Jordan*. Then to see Florence Hammond. ... To a cocktail party at Dorothy Harvey's: Arthur & Gladys Ficke, Harry Harvey, Mabel Luhan, ... Hal Bynner, Ida Rauh. Home for dinner. Ettie Stettheimer & Virgil Thomson who after dinner played his remarkable opera to words of Gertrude Stein: *Four Saints in Three Acts*.[2] Alma & Maurice Wertheim were here, Carrie Stettheimer, Max Ewing, Mabel Luhan who brought Marty Mann, Dorothy Harvey, Emily Clark & Zena Naylor. I went to a drag in Harlem with Harry, Hal, Emily, Virgil & Marty. We picked up Eddie Manchester[3] & went to the Lenox Club where I danced with Louis Cole in drag, & then to Pod's & Jerry's.

1. Film star Rudolph Valentino's widow and Alla Nazimova's lover.

2. The first hearing in America, but the opera was not produced until 1934.

3. One of Ethel Waters's former beaux.

Saturday, 16 February 1929

Home at 7.30. Saw millions of people I knew. Awakened at 11 by the telephone: Marinoff, who spent the night with Reg. . . .

Monday, 18 February 1929

... Reading *The White Girl*, a very interesting book about a girl who passes, by Vera Casparay. Lunch in alone. Sidney Peterson comes in to see me & asks what I think about miscegenation. It seems he is in love with a white girl. . . .

Wednesday, 20 February 1929

... In the afternoon Marinoff & I go to Wanamaker's for a debauch, buying (or planning to buy) a mink coat, a refectory table, & some Madagascar horn birds, a couple of Italian vases, etc. On the way uptown we call on Florence Hammond. Virginia Hammond & Armina Langner come to dinner & go to a movie with Marinoff while I go to take Eddie Wassermann to dinner at Algonquin where Frank Case is dining with a blonde. Then we meet Blanche

[Knopf] at first performance of [Wallace] Thurman & [William] Rapp's *Harlem* at Apollo Theatre, a racy melodrama with plenty of authentic Negro dialogue. . . .

Thursday, 21 February 1929

. . . Read Ralph Barton's *God's Country,* not with too much enthusiasm.[1] Lunch in alone. Then I drive in the snow to Apollo Theatre to get tickets for Meda & Hannah [Ellis] for *Harlem.* . . . Marinoff . . . bought her first mink coat today for 1,950 dollars. . . .

   1. Barton's satirical history of the United States, with many of his irreverent drawings, was a failure with the critics as well as the public.

Friday, 22 February 1929

. . . Read Bowyer Campbell's *Black Sadie* which begins well but is full of ignorance & coincidence. To the Stettheimers' for dinner: Georgia O'Keeffe, Phil Moeller, Henry McBride, Joe Brewer,[1] & Virgil Thomson who plays part of his opera [*Four Saints in Three Acts*]. . . .

   1. Editor at Payson and Clark who published (at CVV's urging) Gertrude Stein's *Useful Knowledge.* Later Brewer became president of Olivet College.

Wednesday, 27 February 1929

. . . Meda & Hannah did not like the play *Harlem* which they saw last night. Julie Hopwood very ill with crisypelis, a trained nurse & feeding through the rectum. I go to Goldfarb's to send her flowers. . . . Home before 2. . . . Dinner at Otto Kahn's: Lord & Lady Weymouth, Lady Lettice Liggins, Lord Beaverbrook. We went to *Jonny Spielt Auf* [by Ernst Krenek] at the Metropolitan & in Gatti's box![1] I went back to see Tibbett[2] after the show. Then we went to Harlem to the revue at Connie's Inn, to the Sugar Cane, . . . & Lenox Ave. Club, & finally to Pod's & Jerry's. Home at 6.

   1. Guilio Gatti-Casazza, director of the Metropolitan Opera House.
   2. Lawrence Tibbett, operatic baritone.

Saturday, 2 March 1929

. . . To the Algonquin where I had lunch with Ethel Barrymore, Constance Collier, Frank Case. Going out I ran into John Floyd (drunk, of course). Bertha Case's maid is ill & I send her some flowers. In calling up Hal Bynner I discover that Arthur Ficke is down here with one arm paralyzed by booze. I drive Constance to the theatre for as far as we can get in the rain & crowded streets (she gets out & walks). . . . Then to Commodore Hotel to see Gladys & a pretty glum Arthur [Ficke]. Then home. . . . I go to Eddie Wassermann, joined by Donald Angus & Harry Block. We go to Don Juan for drinks. Donald gets drunk & goes home. Then Hal Bynner joins us & we all go to Harlem. Club Harlem, where we see Johnny Cobb, Lenox Ave. Club where are Otto Kahn & Horace Liveright. Louis Cole joins us & goes with us to Pod's & Jerry's. Home at 5.30.

Tuesday, 5 March 1929

According to the morning papers Julie Hopwood has left the bulk of her estate to the Jones of Cleveland[1] with a trust fund to support Avery's monkey Pepe Squash. I stayed in all day, very bilious, asleep a good deal of the time. Finished Isadora Duncan's *Russian Days* & reading *Journal of a Slave on a Georgia Plantation*, a bitter arraignment of slavery by Frances Anne Kemble.[2] Lunch in with Marinoff. There are cocktail parties at Eddie Wassermann's & Harry Harvey's which I visit. Ina Claire & Gene Markey come to dinner & spend the evening here.

    1. Julia Jones and her son, civil engineer P. Allan Jones, were close friends of Avery Hopwood's mother, who established a trust for them. Hopwood himself did not mention them in his will. In accordance with his wishes, the bulk of his estate established the Avery Hopwood Awards to young writers through the University of Michigan, of which he was an alumnus.

    2. Better known as the popular nineteenth-century actress Fanny Kemble, who gave up her career to marry into Southern gentry and then regretted having done so.

Saturday, 9 March 1929

Up at 7.30. Cloudy & cold. My biliousness has passed away, but I have a hangover & go to see Jack Schnabel about mss. of Avery's novel & find that Archie Bell[1] has tampered with it & that it belongs to the estate & has to be sold at auction.[2] Take Zena Naylor to lunch at Crillon. Home & lie down. . . . We go to the Fifth Ave. Playhouse to see a Japanese film, which we enjoy & to Toyo Kan's on E. 19th St. for a Japanese dinner. . . . Then with Eddie Wassermann we go to Arthur Richman's. . . . Eddie & I go to the Lenox Ave. Club where we see Louis Cole. I come home & go to bed before 3, leaving Eddie. Marinoff goes home with Reg.

    1. Cleveland, Ohio journalist, a friend of Hopwood.

    2. Hopwood's mammoth roman à clef, titled *The Great Bordel*, disappeared soon thereafter. A copy subsequently surfaced, but it has not been published.

Tuesday, 19 March 1929

. . . Lunch in with Marinoff. Then to see Jeanne Eagels in speaking film, *The Letter* [by W. Somerset Maugham], an amazing picture, especially the fight between a mongoose & a cobra. Marinoff had some people to dinner. I dined chez Eddie Wassermann with T. R. Smith, Harry Block, & Max Ewing. Home at 2, slightly plastered.

Thursday, 21 March 1929

. . . Lunch in with Marinoff & then to Carnegie Hall to hear [Arturo] Toscanini conduct Schubert's C Major Symphony & *William Tell* overture electrically. . . . Nora Holt (just in from Chicago), Langners, & Eddie Wassermann for dinner. After dinner, party for Nora who sang: Arthur Richman, Dorothy Hergesheimer, Alfred & Blanche Knopf, Jimmie Reynolds, . . . D'Alvarez, the Val Dudensings, Harold & Alice Guinzberg, James Weldon & Grace Johnson, Katie Seabrook & a boy named Sherham, Harry Block, Hal Bynner, . . . Walter & Gladys White, Jim & Dorothy Harris, Elmer & Nella Imes, Muriel Draper & someone, Rita Romilly, Donald Angus, . . . Cecil Beaton. . . . They leave about 4. Then a cocktail party at Cecil Beaton's but I don't go.

Saturday, 23 March 1929.

. . . Reg Wallace & Donald Angus come to dinner. Then Donald & I go to Eddie Wassermann's where Clifton Webb & Kim Denman (met) appear. We go to Tony's (next to Don Juan) for dinner & then to Harlem, Lenox Ave. Club, and from there with Louis Cole to 109 W. 136 where we see & do some strange dancing. Home at 5. Marinoff stays with Reg Wallace. Eddie Wassermann is drunk & rude to Donald.

Thursday, 28 March 1929

. . . In the morning I drove to Goldfarb's for flowers. The place is fabulous in its Easter beauty, like a flower show. To Palace to get seats for Meda. Virgil Thomson comes for lunch. After lunch I take a nap & start reading an amazing book called *The Innocent Voyage.*[1] To a cocktail party at Tom Smith's for Texas Guinan[2] and a coupla gunmen. They do not come but Peter Arno & his wife [Lois Long], Zena Naylor, Donald Freeman, etc. Wood Kahler[3] takes Marinoff to the theatre. Eddie Wassermann['s]. Later Duke Ellington.[4] . . . I get simply loaded & go home without dinner around 11 o'clock.

1. By Welsh novelist Richard Hughes, who later changed the title to *High Wind in Jamaica.*

2. Her welcome to customers—"Hello, sucker"—became a catchphrase in the late twenties.

3. One of Regina Wallace's beaux, also a theater escort for Marinoff from time to time.

4. Composer and leader of his own orchestra at the Kentucky Club and the Cotton Club.

Friday, 29 March 1929

. . . To Jac Auer's for exercise & a rubdown. Home for lunch alone, a nap & then I finished reading Richard Hughes's remarkable book, *The Innocent Voyage.* Started Walter White's *Rope & Faggot.* Dinner in with Marinoff. Then we called on Florence & Percy Hammond. . . . Then at 9 on to Lawrence & Armina Langner's farewell party for St. John Ervine[1] who sails. . . . Then on to a party at Katie & William Seabrook's. . . . We go home at 1.30. . . .

1. Irish playwright and novelist.

Wednesday, 3 April 1929

. . . Home around 5. Find Nella [Larsen] Imes's new book [in manuscript] *Passing* here. Read it absorbedly till I have to go out to dinner. Reg Wallace & Virginia Hammond dine here with Marinoff. I go to Joe Brewer's for dinner. Home at 1 & finish *Passing,* an extraordinary story, extraordinarily told. I go to bed & sleep badly. I am so excited.

Thursday, 4 April 1929

Up at 8.30. Warm & cloudy. I get dressed & go to Knopf office where I stir Blanche & Alfred up about Nella Larsen's *Passing,* making quite a scene. Also talk with Geo. Jean Nathan. To Goldfarb's to send flowers to Nella & Joe Brewer. Then to Dorothy Peterson's for lunch. Nella is there. Then to Gramophone Shop & home. Rain. . . . To the Sherry-Netherland to join Blanche & Alfred—their 13th wedding anniversary—for dinner. . . . We go to the St. Regis, dance, etc., till midnight. Home & to bed.

Friday, 5 April 1929

. . . Alfred Knopf . . . tells me they are instituting a selling campaign for Nella [Larsen]'s book [*Passing*]. Donald Angus for dinner. He & I go to opening of Mary Pickford in Movietone *Coquette* at Rivoli. It is terrible. . . .

Saturday, 6 April 1929

Up at 7.30. Cloudy & warm. Dressed, pasted up scrapbooks, wrote letters, to drug store, to music shop to send Duke Ellington records to Margaret Case, to bank for cash, to . . . have a rip in my coat mended, & to Warwick where I collected Louella Parsons[1] & took her to lunch at the Crillon where she got stewed & we had a good time. Home at 3. At 5 a cocktail party: Miguel Covarrubias & Rose Rolanda, just back from Mexico, Mary McKinnon, Max Ewing, Lawrence & Armina Langner, Sara & Lawrence Marsh,[2] Joe Brewer, Donald Angus, Harry Block, Poldark Birnbaum & his brother.[3] Marinoff & I took Harry Block, Miguel & Rose, Donald, Max Ewing & Mary McKinnon to dinner [at] Fornio's, and these except Max to Miguel's where we see many pictures of Mexico, paintings, etc. Then Donald & I go to Joe Brewer's to a party. . . . Home at 3. Marinoff goes to Harlem & gets home after 5.

    1. Hollywood gossip columnist for the Hearst syndicate of newspapers.
    2. Actress Julia Hoyt's sister and her husband.
    3. Martin and Poldark Bierbaum were art dealers; Poldark was an occasional theater escort for Marinoff.

Thursday, 11 April 1929

. . . Lunch in with Marinoff & we go to Philharmonic concert to hear Clemens Krauss[1] conduct. He is very romantic & handsome, & W. J. Henderson[2] with whom I talked after the concert says it is rumored he is the natural son of an Austrian grand duke & a ballet dancer. Home for a minute after the concert then to dinner with the James Weldon Johnsons. Home at 9.30 & to bed. Indigestion. I take Calomel.

    1. Austrian conductor, primarily of opera.
    2. English born musicologist specializing in Wagner and singing.

Sunday, 14 April 1929

Up at 11 o'clock. Cold & cloudy. Read papers. I had lunch & went to bed again till 3. Al Woods[1] just back from Europe came in & we all talk over the transatlantic telephone to Marie Doro in Paris, a thrilling experience. I get quite lit. . . .

    1. Albert Herman Woods was a producer of many farces and on-stage bedroom romps of the period.

Thursday, 18 April 1929

. . . Lunch early. Then Marinoff & I went to sale of Avery [Hopwood]'s effects at Marx Auction Rooms. . . . Later, came home, picked up Nella Imes & Elizabeth Shaffer & took them to cocktail [party] given by Blanche Knopf for Nella. Irita Van Doren, the Seabrooks, Isa Glenn, Grace Johnson, Walter White. . . . I took Alfred, Blanche, & Marinoff & Wood Kahler to dinner at Don Juan. I was drunk & disorderly. Home & in bed by 10.30.

Friday, 19 April 1929

. . . I have quite a splendid hangover. Lunch in with Marinoff. We order a stateroom on the *Majestic* for May 10. Then we walk to Saks, to French Book Shop, to Vantine's, etc. Home around 3.30. I go to bed for two hours. To the Stettheimers for dinner with Phil Moeller. . . . I give a party at Connie's Inn at 11 o'clock. The revue is the dirtiest I have ever seen. Earl Tucker[1] & Midnight Steppers marvellous dancers. Bertha & Frank Case, Gene Markey, Eddie Wassermann, Armina Langner, Blanche Knopf. Home at 3.30.

    1. African American dancer called "Snakehips," widower of Florence Mills.

Monday, 22 April 1929

Up at 8.15. Toujours rain! Dressed, & off to post office & to Jac Auer's for exercise. The rubbers are no good this year & the whole place is run down. Lunch with Marinoff at the Algonquin. . . . Home at 3.30. Rita Romilly comes in later & I sell her Tonny sketch.[1] Marinoff & I go to dinner at Eddie Wassermann's, also Mercedes de Acosta. Then to see Jimmie Johnson's[2] show, *Messin' Around*, at the Hudson opening night. It is so bad we leave after first act. Met Cora Green. Eddie & Mercedes come home with us & stay till midnight.

    1. CVV met the Dutch painter Kristians Tonny through Gertrude Stein in Paris. He was sufficiently enthusiastic about Tonny's work to offer to try to sell some of it in the United States.
    2. James P. Johnson, African American composer of several routine black revues on Broadway, also wrote an opera based on a one-act play by Eugene O'Neill, *The Dreamy Kid,* a piano concerto, and a symphony.

Thursday, 25 April 1929

. . . Picked up Gladys Bentley,[1] a Negro pianist, on W. 46 St., where I saw Porter Grainger, & took her to Eddie Wassermann's where she played at a Thé Dasante for Nella Imes. . . .

1. A 300-pound transvestite who sang her own scabrous versions of popular songs at Connie's Inn and The Clam House in Harlem, often dressed in a white tuxedo. Also known as "Bobbie Minton."

Tuesday, 30 April 1929

. . . To a cocktail party at Max Ewing's for Zena Naylor who is sailing Friday. . . . Home for dinner & then to see *The Little Review* (with Cliff Webb) with Marinoff. . . .

Wednesday, 1 May 1929

. . . Home for lunch. Marinoff, Edna Kenton, Rose Rolanda, A'Lelia Walker. Marinoff takes them to her box party of *Blackbirds.* . . . Marinoff goes to dinner with Reg [Wallace] & Virginia [Hammond] & I take Eddie Wassermann to dinner at the Don Juan. We go to opening night of *Grand Street Follies.* . . . To a party . . . where I meet Ruth Draper. Saw Phil Moeller, Mina Curtiss, Muriel Draper, Albert Carroll, . . . Max Ewing, etc. With Eddie I go to Lenore Ulric's. Sidney Blackmer, Virginia, Reg, & Marinoff there. Home about 3 & to bed.

Friday, 3 May 1929

. . . With Muriel Draper to lunch at the Crillon. . . . Then with Muriel to Anderson Galleries to see Demuth pictures (uninteresting). Stieglitz was there. . . . To Goldfarb's for flowers & with an enormous bunch of lilies I go to tea the Stettheimers give us. . . . Then to a party at Dudley Murphy's where Gladys Bentley sings & plays, Libby Holman[1] sings, Peter Arno shows dirty films. . . . Home at 2.

1. Musical comedy performer, then appearing in *The Little Review.*

Saturday, 4 May 1929

. . . Up with rather a hangover about 8 o'clock. . . . Dressed later & went to party for us at Lawrence & Armina Langner's, . . . home around 4.

Thursday, 9 May 1929

. . . My vaccination is a large size. Packing all day. . . . To a cocktail party at Blanche's for Eddie Wassermann. . . . Home & dressed & to Stettheimers to say farewell. To Rita Romilly's for dinner with Max Ewing, Donald Angus, Regina Wallace. We all go to Bertha Case's dance for us at the Algonquin. . . . Home at 4.

Friday, 10 May 1929

. . . After lunch we go to the docks with our baggage. A farewell supper at Eddie Wassermann's. . . . Blanche, . . . Lawrence [Langner], & T. R. Smith come to the boat to see us & Eddie sail. We had a case of champagne. Meda came down, & Hannah [Ellis], & David [Marion]. Also, Bertha Case, Reg Wallace, Virginia Hammond, Nils Nelson & Geo. Hoy, Harry Block, Walter & Gladys White, Mary McKinnon with a Mr. Quinn, Max Ewing, Muriel Draper, Elmer Imes, Jim & Grace Johnson & Rita Romilly. . . . The boat sails at 10. Eddie & I drink the two remaining bottles of champagne. He is in his cabin with Leonard Poole, the steward, I know. In bed about 12, tranquilized in flowers and friends.

Sunday, 12 May 1929

. . . Walked the deck & had a big lunch. Saw Eddie (just gone to bed at noon) & Eva [Gauthier]. They dine with us downstairs. We go to the smoking room & drink a lot of brandy & soda & retire at 1.30.

Monday, 13 May 1929

Up at 11 & down for lunch, but it is rougher, & I feel rotten, rotten. I go to bed right after lunch & stay there the whole afternoon. Get up for dinner, but we didn't dress, at which I drink a bottle of Montrachet. . . .

Tuesday, 14 May 1929

. . . Wrote a lot of letters. Drank a lot of drinks in the smoking room with Eva, Marinoff & Frank Houston.[1] Dressed. Again in the smoking room, met Eddie who took us to the gala dinner at the Ritz. . . .

   1. A banker and director of the Waldorf Astoria Corporation.

Thursday, 16 May 1929

. . . Dinner with Marinoff downstairs. Later we see Eddie . . . & stay up very late drinking one thing & another.

Friday, 17 May 1929

. . . We dine at the Carlton, sending Eddie to his service flat in St. James Street, but he is lonesome & we invite him to dinner at Simpson's [in the Strand] because we have no living room as yet. . . .

Saturday, 18 May 1929

. . . Lunch with Hugh Walpole. . . . Then with Fania to see Mrs. Patrick Campbell in *The Matriarch* (which we enjoy). . . . Back to the Carlton, G. B. Stern[1] & Edna Thomas came in for cocktails. Then we join Joe Brewer, Eddie Wassermann, & Harold Acton (met)[2] at Savroni's where Joe gives us a marvellous dinner. . . .

> 1. Gladys Brownyn Stern Holdsworth, prolific English writer and author of *The Matriarch*.
> 2. English writer and Oxford aesthete early to endorse T. S. Eliot, Ronald Firbank, and the Sitwell siblings.

Tuesday, 21 May 1929

. . . Lunch with Jack [i.e., John] Van Druten at Savroni's & encountered Adele Astaire. . . . Then in the bright sunlight we motor to the Robesons' new place in Hampstead Heath. We have dinner with Paul, Essie, & Mrs. Goode, & see the baby & the house. . . . Home & to bed about midnight.

Wednesday, 22 May 1929

. . . About 11.30 we trotted over to the Nat'l Gallery. At 1 we went on to Boulestin's where Rebecca West gave a lunch. . . . Then to a party Cecil Beaton gave for us where there were dozens of people & most of the names I did not catch. . . . Home & dressed & to pick up G. B. Stern in the historic Albany. She gave a dinner at the Ivy for us. . . .

Thursday, 23 May 1929

. . . We start out about 12 & stop at several shops on our way to Boulestin's where we give a delightful lunch party for Paul & Essie Robeson, Cathleen Nesbitt, Hugh Walpole. Then Paul, Marinoff & I walk to the City & in St. Paul's. Then we drive back, dropping Paul, . . . & encounter Eddie Wassermann & Joe Brewer. Joe & I drive back to the Carlton & on to a cocktail party at Harold Acton's in his beautiful house in Lancaster Gate. . . .

Saturday, 25 May 1929

. . . Dropped Marinoff at the Ivy where she had lunch with Ruth Chester[1] & on to the Café Royale where Arthur Machen had lunch with me. It is the first time I have been there—and the lunch. A dreadful place which once was wonderful. Walked home around 3. Paul broke his engagement to meet Marinoff at the theatre. She comes home at 5.30 & Eddie Wassermann . . .

calls up & comes over. We go to dinner at the Eiffel Tower & have another dreadful meal. Then leaving Eddie, we go to Arthur Machen's, meeting Mrs. Machen, their son Hilary, & Mr. & Mrs. Jordan of Knopf's. . . . Home about midnight.

    1. Older actress whose career had ended before the twenties began.

Sunday, 26 May 1929

. . . We go off to Hampton Court on a bus & have a grand day with the flowers & picknickers & lunch on the river. Back to town & Tallulah [Bankhead]'s London house. She is back from a tour for the day. . . . We motor in a Daimler to Café de Paris, a divine place on the river where we have dinner. . . . Then we go to the Bat to hear Dwight Fiske sing & finally go to Levison's[1] flat to dance & recoup. Home around 4.30. <u>Soused.</u>

    1. Frankie Levison was Tallulah Bankhead's companion at the time.

Wednesday, 29 May 1929

. . . Dwight Fiske . . . & I have a cocktail at the Mayfair & then went on to the Ritz where I met Marinoff. . . . On to Harold [Acton]'s house. . . . At 4, M. P. Shiel (met) came to see me & stayed about half an hour, and talked most surprisingly. Eddie Wassermann later to say goodbye. He is leaving for Paris tomorrow. . . . Picked up Cathleen Nesbitt later & went to Robesons' for supper. The Jacksons—she is Paul [Robeson]'s girl[1]—also appear & drive us home around 12. Tallulah telephones from Birmingham.

    1. Yolande Jackson, English actress.

Thursday, 30 May 1929

. . . To lunch with Marinoff at Scott's. Then we go window-wishing. . . . On to Oliver Messel's[1] studio where I met him. . . . On to a party at Betty Chester's,[2] given by her & John Van Druten for me & Marinoff. Harriet Cohen[3] played & Leslie Hutchinson sang. . . . Rose McClendon, Edna Thomas, Paul Robeson, Anna May Wong,[4] Auriol Lee,[5] Vyvyan Holland. . . . Back to hotel, dressed . . . for dinner at a quarter of nine. . . . On to the . . . election party on the top floor of Selfridge's store, the most marvellous party I have ever seen, with the crowd in the street below. Everybody there, unlimited champagne, food & music. . . . Home around 4.

    1. English set and costume designer.
    2. One of the "Co-Optimists," a quartet of sophisticated entertainers.

3. English pianist, specializing in Bach.

4. Chinese American actress, soon to become a close friend and, in 1932, one of CVV's first photographic subjects.

5. English actress then appearing in *Milestones,* subsequently on Broadway in *Nine to Six,* also in films.

Friday, 31 May 1929

... Up around 5 & to a cocktail party at Zena Naylor's. ... Then to Dwight Fiske's. We dine at Boulestin's & go on to ... a party for me at Frankie Levison's studio. ... Home around 5.

Sunday, 2 June 1929

... At noon Dwight Fiske called for us & we took a train for West Drayton & Emilie [Grigsby]'s cottage where we had an excellent lunch. ... Back to town at 5. ... Lawrence & Armina Langner, Philip Moeller, appeared & we dragged them around to Tallulah's. ... We lapped up cocktails till 7.30. Then home to dress, on to the Embassy to dinner with ... two insufferably dull people. Michael Arlen dined opposite with his wife. We left early.

Tuesday, 4 June 1929

... Marinoff goes to the Caledonian Market. I pick up Dwight Fiske ... & take him to lunch at Emilie Grigsby's. ... Took Hugh Walpole to dinner at Savroni's & we go on to see Gracie Fields[1] at the Victoria Palace. Then to a party at Gilbert Miller's. Peggy Wood, Leslie Howard,[2] Phil Moeller, Lawrence & Armina Langner, Maurice Wertheim. To bed about 2.

1. English music hall entertainer.

2. English actor, best known as Ashley Wilkes in *Gone with the Wind.*

Friday, 7 June 1929

Marinoff leaves—sunny & cold—on a motor trip with Langners & Phil Moeller. ... I have a few drinks at the bar. ... Then to Savroni's where I meet Harold Acton, Rebecca West, Peggy Wood, & take them to lunch. After lunch Rebecca, Harold & I go to some exhibitions & shops, & Rebecca slaps my face on King Street for some pert remark. ... Then we go to Dwight Fiske's cocktail party for me. ... Then to Rebecca West's for dinner: Constant Lambert[1] ... & Bertrand Russell[2] (met). Home around 12, plastered.

1. English composer of ballet scores and, later, jazz-influenced songs.

2. English philosopher, pacifist, and lecturer whose unorthodox views caused his imprisonment during World War I.

Sunday, 9 June 1929

Beautiful sunny day. Dressed, finished packing, & off at the Euston Station for Carlisle (11.30–6) in Cumberland where I was met by Hugh Walpole's chauffeur[1] & driven 36 miles to Hugh's cottage, Brackenburn, Manesly Park, Keswich. On a lake in the mountains. We have supper & talk & retire around 11.

    1. Harold Cheevers, Walpole's longtime companion and heir.

Monday, 10 June 1929

. . . I drive to Keswich with Harold [Cheevers]. Back for lunch. A little later we drive to Grasmere to Wordsworth's cottage & grave & tea. Back for dinner & to bed at 11. I sleep more fitfully than the night before.

Tuesday, 11 June 1929

Up at 8.30. Dressed, ate a trout for breakfast caught last night. . . . Marvellous bright day, but cool. . . . Lunch at the cottage with Hugh & a nap. Finished Harold Acton's *Humdrum,* a bad book which interests me. Late in a glorious afternoon we had tea & went out on the lake in a motor-row-boat. After a time we stopped in a cove & Harold carried me to shore & Hugh & I walked home. After dinner we talked till 11 & I went to my room & finished mss. of Essie Robeson's book[1] which is fairly rotten. To bed at 12.

    1. A biography of her husband, Paul.

Thursday, 13 June 1929

. . . I take a train for London, arriving at 6.30 at the Carlton to find a great batch of mail, telephone calls. To a cocktail party at one at Zena Naylor's. . . . To dinner at Emilie Grigsby's, alone. Then to St. James Theatre to meet Lawrence & Armina Langner who introduce me to Mr. & Mrs. [George] Bernard Shaw. Went back to see Lynn [Fontanne] & Alfred [Lunt] & over to Langners'. About 1.30 I went to a party given by Sir Basil Bartlett.[1] . . . David Plunkett Greene[2] took me home at 4 & we talked for [*word?*] hours. . . .

    1. English actor and producer.
    2. An accomplished amateur English pianist, more often identified as a six-foot, seven-inch phlegmatic dandy.

Friday, 14 June 1929

. . . Feeling very bilious. The phone rings incessantly. But I manage to dash to the hair-dresser at noon. . . . On to meet David Plunkett Greene for cocktails at Savroni's. Then David & I meet Patrick Balfour[1] & we lunch at the Maison Basque. . . . Then on to keep an engagement with George Moore[2] with whom I spend an hour & a half. Then . . . I meet Pat & David again & we have cocktails. . . . On to Tallulah's, more cocktails. . . . Then on to meet Lawrence & Armina & Phil [Moeller] . . . to hear *La vie Parisienne*. . . . Met Essie & Paul Robeson . . . & told Essie what I thought of her book. Home at midnight.

> 1. English gossip columnist for the *Daily Sketch* until he inherited the title of Baron Kinross.
> 2. Irish writer whose *Confessions of a Young Man* had greatly influenced CVV in his youth. Subsequently, he published articles about Moore, resurrecting one of them for his final book, *Sacred and Profane Memories* (1932).

Saturday, 15 June 1929

Up at 8. Sunny & hot. I have a headache & feel rather bilious. Packing to get out of London. Left for Paris on the *Golden Arrow*. . . .

Monday, 17 June 1929

49 years old. Woke up feeling some better on this sunny, cool day. . . . We . . . walk to the bank, & the Castiglione bar, ending finally at Larue's for lunch. After lunch we walk some more & buy some liquor for my cocktail party at the Bristol: . . . Kitty Miller,[1] Louis Cole, Adelaide Hall, Nora Holt, Mercedes de Acosta, Georgette Cohan,[2] Boonie Goossens, Dan Reagan, . . . Eddie Wassermann, Dagmar Godowsky. . . . With Dan, Boonie, Mercedes & Nora, to dinner at Boileau's. Then home. Fania & I . . . picked up Louis Cole & went to a bar or two. I dislocated my jaw, but it came back automatically before I went to a hospital. Home about 2.

> 1. Katherine Browning Miller, playwright identified with Greenwich Village.
> 2. Stage actress, best remembered for *Diplomacy*.

Tuesday, 18 June 1929

Up at 8.30 with a <u>terrific</u> hangover. Dressed & to Eddie Wassermann's. Drank a few sidecars.[1] We drove to the Castiglione bar & had a few more. . . . I was very tight. From there with Marinoff to the Café de Paris where I picked up Eddie & took him to call on Louis [Cole] who was not in. . . . To the Café de la Paix, & to Virgil Thomson's. Bought some flower pictures on the Quai & home for dinner. God, how drunk!

1. Arguably the most popular cocktail of the year: equal parts of cognac or brandy, cointreau, and lemon juice.

Wednesday, 19 June 1929

In bed all morning with a hangover. Then I recover sufficiently to go to the Castiglione bar & to Larue's where I take Marinoff, Nora Holt, Cecil Beaton, & Eddie Wassermann to lunch. . . . Home around six. Hot. Colin McPhee & Jane Belo[1] joined us. We went to the Carlton for a drink where I saw my old friend, the barkeeper, & ran into Dagmar Godowsky & Artur Rubinstein.[2] Then we went upstairs & met Leopold Godowsky.[3] Dinner at the Manoir Tokay, & then we went to the Bal Musette on the rue de Lappe. Danced till about 11.

1. McPhee and the photographer Jane Belo were then living together.
2. Polish pianist whom CVV had known since 1913 at Mabel Dodge's Villa Curonia at Florence.
3. Russian pianist and composer, Dagmar Godowsky's father.

Saturday, 22 June 1929

. . . To the Castiglione bar, then to meet Marinoff at Brasserie Universelle. We try to do some shopping after lunch, but everything is closed. I come home. Then go out . . . to Virgil Thomson's. I meet a boy called Grosser[1] & Virgil & I go to Bernard Faÿ's[2] where I see Kristians Tonny. . . . Back to the hotel where I pick up Fania, Nora Holt, & Milton Woldman.[3] We dine at Boileau's & go to Bal Coloniale where we . . . see Countee Cullen. . . . From there Nora, Fania, Milton & I go to Costa's where I . . . meet Bob Scanlon, publicist, & finally go to Bricktop's. She sings for us. Home at 3.30.

1. Painter and designer Maurice Grosser, Thomson's longtime companion. Grosser invented a scenario for the Thomson-Stein opera *Four Saints in Three Acts*.
2. French historian and biographer of American subjects, later found guilty of and imprisoned for collaboration with the Nazis in Paris.
3. Nora Holt's momentary companion, doomed by CVV, writing to Marinoff, to be identified as "sweet but quite dull, I think," 11 June 1929.

Sunday, 23 June 1929

Up at 9, with a hangover and <u>remorse.</u>

Monday, 24 June 1929

Slept almost too well, awakened at 8, very cross & nervous. . . . Cocktail party: Kristians Tonny, Virgil Thomson, Louis Cole, Maurice Grosser, Nora Holt, Rose Wheeler, Dagmar Godowsky, a Miss Chanson (colored) whom Nora brought, George Hugnet. . . . Nora stayed to dinner & after dinner she & I picked up Tonny, Hugnet, Grosser, & Thomson & take them to the rue de Lappe. After—we went to Costa's Bar in Montmartre. Saw Louis Cole . . . who took us [to] this Music Box review where we saw Earl Tucker, Georgette Cohan & Harry Glynn. Home about 4.

Tuesday, 25 June 1929

. . . Not feeling so good. Dressed & went to Castiglione bar for a cocktail where I met Virgil Thomson & Maurice Grosser & took them to lunch at Voisin's. . . . Back to the hotel & then to Nora Holt's. . . . We went to the Crillon bar for drinks. Then Marinoff arrived & to . . . the rue de Lappe where we saw Mohamed the Arab who went with us to Costa's Bar where we danced, etc., till 1.30. . . .

Friday, 28 June 1929

. . . Lunch with Marinoff . . . chez Drouant, rue St. Augustin. Before that we had cocktails at the Castiglione bar & ran into . . . Ralph Barton.[1] After lunch home & then I amused myself in the rue St. Sauveur. Then . . . to tea at Natalie Barney's. Louise Bryant was there. . . . To a cocktail party at Elsie Arden's:[2] . . . Nora Holt (who sang), Louis Cole (who danced). . . . On to dinner with Nora at the Cabaret. Then to the rue de Lappe where I met a charming boy. On to the Tribonlette (first time) & to Costa's where I get into an argument. Then with Nora & Louis to the Music Box. . . .

> 1. By 1929 Barton's manic depression had begun to control his life. He had just returned from the South of France where he had offered to shoot his fourth wife, Germaine Tailleferre, in the belly to abort their unborn child. He committed suicide in 1931.
>
> 2. American actress and singer whose career was made largely in England.

Sunday, 30 June 1929

. . . It is the day of the Grand Prix. Up about 10 & fool around the morning. Lunch in with Marinoff. Out for a few drinks & amused myself rue St. Sauveur. . . . Home about 6, & out again to Alice Brady's[1] at the Chambord. . . . Ralph Barton . . . & Alice meet. I leave, call on Nora . . . & we dine at the Cabaret. Go [to] rue de Lappe where we pick up a charming Spaki & take him to Costa's bar. See Casca Bonds[2] there. Home around 2.

1. American actress, later to appear in Eugene O'Neill's *Mourning Becomes Electra*.

2. An aspiring African American tenor, one of A'Lelia Walker's homosexual acolytes.

Monday, 1 July 1929

. . . To lunch with Katie Seabrook & Marinoff at the Castiglione bar. Then I go to Cleris to order a bracelet for Louis Cole's birthday. To La Samaritaine for a bournous de Spaki which I do not find, to the Palais Royale et home. . . . Marie Doro telephones & comes to dinner with us. After she goes we go to bed. I spend an hour with Nora who is leaving for London tomorrow. . . .

Thursday, 4 July 1929

. . . I do not feel so good. But after a while I stroll out, run into Ralph Barton on the rue St. Honore, take him for a drink at Castiglione where he tells me he still loves Carlotta Monterey & does not want her to marry O'Neill. On to lunch chez the Duchess de Clermont-Tonnere,[1] Natalie Barney, Colette (met),[2] . . . Daniel Halevy (son of the great Halevy)[3] & a young man. After, Romaine Brooks.[4] Marinoff is still sick, so I come home. Mercedes de Acosta comes in. Later I visit the . . . Boeuf sur le toit for a cocktail. Home for dinner with Marinoff. Then off to Fouquet's for a drink on the terrasse. Then rue de Lappe, where I found the Spaki, took him to the Moulin Rouge where I find Louis Cole. Later we all go to his birthday party. . . . Home about 4. The Spaki left at 3.

1. Elisabeth de Gramont, titled Frenchwoman in the social circles of Gertrude Stein and Natalie Clifford Barney.

2. Sidonie Gabrielle Colette, after Marcel Proust arguably the greatest French writer of the twentieth century.

3. Jacques François Halevy, nineteenth-century composer of many operas, now largely forgotten.

4. European-born American painter and Natalie Clifford Barney's longtime companion.

Friday, 5 July 1929

Up at 9, determined to be good! Sunny & warm. Not feeling so bad. Marinoff's cold is better and she gets up & goes out with me. We go to . . . the Brasserie Universelle for lunch. . . . Then I go to the Jardin d'Aulimation (for the first time) to see the Negresses with the saucer mouths, which makes me physically ill. . . .

Saturday, 6 July 1929

. . . Call Nora up & find her in bed. She has flown back with David Plunkett Greene & had an amour on the plane. We join her & go to a dull cocktail party. . . . Then we dine at the Canneton, very expensively, & come home & retire, passing up an evening with David Plunkett Greene & his boy friends.

Sunday, 7 July 1929

. . . Later in the afternoon Nora & David Plunkett Greene arrive. In an hour we leave David. Nora, Fania, & I go to a cocktail party chez Katie Seabrook. Man Ray[1] is there. . . . Nora sings, Nora & Fania take off their clothes. It is very wild.

    1. Emanuel Radnitzky, American photographer and avant-garde filmmaker.

Thursday, 11 July 1929

. . . Nora Holt appears at 4 & at 6 Rita Romilly, fresh from America. They both dine with us. At 8 we embark for the Quai d'Orsay & the express for Madrid at 8.40. Train has a horrible roadbed & we don't sleep at all.

Sunday, 14 July 1929

. . . We went to our first bull fight at the Plaza de Toros at 6 o'clock. Walked back after at 9 o'clock. Had some beer & heard La gran vic at the Theatro de la Corrida. In bed about 12.30.

Monday, 15 July 1929

Up early & drove to Toledo in a taxi-cab where we spent the day. Lunch at the Castellia. At night . . . to Botini's for dinner & then we . . . go to see a street "verbena," a kind of fiesta. Very delightful. We leave all the Madrilenos still making whoopee at 2 o'clock. Go to bed.

Friday, 19 July 1929

. . . Saw storks on their nests & flying for the first time. The walls of Avila, the cathedral, etc. Home by way of the Escorial. Lunch at the Hotel Ingeles. Early dinner & to bed.

Saturday, 20 July 1929

Up early & off by train to Granada at 9.50. A delightful day. Lunch on the train. Not too hot, not too dirty. . . . Drove to the Washington Irving Hotel & arranged one of the royal suites. Slept well. <u>Cold.</u> No <u>mosquitoes.</u> Dinner in the garden before retiring.

Tuesday, 23 July 1929

. . . In the afternoon we left on a Pullman car for Seville, a charming ride through fabulous olive groves. . . .

Friday, 26 July 1929

. . . To the hotel for lunch and at 3.25 we set out for Cordoba on a train arriving in time to see the mesquita, with a guide, before dinner. The Hotel Regina was noisy & the food was none too good. There was a cinema in the bull ring opposite the hotel which let out at 1 o'clock, & the children noisily strolled home.

Sunday, 28 July 1929

. . . At 5 we drove to the bull ring & saw a very bad fight with an enormous crowd. During the torture of the fourth bull, it began to pour & we escaped soaking wet. We came home, changed our clothes, dined & went to bed at 11. Slept well anyway. It rained all the evening.

Tuesday, 30 July 1929

Up early & took the train for Paris at 10.05. I had indigestion & a bad headache and didn't eat my dinner. Played solitaire all day. Hot & dirty. But saw from the window the Escorial, the walls of Avila, the ruined castle at Medino del Campo, & the cathedral at Burgos. . . .

Wednesday, 31 July 1929

. . . Found Paris cold, & later in the day rainy. . . . Before lunch I went to the Carlton for a manicure & a haircut. . . . Then to Rita Romilly's where we met an Englishwoman & Ethel Waters, her man, Eddie Matthews, just arrived in Paris. We went to the Viking for dinner & then to the rue de Lappe. . . . We took Ethel Waters & her friend home & where I picked up Marinoff. She passed out after two cocktails, & took her to Costa's bar where we had supper. . . . Home at 3.30 (Oh, how drunk!). Decided to go to America & at 2 o'clock call . . . at the French line & secure passages on the *Ile de France.*

Saturday, 3 August 1929

. . . We go to Bricktop's to pick up Ethel Waters. I see Brick & her man & her mother & we meet Allegretta, Ethel's adopted child, & Eddie Matthews & Ethel go with us to the Bal Coloniale where we . . . see Eric Walrond. Then to the rue de Lappe where we encounter many of our old friends. Then to Costa's bar for ham & eggs & home around 2.

Tuesday, 6 August 1929

. . . Lunch with Marinoff at the restaurant Franco-Italien. Then to the Gare Quai d'Orsay where we are met at the station by Carlotta [Monterey] who drives us to her Chateau du Plessis at St. Antoine du Rocher where we see Eugene O'Neill, have dinner, & talk all the evening. We have separate rooms but Marinoff is afraid & sleeps with me.

Thursday, 8 August 1929

We get up to a sunny cool morning at 9 & I say goodbye to Carlotta & Eugene, leaving on the 11.21 for Paris. . . . Take Emilie Grigsby . . . & Virgil Thomson to dinner at Larue's. . . . Marinoff & Emilie then leave us & we go to the rue de Lappe where we amuse ourselves. Then to Costa's Bar. To La Feniche where we find Ethel Waters & Bricktop & take them to the Petite Charmine. Back to Costa's where we see Louis Cole. On the way home we stop at the Begonia Bar, rue St. Honore. Home about 3.30.

Friday, 9 August 1929

. . . Virgil & I lunch at La porte jaune in the Bois de Vincennes. It is very amusing. Then we visit a place in the Place de la republique & finally end up in the rue St. Sauveur where I get very drunk. Home at 8.30 & then stagger out again without any [*drink?*]. Meet Harold Jackman at the Café de la Paix who introduces me to Claude McKay.[1] I am very soused by now & stagger in around midnight.

1. African American poet and novelist subsequently ranked with Langston Hughes and Countee Cullen as the most significant writers of the Harlem Renaissance.

Monday, 12 August 1929

Up betimes . . . & meet Julian Green at the Castiglione Bar & he takes me to lunch at an Alsatian restaurant & tells me all about himself & Robert de St. Jean.[1] We go to Weber's for awhile & then I introduce him to the rue St. Sauveur. He leaves me there. Later Marinoff & I call for Katie Seabrook & take her for a charming dinner at the Pavilion du Loi in the Batteau Charmante. Marinoff has one of her tempers & I go home around 10.

    1. Julian Green's longtime companion.

Tuesday, 13 August 1929

Up at 8. Dressed & finished packing & met Julian Green downstairs. Then we drove to his home—an elaborate one furnished in American Victorian furniture. Then we walked through the Trocadero Gardens . . . where we took a taxi & we drove to the Castiglione Bar where he left me & I met Marinoff. An amazing young man full of insane desire. Marinoff & I drove to Larue's for lunch & met (by accident) Ralph Barton who had lunch with us & told us he too was sailing on the *Ile de France*. . . . Arrived at [Le] Havre we discover that the boat (recently out of drydock) is not sailing till tomorrow at 2. . . .

Thursday, 15 August 1929

Up early. Went on deck. Go read in salon. Drank with Ralph. Lunch with him & Marinoff. Later with Ralph & Lillian Gish. A nap later. Gish had dinner with us. Ralph, Fania & I sat around the smoking room till nearly 12 when we went to bed.

Sunday, 18 August 1929

. . . Making out customs declaration. . . . Late in afternoon talked with Ralph & a moron called Joe Moore. Dinner, a while in the smoking room & to bed.

Wednesday, 21 August 1929

. . . In the afternoon I do a few errands & then join Dudley Murphy at the RCA Studios where he is doing a film of *Black & Tan Fantasie,* with Fredi Washington & Duke Ellington. I am photographed with them. Home. Edna Kenton comes in. To Eddie Wassermann's for dinner, Muriel Draper also. After dinner Harry Block, Max Ewing, T. R. Smith, Arthur Richman, Nella & Elmer Imes, Regina Wallace, Joe Brewer. Home around 12.30.

Thursday, 22 August 1929

. . . Get dressed & go to see Jacob Schwebel in the morning about Avery [Hopwood]'s estate. Back home & to the Knopf office with Marinoff. We lunch with Blanche & Alfred & learn that Aaron Douglas has not yet started on the *Nigger Heaven* drawings announced for this fall.[1] At 4.30 Tony Salemme appears with his very beautiful head of Ethel Waters. . . .

    1. Knopf planned to issue a limited, illustrated edition of CVV's novel. Several artists were considered before the English E. McKnight Kauffer was engaged for the job.

Saturday, 24 August 1929

. . . In the afternoon I went to see Bessie Smith in the talking film version of *St. Louis Blues* at the Rialto. Home late in afternoon. Virginia Hammond came to dinner & with her & the Imeses we go to see King Vidor's film (Negro) *Hallelujah* at the Lafayette Theatre. After that I leave them (Marinoff goes home with Virginia) & meet Eddie Manchester & Donald Angus & we go to Pod's & Jerry's for the Negroes, meeting a number of old friends & acquaintances. Home around 4.

Wednesday, 28 August 1929

. . . Arthur & Gladys Ficke come in for cocktails & later Marinoff brings Ray Goetz[1] in. Then Marinoff & I dine with Reg Wallace at Leone's. I get quite drunk. They leave me to see *Hot Chocolates* & I go to see Ethel Waters in a picture at the Winter Garden. Home around 11 & to bed. I write Edna Kenton & offer her a trip abroad.

    1. Translator and adaptor of French plays.

Friday, 30 August 1929

. . . Langston Hughes comes for dinner, with the mss. of his new novel[1] & later Donald Angus who spends the evening here. We talk & drink & make music. In bed about one, quite lit.

    1. *Not without Laughter,* published by Knopf the following year.

Monday, 2 September 1929

Up early & take the 11 o'clock train for G[reat] Norwalk, where we are met by Armina Langner. We spend the day with her & Lawrence. . . . Home about

10.30. I do not want a country house. Reading the mss. of Langston Hughes's novel on the train.

Wednesday, 11 September 1929

... Took Marinoff to the train ... & she left for the Langners' country place in Larchmont. .... Donald [Angus] came to dinner & at 9 we went to a party at Joe Brewer's: Monroe Schoen, Jimmie Cole (met), Ray Whitehead (met), Ray Mills, Jimmie Whitehall, & several others. Home about 2.

Thursday, 12 September 1929

... Up at 8—cool—with a hangover. To Dr. Clooney to have my teeth cleaned. To post office. Saw Helen Westley hanging over balcony of Guild Theatre. To music store on 42 Street. Then for Muriel Draper. Joe Brewer, Jim Whitehall, & Ellery Larsen[1] there. We took the first two to lunch with us at the Crillon & had a very gay time. Later took Muriel to get some pictures, left my watch, a trifle faint by perspiration at Walker's, & came home to find Paul Robeson's head by Jacob Epstein here. Caught 5.05 with Eddie Wassermann to White Plains where we went to Alfred's birthday party. Sam Knopf drove Eddie & me to town & we stopped up in Harlem at Pod's & Jerry's.

    1. An aspiring novelist who wrote unsuccessful imitations of Gertrude Stein.

Friday, 13 September 1929

Up at 7, with a hangover & nervous. .... Ralph Barton for lunch. .... Langston Hughes comes in & I give him back his mss. Dinner in alone. After dinner Jimmie Cole who spends the evening here.[1] In bed about 1.30.

    1. This is the first occasion on which CVV recorded a visit from a black call boy.

Saturday, 14 September 1929

... To the Crillon with Max Ewing for lunch. After lunch we went to ... Dorothy Caruso's shop where I made a barking record. Max drove home with me. Later Rhea Wells, who is leaving for Europe, comes to say goodbye & bored me. I give him a hundred dollars. John Floyd calls up to ask me to re-write Avery's book. Donald Angus comes for dinner. After dinner Jimmie Cole. About midnight we all go to a drag at Manhattan Casino which for roughness, boldness, etc., surpasses any I have ever seen. .... We stay till about 3 when I lose Donald & move on to Pod's & Jerry's with Jack Barker & Jimmie Cole. It is very brilliant. .... Home about 4.30.

Tuesday, 17 September 1929

... Feeling fine, but the continued hammering & riveting on the new Hotel Wellington are quite nerve-wrecking. In all day. Lunch in with Marinoff (quite temperamental) & dining with her & Regina Wallace who went to a movie. I read (en fin) D. H. Lawrence's *Lady Chatterly's Lover*. In bed around 10, and slept well. Two copies of Taylor Gordon's *Born To Be*[1] arrive.

> 1. CVV supplied an introduction to this autobiography; Muriel Draper revised Gordon's manuscript for publication.

Saturday, 21 September 1929

... We put up the fall hangings. ... Marinoff has another outburst of temper. I am beginning to worry about her. Regina Wallace comes in. At 7 we go to the Stettheimers' to dine with the 3 sisters & Frances Seligman. Home around 10, & to bed.

Monday, 23 September 1929

... Take Donald Angus & Regina Wallace with us to dinner at Leone's. Marinoff goes home with Reg. Donald stays all night with me. Marinoff & I had quite a wild fight, but make up over the phone.

Thursday, 26 September 1929

... Finished reading *Ultima Thule* [by Julian Green]. Out to jewelers & to Algonquin for [lunch]. Home for a nap & reading *Les Clefs de la Mort* [by Julian Green]. Both of these books marvellous & <u>depressing.</u> To a cocktail party at Ruth Baldwin's[1] place, ... and I met a lot of lesbians. Home for dinner with Marinoff (who spent the day having her hair dyed, after a year of it whiteish) & to see *See Naples & Die* with her. ...

> 1. Silent film actress.

Sunday, 29 September 1929

Up at 7. (Daylight saving time ceases today.) Cloudy & cooler. ... Donald Angus comes over with a troubling story of what happened last night & I give him some money.[1] ... I take Harry [Block] ... to dinner at the Don Juan where I see Bill Benét. Home and to bed. At 11 I collect Rose Rolanda (last minute substitute for Julia Hoyt) & go to opening of the new show at the Cotton Club, with Muriel Draper & Eddie Wassermann. Met Jimmie Durante.[2] Then to Pod's & Jerry's. ... Home around 5.

1. Angus had been beaten up and robbed by a male prostitute in Harlem.

2. American vaudeville comedian, nicknamed "Schnozzola" because of his large nose.

Friday, 4 October 1929

. . . I took Tom Rutherford to dinner at the Don Juan. Then we went to Lafayette Theatre & ran into Rosamond Johnson. Jack Johnson[1] was on the bill & we went back to meet him later. Nothing could be sadder than a deposed champion in his decline. . . . After this we went to Catagonia Club and Pod's & Jerry's & then to the Cotton Club. Talked with Duke Ellington. Came home around 2.30. . . .

1. African American champion heavyweight prizefighter.

Monday, 7 October 1929

. . . Reading a stupid lascivious book called *Une matinée libertine*[1] & *Scarlet Sister Mary* [by Julia Peterkin]. Meda is moving to a place of her own & we shower [her] with a lot of old china. We and Wood Kahler dine with Regina Wallace & spend the evening there. Home, quite soused, around 12.30.

1. An illustrated book of lesbian pornography in an edition of 100 copies, of which CVV had added one to his extensive library of homosexual literature. He recommended that this be given to the Beinecke Rare Book and Manuscript Library at Yale, but his literary trustee, Donald Gallup, gave it to CVV's most intimate friend after 1931, Mark Lutz. (Except when they traveled together, they wrote daily letters to each other for thirty-three years.) The homosexual collection was subsequently given to the Boatwright Memorial Library at the University of Richmond, where Lutz had been a student, but it was never catalogued there and simply disappeared.

Wednesday, 9 October 1929

. . . Marinoff out for the day. I have Max Ewing for lunch. Otherwise I read Gilbert Seldes's *Wings of the Eagle,* an excellent novel but nothing original, & slept for an hour. I go to Eddie Wassermann's at 6 & find his two old nurses there. Later Muriel Draper & Fania for dinner & Fania goes to the theatre. We rearrange Eddie's park room for him & finally, joined by Max Ewing, go to a party at A'Lelia Walker's. Fania comes in later. . . . Home at 1.30.

Saturday, 19 October 1929

. . . My cold is still with me. Walked to Crillon by way of Holliday Bookshop. . . . Later Donald Angus, George Hoy, & Tom Rutherford arrive & we dined at the Don Juan. Came back & played records, etc., till nearly four, Tom being the last to leave, very tight. Harry Glynn comes in about midnight with two bottles of absinthe.

Sunday, 20 October 1929

. . . My cold persists. I spend the day clearing up the house, reading papers, writing letters, etc. Lunch in with Marinoff. . . . I do not intend to go out at all, but late in the afternoon Nils Nelson calls up & I join him at the Biltmore, take him to the Don Juan, to Nella Imes . . . and we go with Nella to the Cotton Club where we are turned down because the party is "mixed." From there to Pod's & Jerry's where I find some difficulty in getting rid of Nils who has become obnoxious. Home at 2.

Wednesday, 23 October 1929

. . . To Knopf & . . . talked . . . about drawings for *Nigger Heaven.* Saw work of Elmer Campbell[1] & Charles Sandford & selected Campbell's work. Then walked up the Avenue, finally to Don Juan where I ran into Isa Glenn & Bayard Schindel & they lunched with me. Home at 2.30. . . .

    1. African American artist, *Esquire* magazine's premiere cartoonist in the thirties and forties, E. Simms Campbell.

Friday, 25 October 1929

. . . My nose is still running, but I feel pretty well, considering. I read *Hanna.* Lunch in with Marinoff. Then to Philharmonic Concert with her, Toscanini conducting, a wonderful performance of *La Mer* [by Claude Debussy]. *Hanna,* like all of Tom Beer's books, made up of thousands of minute & forgettable details. Seldom a memorable fact or picture emerges. Regina Wallace came for dinner & after dinner we go to bed. (Not Reg! She goes home.)

Saturday, 26 October 1929

. . . I wash my hair for the first time in four weeks in spite of fact that my cold persists. . . . To Goldfarb's, to the Don Juan where I take Aaron Copland to lunch. He comes home with me after lunch & I play Spanish records. Later with Marinoff to Ellen Glasgow's to tea, Hotel Chatham. . . . Home at 5, meet Tom Rutherford. We dine at Leone's & go to the Don Juan for a drink. Then to Pod's & Jerry's where we get very drunk & run into Eddie Manchester who takes us to the Clam House. Home at 5.

Sunday, 27 October 1929

... Marinoff out all night because Louise Bryant tried to commit suicide at the Brevoort & she goes down there with the Langners. .... Late in the afternoon we gave a cocktail party: Ellen Glasgow, Joan Carr (met),[1] Aaron Copland, Donald Angus, [Marguerite] Namara & Mildred Lord, Lawrence & Armina Langner. The last 4 stayed to supper. .... In bed about midnight.

1. Aspiring English actress who retired early from the stage to marry Viscount Moore.

Tuesday, 29 October 1929

... To the post office for some records from Madrid, which I played with delight when I returned. Then to Don Juan for lunch with Irita Van Doren. .... Late in the afternoon to cocktails chez Auriol Lee at the Elysée. She is sailing tomorrow on the *Berengaria.* Jane Cowl, Eddie Wassermann, Ernest Boyd, Alice Patterson,[1] Arthur Richman, Virginia Hammond, ... etc. Home for dinner & then to Lawrence & Armina Langner's where we find Djuna Barnes, Helen Westley, Phil Moeller, & are later joined by Louise Bryant with long stories about her separation from Bill [Bullitt]. Home about midnight. Jane Cowl tells us that Klauber[2] is out of his mind & in a sanatorium.

1. Alice Patterson Guggenheim, *Newsday* publisher.
2. Adolphe Klauber was drama critic for the *New York Times;* Ernest Klauber was a theatrical producer. It's not clear which man CVV is referring to.

Wednesday, 30 October 1929

... Paul & Essie Robeson for dinner. Paul lingers on & talks about himself & his voice & his tangled love affairs till midnight.

Thursday, 31 October 1929

... Victor Wittgenstein was giving a party, but calls it off. After the low stock number, no one will come.[1]

1. Neither here nor until 13 November does CVV otherwise allude to the stock market crash on 29 March 1929.

Saturday, 2 November 1929

... I have a pretty hangover. Pay bills, etc. At noon I go to Goldfarb's & send some flowers to Dorothy Peterson & Carmel Myers (who opens at the Palace today). Then to Don Juan for a coupla cocktails. Then to Dorothy

Peterson's for lunch. Nella Imes & Tom Rutherford there. Nella & I go to Bob Chanler's but he has gone back to Woodstock [New York]. We walk to the corner & see some very beautiful cats in a window & have conversation with their owner. Then take a bus uptown. . . . Donald Angus comes to dinner. We go to Hall Johnson's concert. . . . We then come [to] Don Juan for a drink where we run into Tom Smith. Then to Eddie Wassermann's. . . . Then to Catagonia Club with Donald where I see Elmer [Sims] Campbell, Clara Smith, Bernia Austin, . . . & many others. Later to the Clam Bake [i.e., House]. . . . Home around 3.

Sunday, 3 November 1929

. . . Late, Fania and I went to a cocktail party at Lloyd Morris's:[1] John Erskine (met),[2] Donald Angus, Ettie Stettheimer, Rita Romilly, . . . Arthur & Marion Spingarn, . . . George Hoy, Nils Nelson, Eddie Wassermann, Max Ewing, Muriel Draper. The last 3 with me to Eddie's, & then Max & Muriel dine with me at Leone's & come to the house where we play Spanish & Tauber[3] records till 1.30 when Marinoff gets home after an evening with John Emerson.

> 1. American social historian; CVV is thinly disguised as "Paul Follett" in Morris's novel *This Circle of Flesh* (1932).
> 2. American critic, musician, educator, and author of satirical historical novels and several books on music.
> 3. Richard Tauber, popular Viennese opera and operetta tenor.

Wednesday, 6 November 1929

. . . To Tom Smith's, had a cocktail or two, & took him to lunch at the Crillon. . . . Eddie & I went to Tom's for half an hour & then to Harry Glynn's. Home at 5 to find Frederick Richardson, a friend of Henry [Blake] Fuller's here, who read me some of Fuller's last letters & told me amazing stories of the man's actual poverty. Dinner in with Marinoff & to bed before 7.30. I had an astonishing dream or two, but slept till 9 . . .

Thursday, 7 November 1929

. . . this morning! Sunny & cold. Feeling splendid, but do not get anything important done. . . . Rose Rolanda came in with Marinoff. Dinner at Reg Wallace's with Marinoff & Donald Angus. Donald & I & Rose go to the Cotton Club, to Catagonia Club, & to Clam House. . . . Home at 5. Marinoff at Reg's for the night. . . .

Saturday, 9 November 1929

. . . Joined Donald for dinner at Don Juan. Back to the house. Jimmie Cole came in. We three went to Harlem. . . . Catagonia Club & Clam House. Home around 4.30. Marinoff at the Equity Ball arrived about the same time. Nils Nelson killed in a speakeasy this morning.

Tuesday, 12 November 1929

. . . Arranged with Covarrubias to do drawings for N.A.A.C.P. benefit program. To lunch with Eddie Wassermann at Crillon after stopping to see Stella Block drawings at Montross Galleries. . . . Then Eddie & I go to Knoedler's to see Renoir exhibit. Also saw Lee Simonson. Home. . . . Knopf's art editor . . . comes in & I tell him that Elmer [Sims] Campbell cannot do the *Nigger Heaven* drawings. Marinoff goes to theatre. I go to Don Juan & to Algonquin for dinner. . . . Home at 8. Jimmie Cole comes in.

Wednesday, 13 November 1929

. . . The stock market situation is very alarming. Reading desultorily. Lunch in with Marinoff. In the afternoon I actually write what may be a chapter of something.[1] D'Alvarez suddenly appears & stays till we dine at Eddie Wassermann's. . . .

    1. *Parties*, originally titled "Scenes from Contemporary New York Life" which later became its subtitle.

Friday, 15 November 1929

. . . Marinoff goes to the country with her brother & I write—more successfully—on the second chapter of what may turn out to be a novel. Lunch in alone. Paul Robeson comes in, & earlier a bootlegger. Lie down for awhile. . . . Later Donald Angus. We dine at the Algonquin . . . & go to the Palace to see Jimmie Savo,[1] Jimmy Durante (marvellous), & Helen Kane.[2] . . .

    1. Vaudeville and nightclub comedian whose popularity rested largely on his song "One Meatball" ("You gets no bread with one meatball").
    2. Musical comedy actress known as the "Boop-Boop-a-Doop Girl."

Thursday, 21 November 1929

. . . Worked on my novel, such as it is. Jack Marinoff calls Fania up (for money, no doubt) & she goes to meet him. . . . Marinoff has a bad session with her brother & so I take her over to the Don Juan for cocktails & get her drunk. Home for dinner. Then to Bob Chanler's. . . .

Sunday, 24 November 1929

. . . We do not go out till dinner time when we dine at Leone's. Rain. Then to Theatre Guild rehearsal of *The Game of Love & Death*. . . . We took Armina Langner & Chief Long Lance (met)[1] home with us & Lawrence (who had taken Joan Carr) came after. . . . They left about 3.

> 1. Blackfoot Indian, popular in the late twenties because of his personality and his ceremonial dances. He was later accused of being an African American and only passing as a Native American.

Monday, 25 November 1929

Up at 9, with a terrific hangover. Cold & clear. Waste the morning. . . . Lunch in with Marinoff & took a nap. Late, went to Goldfarb's & called on Joan Carr, taking her to Max Ewing's. . . . Then to Eddie Wassermann's. . . . Then to Harry Glynn's with Eddie. We . . . proceeded to a speakeasy on Third Ave. for dinner. Then to a dive (for stevedores off boats) on W. 19 St. En route we picked up Tom Measor. Home in a deplorable state around 3.

Tuesday, 26 November 1929

Up at 10.30. It took me all the morning to dress. . . .

Wednesday, 27 November 1929

. . . I am shaky & nervous. Read Long Lance's very interesting account of Indian life in the Northwest & lunched in with Marinoff (sausage & waffles). Slept all the afternoon. Get up to go to a cocktail party at Cecil Beaton's at Ambassador. Henry McBride asks me to write an article about Florine [Stettheimer] for *Creative Art*. . . . Home & dressed. To dinner at Algonquin with Victor Wittgenstein & Marinoff who went to theatre together. I go to opening of Cole Porter's *Fifty Million Frenchmen* with Harry Glynn. . . . Then to a party at Arthur Richman's. . . . Then to Harlem with Noel Sullivan, . . . Donald Angus, to a drag at Manhattan Casino, Pod's & Jerry's where Alice de la Mar turned up, to Clam House, to Lenox Club, where we had a strange adventure with a Southern lady, then with Noel . . . to Eddie Wassermann's. Home at 8.30 A.M.

Thursday, 28 November 1929

Up at 11 for a manicure. Lunch & to bed again. Cold & clear. I feel all right. Up for good at 3.15. . . . We had . . . a buffet Thanksgiving dinner with two geese: Emma & Elizabeth [Shaffer], Covarrubias & Rose Rolanda, Tom Rutherford, Donald Angus, Nella & Elmer Imes, Edna Kenton & Eddie Wassermann. They left about one.

Friday, 29 November 1929

Up at 9.30. Clear & cold. Tried to write, but with no effect . . . & after lunch in went to bed. . . .

Monday, 2 December 1929

Horrible dreams last night. . . . Marinoff wrote Jack [Marinoff] & lends him $4,000 on his land deal. When she comes home I learn that my account is overdrawn & I go to the bank to learn that it is $467.70 overdrawn! To Goldfarb's & to a cocktail party at Joe Brewer's: . . . Libby Holman, Clifton Webb, Eddie Wassermann (at his worst), Muriel Draper. . . . I go home at 7 for dinner with Reg Wallace. She & Marinoff go to the theatre. Jim Cole comes to see me. They return home about 12, & I retire.

Wednesday, 4 December 1929

Up around 8.30. Feeling swell. I have never slept or [eaten] so much as nowadays, it seems to me. Clear & cold, the roofs still covered with snow. Writing, also a great deal of telephoning with & for Walter White for the N.A.A.C.P. benefit on Sunday night. Called Clara Smith & Clifton Webb. After lunch I take 5 bottles of sauterne to the Stettheimers & get some songs from *50,000,000 Frenchmen* for Nora [Holt]. Home again at 3. Emily Clark came to see me. To a cocktail party for his [Robert's] brother, Wm. Astor Chanler. . . . Home, dressed & dined at the Stettheimers' with Marinoff, Frances Seligman, Georgia O'Keeffe, Carl Van Doren, H. L. Mencken, Steichen, & Henry McBride. Home at midnight.

Thursday, 5 December 1929

Slept fitfully, dreaming, curiously enough of [Manuel de] Falla's *7 Spanish Songs*. Up a little after 7. Cloudy & cold. My account comes through at the Harriman Bank (cheque arrives from Chicago). Writing cheques & on my novel (?). Lunch in alone (gefülte fish). Then to post office, Goldfarb's, &

Knopf office where I see some interesting drawings for *Nigger Heaven*. . . .
Home for dinner: Juliet & Arthur Hornblow, Leopold Godowsky, & Florence
Reed. . . . Armina [Marshall], Chief Long Lance. Fania & I went to a party at
Clara Smith's. Then to the Clam House where we see Gladys Bentley. . . .
Home at 4. Marinoff stays with Armina.

Sunday, 8 December 1929

. . . Joan Carr, Donald Angus, Rita Romilly, & T. R. Smith come for cocktails,
and we take them to dinner & the N.A.A.C.P. benefit at Forrest Theatre which
is a huge success. Afterwards we go to a party at the Dark Tower. During the
evening we see Covarrubias, Rose Rolanda, Marion & Arthur Spingarn, . . .
Jim (just back from Japan) & Grace Johnson, Rosamond, Nora, & Mildred
Johnson, [Mac] Stinnett, Harold Jackman, . . . A'Lelia Walker, Mamie White,
Clara Smith, Nella & Elmer Imes, Eddie Wassermann, . . . Lloyd Thomas,
Taylor Gordon, Geraldyn Dismond, Walter & Gladys White, Max Ewing. . . .
What a swell time.

Monday, 9 December 1929

. . . Lunch home, Mahala Douglas, Florence Reed, Virginia Hammond. After
lunch lie down for an hour. To Jac Auer's. (Marinoff goes out early, to dinner with Armina Langner, to theatre with her, & to spend the night with her.)
Donald Angus for dinner & later Jimmie Cole. They stay till midnight.

Tuesday, 10 December 1929

. . . To a party at Max Ewing's late: . . . Mamie White, Marguerite Namara, . . .
Donald Angus, . . . A'Lelia Walker, Tom Rutherford, . . . Covarrubias & Rose
Rolanda, McCleary Stinnett, Harold Jackman, Taylor Gordon, etc. I came
home to a dinner with Bob Chanler & Louise Hellström, Beatrice & Bobby
Locher, which bores me to death. They leave at midnight.

Monday, 16 December 1929

Up early & to work. A bright beautiful day. . . . I take Muriel [Draper] to lunch
at the Crillon & we spend the afternoon together, drinking & talking, ending at the Don Juan. Then I come home & dress &, quite drunk, go to Max
Ewing's for cocktails. . . . Eddie Wassermann & I dine at the New Jungle &
then go to Carnegie Hall where we join Florence Reed's box party for Iturbi's

first New York recital, an exciting event.[1] . . . Later Eddie & I get very drunk at the Don Juan. Home around one.

1. Spanish pianist José Iturbi.

Tuesday, 17 December 1929

. . . Have a hangover & am depressed. To Jac Auer's. Then to Frances Seligman's for lunch. . . . Home & nap for an hour. Dinner with Nellie & Sam Knopf at their place in Carlton. . . . Then we go to see a play called *Young Sinners* [by Elmer Harris]. . . . Then Marinoff & I join a party . . . & we all go to Harlem to the Savoy to see the very remarkable "Lindy Hop."[1] . . .

1. An athletic ballroom dance that soon replaced the Charleston and the Black Bottom in popularity.

Wednesday, 18 December 1929

. . . Feeling rather bouleverse by the season & the number of people I am seeing. I think it would be wise for me to withdraw from life for a while. Emily Davies[1] calls for me & we go to a farewell breakfast given by Lilyan Tashman[2] at the Sherry Netherland where there is food & champagne in abundance. Lilyan does not make the train. . . . About 2.30 I leave & go to the bank where I collect some Christmas money. Home around 3.30. Doing odds & ends, silly things. Reg comes to dinner & goes to theatre with Marinoff, & Jimmie Cole comes to see me. I go to bed about 11.

1. Freelance journalist.
2. Hollywood movie star.

Thursday, 19 December 1929

. . . Cocktail party for Paul & Essie Robeson: Frances Alda, Ruth Hale, Rita Romilly, Amanda Seldes, Frances Seligman, Mercedes de Acosta, Irita Van Doren, Virginia Hammond, Rose Rolanda, Joan Carr, Armina Langner, . . . Mary McKinnon, Emily Davies, Mr. & Mrs. Benno Moisevitsch & Mr. Tate (their manager), Heywood Broun, Chief Long Lance, Eddie Wassermann, Gilbert Seldes, Max Ewing, . . . Arthur Spingarn, Sam Knopf, . . . Percy Wassermann, Covarrubias, A. K. Mills,[1] Donald Angus, Aaron Copland, Arthur Richman, Kendall Messner,[2] Lloyd Morris, Joe Brewer.[3] A few stayed to supper but left early. In the midst of this Essie Robeson tells me the book about Paul on which I had given her advice she has sold to Harper's. This puts me in a frightful anger & I have a sudden sore throat.

1. Eventually an associate with the Edison Institute after a career in public relations in New York.

2. Julian Messner's brother and partner in publishing.

3. A perplexing guest list (assuming that CVV listed everybody) at this large party for the Robesons because there were no other African Americans present.

Friday, 20 December 1929

. . . Presents & telephones, etc., all the time. My sore throat persists. . . . Donald Angus for dinner. Marinoff goes out with Birnbaum. Tom Rutherford comes in later & after Donald leaves is silent for several minutes & then says: "I hate to come here because I feel that I am boring you, & anyway I think you are damn superficial." Myself: "Then why do you?" He: "Because I am fond of you, I suppose, & then from a sense of duty." Myself: "I don't know what you are talking about, but if you feel that way I advise you not to come." He goes with a goodbye & "perhaps I shall see you five years from now." I retire about 11. Nik Muray gives a party at night. We do not go.

Saturday, 21 December 1929

. . . Dinner with Jane Belo & Colin McPhee in their duplex apartment on Sullivan Street. They give us two drip coffee cups. Aaron Copland is there & we take him along to Bob Chanler's where we find Grace & Jim Johnson, A'Lelia Walker & Lloyd Thomas, Taylor Gordon, Joan Carr, Alfred de Laigre,[1] Lawrence & Armina Langner, Gilbert & Amanda Seldes, . . . Louise Hellström, Eddie Wassermann, etc. Eddie, after some offensive talk infuriates me & I call him "a cheap kike," "a low worm," etc. We drive Aaron home & get home by two.

1. Producer and director of plays, in a long partnership with Richard Aldridge; in the twenties he was a stage manager and appeared with Marinoff in *The Love Habit*.

Sunday, 22 December 1929

. . . At 5 o'clock we go to Max Ewing's to a party for Paul Robeson (who of course does not appear). . . . After this Fania and I go to the Algonquin to dine (where we see Yolande Jackson, Paul's girl, here to play in *Jew-Suss*. She is embarrassed). Home & to bed early.

Tuesday, 24 December 1929

. . . Eddie Wassermann calls up & asks me to dinner! I go out to send telegrams & flowers. Home for lunch. . . . Nora Holt supposed to arrive on the

Leviathan but we do not hear from her before we leave on the 4.50 train for Carmordale, with Helen Westley & Phil Moeller. We are met by Lawrence Langner & drive to his country house. . . . Dinner & a Christmas tree. In bed about 11. A swell time. I keep Marinoff awake by snoring.

Thursday, 26 December 1929

. . . Marinoff packing. Eddie Wassermann comes in to say goodbye to her & weeps over his reconciliation with me. . . .

Friday, 27 December 1929

. . . Housewarming at Rita Romilly's new place, East River & 52 St. . . . Muriel Draper . . . persuaded me to give 25 dollars to a Negro steward at Sing Sing. . . . Nora [Holt] sings. Home around 3 very drunk.

Saturday, 28 December 1929

. . . Marinoff sails for California.[1] . . . I go to the Biltmore & have an hour's massage at Jac Auer's. Then to Don Juan for lunch & home for a nap. Dinner at the James Weldon Johnsons', an old fashioned southern supper: Jack & Grayce Nail, Rose & Miguel Covarrubias (who has agreed to illustrate *Nigger Heaven*), . . . Rita Romilly, Muriel Draper, Eddie Wassermann, . . . Herbert Gorman, Rosamond Johnson later. A few of us go to Pod's & Jerry's & the Clam House. Home around 2.

    1. By way of the Panama Canal and a chaste shipboard romance with the actor Walter Houston, Marinoff went out to Hollywood to test for talking films.

Sunday, 29 December 1929

. . . At 3.30 James Cole comes to see me. He leaves at 5 or so. I dress & go to Clif Webb's where are Marilyn Miller, Cole Porter (met),[1] . . . & E. Wassermann, Gladys Bentley singing. From there I go to Virginia Hammond's for dinner: Florence Reed & Eddie Wassermann. We go to Iturbi's concert at Carnegie [Hall] where we are joined by Alfred & Blanche Knopf. . . . On to Stinnett's for drinks & on to a party . . . where are A'Lelia Walker, Taylor Gordon, Blair Niles,[2] Heywood Broun, Ruth Hale, Bernice Abbott,[3] Olivia Wyndham,[4] . . . etc. I pick up Nora Holt & we go to the Clam House where are Rose & Miguel [Covarrubias], Pod's & Jerry's, & The Nest, . . . to Lenox Club. . . . Home at 6.A.M.

    1. Composer of popular songs and scores for musical comedies.

2. English writer Blair Rice, who divorced explorer William Beebee to marry architect Robert Niles. She wrote *Strange Brother,* a sympathetic homosexual novel with scenes occurring at The Clam House.

3. American photographer.

4. English heiress, in a ménage à trois with African American actress Edna Lewis and her restaurateur-husband, Lloyd Thomas.

Tuesday, 31 December 1929

. . . Dinner at Eddie Wassermann's: Nora Holt, Blanche Knopf, Emily Davies, Stinnett, Covarrubias, Rose Rolanda. At 11 we move on to Muriel Draper's party (with Witter Bynner) where during the course of the night pretty nearly everybody turns up. I have a row with Blanche Knopf because she goes off to Bessie Lasky's[1] without me. Home (with Donald Angus) around 5.

1. Wife of film producer and director Jesse L. Lasky.

Dudley Murphy, Duke Ellington, Carl Van Vechten, and Fredi Washington on the set of *Black and Tan Fantasie,* 1929 (photographer unknown; Carl Van Vechten Papers, Manuscripts and Archives Division, New York Public Library, Astor, Lenox and Tilden Foundations)

Carl Van Vechten, Antonio Luhan, and Witter Bynner in Taos, New Mexico, 1927 (photographer unknown; Van Vechten Trust)

Carl Van Vechten and Lois Moran in Hollywood, 1927 (photographer unknown; Van Vechten Trust)

Aileen Pringle on the set of *Adam and Eve,* 1927 (photographer unknown; editor's collection)

Frank Case, Carl Van Vechten, Flora Zabelle, Emil Jannings, Bertha Case, and Jesse Lasky in Hollywood, 1927 (photographer unknown; Van Vechten Trust)

Carl Van Vechten and Fania Marinoff, 1930 (French carnival photograph; Van Vechten Trust)

Armina Marshall and Lawrence Langner, 1932 (photograph by Carl Van Vechten; Yale Collection of American Literature, Beinecke Rare Book and Manuscript Library, Yale University)

Jimmie Cole, 1932 (photograph by Carl Van Vechten; Yale Collection of American Literature, Beinecke Rare Book and Manuscript Library, Yale University)

Carl Van Vechten and a lion cub at the Berlin Zoo, 1930 (photographer unknown; Van Vechten Trust)

Fania Marinoff on the cover of New Masses, April 1928 (illustration by Frank M. Walts, Yale Collection of American Literature, Beinecke Rare Book and Manuscript Library, Yale University)

Carlotta Monterey and Eugene O'Neill, 1932 (photograph by Carl Van Vechten; Yale Collection of American Literature, Beinecke Rare Book and Manuscript Library, Yale University)

Gertrude Stein at Bilignin, 1934 (photograph by Carl Van Vechten; Van Vechten Trust)

Alfred A. Knopf, publisher; Carl Van Vechten, novelist; Texas Guinan, speak-easy queen and contract witness, 1930 (photographer unknown; Van Vechten Trust)

Parties advertisement, 1930 (illustration by Roese; Van Vechten Trust)

Carl Van Vechten and Fania Marinoff, 1930 (photograph by Nickolas Muray; Carl Van Vechten Papers, Manuscripts and Archives Division, New York Public Library, Astor, Lenox and Tilden Foundations)

Carl Van Vechten, 1934 (self-portrait; Van Vechten Trust)

1930

"Quite a hangover. I don't see
how I can ever work again.
Something has happened
to my ability to create."

Fania Marinoff was in Hollywood while Van Vechten continued to work on *Parties,* but his subterranean life in shady Harlem cabarets and in private liaisons took up a share of his time. In June he and Fania Marinoff left New York for an extended European holiday. They spent two weeks in London, then two in Paris, before embarking on another chauffeured tour, this time to include the Rhône Valley, where they visited Gertrude Stein and Alice B. Toklas at their summer home in Bilignin. Later, by train they traveled to Berlin, where Van Vechten was easily caught up in the nightlife of the homosexual "boy bars," as they were called. The Van Vechtens returned to New York in mid-September to face nearly uniformly negative reviews of *Parties* but also to stare through an alcoholic blur at "The Splendid Drunken Twenties" that soon enough would collapse under the weight of the Depression.

Saturday, 4 January 1930

. . . With Donald [Angus] went to Alhambra Theatre where we saw a show with Clara Smith. Afterwards went back stage & found our old friend Pedro (a waiter at Small's) at the door. . . . Then to [Isamu] Noguchi's[1] show to see his head of Gladys Bentley. . . . Home & Jimmie Cole comes & sees me. Later, Donald. They both stay all night.

    1. Japanese American sculptor and designer, one of CVV's early photographic subjects.

Tuesday, 7 January 1930

. . . Hugh Walpole came to dinner, tired after his lecture, fidgety & argumentative. I took him to the opening of Mary Ellis & Basil Sidney in *Children of Darkness* by Edwin Justus Mayer & he went to sleep. So after the first act I took him away & dragged him to a speakeasy where we sat for an hour when he left. . . .

Wednesday, 8 January 1930

. . . Worked on Chapter IX & found myself going right along. Lunch in alone. Then went to Benhauer's to have some clothes let out (I am getting quite fat). . . . To Reg Wallace's for a cocktail party. . . .

Thursday, 9 January 1930

. . . Worked on my book. Lunch in alone. Slept for two hours. Up and off to Blanche Knopf's for cocktails. She is so thin now that she is scraggly, & she is back to her old supercilious manner. . . . Then come home where I am joined by Jimmie Cole who stays the night.

Sunday, 12 January 1930

. . . Donald Angus comes for me at 4.15 & we drive to Jim & Grace Johnson who give a party for Nora Holt, an extraordinary occasion. . . . Nora, Donald & I drive from there to Nils Nelson's[1] & George Hoy's on Cornelia Street. Cocktail party. . . . Then Nora, Donald & I go to the Napoleon on MacDougal for dinner. . . . Hence to Harlem, to Nora's apartment . . . & to Lafayette to see Josephine Baker[2] in *The Siren of the Tropics*. She is marvellous. Then to the Clam House where Gladys Bentley plays. . . . Home around 2. Donald very drunk and grumbly.

1. Apparently, Nelson had not been killed in a speakeasy two months before. He and Hoy were then living together, briefly, until Hoy married Marguerite Namara.

2. African American entertainer who starred in Caroline Reagan's *Revue Nègre*, became an international star, and later acted in French films.

Tuesday, 14 January 1930

More rain. Feeling blue & incompetent & managed to waste another morning. To lunch at Rita Romilly's with Nora Holt. Taylor Gordon came in & went out with me. He made a cryptic remark about one "T. Coles."[1] Home. Covarrubias came in & talked about the illustrations for *Nigger Heaven*, and later Langston Hughes who stayed to supper. He goes early. . . .

1. CVV's arrangement with Jimmie Cole was no secret in Harlem.

Wednesday, 15 January 1930

. . . I am very blue, but I write quite easily & merrily, if somewhat scholarly, both before & after lunch. . . . Late in the day I learn by the papers that a woman was found dead in Dudley Murphy's apartment. And, rather to my horror, I put a lobster in boiling water for bouillabaisse. The bouillabaisse is marvellous. Gladys Unger comes to dinner, & Emilie Grigsby & Chief Long Lance. They leave about 12.30.

Thursday, 16 January 1930

Up at 8 with something of a hangover. Wrote a little, lay down a little. . . . Lunch in. Then went to Iturbi's third & last concert at Carnegie Hall. Got very tired during the 12 Liszt etudes, but woke up in the encores. Eddie Wassermann with me. . . . Home & into Boivin pyjamas & my purple Babini robe-party regalia:[1] Nora Holt, Donald Angus, Stinnett, Mercedes de Acosta, Rita Romilly for dinner. After dinner Adelaide Hall who danced & sang, Geoffrey Gwythers who played, Dudley Dickson who danced & sang, Chief Long Lance who danced an Indian dance, . . . Miguel Covarrubias & Rose Rolanda, Joan Carr & Alfred de Laigre. Nora sang & Stinnett danced. Taylor Gordon who sang, Langston Hughes, Lawrence Langner with a Mrs. Landis. . . . Later Noguchi with a Miss Thorn. Eddie Wassermann. The party ended about 4. <u>Very</u> successful.

1. This is the apparel that led Lawrence Langner to write in his autobiography that CVV looked like the Empress of China gone berserk. That casual simile was embroidered upon by subsequent writers until CVV was identified as someone who frequently dressed in drag. He never did.

Saturday, 18 January 1930

Up at 12. Wakened by Meda after she had rung the bell for an hour. Hang around all day resting, etc. Bad weather. At 5 Elmer Imes came in to tell me that Nella [Larsen], in her recent story in the *Forum,* has been accused of plagiarizing a story by Sheila Kaye-Smith.[1] Donald Angus for dinner & the evening. Then at 11, I go to a dance given by Bertha Case. Joe Hergesheimer, Chief Long Lance, Clif & Mabel Webb, Marguerite D'Alvarez, . . . E. Wassermann, Mary McKinnon, Leslie Howard, Marc Connelly, . . . etc. I took Gladys Unger home at 4.

> 1. Larsen denied the accusation, and several supporters agreed with her that the similarities in the stories was merely coincidental; even so, CVV was the only one to defend her publicly, in an open letter printed in *Forum,* where Larsen's story had been published.

Sunday, 19 January 1930

. . . Donald Angus arrives at 4.30 and makes the grand tour with me: Florence Sternberger's. . . . Ellery Larsson's, . . . a big party for Gilda Gray. . . . We stopped for Nora Holt & all went to a party at A'Lelia Walker's which was so crowded you couldn't see: Everybody up & downtown were there. Adelaide Hall sang. We left to go to Stinnett's, also Eddie [Wassermann], Blanche Knopf, . . . & Clif Webb who tried to shake us. We went to the Clam House. . . . Home at 4. Donald lost his job at Jay Thorpe's.

Thursday, 23 January 1930

. . . To Fannie Hurst's where I see Elisabeth Marburg, Laurence Rising,[1] Rupert Hughes,[2] Chief Long Lance, D'Alvarez, & Dorothy West[3] (who is waiting on the door). Then to a party to show me new modern rooms done by Lee Simonson at an apartment on Park Avenue. . . . I stay for a few minutes, go home & dress & go to dinner at the Langners': Emilie Grigsby & the Knopfs. We go to *Red Rust.*[4] Then I bring Emilie home & go to D'Alvarez. . . . To bed about 1.30.

> 1. Playwright for the Dolly Sisters in *His Bridal Night.*
> 2. Playwright, best remembered for *The Cat Bird* (1920).
> 3. Boston poet; the youngest of the African American writers later identified with the Harlem Renaissance.
> 4. A Russian play by Kirchon and Ouspensky translated by Frank and Virginia Vernon.

Saturday, 25 January 1930

. . . Lunch at the Algonquin with Ettie Stettheimer. . . . Ettie & I go to premiere of *Sadko* [by Nikolay Rimsky-Korsakov] at the Metropolitan. All the
old timers are still there. . . . Home at 6. Donald Angus for dinner. We call
up Jimmie Cole & around midnight he takes us to a party . . . on Edgewater
Ave. A lot of pleasant people are there. Jimmie & I leave around 3 & go to the
Clam House where we see Gladys Bentley. . . . Home at 4 with Jimmie.

Sunday, 26 January 1930

Get Jimmie up at 11.15 and his breakfast. A bright, sunny day, & I have a terrific
hangover. . . . At 5 Donald Angus calls for me & we go to Tom Howard's[1] for
cocktails. . . . I amuse myself by being fearsome. At 6.30 Kay Mills drives me
to Clif Webb's where there is another cocktail party. I get very drunk & go
home that way. Nora Holt sings. Libby Holman sings, B[eatrice] Lillie, Louise
Brooks,[2] Marilyn Miller[3] who dances, Eddie Wassermann, Blanche Knopf, &
a lot of others.

    1. Musical comedy performer, notably in the *Greenwich Village Follies*.
    2. American actress best remembered for a German film directed by G. W. Pabst,
Lulu.
    3. Popular musical comedy performer.

Monday, 27 January 1930

. . . I have a hangover & feel frightful. . . . Took Donald to lunch at the Crillon
after going to Stewart's for a bracelet for Jimmie [Cole] & Goldfarb's. . . .
Stuart Rose comes to see me at 5. He leaves at 6.30. I pick up Donald & we go
up after Nora. Sleet & rain. I take her to the Dark Tower[1] for dinner. Florence
[Embry] Jones joins us. And later Edna Thomas. With Edna & without Florence we go to the Lafayette Theatre to see Butterbeans & Susie & a terrible
show. Home early & sleep badly. . . .

    1. A'Lelia Walker's salon for young black artists and writers and older white
patrons and supporters had become a "tea room," a common epithet for a speakeasy.

Saturday, 1 February 1930

Up very early. Get Jimmie's breakfast for him, & get him off before 10
o'clock. . . . At 4.30 I go to Max Ewing's to see two heads he has done of Muriel
[Draper]. . . . Then I go to twentieth wedding anniversary of Grace & Jim

Johnson. . . . Then home to meet Donald Angus & Jimmie Cole & we go to a party some friends of Jimmie's are giving. Jimmie comes home with me at 1.30.

Tuesday, 4 February 1930

. . . Dressed & called for Emilie Grigsby (at the Barclay) in the rain. I take her & Blanche Knopf & Eddie Wassermann to the Crillon for dinner & then we went to see Katharine Cornell in *Dishonored Lady,* a bad play & a bad actress, but the house is brilliant. . . .

Friday, 7 February 1930

. . . In the afternoon I go . . . to Noguchi's exhibition. . . . Then to Stieglitz's new gallery where I see O'Keeffe's pictures & herself. Then for Emilie Grigsby to a party at Blanche Knopf's: Florence Vidor, Heifetz, Adele Astaire, Fannie Hurst, Ralph Barton, Armina & Lawrence Langner, Dorothy Dicksen,[1] Geoffrey Gwythers, Geo. Jean Nathan, Nora Holt (who sings), Phil Moeller, Irita Van Doren, Arthur Richman, etc. From there I go with Nora to a party given by Geraldyn Dismond at 113 W. 136 St: Harold Jackman, Stinnett, Alberta Hunter, . . . Louis Cole! etc. On to dinner with Gilbert & Amanda Seldes. . . . Home around 12.30.

1. Actress in musical comedies and revues.

Sunday, 9 February 1930

. . . Lunch chez Marguerite D'Alvarez. . . . At 6 I go to Bertha Case's cocktail & supper party. . . . Later, Nora [Holt] & I went to Harlem: Small's Paradise, Pod's & Jerry's, the Clam House, The Nest, & Lenox Ave. Club where we stayed until 7.30. Saw Louis Cole, . . . Snakehips [Earl Tucker]. Met Nina Mae McKinney,[1] Jazz Lips Richardson.[2] Home around 8.

1. African American singer and actress on stage and in films (sometimes uncredited).

2. African American actor in *The Green Pastures* and *Hot Chocolates.*

Friday, 14 February 1930

. . . I work on second chapter (2nd draught) of *Parties.* Lunch in alone. Met Joan Carr at Carnegie Hall. We hear Philharmonic concert. Then to Don Juan for a drink. Home. Edna Kenton comes to dinner & spends the evening. She refuses to take European trip I have offered her. . . .

Monday, 17 February 1930

. . . Got Jim [Cole]'s breakfast & sent him away. Alfred telephones that Covarrubias has found himself unable to do the illustrations for *Nigger Heaven.* This is getting to be funny, how everybody fails on this book. Worked most of the day on Chapter III of *Parties.* . . .

Monday, 24 February 1930

Jimmie leaves at 10. . . . Hangover. Scolding letter from Marinoff, & accounting of Avery Hopwood's estate arrive. . . . Edna Aug comes in at 4 with her dog & makes a scene. Dinner in alone. Then I go to a party at Walter White's for Sonia Jones, the Cleveland violinist: Nora Holt, . . . Taylor Gordon, Grace Johnson, . . . Aaron & Mrs. Douglas, Nella Imes. Home around midnight & to bed.

Tuesday, 25 February 1930

. . . Late in the afternoon Florine Stettheimer . . . & Donald Angus for dinner. We go to dress rehearsal of Marc Connelly's Negro play, *The Green Pastures,*[1] which is marvellous. All the people—black & white—I know interested in the subject were there. Afterward, Muriel Draper, Max Ewing & I go to Don Juan to talk it over. Home around 2.

> 1. An all–African American cast in a play based on *Ol'Adam and His Chillun* by Roark Bradford that recounts Old Testament stories through the devout beliefs of Negroes in a more innocent age where angels have wings and fish fries are popular in heaven. It was phenomenally successful.

Wednesday, 26 February 1930

. . . Rita Romilly for dinner & we went to *The Green Pastures,* an even greater experience than the night before. . . . I went backstage to congratulate Marc Connelly & met Richard B. Harrison who plays God, a magnificent performance. He asks me for a copy of *Nigger Heaven* & will get one.

Thursday, 27 February 1930

. . . Witter Bynner, Nora Holt, & Nella Imes for dinner. After dinner Nina Mae McKinney, Louis Cole, & Tom Rutherford. Nora & Nina sing & Louis dances & Tom sings his Blues. The last to go about 3.

Friday, 28 February 1930

Up at 9 . . . with rather a hangover. I managed to get a little—not very much—work done before I called for Carrie Stettheimer & took her to lunch at Don Juan & the Philharmonic concert. Toscanini is back, his performance of the *Tannhauser* bacchanale thrilling. Then to the Stettheimers' for a few minutes. Saw Mrs. Stettheimer & to a cocktail party. . . . Home at 8.30 & Jim Cole comes in for a couple of hours.

Saturday, 1 March 1930

. . . Out to cable Picasso to ask if he will illustrate *Nigger Heaven*. . . . Later Donald Angus arrives. He has lost his job at Hickson's & is very discouraged. I take him to dinner at Leone's. . . . Then I go to a party at the Langners' & spend most of the evening talking about *The Green Pastures*. . . . Blanche Knopf brings Thomas Wolfe (met).[1] . . . But later I depart with Horace Liveright, . . . Ben Ray Redman & Frieda Inescort . . . for a drink. Home at 4.30.

    1. American novelist. Wolfe memorialized this and a later encounter in two of his novels, *The Web and the Rock*, in which CVV is the writer "Van Vleet," and *You Can't Go Home Again*, in which he is "Stephen Hook."

Tuesday, 4 March 1930

. . . Marinoff telegraphs she is arriving the 18th. . . . At 5 o'clock I go to a party given in the office by Blanche Knopf. . . . Met Dashiell Hammett[1] & talk with Mencken, Henry Seidel Canby,[2] . . . Nella Imes, James Weldon Johnson, Louis Sherwin, etc. Home, change my clothes & off to Marguerite D'Alvarez for dinner. . . . Home about 1, quite soused.

    1. American novelist whose detective fiction CVV endorsed with dust jacket blurbs.

    2. Literary critic, co-founder of the influential *Saturday Review of Literature*.

Thursday, 6 March 1930

Up at 8 with quite a hangover. Warm & sunny. Wrote Chapter XI. To lunch at office with Blanche Knopf & Hugh Walpole, then to Sprinchorn exhibition . . . & to antique show at Grand Central Palace. . . . Home at 4 & lie down for an hour. Up & dress & to Fannie Hurst's for dinner. . . . A fortune teller (colored) named Nancy appeared & told us all a lot of junk.[1] Home early (around 1).

    1. Almost immediately, CVV built this encounter with the occult into a scene in *Parties*.

Thursday, 13 March 1930

. . . Up at a quarter of nine with rather a hangover. . . . Working on Chapter XVIII, perhaps not inspired but t'will serve. I still don't know what this book is about. . . . Tom Rutherford for dinner & later McCleary Stinnett. We all go to the Centre, Glynn's new place, very dull. Then Mc & I go on to Muriel Draper's party . . . where I meet Eugene McCown[1] & fight with him at once. . . . Home around 3, very drunk.

    1. Temperamental expatriate writer and café society pianist in Paris.

Wednesday, 19 March 1930

. . . My indigestion is a little better. Marinoff is nervous & cross. Donald Angus is sick. Jimmie Cole writes he has lost his job. Nevertheless it is sunny & clear & I go to work on Chapter XV and make it. . . . Dinner in with Marinoff. We go to see Mei-Lan-Fang.[1] Then to a party at the Langners'. . . . Home at 3.

    1. Chinese actor in recitals of ancient Oriental mime and dance.

Monday, 24 March 1930

. . . To Eddie Wassermann's for dinner, Marinoff & D'Alvarez. We go to see *The Last Mile.*[1] Then to Harlem to Small's Paradise to see the new revue with Andy Razaf's song, "Go Harlem," which contains the line:

"Go inspectin'
Like Van Vechten!" . . .

    1. Play about capital punishment starring Spencer Tracy.

Wednesday, 26 March 1930

. . . At a quarter of 3 Marinoff leaves for Atlantic City—in a highly nervous state. I lie down after she has gone. . . . To dinner chez Mercedes de Acosta. . . . Eddie Wassermann . . . & I go to see new revue at Lenox Club. See Louis Cole. Home around 3.

Friday, 28 March 1930

. . . For dinner: Ethel Waters, Eddie Matthews, & Nora Holt. After dinner Tom Rutherford, Donald Angus, Louis Cole, Rita Romilly. . . . Nora & Ethel sang, & the party lasted till about 3. I got very tight. . . .

Saturday, 29 March 1930

. . . I have a hangover. To dinner with Channing, Anna, & Helen Pollock. . . . The conversation, as usual, was asinine & unbeautiful & I left early. James Cole comes to see me at 11.30. Invited to a party chez Ben Ray Redman, but don't go.

Monday, 31 March 1930

. . . I don't feel so good but I write Chapter I of third draft of *Parties*. Lunch in alone. Visit Blanche Knopf & decide about binding & format for *Parties*. . . . Dinner in with Marinoff & then we go to see Argentinita[1] at the Booth Theatre & love her. . . .

    1. Spanish dancer making her debut in the United States.

Friday, 4 April 1930

. . . We walk to Knopf office to drop off an anniversary present for Blanche & Alfred. On to Philharmonic concert. Toscanini conducts *Götterdämmerung* Funeral March to commemorate death of Cosima Wagner.[1] To a tea at the Stettheimers'. . . . Home early. Dressed & went to St. Regis. Alfred & Blanche have an anniversary party. Dr. Logan Glendenning & his wife—he gets drunk & tells bad stories very badly—Mencken, E. Wassermann, Dorothy Hergesheimer, Nellie & Sam Knopf. Later we go to the hotel & Florence Vidor & Heifetz join us. Home around 2.30.

    1. The wife of the composer.

Saturday, 5 April 1930

Up at a quarter of 9, feeling all right, but Marinoff has a terrible hangover & stays in bed. . . . Dinner home with Marinoff. I lie down for an hour & then go to a party Ethel Frankau[1] & Aline Bernstein[2] give for Emily Davies. . . . On to a party Blair Niles & Taylor Gordon give: Bud [i.e., Rudolph] & Pearl & June Fisher, Alain Locke, Langston Hughes, Dorothy Peterson, Inez Wilson,[3] Sidney Peterson, Georgette Harvey (whose quartet sings), Elsie Arden, Max Ewing who brought Eugene McCown, . . . E. E. and Ann Cummings, etc. Muriel & Smudge[4] & I go to the Lenox Club, 5, stay till 6 o'clock. Louis Cole sits with us.

    1. Aline Bernstein's sister, with whom she lived at the time.
    2. American stage set designer, Thomas Wolfe's mistress.

3. African American actress and administrator of the Harlem Experimental Theatre.

4. Muriel Draper and her younger son, Saunders.

Sunday, 6 April 1930

Get up at noon with quite a hangover. . . . Dressed by four. Rain. To a cocktail party at Rita Romilly's. . . . To a supper party given at the Sherry-Netherland by Blanche & Alfred Knopf for Emily Davies: Nora Holt (who sang), George Gershwin who played, . . . Armina & Lawrence Langner, Eddie Wassermann, Bennett Cerf,[1] George Oppenheimer. Cerf drove us home about midnight.

1. Publisher who had just purchased the Liveright Modern Library to issue through his new Random House.

Saturday, 12 April 1930

. . . Work on Chapter X. Then I . . . pick up David Plunkett Greene & take him to the Don Juan for cocktails & to the Crillon for lunch. After lunch I take him to the Grand Central to show him the station. . . . Home at 5 & off again directly (alas) to Doris Ullman's[1] for tea. . . . Marinoff goes to her sister's and then I lie down for an hour. My cold is bad. Then to Harlem: Grace Johnson for a moment, then to Nora Holt's. . . . We go to Small's Paradise to see review. Then to Clam House, Gladys [Bentley] singing. The crowd was marvellous. . . . To Lenox Club. Home around 6.

1. American photographer who had made a series of portraits of CVV in 1929.

Tuesday, 15 April 1930

. . . Lunch in alone & wrote all day on chapter 12 & 13. Reg Wallace & Rita Romilly come to dinner & we all go to see Jed Harris's production of *Uncle Vanya* (first night) with Lillian Gish, etc. Then Marinoff & I go to Heifetz's party at his place, 247 Park Ave. . . . Heifetz with a chamber orchestra plays the [Ernest] Chausson concerto. An enormous party. . . . I go home at 2. Marinoff returns at 3.30. Cold & rain.

Friday, 18 April 1930

. . . I work all day on Chapter XVII. Lunch in with Marinoff. Rain. We give a cocktail party for David & Richard Plunkett Greene & Ruth Baldwin & use 7B[1] as a cloak room: Adelaide Hall, Langston Hughes, Marsden Hartley, Nella Imes, Bertha Randolph, Jack Carter, Jim & Grace Johnson, Walter & Gladys

White, Blanche Knopf, Eddie Wassermann, Nora Holt, Bruce Nugent, Dorothy Peterson, . . . Rose McClendon, . . . Lloyd & Edna Thomas, Eddie Manchester, Herman Sartoris, Stinnett, Elsie Arden, Nora Johnson, Rita Romilly, Marty Mann, Muriel Draper, Olivia Wyndham. Gladys Bentley sang. A few of us went to dinner at a place on Broadway & then to Kirkpatrick's Minstrels at Royale Theatre—dress rehearsal—where I saw many more people. David, Nora, & I went to the Clam House where I saw Susie Seligmann & her husband. I come home at 1.30.

1. Recently CVV had arranged with the manager of his building to use a vacant apartment on his floor for storage.

Saturday, 19 April 1930

Up at 8. Cloudy. Dressed & went to Jac Auer's, . . . to Don Juan for a drink, & then to Crillon where I meet Marinoff for lunch. . . . Home around 4.30. I sleep for an hour. Regina Wallace comes to dinner & I lie down again before going to Harlem to join Nora Holt, the [David and Richard] Greenes, Ruth Baldwin, Marty Mann, Dr. [Geoffrey] Nurse (in whose speakeasy we have supper). Then to Connie's Inn for new show. I go back to see Edith Wilson (not in the show), Roscoe Simmons,[1] Al Moore, Earl Tucker, . . . on the way to a drag at Renaissance Casino. On to the Clam House which is riotous. . . . Home around 4.30. . . .

1. African American political activist Roscoe Conkling Simmons, who seconded the nomination of Herbert Hoover for president. He was a regular columnist for the *Chicago Tribune.*

Sunday, 20 April 1930

. . . Late in the afternoon we go to Chinatown & have a grand time & then to a supper party at Eddie Wassermann's. . . . I get very drunk. Later we go to a party of Taylor Gordon's but I was too drunk to know what happened there. . . . Home around 2.

Tuesday, 22 April 1930

Wrote Chapters XVIII & XIX. Lunch in alone & finished typing third draught of *Parties.* . . . Nora Holt calls for me & we dine at Jacques de Walter Gaffney's on Madison Ave. in great style. . . . The Greenes, Ruth [Baldwin], Nora & I leave early to take the Greens to the boat. They are sailing on the *Berengaria!* . . . Marty Mann & I go to Lloyd & Edna Thomas's. Taylor Gordon there. I get very drunk. Then to the Clam House. Home around 3.30.

Wednesday, 23 April 1930

. . . Marinoff hates *Parties* which she read last night. She's probably right.

Thursday, 24 April 1930

. . . Finished correcting *Parties* & sent it over to Knopf. Marinoff tells me she hates the book in no uncertain terms. . . .

Friday, 25 April 1930

. . . Lunch at Don Juan with Donald Angus. . . . Came home. Alfred Knopf calls up to tell me he likes *Parties* and that it is the New York *Heartbreak House*.[1] Later, Blanche calls up with enthusiasm. I telephone Lawrence that I will dedicate it to him & Armina. Eddie Wassermann meets me at Don Juan & we dine at Leone's, then go to Alhambra. Meet Alain Locke on 7 Ave. Then to Louis Cole & Clam House where we find Eddie Manchester & telephone Nora to join us, ending at the Sheik Club, . . . an awful bore. Leave at 2 & take Nora home.

> 1. George Bernard Shaw's play about the moral and emotional impotence of the ruling classes in England on the eve of World War I.

Monday, 28 April 1930

. . . I have indigestion & a bad tooth & Lawrence Langner gets funny with a luncheon engagement so I get bad-tempered. To Dr. Cloney's at 12. He thinks my tooth is sensitive but not ailing. . . . Dinner in & then we go to see *Strike Up the Band*. Home & to bed & have a horrible time with teeth. No drug helps & I am awake all night. . . .

Wednesday, 30 April 1930

Up at 7.00 with a blinding toothache. Dressed and went to see Dr. Cloney. . . . He takes out a nerve & I come home & lie down. . . . Get drunk & go to bed.

Friday, 2 May 1930

. . . Lunch in with Marinoff. Then to Goldfarb's & Knopf office where Texas Guinan came to witness my contract for *Parties* & was photographed with me & Alfred. Home at 4. Joe Brewer, Kate Seabrook, Armina Langner, Stinnett, Nella Larsen for dinner. Lawrence Langner came later & we went to N.A.A.C.P. party at the Saratoga—unbearably hot. Everybody was there & among others who entertained were Adelaide Hall, Nora Holt, Jimmie

Daniels,[1] Broadway Jones.[2] . . . I talked with Adelaide, Nora, . . . Harry Glynn, . . . etc., & met Caspar Holstein.[3] Later to the Clam House, an amazing sight, for an hour. Home at 5.00. . . .

1. Young African American soon to reign in café society as pianist and singer.

2. African American musical comedy performer.

3. African American bolito king in Harlem who invented the numbers racket in which one bet on three-digit numbers drawn from the daily stock market reports. The odds were 600-1. Holstein was another African American celebrity thinly disguised in *Nigger Heaven*.

Sunday, 11 May 1930

. . . Spent the morning clearing out storeroom & putting blankets away. Lunch in with Marinoff. Then with Reg Wallace we drive to the Bronx Zoo & inspect it. Returning around 6 we go to Miyako's for dinner. John Durkin, our favorite elevator boy, is very drunk. . . .

Tuesday, 13 May 1930

. . . Late in afternoon Blanche Knopf gives a cocktail party for Wm. Aspenwall Bradley.[1] . . . Armina & Lawrence Langner came here for dinner with us & Fania & I go to see Nazimova in *A Month in the Country* but are so bored we leave after Act II.

1. Paris-based American literary agent.

Wednesday, 14 May 1930

. . . Late in the afternoon Colin McPhee & Jane Belo who are to be married & sailing on Friday come in to say goodbye. Also Joan Carr who sails tomorrow. Eddie Wassermann arrives & I take him to dinner at Leone's & to a wrestling match at Mad. Sq. Garden which bores me. Then to Michel's for a couple drinks. It rains heavily. I drive Eddie home & come home myself. A lot more stocks arrive from Avery Hopwood estate.

Thursday, 15 May 1930

. . . Lilyan Tashman & Edmund Lowe[1] for dinner. Marian Beale, a fiasco for service. Then we take Lilyan & Ed to *The Green Pastures*. Afterward to Bob Chanler's for a party, for a minute, & then to Don Juan for a couple of drinks. Home about 2.

1. Popular film stars, married to each other.

Friday, 16 May 1930

. . . Start third reading of *Parties* galleys. . . . We give a cocktail party for Lilyan Tashman & Edmund Lowe. Margalo Gilmore, Texas Guinan, Frank Case, Ben Ray Redman, . . . Edith & Sam Hoffenstein, Dashiell Hammett & Nell Martin,[1] . . . Grace & Jim Johnson, Alma Wertheim, . . . Constance Collier, Mercedes de Acosta, George Gershwin, Blanche Knopf, Sam & Nellie Knopf, . . . Edward Wassermann, Wittgenstein, Comte & Comtesse de Forceville,[2] . . . Bayard Schindel & Isa Glenn, Regina Wallace, Long Lance, T. R. Smith. . . . The party was over about 8.30 & I took Eddie Wassermann to dinner at the Crillon & came home to bed at 10.

> 1. American minor actress, law student, migrant worker, newspaper journalist, novelist (*Lovers Should Marry*), vaudevillian, and in 1930 Dashiell Hammett's mistress.
> 2. Clarita and Philippe de Forceville.

Tuesday, 20 May 1930

. . . According to the papers Paul Robeson made a great success in *Othello* last night, & Long Lance didn't do so well in his picture, *The Silent Evening*. . . . Lunch at Algonquin for Marinoff. Then to Macy's to find new brocade to cover our couch. Home for a couple of hours. Then to a cocktail party at Ben Ray Redman's (and Frieda Inescort). . . . On to a cocktail party at Sam Hoffenstein's. . . . Home at 6.30. . . . Alfred & Blanche & Mencken for dinner. Texas Guinan expected but did not come.

Wednesday, 21 May 1930

. . . At noon I go to Nickolas Muray to be photographed. Fania comes later & is photographed with me. Then we dip into . . . Cook's for a plan of the *Mauritania*. . . . To Algonquin for lunch. . . . Then to see Ellen Glasgow at the Chatham. . . . Then to E. Wassermann's party for Lilyan Tashman & Ed Lowe. . . .

Friday, 23 May 1930

. . . Marinoff tells me that Nell Martin is having a baby by Dashiell Hammett & that Lil [Tashman] discovered Ed Lowe in bed with Constance Bennett.[1] . . .

> 1. Popular film star, notably as a ghost in the *Topper* movie series.

Saturday, 24 May 1930

. . . Sent a cablegram to the [London] Carlton engaging rooms. To Jac Auer's. Then to the Sherry-Netherland where Eddie Wassermann & his sister picked up Lil Tashman & Ed Lowe & took us to lunch at the Don Juan. Marinoff was there for a moment. . . . About 4.30 we take down all the curtains & send them to the cleaners. Dinner in with Marinoff & then I go to sleep for an hour. Eddie Wassermann comes for me at 9.30 & we inspect two speakeasies: Tony's where we have a talk with Tony & he gives us his unfavorable views of Mussolini, & The Iron Gate where we see . . . Bill Benét, Monte Woolley,[1] Ernest Boyd, etc. Then to the Clam House where we see . . . Gladys Bentley. Home at 1.30.

 1. Little-known, bearded eccentric actor until he appeared in *The Man Who Came to Dinner,* both the play and film, mimicking acerbic critic Alexander Woollcott.

Thursday, 26 May 1930

Up at 7.30 with rather a hangover. Cold & cloudy. Dressed & went to . . . Brentano's: ordered cards for "absent from N.Y." To sub-treasury on Wall Street for new passport, & on to a Spanish restaurant where I had lunch with Eddie Wassermann. Home to find my page proofs. Read a couple of chapters. Then took a nap. Langston Hughes came to see me. His patron[1] has failed him & he borrows some money. We go to dinner at Clarita & Philip de Forceville's. . . .

 1. Charlotte Osgood Mason, eccentric, wealthy, white patroness of several young African American writers and artists, including Aaron Douglas, Langston Hughes, and Zora Neale Hurston.

Thursday, 29 May 1930

. . . I read page proofs. Ettie Stettheimer comes for lunch & reads 2nd chapter for German mistakes but doesn't find any.[1] . . . Regina Wallace came for dinner. After dinner I go to Tony's for a coupla drinks & then to Rhea Wells's party. . . . Home around 1.30.

 1. In *Parties,* a German character uses her native language from time to time. CVV spoke no German.

Friday, 30 May 1930

Decoration Day. Up at 8, with a hangover. . . .

Saturday, 31 May 1930

Up at a quarter to eight with quite a hangover. . . .

Wednesday, 4 June 1930

Up at a quarter of nine with a pretty hangover. . . .

Thursday, 5 June 1930

. . . At 4 Eddie Wassermann comes in & later we go to a cocktail party chez Kay Mills, where the cocktails are bad & the company ordinary. . . . From there with Eddie to . . . the Plaza where we had dinner, Marinoff joining us. Then to 44 St. Theatre to see Norman Gaulder's extraordinary production of *Lysistrata*. Later to Tony's & Iron Gate, both of which bore me now.

Friday, 6 June 1930

. . . Lunch with Blanche & Alfred. After lunch went to Doris Ullman's & spent the afternoon drinking martinis. . . . At 5 came home. Edwin Knopf came in. At 7 went to dinner with . . . Regina Wallace & Everett Ships[1] at Leone's. Then to Tony's, where we got drunker. . . . I suggest to Tony that he write a book. . . . Then we went to a party given . . . for Lily Damita:[2] . . . George Gershwin, Ralph Barton, etc. Home at 2.30. My ankles are swollen.

    1. Regina Wallace's current but only momentary beau.
    2. American musical comedy performer.

Tuesday, 10 June 1930

Up at 7.30. Cloudy & rain. All day <u>packing.</u> . . . Late in the afternoon Zora Neale Hurston arrives, Langston Hughes, Ettie Stettheimer, T. R. Smith, Armina Langner. Dozens of people telephone. Marinoff & I have dinner in together. After dinner Rita Romilly comes in & bothers us. The Gilbert Seldeses give a party—they sail tonight—to which we do not go. I read a little in *Poor Nigger*[1] & then go to sleep, circa 10 o'clock.

    1. There was no outcry in the black press over the title when this collection of essays and stories by Orio Vergani was published, four years after *Nigger Heaven*. It was translated from Italian by W. W. Hobson.

Wednesday, 11 June 1930

. . . Farewell to Meda & with our trunks to the Cunard Line Docks, <u>and</u> sail on *Mauritania* at 5 o'clock. B109, biggest & best single room on the boat. Max

Ewing, E. Wassermann, Blanche Knopf (who introduces me to the purser), Taylor Gordon, Donald Angus come to say goodbye (& with Rita Romilly, too late). We dine & go to bed early. Fog & a fog horn, but I slept well.

Thursday, 12 June 1930

. . . Meet Mahala Douglas & had a swell lunch with her & Marinoff. Very calm & feeling fine. Later, to bed for a nap & reading *Petal of the Rose* [by Charles Pettit]. Dressed & dined with Mahala & Marinoff. Champagne, etc., & spent the evening in the lounge. In bed about 12.

Tuesday, 17 June 1930

Up at dawn, and off the boat at Plymouth. . . . We arrived in London around 3, and found the porter from the Carlton waiting for us and drove to the Carlton to find same room I had when I was sick, 175–76, and all the old waiters, elevator attendants, etc. A sudden rainstorm. We unpack. Fifty years old today. We celebrate by dinner at the Ivy & to see the *Cochran Revue*. [Leslie] Hutch[inson] speaks to us from the orchestra.

Friday, 20 June 1930

. . . It gets hotter during the night & Marinoff gets nervous with the hotel music & my snoring.

Tuesday, 24 June 1930

. . . We started off early & went to the Wallace Collection with more boule than we ever saw before. Then to the Robesons for lunch & saw the baby. Paul drives us home at 2. . . . At 4 we call on Mr. George Moore & find him as enlivening as ever. He . . . says there are no such things as thoughts, only words, & we met his Tabby Persian, Sam. Then to Jacob Epstein's: his wife is there & we see his new marble fecundity & his head of Robeson. On to Simpson's [in the Strand] for dinner & to see *Othello* again. Went back to see Paul after the play & then home to bed.

Wednesday, 25 June 1930

. . . To the Tate Gallery alone & much edified by the Blakes, the French room, etc. Back to the hotel & to lunch at Sovrani's with Marinoff, Rebecca West, & Evelyn Waugh. . . . Then to Cecil Beaton's cocktail party: . . . Oliver Messel, Lady Ravensdale, Lady Wayworth, Lord Weymouth, Tallulah Bankhead, Patrick

Balfour & his sister, Dwight Fiske, Ethel Barrymore, etc. . . . Home to dress, & . . . on to Patrick's birthday party. Elinor Glyn, etc. . . . Home at 3. . . .

Thursday, 26 June 1930

. . . Off to the British Museum at 10.00 & bowled over by it. I had forgotten its wonders.

Friday, 27 June 1930

. . . After lunch we go to the Albert & Victoria Museum. Back to the hotel at 5. I go to a cocktail party at Kim Peacock's[1] (skipping one at Dwight Fiske's) & then go to see McKnight Kauffer & Marion Dorn,[2] where Marinoff was. Then we go to the Ivy for dinner. Later to the Carlton & then they take me to the Gargoyle Club. About one I go to a party . . . where I meet Rex Evans[3] & see Frankie Levinson. Home about 3. . . .

    1. Actress in silent films.
    2. English artist E. McKnight Kauffer, called Ted (for Edward), and his actress wife.
    3. Character actor in films.

Sunday, 29 June 1930

Twenty years ago I was married in London, Christ Church, . . . and we had our wedding breakfast in the Carlton Hotel where now I am living.[1] . . .

    1. CVV's first marriage, to Anna Snyder, ended in divorce in 1912.

Thursday, 3 July 1930

. . . Homesick. I don't seem to like Paris at all this time. . . . At 4 I go to meet Julian Green at Weber's and presently we stroll to rue de Siene for photographs which we do not find. Then we go to Montmartre in search of Louis Cole & he turns up on the street. Julian disappears. Louis & I talk at a café & watch Harlem go by. . . .

Monday, 7 July 1930

. . . I feel fairly rotten & very depressed. Met Marinoff down town & we run into Marc Connelly & Alice de la Mar. The latter lunches with us at Larue. I go to see her late in the afternoon. We dine with Mahala [Douglas] at Joseph's: chicken flambé, which makes me sick. . . .

Tuesday, 8 July 1930

Up late & so many people telephone that I do not get away from the hotel till 12.30. I have a cocktail at Castiglione Bar & then meet Marinoff & George Jean Nathan & Lillian Gish for lunch at Larue. . . . At 5.30 meet Marinoff & Marc Connelly at Castiglione Bar. I take Robert de St. Jean & Julian Green to Boilieau for dinner. Then they take me to see a private film, *L'Age d'Or* [by Salvador Dali and Man Ray] at the Vicomte Charles de Noillaes. . . .

Thursday, 10 July 1930

Up at 7.30, with a hangover. Hot & rain. Very depressed, but got dressed & had lunch at the Franco-Italian restaurant & then went to the Lewis Agency to arrange about a tournée. . . . Then with the Russian chauffeur I discovered yesterday, Fania, D'Alvarez, Leche[1] & I go (1) to Larue for dinner, (2) to Boeuf sur le toit (saw Louis Cole), (3) we get rid of Leche who is very boring & go to Violette Murat's.[2] . . . Home about 2.30.

    1. French novelist Alain de Leche.

    2. Minor royalty in café society, often identified in lesbian circles.

Friday, 11 July 1930

. . . At 11.30 M. Lewis [Agency] arrived with a Voisin car & a chauffeur named Louis with whom we took a drive in the Bois & engaged for our southern trip. . . . We got home late in the afternoon & I lay down & read *Sir Goldberg's Party*, by Alain Leche, a rotten book. Then dressed & we went to Boonie Reagan's for cocktails.

Sunday, 13 July 1930

. . . Lunch at Escargot with Marinoff & then to Marche aux puces where we had extraordinary luck & found 4 carved Negro chairs, oyster plates, & some amusing figurines. Home with them. Then to a bar on rue Fontanne, to dinner at Auberge du Clos, to a Negro dance, Quai de Berli, to the rue de Lappe, much changed, where nevertheless I met some of my old friends. . . . Later we saw them again at Grand Ecart together with Louis Cole, Elisabeth Welch,[1] Olivia Wyndham, & Marty Mann. I picked up Tony Gardenia[2] & we went to Bricktop's . . . & to a place on Place du Terte for supper. Home at 7.

    1. African American singer who abandoned the United States for a long and successful career in England.

    2. English professional wrestler. The habit of collecting people from various alien

social groups was not uncommon in the twenties, as CVV's brief encounters with a number of surprising companions referred to in his daybooks suggest.

Wednesday, 16 July 1930

About 9.30 we started off in a Voisin driven by Louis, in the rain. . . . At La Prondene, a charming hotel at Jouy we stopped for déjeuner & who should appear opposite us but Sacha Guitry & Yvonne Printemps.[1] She looked at us, & perhaps recognized some one who had recently seen her from the front row. We went on to Chartres. Occasionally the sun came out but here it rained & was rather dark in the cathedral. We stopped at Vendôme to see the beautiful Eglis de la Trinite, and arrived at Eugene & Carlotta O'Neill's Les Plessis, outside of Tours, at 6.30. Dinner & in bed by 10. Slept none too well.

 1. French director and writer and his wife, who sang in musical comedy.

Thursday, 17 July 1930

Up at 8.30. Rain, but we started out bravely in the motor. Got to Langeois in pouring rain. Saw the chateau. Lunched at the Lion d'Or and went down the Circe, crossing the Fonteurault, stopped to see the church at Candes. Then went on the Chinon, and finally inspected Azaz-le-rideau before coming back to dine with the O'Neills at 6.30. In bed about 10.30, slept well, as Miss Marinoff crawled in with me.

Friday, 18 July 1930

. . . Carlotta drove with us to Blois where we had lunch at the restaurant François I & saw the chateau. On to Ambroise for another inspection & then on to Clemenceaux. Home for dinner & Eugene O'Neill told us about his play, a trilogy of New England called *Mourning Becomes Electra*, based on the Greek trilogy. It is to be completed in another year. To bed about 11. . . .

Monday, 21 July 1930

. . . We get into Toulouse—after a tire explodes outside—at 11, & waste an hour there, driving through the dark from 12–1.30 to Carcassone, driving up to the old Cité & into the hotel, a porter meets us & puts us to bed.

Thursday, 24 July 1930

The car is ready so I make an effort to get off to Barcelona but Louis had no breakfast & we can get no visas so we compromise by going to Nimes. . . . See Ramon Novarro in *Ben Hur* in the Roman arena. . . .

Friday, 25 July 1930

. . . Through Arles, Taradcan, Aix-en-Provence. Lunch in Marseilles, bouillabaisse in the Vieux Port. Then after a brief stroll we are off for Cassis-surmer where we find Colin McPhee and Jane Belo ensconced in a cottage on the mountain. . . .

Saturday, 26 July 1930

. . . Wakened early, by an unearthly din. The noisiest square I've ever been in. We are leaving [Toulon] immediately, & I tell Louis to get ready, but after an hour on the Quai & lunch there we telephone the hotel we will stay. In the afternoon I manage a nap but about 5.30 we stagger over to Willie Seabrook's studio & find him & Marjorie Worthington (met), go to dinner with them. . . . Out for a ride on the ocean, back for fines at the Cosa de la rade, & finally . . . to the bal musette, rue Lafayette, & to a whore house. Home about 1.30.

Sunday, 27 July 1930

. . . Terrible din as usual, but fooled around the hotel till eleven, when I went downstairs, paid my bill, met Louis & sent the baggage down. Then we went to see Willie Seabrook & Marjorie Worthington & she showed us how a girl looks in a black corset & nothing else. Then we had a couple of bottles of champagne & embarked for the Restaurant Lyonnaise for lunch. . . . A little later we drove into Cannes. . . . We had dinner in the garden at the Victoria & later Marguerite D'Alvarez came to see us. . . . In bed at 10 & slept pretty well except for mosquitoes.

Monday, 28 July 1930

. . . In the afternoon we go for a walk, very hot, and at 4 drive to Juan-les-Pins to see where Avery [Hopwood] died & Cap d'Antibes. Back for dinner at the Relais Coques in the public square, with a band, & to bed at midnight. Quite soused. Mosquitoes & hot.

Thursday, 31 July 1930

. . . At one o'clock, with Louis and the car, we picked up D'Alvarez & motored to Eden-Roc for lunch. . . . We drove on after lunch through Villefranche & then to Monte Carlo, meeting Charles Inglefield, the 71 year old fairy. . . .

Monday, 4 August 1930

. . . We were out [of Valever] by 9, and started off in the car for Le Puy, a drive with gorgeous views, by a quite perilous road . . . & saw the cathedral & the Black Virgin & started back, but we were tired, & Louis was aggravating, . . . & we got back very late in a bad temper. . . .

Tuesday, 5 August 1930

. . . We started off for Belley at 1.15. It got gradually brighter & in spite of a puncture we made Belley before 4.30. Went to the Hotel Pernollet, found our letters & drove out to Gertrude Stein's lovely place at Bilignin at 7 o'clock & stayed for dinner. Home at 10.

Wednesday, 6 August 1930

. . . At noon we start off for Bilignin where we lunch with Gertrude Stein & Alice Toklas. Then in the car over Lac de Bourget to Chambery & Les Chalmetier, home of Rousseau. Back to Aix-les-Bains where we dine & drive back to Belley at 11 o'clock.

Thursday, 7 August 1930

. . . I am troubled with indigestion, too much "vin du pays."

Friday, 8 August 1930

. . . As we go further on this trip Louis becomes more & more aggravating. He will not drive slowly, or stop, or do anything else that we ask of him easily, altho he is never rude. . . . To Paris where we arrive in front of the Michel at 5.45. . . .

Thursday, 14 August 1930

. . . After lunch Marinoff & I went for a long walk on the Boulevard & to the Musée Grevin, & then we came home to find a cablegram from Bricktop. It was her birthday & she gives a party at Flousce (her place). We go up at once & were the only ofays[1] there. . . . We came home at 11, quite lit & have indigestion in between.

1. Pig-Latin for "foe," a commonly popular slang word among African Americans for white people.

Friday, 15 August 1930

. . . Feel quite improved. Apparently my system craves gin! Anniversary. *Parties* is published today & 18 years ago Marinoff & I had our first "party"![1] . . . This is Assumption Day. Everybody in Paris closed till Monday.

    1. CVV and Marinoff had met in July, then for a second time on August 11; four days later their affair began and continued until their marriage on 21 October 1914.

Saturday, 16 August 1930

. . . Paris is quiet & lovely on this holiday. . . . We go to . . . Le Torque & Sibyl Kemp's cottage, a charming affair, but there is not enough to drink & after dinner (she has been rude & overbearing to Emilie [Grigsby]) she leaves to play at the casino. . . . Marinoff comes into my wing to sleep & we retire about 10 in a 3/4 bed. I am <u>very</u> cross.

Sunday, 17 August 1930

. . . It appears that Sibyl Kemp came in at 8.45 this morning. Nevertheless, she stumbles out to go to Boulogne. . . . I have difficulty getting a seat on a Pullman, but finally land one & we leave for Paris, arriving about midnight. . . . This is one of the worst weekends I have ever spent.

Wednesday, 20 August 1930

. . . Spent morning packing. . . . Edna Thomas & Man Ray to lunch. After lunch I went back to the hotel & collected Fania & we went off to the Gare du Nord & took the *Nord Express* for Germany. Had a swell dinner & went to bed. Awakened at 12 by a stupid customs inspector.

Thursday, 21 August 1930

. . . Breakfast & in Berlin before 9. . . . After a bath I wandered to the bar about 11 o'clock, & then I wandered out . . . Unter den Linden. . . . Later we met Muk de Jari in exaggerated Tyrolean costume. . . . Then I go to the Eden Bar. Back to the hotel for dinner & see a very tiresome piece, *Victoria and Her Hussar,* at the Metropol Theater. After a beer, home at midnight.

Friday, 22 August 1930

Up at 8, we have a nice fight. Sunny & warm. Dress & go to the bar. . . . Then we go to the Frederichs Museum, . . . & to the Royal Palace. . . . We dine at the Bristol & Ernst Syzamatolski, a friend of Dagmar [Godowsky]'s, appears to take us out. We go to Johnny's Night Club, to the old & new Eldorado & to the Silhouette where I meet Fritzi. Home around 3. My first night in the homosexual clubs of Berlin.

Saturday, 23 August 1930

... After lunch we go to the zoo and the aquarium. Then meet Noel Murphy & Syzmatolski at the Eden Bar. A pretty whore turns up. .... Then on to the Kleist-Kasino, a bar where boys meet, the Johnny Club, the Jockey, where there are beautiful posters of Mistinguette,[1] & to the Silhouette where I talk to Fritzi. Marinoff & Noel go home about 9.30 but I stay till midnight with Ernest.—Rats.

    1. Ageless French chanteuse CVV had admired since his first encounter with her in 1907.

Sunday, 24 August 1930

Up at 9 with quite a little hangover. .... Later . . . Marinoff & I go to *Die Meistersinger* at the Staatsoper, a marvellous performance. We got our food between acts.

Monday, 25 August 1930

... We dress & motor to Potsdam where we spend the day inspecting the palaces. .... Home around 5.30 . . . & to Muk de Jari's who has promised to go out with us. This he doesn't do. He is in bed & there is a Serbian there & also a Viennese who goes home when I do, about one o'clock.

Tuesday, 26 August 1930

... We walked to Neue Museum to see Egyptian collection. Then to zoo where we were photographed with lions. .... Interviewed in the morning by Bernhard Kruger of the *8 Uhr Abenblatt* (it appeared in the evening) & at 6 o'clock by Ziemer of the *Chicago Tribune.* To Eden Bar where we meet Noel Murphy & Georg Doertelback & I took them to dinner at the Atelier. Then we went slumming. He took me many places, but left the girls after the first two. About 2 o'clock ran into Zena Naylor, Derek Jackman, Eddie Bonehard, etc., at Johnny's. From there, dropping Doertelback, we went to the Silhouette where I saw Fritzi & later Bender's Nightclub where we stayed till 5. Derek drove us home in his car.

Wednesday, 27 August 1930

Up at 9.30 with a hangover. . . . We went to lunch at the Bristol, I went to sleep for a couple of hours. At 5.30 I got dressed & met Zena & Derek for a drink. Then had dinner with Marinoff at Mutzbauer's, & we went to see *Die Wunderbar*. Met Zena & Derek at the Eden Bar (Marinoff went to bed) & we went in search of the Hohenzollen . . . which we finally found. Then to the Hollandais, to the Eldorado, . . . to the Silhouette where we finally went to the waiters' private club with Fritzi & Franzl. Home about 5.

Thursday, 28 August 1930

. . . Met Marinoff for lunch at Peltzer's. . . . Then we went to a shop . . . & had a debauch. Came home & packed. Then met Zena & Derek Jackson in the Adler's Bar. . . . & took them to dinner at the Bristol. We left Berlin at 10 o'clock. I am very sad. I adore the place. To bed at once, but didn't sleep very well.

Saturday, 30 August 1930

. . . Picked up the Sunday papers for Aug 17 to read two filthy notices for *Parties*. Meet Marinoff in the Castiglione Bar. . . . Then to rue de St. Piers where I bought a beautiful paperweight & an obscene box. . . . We are all moved into a proper two rooms. Dinner at the Cabaret & to bed early. But horrible noises from American drunks during the night.

Sunday, 31 August 1930

. . . A horrible lunch with Marinoff chez Paracis, Place de l'Alma. Don't go there again. Then we went to the Louvre & saw many things . . . I had never seen before, but the pictures are so badly arranged & so dirty & the whole place so filthy that the general effect is no good. Home at 4. The court of our hotel resounds with noisy American voices. . . .

Wednesday, 3 September 1930

. . . Meet Virgil Thomson at Castiglione Bar. . . . With Marinoff went to . . . Emily Davies: Marcel Herrand[1] & an English ass were there. To the Cabaret for dinner & to bed early.

1. French actor who had recently performed pieces by Hugnet and Thomson.

Saturday, 6 September 1930

Up at 9. Hangover. Cloudy, even rainy. First copies of English *Parties* arrive. . . . Then to Castiglione Bar, meet Marinoff at Larue's for lunch. . . . Virgil Thomson comes after me at 3 & we go to a place where he plays his new funeral dance & one of his sonatas for me. . . . Home at 6. We collect Marie Doro at the Scribe. . . . Later we try to go to the Taverne de Paris but it no longer exists. Where are those lovely paintings? We go to Chez Graf, then I take the girls home & go back to Bricktop's till 3.30. . . .

Sunday, 7 September 1930

Up at 9 with quite a hangover. Packed in the morning & lunch in. Then I drive to see Notre Dame & played about a bit. . . . At 4 Man Ray & his girl appeared. We had some drinks. Then went chez Les Vikings for some wine, & finally to the Coupole where Marinoff & I had dinner and afterward I went to the Bobino Music Hall, rue de la Gaite, an entrancing place. Home very tired later.

Wednesday, 10 September 1930

. . . Walk to town, stopping in the bookshops looking in vain for *Parties*. Stop in Castiglione Bar to say goodbye to my pals. On to Larue's for lunch. More farewells. . . . Then we go together, Marinoff & I, to the Madeleine which I have not entered for years. Later I go to the Café de la Paix, to Khaki, now feeling fairly fit. Have a couple of drinks of Pernod & set off for Said's but I do not stop there. Back to hotel, very lit by now and soon Ted Kauffer & Marion Dorn appear from London, Ted with eight marvellous *Nigger Heaven* drawings.[1]

> 1. Kauffer produced a full set of illustrations for *Nigger Heaven*, but the long-delayed limited edition was never published because the Depression had dried up the market for expensive books.

Sunday, 14 September 1930

Woke at 7.45 to a stormy, pitching sea. The boat lifted in the air several feet & then dropped, but nothing in the cabin was upset. I stayed in bed all day. . . .

Thursday, 18 September 1930

Spent entire day unpacking, talking to Mr. Torrson about new apartment, etc.[1] Lunch & dinner in. Elmer & Nella [Larsen] Imes to dinner. They are talking of separating. She goes abroad on a scholarship tomorrow & he goes to Fisk.[2] We sent them home early & went to bed.

    1. Marinoff and CVV had decided to take the adjacent three-room apartment, breaking through a dividing wall, thereby nearly doubling their space, creating a library, sewing room, and "Victorian Room," the latter centered on his mother's square rosewood piano.

    2. Imes, a physicist, had returned to his teaching position at Fisk University. Larsen was aware of his affair with a white administrator there, Ethel Bedient Gilbert.

Friday, 19 September 1930

. . . To a cocktail party Blanche gives for me: Nora Holt (who sings), Jimmie Durante, Texas Guinan, Jesse & Bessie Lasky, Carl Van Doren, Joe Brewer, Matt Moore, Mankewicz,[1] G. J. Nathan, Elmer Adler,[2] Max Ewing, Nell Martin, Isa [Glenn] & Bayard Schindel, Frances Seligman, Mercedes de Acosta, Lenore Harris, Auriole Lee, John Van Druten, Arthur Richman, T. R. Smith, Eddie Wassermann, Reg, Judith Anderson, Wood Kahler. Blanche, Fania, & Lawrence & Armina Langner dined at Don Juan and to bed about 11, very tight.

    1. English playwright and film producer Wolf Mankewicz.

    2. Book designer for Alfred A. Knopf, editor of *The Colophon,* an extravagant literary quarterly; also editor of *Breaking into Print,* a book of essays by twenty significant writers of the twenties about their early publishing experiences.

Saturday, 20 September 1930

. . . Donald Angus & Reg Wallace for dinner. Later, went to a party at A'Lelia Walker's with Rita Romilly: Ivor Novello, Blair Niles, Casca Bonds, . . . Sterling Suftin, Bud Fisher, . . . Harold Jackman, Countee Cullen, Edna & Lloyd Thomas, Max Ewing, Lucile Randolph, Catherine Johnson, Gladys White, Gloria Swanson (the Chicago black drag), etc. It was so crowded that Rita & I went to Clam House with Harry Glynn. . . . Home around 4.

Wednesday, 24 September 1930

. . . Painters working slowly. . . . Lunch in. Then Marinoff & I go to Stern's & Macy's to look at big rugs & select a couple. Also to see General Electric refrigerators. Also to Gurnn & Latchford's where we buy a 3 story Tansu chest. Home around 5, Marinoff goes to dinner & the theatre, & Donald Angus goes to dinner with me at Don Juan & comes back to house. Also, James Cole comes in & spends the evening.

Thursday, 25 September 1930

. . . The door is knocked through between the two apartments. . . . Dress & go to Tony's for a cocktail, then to a party . . . at Peter's, 52 W. 53 Street.

Friday, 26 September 1930

. . . Carpenters & painters at work. I spent the day more or less hanging over them. As a result, some things got done. Lunch in & dinner in. Reg Wallace comes for dinner & unexpectedly James Weldon Johnson. Late at night I go to a party Ruth Baldwin gives for Edna Thomas: Olivia Wyndham, . . . 3 boys, A'Lelia Walker, Rita Wellman, Inez Wilson, Lloyd Thomas, Iris Barry,[1] Stinnett, . . . Taylor Gordon, David Plunkett Greene, Fredi Washington, etc. About 2 Nora Holt . . . & I go to Lenox Club. . . . Home about 5.30.

  1. Film critic for the *Daily Mail* in London; later a film historian and eventually head of the film department at the Museum of Modern Art.

Saturday, 27 September 1930

Up at 10 with a hangover. . . . Lunch with Muriel Draper & Eddie Wassermann at Don Juan. . . . After lunch Marinoff & I go to Macy's for shelving, etc. Home late, dressed & met Eddie for dinner at the Crillon & then to see Auriol Lee in *Nine to Six.* Marinoff & Lenore Harris went together. We went back to see Auriol. Then Eddie & I went to a drag at the Alhambra in Harlem, very delightful. Cool, not too crowded. Lots of Negroes & not too many spectators, Harry Glynn was there with . . . Eddie Manchester, Jules Bledsoe. Went home about 2.

Monday, 29 September 1930

. . . At night Marinoff (with Percy Hammond) & me (with Lenore Harris) to go to see Gilbert Miller's production of two Molnar plays (Joan Carr is in them). . . . Then to a party at Eddie Wassermann's: Clarita de Forceville, Florence Sternberger, Lewis Milestone,[1] Matt Moore, Auriole Lee, Francine Larrimore,[2] Judith Anderson, Blanche Knopf, Arthur Richman, . . . Louis Bromfield, John Peale Bishop.[3]

  1. Film director and producer.
  2. Popular actress in a succession of plays; her name kept many of them running.
  3. American poet and novelist, also in collaborative writing with Edmund Wilson.

Wednesday, 1 October 1930

. . . I go to Tony's at 7 o'clock & . . . . dine at Muriel Draper's, 312 E. 52 house for the first time. The Lochers are there. I get quite tight when Muriel asks me for some money to have Ellery Larsson psychoanalyzed. I refuse, take taxi up town, collect Nora Holt . . . & go to the Savoy. David Plunkett Greene, Fania with Wood Kahler, Al Moore, Opal Cooper,[1] A'Lelia Walker, Mamie White, Billie Cain,[2] Max Ewing, Lloyd Thomas, etc. I get very drunk & am dragged home at 3.30.

    1. African American actor in the Lafayette Stock Company.
    2. Entertainer at Small's Paradise.

Monday, 6 October 1930

. . . Lunch in with Marinoff. Her new French maid, Marcette, arrives. Dinner with Reg at a French place. Then she & Marinoff go to the theatre. I come home & expect James Cole. As he doesn't arrive, I call up Donald Angus who comes over. He has been promoted at Jay Thorpe's & his salary raised.

Tuesday, 7 October 1930

. . . Dinner with Marinoff & Judith Anderson at Eddie Wassermann's & we go to see *Brown Buddies* with Adelaide Hall & Bill Robinson (his arm in a sling from a bullet wound). . . . Then to a party at John Van Druten's. . . . Home at 2.30.

Thursday, 9 October 1930

. . . Meda arrives surly & almost immediately has a run-in with Marinoff as to whether she shall make the bed. The place is in an uproar. Marinoff goes out & I have lunch in alone. . . . Just before Edna Kenton arrives for dinner, Meda announces Blanche Knopf in a mumble. Marinoff calls her down & soon Meda is on her way. Marinoff finishes getting dinner & serves it, for Wood Kahler too, who was taking her out. There is some heavy drinking, & the guests only depart at 1.30. Meda does not even say goodbye. That is how she repays our affection & kindness.

Friday, 10 October 1930

. . . It seems a great relief to have Meda gone. I take Joan Carr to lunch at the Crillon & then we go to the Philharmonic Concert. We come home to the house to collect Fania & go to Ivor Novello's to meet Gracie Fields. Others were there. Home & dress & go to Arthur Richman's buffet supper for Ina Claire.

Saturday, 11 October 1930

At 11 Alice & Leon Monnier came to see us & agree to come as servants for 45 dollars a week.[1] In the afternoon we start to clean out Meda's very dirty cupboards. Then at 4.30 I go to a cocktail party at Doris Ullman's. . . . Home at 6.30, & we take Donald to dinner at Leone's. Home & to bed about 11.30.

    1. Nearly five years had passed since Fania Marinoff had dismissed Alice, her "French maid," as unsatisfactory.

Wednesday, 15 October 1930

. . . Alice & Leon are difficult to get adjusted to. At 1 I meet David Plunkett Greene at the Don Juan. Afterward I go to see Walter White at the N.A.A.C.P. to see some drawings by Hale Woodruff, Negro painter in Paris. Then to Holliday Book Shop, to florist, flowers for Joe Brewer, & home. Mencken & Mrs. [Sara Haardt] Mencken, Blanche & Alfred Knopf for dinner, not too well served & very slow, with Alice & Leon. This couple is getting on my nerves. On to *Three Is a Crowd* with Clif Webb, Libby Holman, & Fred Allen.[1] Afterwards to a party given at the Elysée: . . . Libby & Clif, . . . Richard Barthelmess, . . . Florence Eldridge, Frederic March, Cole Porter, Ivor Novello, Lillian Braithwaite, Harpo Marx,[2] King Vidor, Judith Anderson, Ina Claire and home around 5.

    1. Vaudeville comedian in musical revues who then migrated to radio for a long and successful career.

    2. The silent, harpist Marx Brother, first in vaudeville, then on Broadway, and subsequently in films. CVV encountered Groucho, the annihilating, punning, most verbal of brothers shortly afterward. The Marx Brothers were then appearing on Broadway in *The Cocoanuts* by Irving Berlin.

Thursday, 16 October 1930

. . . Sunny & cool but everything is wrong in the kitchen & Marinoff is ready to fight with Alice & does so. As a consequence we have a terrible morning which culminates in a man coming to tune the piano. We go to the Algonquin . . . & fight during lunch. . . . Home to a terrible dinner & another fight & to bed early. . . .

Friday, 17 October 1930

. . . We decide to let Alice & Leon go at once. They are worthless, and so after lunch they do go, & not unwillingly, but by now I am a wreck. Marinoff goes out & when she returns . . . she cooks dinner & Donald comes in. . . .

Saturday, 18 October 1930

A terrible day. . . . I go to lunch with Eddie W. & talk about servant problem with Bertha [Case] at Algonquin. Walk home & find Rita Romilly here & Marinoff becomes hysterical again. But towards night, calm descends. Bertha's Sara [Victor] has found us a servant, perhaps. Marinoff goes out to dinner, etc., with Wood Kahler. Donald comes for me, I take him to Tony's for cocktails & the Crillon for dinner. Then we come home & Jimmie Cole calls in. Later he takes us to a party in Harlem where we find George Hoy & his sister. On the way to Clam House, . . . to Lenox Club, where I see Lena Wilson, etc. We take Neil Laurencie[1] along & later he & Donald leave us & he tries to beat Donald up. Home around 6.

    1. An acquaintance of Jimmie Cole's from the party.

Monday, 20 October 1930

. . . No servant yet. Marinoff & I fight most of the day. . . . We dine at Algonquin . . . and go to Lenore Ulric's opening in *Pagan Lady.* Afterwards a party at Blanche's where comes Lenore, Sidney Blackmer, Eddie & Judith [Anderson], etc. Later we go to Judith's & while I am sitting drinking, my cock strolls out! Home about 1.30.

Tuesday, 21 October 1930

. . . Our first cocktail party in our enlarged quarters: Frederick March & Florence Eldridge, Judith Anderson, Lenore Ulric & Sidney Blackmer, Anna May Wong, John Van Druten, Eddie Wassermann, Van Vechten & Angevine Shaffer, Donald Angus, Lillian Braithwaite, Armina & Lawrence Langner, Blanche Knopf. . . .

Wednesday, 22 October 1930

. . . To Judith Anderson's to a cocktail party for Blanche Knopf: Maurice Gest, Arthur Richman, Joan Carr, Condé Nast, Groucho Marx, Alfred Knopf, Harry Glynn, Jack Colton, Bennett Cerf, . . . Emily Clark, & hundreds of others.

Eight of us go to Ethel Waters in *Blackbirds*. Then with Eddie I go to a drag at the Savoy. Home at 1.30.

Monday, 27 October 1930

. . . Two new maids come. Edith Ramsay . . . as cook, etc., & Marinoff's French maid, Valentine Aubert. Bob Chanler's funeral, to which we do not go. . . .

Friday, 31 October 1930

Up at 8.30. Cloudy & cool, with quite a hangover. . . . At 12 I go out to send flowers to Ethel Waters on her birthday. . . . Colin McPhee comes in at 4. Then I go to a party at Lenore Harris's. . . . Home with Eddie Wassermann for dinner. Then we go to Iturbi concert. . . . Later to a party at Dreiser's, where I take Eddie. . . . Home around midnight.

Saturday, 1 November 1930

. . . Before I am through breakfast the electrician is here to install the radio. John Colton comes for me & takes me to a new Tony's, 42 W. 53 St. . . . Marinoff goes to the Langners' in the country. Donald comes for me at 7 & I take him to dinner at the new Tony's. Then to house again to hear Lotte Lehmann sing *Tannhauser* in Chicago. Then to a party. . . . Donald went to Harlem with me & we were out till 4 o'clock. . . .

Sunday, 2 November 1930

. . . At noon heard H. G. Wells on the radio. . . . In the afternoon listened to the Philharmonic over the radio. James Cole came in for an hour. Then I visited Donald Angus at the Wellington. . . . At 6.30 I go home to find the Langners with Marinoff & I take them to the New Tony's where we have a swell dinner. . . . Home about 9 & listened to Gigli[1] over the radio.

    1. Operatic tenor Benjamin Gigli.

Monday, 3 November 1930

Eddie [Wassermann] & I go to see Kid Chocolate fight La Barba at Madison Sq. Garden. It is not a good fight & I have such a cold I don't enjoy it. Invited to Colin McPhee's after but come home instead, as I am not feeling too good. French & Czechoslovakian translations of *Spider Boy* & *Nigger Heaven* arrive. Also pocketbook of *Lords of the Housetops*.[1]

    1. A book of stories and essays about cats that CVV had edited for Knopf in 1922.

Wednesday, 5 November 1930

. . . Louis Bromfield comes to see me at 4, Max Ewing at 5, Sidney Peterson at 6. Donald comes to dinner & Max stays too. After dinner Zena Naylor. I give her a bawling out, say I'm tired of hearing her talk about her lovers. She gets sore & goes home about 12. Max stays till 1.30. Very drunk, I retire.

Thursday, 6 November 1930

. . . We have dinner in & go to see George Gershwin's *Girl Crazy* of which one act satisfies us. So we come home & dress & go out with Sidney Blackmer, Lenore Ulric, Eddie Wassermann, Armina Marshall . . . to a party at Texas Guinan's club where I meet Jean Malin[1] & Ernst Lubitsch[2] . . . and have a sweet talk with Texas who promises to take me to dinner with the Everleigh Sisters.[3] Home at 4.30.

   1. French transvestite entertainer.
   2. Hungarian stage and film director.
   3. When CVV was a college student in Chicago, the Everleigh Sisters ran a celebrated brothel. CVV played the piano there occasionally for tips and in his old age remembered that there was a fountain in the foyer. "All the best people used to fall in," he wrote.

Friday, 14 November 1930

Awakened by the telephone at 6 in the morning. It is Elizabeth [Shaffer Hull] in Los Angeles with the news that Emma [Van Vechten Shaffer] died this morning. I am more upset than I have been for years. . . .

Monday, 17 November 1930

Up at 8 after sleeping about 12 hours. A reassuring telegram from Van Vechten Shaffer who arrived in Los Angeles last night. . . . At 11 o'clock this morning Emma's funeral. . . . Late in the afternoon I had quite an enterprising row with Marinoff after she locked herself in her room & couldn't get out. Finally released by the engineer of the Hotel Wellington. . . .

Wednesday, 19 November 1930

. . . The Bromfields, Muriel Draper & Joe Brewer for dinner. At midnight Marinoff & I go to a party Fred March & Florence Eldridge throw at the Sherry-Netherland: Claudette Colbert (met),[1] Jack Colton, Ernst Lubitsch, . . . Eddie Wassermann, Lenore Harris, etc. Home around 2, very drunk.

   1. French Canadian actress and later a movie star.

Thursday, 20 November 1930

Up at 8 with a terrible hangover. . . . We drive to Lawrence Langner's to leave Zora Hurston's play, *Mulebone*[1] (which I heard with pleasure today) & then to Willie Seabrook's, 66 Fifth Ave. He & . . . Marjorie Worthington take us to dinner at the Brevoort. Home around 10 & in to bed.

> 1. Langston Hughes collaborated with Hurston in writing the play. CVV gave it to the Theatre Guild for consideration, he thought, with their permission. Langner then passed it on to the Karamu Playhouse in Cleveland, Ohio. Hughes had not been consulted.

Saturday, 22 November 1930

. . . Reg Wallace . . . goes to the theatre & spends the night with Marinoff. I collect Donald Angus & go to Belle Livingston's[1] & meet Jack Colton who has brought a young Yale boy over for an audition. . . . Jack, Donald, & I dine chez Tony (E. 53) & go to Sterling Suftin's to see his amazing moving pictures.[2] He has a crowd in. . . . Donald takes away with him a boy named David Ayers when we go to Harlem. To Clam House, Lenox Club, etc., & back again with Jack Barker. I get home at 7.

> 1. Key club queen of speakeasies; she promoted Bricktop into stardom.
> 2. Donald Angus recalled that the films were homosexual pornography.

Sunday, 23 November 1930

Awakened by Marinoff at 12. A beautiful day. I have a hangover. After I read the papers we go to Geraldine Farrar's[1] concert at Carnegie Hall. She looks lovely & sings marvellously, almost better than I have ever heard her before. . . . Then to the Algonquin for dinner. . . . Home & to bed shortly after 8, after I listen to Ernestine Schumann-Heink croaking out "Ah mon fils" on the radio.[2]

> 1. American soprano at the Metropolitan Opera House, with a cult following called "The Gerryflappers," organized by Max Ewing. "Flappers" are open galoshes.
> 2. American contralto at the Metropolitan Opera House, reigning there in an earlier era.

Tuesday, 25 November 1930

. . . Went to join Alfred Knopf at his office with Marinoff & we went to a re-markable lunch given by Sam Kaplan[1] in his office on Vestry Street: goose, roast beef, boiled beef, etc. Mencken was there. . . . [To] Kay Mills to a cock-tail party, all the old ones. . . . Then home, dressed, Muriel Draper & Eddie Wassermann for dinner & we went to opening night of Ethel Barrymore in

Scarlet Sister Mary. . . . The event was embarrassing.[2] Then Marinoff, Eddie & I went to a party at the Langners'. . . . Home around 2.

1. An Indiana author.

2. Based on a novel about African Americans, by white author Julia Peterkin, the play starred Ethel Barrymore in the title role, and Estelle Winwood, both wearing blackface makeup, in a cast with fifteen African American actors.

Monday, 1 December 1930

. . . Bobby Locher comes for lunch & designs a screen for us, taking away Pollock's drawings.[1] Writing letters, etc. Poor Harry Block arrives, very poor and asks for some money, & gets it. . . . Arthur Richman, Eddie Wassermann, Armina Langner come to dinner. Hannah [Ellis] helps Edith [Ramsey]. We go to see Arthur Hornblow's translation from the French: *A Kiss of Importance* with Basil Rathbone & Ann Andrews. . . . Our dinner guests come home after the play & they stay till 2.

1. British paper doll sheets for pantomime puppet theaters popular as home amusement in the nineteenth century were used to decorate a three-panel folding screen.

Tuesday, 2 December 1930

. . . After lunch . . . I meet Eddie Wassermann & Anna May Wong & went with them to the Six Day Bicycle Race at Madison Sq. Garden. Home again at 4.30. . . . Marinoff arrives to tell me she has fired Edith. I go to Eddie Wassermann's where I meet Alec Waugh.[1] I take them & Harry Glynn to dinner at Tony's (East 57 Street). Alec gets drunk & leaves & Harry goes off to meet a girl. Eddie and I, unable to arrange a party, go home. . . .

1. English travel writer, Evelyn Waugh's brother.

Wednesday, 3 December 1930

. . . Everybody seems calmer. Marinoff, it seems, later told Edith she could stay. I finished reading Mabel [Dodge Luhan]'s remarkable *Lorenzo in Taos*. Alec Waugh came to lunch. After lunch I . . . visited Bobby Locher to find out about the screen he is making for me. Marinoff lunches with Bessie Lasky & dinner with Frank Case & goes to the theatre. I go after Donald Angus & take him & Sandy Meisner[1] to dinner at Eastside Tony's. Then after dinner I come home to greet James Cole. Later, after he has gone, Donald, Sandy, & Aaron Copland come in & stay till 2. I go to bed. Marinoff gets in later.

1. American theater designer Sandford Meisner.

Thursday, 4 December 1930

. . . At 5.30 Max Ewing, Sam & Nettie Knopf appear & we all go to see Marlene Dietrich in *Morocco*. Then I take them to dinner at Tony's (Eastside) & later Max & I go to opening of Lucile & Jack [Harper]'s Armistice Club. Home around 11.30.

Sunday, 7 December 1930

. . . Sending out invitations to 2 cocktail parties. Also putting away old letters. Lunch in with Marinoff. We have quite a lovely old fight. To a cocktail party at Fannie Hurst's where I meet Mr. & Mrs. Otis Skinner[1] & Maxwell Anderson.[2] The Laskys, Percy Wassermann, Alec Waugh, Henry Hadley,[3] Clayton Hamelton,[4] . . . etc. I leave with Eddie & at his house we are joined by . . . Donald Angus, Jack Colton, Kay Mills & go to dinner at Leone's & to the N.A.A.C.P. benefit at Waldorf Theatre, sit in the first row, & seeing Adelaide Hall, Bill Robinson, Ethel Waters, Duke Ellington, Clarence Darrow, etc. Heywood Broun & Woollcott as announcers. Saw Jim & Grace Johnson, the Nails, Lucile Miller, David Plunkett Greene, Ruth Hale, . . . Walter & Gladys White, Grace Valentine, Dorothy Peterson & her father, Inez Wilson, . . . A'Lelia Walker, Mamie White. . . . Late night at Eddie's. Home at 4.

1. American actor and his wife.
2. American playwright recognized for his blank verse dramas.
3. Conductor of the Manhattan Symphony Orchestra.
4. Dramatic critic for *The Forum*.

Tuesday, 9 December 1930

. . . Polish edition of *Nigger Heaven* arrives. . . . To party at Eddie Wassermann's. . . . Home for dinner and then go to Max Ewing to hear Elsie Arden sing. Florine & Ettie Stettheimer who go home with me, Gilbert & Amanda Seldes. Home around 12.30.

Wednesday, 10 December 1930

. . . The party: Emily Davies who came with a man named Frazier, . . . Val & Bibi Dudensing, Julia Hoyt, Lawrence (who told me he likes Zora [Neale Hurston]'s play, *Mulebone*) & Armina Langner, Gladys Unger, Lois Moran who brought her aunt, Rita Romilly who brought George Davis[1] & another man, Reg Wallace, Jesse & Bessie Lasky & their son, Davidowa,[2] Mildred Knopf, Joan Carr, . . . Mary Lewis, Lenore Harris, Rosalie Stewart,[3] Bennett Cerf, Robert [Morss] Lovett, Victor Wittgenstein, Edward Wassermann, . . .

Donald Angus, Jack Colton, . . . Tom Smith, David Plunkett Greene, Percy Wassermann. I go to dinner with Eddie Wassermann quite drunk & then turn up at a party at Joe Brewer's. . . .

1. Editor at *Harper's Bazaar.*

2. Russian émigrée, often importuned to wear pearls belonging to other women because her flesh was reputed to "feed" them and thereby add to their lustre.

3. Three actresses whose careers may not have succeeded. Mary Lewis, for instance, seems to have appeared only in the *Ziegfeld Follies of 1922.*

Thursday, 11 December 1930

. . . Went to a cocktail party at Jesse Lasky's, held in the Barbizon-Plaza. . . . Home & dressed & go to Eddie Wassermann's to dinner with Aldo and Adele Lewisohn. We go to the Philharmonic concert in Adele Lewisohn's box, with . . . a young Englishman. After the concert Aldo, Eddie & I go to Tony's for a couple of drinks. . . .

Friday, 12 December 1930

. . . I take Marinoff to lunch at the Crillon. . . . Drive by Goldfarb's on way home to send some flowers to Wesley Hill, the Angel Gabriel of *The Green Pastures,* just killed by a taxi cab. Home for a big party. . . . Marinoff leaves in the middle of it for White Plains with Alfred Knopf. These are present: Dorothy Hergesheimer, Esther Root Adams, Doris Ullman, Noma Way, Georgia O'Keeffe, Gilbert & Amanda Seldes, Robert & B[eatrice] Locher, Mildred Whitall, Lenore Ulric & Sidney Blackmer, Muriel & Smudge Draper, Mercedes de Acosta, Fannie Hurst, Mary Lewis, Alma Gluck Zimbalist,[1] J. W. Johnson, Willie Seabrook, Katie Seabrook, Marjorie & Lyman Worthington. . . . Mrs. Geo. Dangerfield,[2] Colin McPhee, Aaron Copland, Ettie & Carrie Stettheimer, Pauline Lord[3] with a Miss Reese, Noel Murphy, Armina & Lawrence Langner, Florence Sternberger, Margaret Moran,[4] Frances Seligman & her son-in-law Newell, Eva Gauthier, Lorna Lindsley, John Emerson, Anita Loos, Reg Wallace, Eddie Wassermann, Ellery Larsson, Henry McBride, Arthur Richman, Frank Case, Alec Waugh, Zena Naylor, Harry Glynn, Max Ewing, K. Mills, Donald Angus with a friend, Lewis Galantiere, Sarah Marsh & Sidney Blackmer, Sogata, Ada Neyland,[5] Demuth, De Laigre, Joan Carr. After it was over, about 8 o'clock I take Sogata to the Iron Gate & he comes back here to stay till 12.

1. American contralto at the Metropolitan Opera House, wife of violinist Efrem Zimbalist.

2. Wife of the literary critic and reviewer.

3. American actress.

4. A singer before World War I, she was the mother of Hollywood juvenile Jackie Moran.

5. CVV's cousin, daughter of his mother's brother Charles Fitch.

Saturday, 13 December 1930

. . . I take Emily Clark to lunch at the Crillon. Eddie Wassermann is there with Mercedes de Acosta. . . . I go home about 4. A little later I join Eddie Wassermann for cocktails at Harry Glynn's. We collect Zena Naylor & . . . David Plunkett Greene . . . & Rita Wellman. I have a row with Eddie and David & go alone to dinner at the Don Juan. Home & Jim Cole comes in. Later Donald. We go to Harlem. I am frightfully lit. To the Nest & the Clam House. . . . Home. God, soused. . . .

Friday, 19 December 1930

. . . To a cocktail party at Alec Waugh's. . . . Then to a cocktail party at Eddie Wassermann's. . . . Harry Glynn, Donald Angus, Eddie, . . . Zena Naylor & I went to a 3rd St. Club. Everybody was very drunk & disagreeable & Donald & I left about 1. Invited to a party at Mrs. Astor's but don't go.

Saturday, 20 December 1930

. . . Reg Wallace comes to dine with Marinoff who has too much of a cold to go out. Ada Neyland & Tom Rutherford arrive. I take them to East Side Tony's for dinner where I meet up with . . . Donald Angus. We go to Iron Gate for drinks. . . . On to the Savoy, the Clam House (where Gladys Bentley sings & I see Sherrill Schell) & finally Clarence Robinson's[1] place where we meet Al Moore, Marjorie Sipp, Zena Naylor, . . . Harold Jackman, . . . Eddie Manchester, Billie Cain, Ada Burns, Georgette Harvey, Alma Smith,[2] etc. Ada Fitch passes out & we go home around 5. . . .

1. African American performer, later in films.

2. Except for Zena Naylor, those in this roster were all African American entertainers.

Sunday, 21 December 1930

. . . With Max Ewing went to hear Dr. Magnus Hirschfeld's lecture on sex at Labor Temple. It lasted (with slides) 3 hours (in German). . . .

Wednesday, 24 December 1930

... We pack, open presents, etc., & go on train to Wilton to the Langners for Christmas with Eddie Wassermann & Philip Moeller. Lawrence's two children, Phyllis & Philip, are there. We have a turkey dinner & Xmas tree & to bed about 12.

Thursday, 25 December 1930

Up at 9.30. Snow & cold. Beautiful Christmas day. . . . We are greeted by a voice over the radio: "Good morning, the makers of Odorono & Cutex wish you a Merry Xmas." ...

Friday, 26 December 1930

... Lunch in with Marinoff. A swell Philharmonic concert. Come home to find a real cri de coeur from Edna Kenton, begging for money. I'll send her some tomorrow. To the Seldeses for cocktails. . . . We pick up Reg Wallace & come home for dinner & go to see Marika Catabouli in a modern Greek version of [Hugo von] Hofmannsthall's *Elektra*. . . .

Saturday, 27 December 1930

... Lunch at Don Juan with Zena Naylor. . . . Later to a party at George Hoy's & Nils Nelson's. . . . Back home for dinner. To a party at Rita Romilly's. . . . Later Donald Angus, Eddie & I with Nora went to . . . Harlem. . . . Home at 6. (P.S. Went to the bank & sent E. Kenton $500.)

Monday, 29 December 1930

... Alfred Knopf comes to lunch. After lunch . . . James Weldon Johnson, Langston Hughes, W. B. Seabrook, & Aaron Copland come to meet Dr. Magnus Hirschfeld who arrived half an hour late, followed by George Sylvester Viereck. The occasion was a huge success. Later Marinoff & I dine alone. In the evening Donald Angus comes in & we gossip & play records. The Viking Press gives a tea for the Grand Duchess Marie to which I do not go.

Wednesday, 31 December 1930

Up at 7.30 with a hangover. Cold & clear. Bobby Locher comes in to look at screen & Mildred Whitall comes to mend it. . . . Mr. Townesson puts up tie-backs, great amethyst flowers in drawing room. . . . I give a small cocktail party: . . . David Plunkett Greene, Olivia Wyndham, Rita Wellman, Tom

Howard, Kay Mills, George Hoy, Nora Holt, Donald Angus, Al Moore, Martin Wilson. Marinoff & I dine chez the Laskys with Bertha & Frank Case, Heifetz & Florence Vidor. Then joined by several others including Anita Loos we go to a party Frank Case & Jesse Lasky give at the Algonquin: Ina Claire, Joan Crawford, Doug. Fairbanks, Jr., . . . Anna May Wong, E. Wassermann, Clif Webb, Geo. Cukor, . . . etc. About 3 Marinoff & I go on to Muriel Draper's where there is an enormous crowd drunk. . . . We leave. Donald Angus & I go to . . . Harlem. . . .

INDEX

Carl Van Vechten (1880–1964) was, successively, an influential music, drama, and literary critic, a popular novelist, and a gifted amateur photographer. He was well known for popularizing African American culture in the 1920s, for his financial and moral support for its artists, writers, and musicians, and for founding the James Weldon Johnson Memorial Collection of Negro Arts and Letters at Yale University. His many books include his magnum opus about cats, *The Tiger in the House,* and his Harlem novel, *Nigger Heaven,* reissued by the University of Illinois Press in 2000.

Bruce Kellner is an Emeritus Professor of English at Millersville University and Successor Trustee for the Estate of Carl Van Vechten. He has published four other books about Van Vechten (a biography, a bibliography, an edition of his correspondence, and a collection of his writings about African American arts and letters), as well as books about the artists Ralph Barton and Charles Demuth, the writers Gertrude Stein and Donald Windham, the Harlem Renaissance, and, most recently, a memoir, *Kiss Me Again: An Invitation to a Group of Noble Dames.*